THE LETTERS OF GERBERT
WITH HIS PAPAL PRIVILEGES
AS SYLVESTER II

NUMBER LX OF THE
RECORDS OF CIVILIZATION
SOURCES AND STUDIES

THE LETTERS OF
GERBERT

WITH HIS PAPAL PRIVILEGES

AS SYLVESTER II

Translated with an Introduction by
HARRIET PRATT LATTIN

COLUMBIA UNIVERSITY PRESS
NEW YORK MCMLXI

Library of Congress Catalog Card Number: 60-5012

Published in Great Britain, India, and Pakistan
by the Oxford University Press
London, Bombay, and Karachi

Printed in The Netherlands

RECORDS OF CIVILIZATION
SOURCES AND STUDIES

EDITED UNDER THE AUSPICES OF THE
DEPARTMENT OF HISTORY, COLUMBIA UNIVERSITY

PREFACE

THE TENTH CENTURY has been a neglected spot in history. So much of it has been lost, so much changed, and so much merged into the seemingly more striking following century. Fortunate we are, then, that Gerbert's letters survived, for life and movement pulsate through them, and the last quarter of this century comes alive with the same types of people to be met with anywhere, anytime. The universality of human nature is apparent in every one of Gerbert's letters.

In addition to this aspect of modernity in the letters they characterize a highly individual person, one who was passionately devoted to the ideal of a strong church and a strong political power—embodied by the German Empire—working together closely and harmoniously. The letters reflect his extensive travels and wide acquaintance. Conflict precipitated many of them and this fact heightens their dramatic impact. Even though individualized in these tenth-century letters they are the same universal conflicts resulting from political expediency, greed, ambition, indifference, treachery, envy. A few letters attempt to satisfy the intellectual curiosity of friends and pupils.

Through the years I have owed much to Professor John La Monte, who suggested the translation, to Professors Edgar Holmes McNeal and Paul Schaeffer for their helpful guidance in translation problems, and to Professor Austin P. Evans for his detailed, keen criticisms of the complete translation. I am grateful to Professor Father Joseph Fenton of Catholic University for advising me to include also the translation of Sylvester II's (Gerbert's) papal documents. Thus far, the number of such papal documents available in English has been very limited.

This translation could not have been completed without the valuable assistance of many librarians and the greatly appreciated use of the facilities of their libraries: Miss Donna Root, and Mrs. Arlene W. Colegrove, and the Cleveland Public Library; Mr. Walter B. Briggs, Miss Alice Reynolds, and the Widener Library of Harvard University; the University of Michigan Library; the Staatliche Bibliothek in Bamberg; the Deutsche Staatsbibliothek in Berlin; the Rijksuniversiteit Bibliotheek in Leiden; the Bibliothèque Nationale; the Vallicelliana Library in Rome; Cardinal Eugene Tisserant and the Vatican Library; and especially Miss Maude Jeffrey, Miss Alice McKee, and the Ohio State University Library.

To the perceptive editor of the Columbia University Press, Mrs. Kathryn W. Sewny, go my deepest thanks for transforming my ungainly manuscript into a printable work.

HARRIET PRATT LATTIN

Columbus, Ohio
December 14, 1959

CONTENTS

The illustration facing page 364 is a facsimile of the end of Letter 261 showing Gerbert's signature in Tironian notes.

INTRODUCTION

*The "List of Abbreviations Used in the Notes and in the Bibliography"
will be found on pp. 391-92.*

INTRODUCTION

GERBERT

Gerbert,[1] noted scholar, famous teacher, celebrated as the introducer of certain elements of Arabic learning into Latin culture, was born of poor but free parents in or near the village of Aurillac in south-central France some five or ten years before the mid-tenth century. In early childhood he entered the monastery of St. Gerald in Aurillac [2] where he received a thorough education in Latin grammar. Here he remained until the year 967 when the count of Barcelona, Borrell II, on a pious visit to the monastery, was so favorably impressed by him that Borrell gained from the abbot the required permission (*licentia*) for Gerbert to seek further education in Catalan Spain.

Borrell entrusted him to Atto, bishop of Vich. However, a catalogue of the library of Vich cathedral at that time and the extant manuscripts from Vich reveal nothing from which Gerbert could have profited to such a degree as his later teaching reveals he did from study in Spain. Only one place in Catalan Spain could have furnished the necessary intellectual substance for expanding his education, and that was the monastery of Santa Maria de Ripoll.[3] Gerbert undoubtedly

---

[1] For a few of the biographies of Gerbert see the Bibliography under Richer (III.xliii ff.), Bzovius, Lausser, Barse, Barthélemy, Bubnov, Werner, Picavet, La Salle de Rochemaure, Leflon, Olleris, Havet, and Lattin, *Peasant Boy*.

[2] G. Bouange, *Saint Géraud et son abbaye* (2d ed., 2 vols. Aurillac, 1881).

[3] An inventory of the movable property of Vich cathedral, drawn up in 957, lists 51 manuscripts, not one of which was a text for the study of the liberal arts. Villanueva, VI, pp. 273-74; and R. Beer, "Die Handschriften des Klosters Santa Maria de Ripoll," SBW, CLV (1907), Abhandlung 3, pp. 53ff. Beer first suggested Ripoll as the center where Gerbert studied in Spain.

continued to be under Bishop Atto's charge and perhaps gained from him some instruction in the mathematical disciplines.[4]

When Count Borrell wished to revive an archbishopric for Catalonia, whose onetime head, Tarragona, had long been under Saracen control, he needed just such a learned and astute man as Gerbert, whose ready wit and oratorical ability could aid him in his personal appeal to Pope John XIII. So, in December, 970, Gerbert accompanied the count and Bishop Atto to Rome.

Pope John was not only delighted by Gerbert's unusual brilliance, but even retained him in Rome in order to profit by the stimulation of association with him. Later, the pope sent him to Emperor Otto I in the belief that Otto, too, would enjoy having in his entourage this young man with his keen, inquiring mind.[5]

It was in Otto's court that Gerbert, who had grown to manhood in a region where the petty nobility was strong and the king was weak, became enamored of the Germanic-Roman idea of an empire great and strong enough to bring order to a disordered world. Here, too, he experienced the thrill of teaching an eager, receptive mind like that of the sixteen-year-old Otto II, who added spice to the teacher-pupil relationship by a wit that matched his own. And here, too, there crystallized within him the need and urgent desire for a more comprehensive study of oratory, both rhetorical and dialectical.

A chance meeting with Gerann, archdeacon of Rheims, on the occasion of Otto II's marriage with the Byzantine Theophanu in St. Peter's at Rome, on April 14, 972, turned Gerbert's attention to this flourishing northern center of culture, and he promised Gerann to join him later in Rheims.

Rheims was all that could have been desired by a poor cleric who,

---

[4] "Under his [Atto's] supervision he pursued mathematical studies thoroughly and successfully." Richer iii.xlii.

[5] Whether Gerbert actually took monastic vows at St. Gerald remains unsettled. When he first appears in Richer's *Historia* (iii.xliii), he seems already secular-minded, and later still more so. If he had become a monk, possibly Pope John XIII freed him from his vows. His later acquisition of property and books was in direct contradiction of the monastic vow of poverty, yet he prided himself greatly upon his uprightness (*honestas morum*). A papal annulment offers a solution for this paradox. Gerbert was ordained to the priesthood by Archbishop Adalbero of Rheims at some time after 972. *Concilium Mosomense* in Olleris, p. 246.

by now, was fired with a burning desire to become a noteworthy teacher. Nearby were several libraries, well supplied with manuscripts, and close at hand at least five scriptoria were active in producing more manuscripts. Moreover, Archbishop Adalbero of Rheims was eager to improve his clergy's earnestness, zeal, and depth of knowledge. The location of the city made it the crossroads for commercial and intellectual interchange and easily accessible to students from everywhere. A pupil was already awaiting Gerbert's arrival in Rheims, since Gerann had offered to exchange his lessons in dialectic for Gerbert's teaching of the quadrivium.

The next eight years passed all too quickly as Gerbert busied himself to revise and expand the curriculum along the lines of Cassiodorus' outlines of secular studies,[6] while he pursued his own studies and researches and at the same time acted as a secretary to Archbishop Adalbero (Letter 1).

It is not known whence Gerbert was able to secure the considerable number of Boethius' logical works which he formed into a corpus for his teaching, since the manuscripts of this corpus, although it was almost identical with that of Cassiodorus, do not antedate Gerbert.[7] The love for dialectic and the keen appreciation of its subtleties remained a prime concern throughout Gerbert's life so that even during voluntary exile in 997 he tried to turn the minds of the nobles and clergy of Otto III's court to this mental gymnastic, and eventually prodded himself into writing a short tract for Otto III himself called *De rationali et ratione uti* (On The Rational and the Use of Reason).[8]

Just as Cassiodorus' outlines for the subjects of the quadrivium were extremely sketchy, so the teaching of these subjects had heretofore proceeded in a faltering, hesitating, and confused fashion. Moreover, these mathematical studies were suspect as proper subjects of study by the clergy. Still further difficulty was caused by the emphasis of the Greeks, reiterated by Boethius,[9] on the theoretical aspects of these

---

[6] *Cassiodori Senatoris Institutiones*, ed. R. Mynors (Oxford, 1937), Bk. II, trans. L. W. Jones under the title *An Introduction to Divine and Human Readings* (Records of Civilization, XL; New York, 1946). See also Lattin, "Eleventh Century MS Munich 14436," *Isis*, XXXVIII (1948), 222-24; and Lattin, *Peasant Boy*, pp. 79ff.

[7] Lattin, "Eleventh Century MS Munich 14436," *Isis*, XXXVIII (1948), 222-24.

[8] In Olleris, pp. 297-310.

[9] *De musica* I.xliv.

branches of learning. In order to compensate for the inadequate material available in Latin for the study of the parts of the quadrivium and to render them more comprehensible, Gerbert turned to their practical aspects and in each case provided a new and visible tool.

For arithmetic he prepared an abacus upon whose surface with amazing speed he dextrously manipulated counters bearing the nine Hindu-Arabic numerals whose use he thus introduced to Latin Europe outside of Spain.[10] For music he insisted upon the use of the monochord for the establishment of the correct pitch,[11] especially in organ pipes, and he apparently introduced finger technique in place of hand technique in the playing of organs. Moreover, he insisted that actual instruments (in his own case, organs) were a necessity in music study. In geometry we know of nothing practical that he introduced except the use of the abacus for solving arithmetical problems resulting from practical surveying; perhaps, he made use of the astrolabe, though this latter seems doubtful. In the field of astronomy he designed some instruments, both for observing and for teaching, and he insisted upon actual astronomical observations.[12]

The impact of Gerbert's teaching of the quadrivium upon one pupil can be noted in his earliest letters, directed apparently to Constantine, monk of Fleury, answering queries about these novelties in Gerbert's educational ideas. The impact of all of his teaching is observable in the large number of students whom he attracted to Rheims from places as far distant as Magdeburg.[13]

At the very height of his fame as a teacher, in November, 980, he accompanied his archbishop, Adalbero, to Italy on a political mission to Otto II. They managed to meet Otto at Pavia and accompanied him to Ravenna. There, much to Otto's delight, Gerbert engaged in a strenuous dialectical debate about philosophical problems of definition with Otric, teacher of the school of Magdeburg cathedral.

Otto II was straining every resource of men and materiel in his plan to make himself master of the Italian peninsula by establishing a firm control over the Italian churches and nobles, and by driving the

---

[10] Richer iii.liv.
[11] *Ibid.* iii.xlix.
[12] *Ibid.* iii.l-liii.
[13] *Ibid.* iii.lv.

Greeks and Saracens therefrom. For such a mighty task he needed men of forcefulness, orginality, and loyalty like Gerbert and so he retained Gerbert when Archbishop Adalbero returned to Rheims.

Within a few months Otto II had designated Gerbert as abbot of St. Columban of Bobbio,[14] in northwest Italy, where the local nobles had been quarreling over the abbey and its land possessions. The new abbot's strict interpretation of the land laws was so diametrically opposed to that of the landed gentry far and wide that he was barely able to maintain his precarious position as abbot through complaints, demands, threats, and appeals to Otto (Letters 8, 12, 18, 19). This slender margin of safety was suddenly cut away by Otto II's death, December 7, 983. Gerbert reluctantly abandoned Bobbio and fled to the imperial palace at Pavia, then occupied by the Dowager Empress Adelaide.

Soon after the arrival in Pavia of the Empress Theophanu from the funeral of her husband in Rome, disquieting news from Germany revealed that the Ottonian power was being threatened. The three-year-old Otto III had been elected German king at Verona, June, 983, and was crowned at Aachen December 25th. When the news of Otto II's death reached Germany, Henry the Quarreler of Bavaria, who had been in prison since 978 as a result of his rebellion against Otto II, escaped from prison and seized the little king. Then he bent every effort towards securing support from the German nobility, lay and ecclesiastical, for his own claim to the throne, so that he could act at least as a co-king with Otto III.

To Gerbert the empresses entrusted the delicate but urgent task of trying to hold the German ecclesiastics and certain of the nobility steadfast in their fidelity to Otto III. When he reached Rheims about January 25th Gerbert discovered that Henry had been moving rapidly in securing support from powerful bishops in the western part of the

---

[14] Richer (iii.lxv) omits the period of Gerbert's abbacy at Bobbio and states that he returned to Rheims with Archbishop Adalbero. If true, he must have made a hasty journey and then have rejoined Otto II in Italy. The early letters bespeak a longer association with some of the addressees than the brief visit to the emperor at Ravenna in 980. Furthermore, Ottonian policy dictated the appointment of close associates to these important positions. Finally, the chronology of the early letters is too compressed if Gerbert's appointment came in the early months of 983, as suggested by Havet (pp. x; 1, n. 1; 15, n. 4).

empire—Folmar (Poppo) of Utrecht, Warin of Cologne, Egbert of Trier, Dietrich of Metz. Henry had already arranged to meet King Lothair at Breisach on the Rhine on February 1st (Letter 24), but Henry turned east instead to gather strength in Saxony. He was finally chosen king on March 23d, but never consecrated. Gerbert's forceful appeals to Archbishop Egbert of Trier, Archbishop Willigis of Mainz, Bishop Dietrich of Metz, Duke Charles of Lower Lorraine, Bishop Notker of Liége, and King Lothair of the Franks (Letters 34, 35, 38-43) to prevent Henry from gaining control of western Germany and Lorraine were successful except for Egbert. They agreed that King Lothair, who was as closely related to Otto III as Henry, should assume the guardianship (Letter 64).

Thus, powerful vassals rallied to Empress Theophanu's support upon her appearance in Germany in May, 984, so that she was able to demand and to secure the return of her son Otto (Letter 45). Encouraged by the vassals' fidelity to her, she assumed the guardianship herself, thus excluding both Henry and King Lothair.

Lothair's principal interest in the guardianship stemmed from his claim to, and designs upon, Lorraine. Because of the intensity of Gerbert's devotion to the Ottos and the loyal adherence of Archbishop Adalbero to the imperial political ties of his Lorraine family, both of them were now caught in the whorl of the last frantic attempt of the Carolingians to reestablish control over Lorraine (Letters 24, 48-49, 53-61, 63-67, 69, 70, 86, 95-96, 103, 109). The large number of letters concerned with saving Otto III's throne and with efforts to keep Lorraine in the empire indicate Gerbert's extreme sensitivity to the fluctuations of political events. Henceforth, political activity claimed too much of his time and attention.

However, Gerbert had never understood that, once his mission in northern France was accomplished, he was not to be summoned to the German court where he could devote himself to the strengthening of imperial power. So, over and over again he sent out reminders through and to diverse persons asserting that he remained faithful to the Ottos and would be quickly responsive to a command for his presence in Germany (Letters 29, 45, 51, 79, 102). True, he was still abbot of Bobbio and, as such, was called upon to furnish a contingent of monks and knights for the German war against the Slavs (Letter

102); nevertheless, he dreamed of being a bishop within the German realm (Letters 125, 126).

The incessant warring and interference in the affairs of northern France by the powerful counts of Blois and of Troyes, Eudes and Heribert, and King Lothair's untoward capture of Verdun and its Count Godfrey, brother of Archbishop Adalbero, plunged both Adalbero and Gerbert into dangerously compromising situations. Their activities in behalf of Verdun resulted in an accusation of treason, brought by Lothair against Archbishop Adalbero but extended also to Gerbert (Letters 59, 64).

Hugh Capet, duke of France, had long appeared as more powerful and more kingly than the king himself, Carolingian though Lothair was (Letters 53, 55).[15] The desirability of establishing favorable relations with Hugh had become apparent to Adalbero and Gerbert (Letters 58, 66, 67), and more especially so after Hugh had dispersed a meeting assembled by King Lothair to try Adalbero in May, 985 (Letter 65).

Upon the death of Lothair, March, 2, 986, Louis V succeeded and began to reign under his mother's tutelage. Adalbero and Gerbert seemed restored to royal favor (Letters 80, 81) until Louis suddenly attacked the city of Rheims (Letter 103) after excluding Queen Emma from directing the affairs of government with him (Letter 100). New charges were prepared by the king against Adalbero who was summoned to stand trial in May, 987 (Letter 107).

Louis's death on May 22d removed Adalbero's accuser, and at the same time forced the nobles, asembled to try Adalbero, to consider the problem of the succession to the throne. Gerbert's electioneering, backed by the support of the most powerful ecclesiastic in France—Archbishop Adalbero—resulted in the rejection of the claim of Louis's uncle, Duke Charles of Lower Lorraine, based upon birth, in favor of the elective principle of kingship. The nobles elected Hugh Capet king of the French.

There was a price, however, for securing the support of the German court to Hugh's election, and one bitterly criticized by later generations of Frenchmen. Gerbert hastened to the Empress Theophanu, whom he probably met on the road between Corvey and Frankfort.

[15] Richer iii.lxxxiv.

She assented. The price? Release of Count Godfrey from prison (Letter 109) and the return of Verdun to imperial control (Letter 112).

Gerbert now became not only secretary (Letters 114, 180) to the new king but his adviser on foreign affairs as well. Gerbert's political acumen, great learning, broad international interests, and experience in matters Roman, Spanish, Byzantine, and German greatly impressed Hugh (Letters 119, 120, 129).

Soon, however, Hugh met a real challenge right at home. Duke Charles, far from submissively accepting his exclusion from the throne, quietly set about strengthening and consolidating his forces and supporters. In May, 988, in a surprise attack, he gained mastery of the stronghold of Laon, the Carolingian capital city, and laid hands upon its bishop, Adalbero, more familiarly caled Ascelin, and the Dowager Queen Emma.

Deeming the politically astute Gerbert necessary to his success in gaining the crown, Charles set about to win him over by force if necessary. Gerbert managed to avoid any commitments to Charles and equally well any open hostility to him in his anxiety to effect the release of both Queen Emma and Bishop Ascelin from Charles's imprisonment (Letters 123, 137). Finally, in the summer and fall of 988 Gerbert and Archbishop Adalbero, whom Charles had twice tried unsuccessfully to win over, concentrated their efforts upon dislodging Charles from the citadel of Laon by furnishing men, materiel, and counsel to King Hugh (Letters 130, 139, 143, 145). This was still unaccomplished when Archbishop Adalbero died on January 23, 989.

Through his long, intimate association with Archbishop Adalbero Gerbert was thoroughly familiar with all of the intricacies of the administration of the affairs of this important Rheims archbishopric. He was so confident that he would be elected archbishop (Letter 160) that he turned aside the attractive suggestions of a powerful German (possibly Archbishop Willigis of Mainz) to come to Germany (Letter 158).

But by some miscalculation of judgment Hugh chose Arnulf, a natural son of King Lothair, a cleric of the cathedral of Rheims, and Adalbero's assistant in the king's chancery. Either Hugh was unaware of Arnulf's devotion to his uncle Charles, or he hoped that the ecclesiastical importance of this nephew's position would influence

Charles to abandon his own aspirations, or Charles, to further his nephew's career, may even have offered to capitulate. Whatever the reason, the appointment was counter to the encouragement previously given to Gerbert that he was to be Hugh's choice (Letters 158, 160).

Gerbert was in despair over the election of Arnulf in whom he saw too slender and unstable a reed to bear these weighty responsibilities. Gerbert's reaction, as so often in periods of crises, was to seek solace in intellectual efforts. In this case he turned his attention especially to astronomy (Letters 160, 161).

Arnulf, however, did not turn against him, rival though he had been, but instead commandeered his services as secretary (Letters 164, 165, 168). Gerbert seized the opportunity to influence Arnulf, directly or indirectly, to adopt the same attitudes towards the Ottos that Archbishop Adalbero had held (Letters 168, 177).

Still, Gerbert sensed an undercurrent of treachery and danger at Rheims so he decided to reach out again, but this time more boldly, for whatever Germany had to offer him (Letters 166, 167, 182). Empress Theophanu, however, was intent upon plans for a journey to Rome and could give neither heed nor consideration to Gerbert in spite of all his years of passionate devotion.

Sensitive to disloyalty and fearful of intrigue though Gerbert was, he was unprepared for the blow that Arnulf delivered to Rheims one September night in 989 when he ordered Adalger, a priest of his cathedral, to throw open its gates to Charles and his unruly soldiers. Arnulf had plotted with extreme cunning, for he had convoked a council at Rheims for this very time. Consequently Charles's bagful of prisoners included ecclesiastics and upper nobility, among them the brothers Bishop Bruno of Langres and Count Gilbert of Roucy, the knights Sehard and Rainaud, Arnulf's own brother Richard, and Gerbert. To hide his own complicity Arnulf permitted himself to be led away with the other prisoners to captivity at Laon (Letter 177). Meanwhile Charles, after allowing his own soldiers unrestrained license in plundering the city (Letters 170, 173),[16] forced Gerbert to assume

---

[16] Gerbert's bemoaning the captivity of his friends in Letter 170, but not his own, indicates that he was not incarcerated with them at Laon. His hesitancy in making an immediate attempt to escape from Rheims was due to his sense of duty to the people of Rheims, as shown in Letter 171, and to his increasing doubts whether King Hugh could cope with Charles's rebellion.

the responsibility for the civil and ecclesiastical administration of Rheims (Letters 171, 172, 175, 176, 182).

For eight months Gerbert remained a virtual prisoner at Rheims under constant surveillance (Letter 170) until, in May, 990, he finally escaped to Senlis (Letters 179, 180, 190) where a synod of bishops under King Hugh's guidance was acting upon the ecclesiastical misfortunes of Rheims (Letters 180, 181). After listening to Gerbert's testimony about Arnulf's treachery which was corroborated by Bishop Bruno (Letter 180), the bishops proceeded with excommunication against the captors of Rheims (Letters 185, 186).

Encouraged by Gerbert's escape and presence at his court, Hugh now took up the cudgel in a campaign against Charles. However, at the actual moment of encounter of the opposing troops neither side dared risk joining battle so that a stalemate ensued, to be broken only in March, 991, when the deceit of Bishop Ascelin of Laon resulted in the capture of both Charles and Arnulf.

A council of bishops at St.-Basle-de-Verzy in June, 991, forced Arnulf to vacate his office. Almost immediately Gerbert was elected and consecrated archbishop (Letter 191). Almost a year had elapsed since the bishops at Senlis, as a group (Letter 187), and King Hugh, individually (Letter 188), had written letters by Gerbert's pen to Pope John XV begging him to take Arnulf's case under advisement and then render some judgment upon it. However, partisans of Arnulf and Charles had reached Rome almost simultaneously with those of the bishops and Hugh so the pope postponed his decision as to his jurisdiction over the controversy.

Thus, early in 992 Gerbert and King Hugh learned with dismay that a papal legate, Abbot Leo of St. Boniface and St. Alexius on the Aventine in Rome, was journeying north to investigate the Rheims "affair." Abbot Leo later described events thus: "But when we arrived at Aachen, we found him [Arnulf] already deposed, nor did we receive a response from you. After we returned home, the pope invited you [Hugh and Robert] to Rome; but, indeed, you refused to come to him." [17]

The pope on the one hand and the king and archbishop on the

[17] Olleris, p. 243.

other girded themselves for the ensuing contest over Gerbert's right to the see of Rheims. John XV cited Hugh and Robert to appear before him in Rome. Gerbert, writing for Hugh, invited the pope to visit France (Letter 193).

The controversy became more acute in June, 995, when Abbot Leo traveled north for the second time and held two councils which condemned Gerbert. After the first council at Mouzon on June 2d, Gerbert, suddenly realizing the precariousness of his archiepiscopal title unless approved by the pope, published the *Acts* of the council of St. Basle (June, 991) which deposed Arnulf.[18] To gain powerful supporters in what he hoped would be a more general council of French, Lorraine, and German prelates at Ingelheim he later sent summaries of the *Acts*, which had been composed with an eye to their rhetorical worth, to Bishops Wilderode of Strasbourg (Letter 201) and Notker of Liége (Letter 202). Scandalized at the harsh words uttered by the bishops during the council of St. Basle, as revealed by Gerbert in the *Acts*,[19] and frustrated by the indecisiveness of the two recent councils, Abbot Leo hastened back to Rome.

He had, however, gained one point for papal contentions, which proved to be an opening wedge in the papal effort to secure jurisdiction over the dispute. At Mouzon, Leo had persuaded Gerbert to promise not to celebrate divine services until July 1st, the time of the meeting of the next council. Gerbert had agreed as a matter of obedience, not as an acknowledgment that he was in the wrong.

However, no progress was made at the second council, which met in St.-Rémy of Rheims. There Gerbert made an impassioned plea for himself,[20] and partisans on each side became even more acrimonious and denunciatory. Leo waited until he was at a safe distance from possible physical interference by King Hugh and then declared that the Kings Hugh and Robert and the author of the *Acts* (Gerbert) had been separated from the Church by Pope John.

---

[18] Olleris, pp. 172-236; mentioned by Abbot Leo in his *Epistola ad Hugonem et Robertum reges*, in Olleris, p. 237.

[19] Chap. XXVIII; and Leo, *Epistola ad Hugonem et Robertum reges* (Olleris, p. 237). Gerbert, in his defense at the council of Rheims (995), calls Pope John XV an "enemy of the human race" (Olleris, p. 252).

[20] *Oratio episcoporum habita in concilio causeio*, in Olleris, pp. 251-256. Only Gerbert's speech has survived.

Gerbert protested vigorously (Letters 198, 199), and still continued to discharge his duties as archbishop. He had been a capable administrator during the four years since he had entered upon the office in June, 991. He watched out zealously for any infringement of ecclesiastical rights and privileges (Letters 194, 195, 205-207, 213-16) and continued the high moral tone established by Adalbero (Letters 197, 212). From his own bishops and clergy he demanded the most straight forward and upright, but charitable, behavior (Letters 200, 205-207). The Rheims diocese was profiting from the cessation of the strife of war, and dissatisfaction seemed at a minimum.

The death of one of Gerbert's loyal bishops, Rothard of Cambrai, in August, 995, reactivated the question of the legality of Arnulf's deposition. Herluin, the new candidate, sponsored by Bishop Notker of Liége, who had developed open enmity to Gerbert, feared that consecration by Gerbert might be considered illegal by the pope. Hence, in April, 996, Herluin made the long journey to Rome to receive consecration from the pope himself. Pope John XV, however, had died, and Otto III's cousin, Bruno, now sat on the papal throne as Gregory V. He confirmed the continuation of the papal policy of opposition to Gerbert's archiepiscopal title by carrying out Herluin's consecration. In the accompanying document (JL 3866) Pope Gregory called Gerbert an "invader" of the Rheims see.

Now, indeed, Gerbert felt compelled to carry the account of the Rheims controversy to Rome in person so he hastily prepared for his journey. Gregory V rejected Gerbert's plea for recognition as the legal archbishop by reiterating the papal demand that Arnulf first be restored to his see. Only then would the pope receive the bishops' complaints against Arnulf and render his decision.

On Gerbert's return journey, probably during a stop at the royal palace at Pavia, he encountered Otto III, sixteen years old and recently crowned emperor by Pope Gregory. Otto was captivated by Gerbert's charm, knowledge, and enthusiasm for education, just as his father had been a quarter century earlier. Otto III even put Gerbert's talents to work in writing letters for him (Letters 208-211). However, duties at Rheims soon beckoned Gerbert, while Otto's frail health impelled him to leave the Italian climate behind.

As the news of Herluin's rejection of Gerbert and Gregory's

censure spread through the Rheims archbishopric a sense of insecurity seized the clergy lest they be charged with associating with an intruder archbishop. When a papal council at Pavia, in January, 997, removed from office the bishops responsible for Arnulf's condemnation,[21] Gerbert foresaw an imminent crisis in his affairs (Letters 212, 214, 216-219).

All of his persuasive powers he poured into vigorous protests to Archbishop Siguin of Sens, primate of the French, against Siguin's acceptance of the papal decision because of its inequitableness, injustice, and even illegality. All in vain. The pressure on Gerbert of the complaints of those who were suffering from the cessation of religious services was stronger than arguments and logic. During the first week of April Gerbert capitulated by fleeing to Germany, never to return to France again.

He turned his steps to Otto III at Aachen whom he found nearly ready to depart on a campaign against the Slavs northeast of Magdeburg (Letters 219, 221-22).[22] The warmth of Otto's welcome and his obvious delight in Gerbert's presence were a soothing balm to the prelate's bruised spirit.

Midst all his tribulations Gerbert had never lost his zest for teaching, and soon he was transmitting his enthusiasm for learning to a new and eager pupil—Otto III. In the spring and summer of 997 scarcely a minute of their association was wasted.[23] School became almost more important than war, and court assemblies became not just functions to attend but dialectical debates to be participated in (Letter 232).

While Otto was still campaigning in eastern Germany and Havelland he had bestowed upon Gerbert the estate of Sasbach, near Strasbourg. Gerbert left Magdeburg in July to take possession (Letters 223-224). However, his enjoyment of it was short-lived. First he became ill (Letter 232), and next his ownership was disputed by another claimant (Letter 229).

In a short while, after Otto returned to Aachen from his successful Slavic campaigns, he informed Gerbert of his determination to have the whole of the Rheims dispute brought before Pope Gregory. As

---

[21] JL I, 492; Letter 214, introductory note and n. 5.
[22] DO III 240, 242.
[23] Letters 221 (last paragraph), 226 (salutation), 230, 231, and 232.

Otto left for Italy in October, 997, he invited Gerbert to become his
teacher and a member of his chapel (Letter 230). With alacrity
Gerbert set out to join him in Italy, and for six months he was again
one of the group of men closely associated with Otto. As a member
of his chapel Gerbert functioned particularly as a musician, while
other clerics, along with their religious duties, carried on the govern-
mental business of the chancery.[24]

The object of the Italian journey was achieved. On April 28, 998,
Pope Gregory removed Gerbert from the Rheims controversy by
carrying out Otto III's desire to have Gerbert created archbishop of
Ravenna.[25]

In this second most important ecclesiastical post in Italy Gerbert
carried on a vigorous reform administration. In February, 999, Pope
Gregory V died. Otto III immediately summoned his beloved teacher
to present himself for election as bishop of Rome and hence as head
of the Holy Roman Catholic Church. His election occurred on
Sunday, April 2, 999, and one week later, April 9th, he was consecrated bishop and pope.

The name he chose, Sylvester II (after Sylvester I), was a decla-
ration that emperor and pope agreed on a policy of strengthening and
pushing the bounds of the Christian Roman empire. Both had their
eyes upon the south of Italy, which they strove to bring into the orbit
of the Roman Church and the new Roman empire. There Sylvester,
in the push to the south, began the feudalization of papal lands by
enfeoffing Count Daiferio in return for military service (Letter 249).
Both strove to break Venice's political and spiritual connection with
Byzantium especially as Venice embarked upon conquests in the
Adriatic (Letter 256). Both welcomed Stephen of Hungary to the
fold of the Roman Church and the friendship of the German-Roman
empire [26] as they hoped that the Byzantine Greeks were being thereby
estopped from further activity this far to the west. Both hearkened

---

[24] Letter 227, n. 1.

[25] JL 3883; Kehr, *Italia pontificia* V, 52, No. 166.

[26] Thietmar ɪᴠ.xxviii, "As Waic [Stephen], on his part, was creating episcopal
sees in his kingdom, through the willingness of the aforesaid emperor [Otto III]
and the encouragement of his brother-in-law, Henry, duke of Bavaria, he received the crown and the [papal] benediction." See also *Stephani regis Ungariae
vita minor*, Chap. V, MGSS XI, 228; and *Stephani regis Ungariae vita maior*,
Chaps. VII-IX, MGSS XI, 232-34.

to the plea of Boleslaw of Poland for Roman ecclesiastical organization in his land, but on the political side in this case Sylvester II and Otto III appeared to disagree. Otto certainly seems to have been willing for Boleslaw to become a king, but, for some unknown reason, Sylvester refused acquiescence. Perhaps he was uncertain of the legitimacy of Boleslaw's claim to kingship [27]—a matter in which he was a not unskilled politician.

Sylvester II reached even farther afield. He continued to maintain the slender thread of communication with the far distant Vladimir of Kievan Russia, probably in the hope that the day would come when this Russian prince would give ear to the religious ideas of the West.[28] To the north, Sylvester demanded of King Olaf Trygvvesön greater conformity to Roman usage, especially in substituting the Roman alphabet for the runic, if his was to be recognized as a Christian nation.[29]

Gerbert's exceptional administrative ability and knowledge, as well as the renown of the name which he brought to the papal office, produced increasing respect for it as its high moral tone and ready accessibility to all became apparent. Although as Sylvester II he insisted upon regularly held papal synods, he still clung to his former ideas that most church problems could be dealt with better by local synods where more effort should be made to reach agreement.[30]

"Against all schisms I will defend the unity of the Church, even by my death, if so decreed," he had written to the French Queen Adelaide (Letter 221). In every corner he tried to effect this unity. Arnulf he accepted as archbishop of Rheims (Letter 244). Petroald he recognized as abbot of Bobbio.[31] He exerted himself to the utmost to prevent Germany from splitting apart ecclesiastically in the acrimonious dispute between Archbishop Willigis of Mainz and Bishop

---

[27] A. F. Czajkowski, "The Congress of Gniezno in the Year 1000," *Speculum*, XXIV (1949), 352-54.

[28] *Polnoe sobranie russkikh lietopisei, isdannoe po Vysochaishemu Povelieniiu Arkheograficheskoiu Kommissieiu. IX.Lietopisnyi sbornik, imenuemyi Patriarsheiu ili Nikonovskoiu lietopis'iu* (St. Petersburg, 1862), p. 68.

[29] J. G. von Eckhart, *De origine Germanorum eorumque vetustissimus coloniis, migrationibus ac rebus gestis libri duo,* ed. C. L. Scheidius (Göttingen, 1750), p. 192.

[30] Letters 256 and 257.

[31] DO III 335.

Bernward of Hildesheim over the jurisdiction of the nunnery of Gandersheim.[32] He gave encouragement and advice to the leaders in Catalan Spain, ecclesiastical and lay, who were striving to promote Christian stability in this region and to push the Christian borderland farther to the south (Letters 251, 255, 260, 261). To those who petitioned to be taken under the direct protection of the papacy, i.e., of St. Peter, he gave assent (Letters 235, 237, 241, 243, 245, 247, 250, 252, 254, 259). Thus, short though Sylvester II's papal reign was (April 9, 999–May 12, 1003), the period was one both of growth and consolidation for the Church.

Why does Gerbert command our attention? Foremost is the admiration which is always aroused for an individual of obscure origin who rises to heights of success through sheer ability and diligent use of his talents. Those who have seen in Gerbert only an ambitious self-seeker forget how many years he obeyed the Biblical injunction, "Seek ye first the Kingdom of God," which he found principally in devotion to learning, and that only afterwards did he discover how "all these things are added unto you," and added because the world valued his way of seeking the Kingdom of God.

Next, he insisted that education must be based upon Greek knowledge, and that theology should be approached only after a thoroughly organized intellectual preparation which should include knowledge of all of the liberal arts, not simply those of the trivium. The courage with which he pursued the teaching of the frowned-upon subjects of the little understood quadrivium is only occasionally matched in history. He broke with all tradition in his devising of charts, models, and instruments for demonstration to his students and for handling by them,[33] and he revived the Greek habit of actual forensic practice before a skilled teacher of public speaking (a "sophist") by students prepared by himself in dialectic and rhetoric. In his efforts to fit the teaching to the students instead of the students to the teaching Gerbert ranks among the greatest teachers.

In the politics of the end of the tenth century he played the most

---

[32] Thangmar, *Vita Bernwardi*, Chaps. XXII, XXVIII-XXX; Tschan, *Saint Bernward of Hildesheim*, I, 153, 157ff., 165-81.

[33] Richer III.lxix-liv; Letter 105; Lattin, "Astronomy," in "Symposium on the Tenth Century," *Medievalia et Humanistica*, IX (1955), 13-17.

important part of any single individual. He helped to save the German throne for the Ottonian family. He belittled the abilities of the last Carolingians and was an important factor in the election of Hugh Capet as king of the French. Then he struggled to keep Hugh firmly established on the throne. He endeavored to nip the nascent power of Otto III's chief Italian rival, Arduin, margrave of Ivrea. Above all, he worked side by side with Otto III towards a world-embracing Christian Roman empire.

With Gerbert, practical number work (logistics) for the first time gained an equal status with theoretical number work (arithmetic) as a subject of formal advanced teaching.[34] He developed speed in arithmetical operations through his revival of the use of the abacus and his introduction from Spain of the nine Hindu-Arabic numerals (without the zero).[35] Also, he brought with him rules for their use, which he wrote out in an elaborated form,[36] and which became the accepted basic work about the use of the abacus and the subject of numerous commentaries by contemporary and later writers.[37] For two hundred years after Gerbert's time the abacists reigned supreme and only slowly retreated before the onslaught of the zero with its fantastic properties. The abacus and Gerbert were so identified that Gerbert's name almost supplanted the word "abacist" as men spoke, instead, of a "girbercist." [38]

Gerbert has seldom found a place in the histories of astronomy because he propounded no new astronomical theory nor made any discoveries. Yet the ready acceptance accorded Arabic astronomy in the following centuries was, in large measure, attributable to the impetus Gerbert gave to the study of the heavens. One of his first letters describes his labor in contriving a precursor of the telescope (Letter 2).

One who would understand the medieval mind should immerse himself in Aristotelian dialectical studies, transmitted through the sixth-century Boethius. Although outlined by Martianus Capella and Cassiodorus, and by Isidore, copying the latter, they were first

[34] Letters 6 and 7.
[35] Richer iii.liv.
[36] Bubnov, *Gerberti opera mathematica*, pp. 8-22.
[37] *Ibid.*, pp. 245-84.
[38] *Ibid.*, p. 291.

effectively taught by Gerbert.[39] Had he accomplished nothing more
than this, Gerbert would still be worthy of our attention, for dialectic
became the backbone for orthodoxy on the one hand and the support
of heresy on the other. Pious churchmen now began to worry that
Boethius was supplanting the authority of the Church Fathers.[40] The
remaining portions of the Aristotelian logical corpus which became
part of Western European thought in the twelfth century were
integrated into the whole fabric only on the solid foundation of
Gerbert's organized teaching in the tenth.[41]

Like many an inspiring teacher from Socrates onward, Gerbert
wrote but little, and of this little, the most interesting part is only
occasionally didactic, consisting, as it does, of his own letters and
papal privileges, and the letters he wrote for others. Only the letters
and privileges will be discussed here.

MANUSCRIPTS AND EDITIONS OF THE LETTERS

The letters written before Gerbert became Pope Sylvester II may
be divided into two groups. The larger group, for convenience called
the "Collection," has been based on copies which Gerbert retained on
parchment sheets and which he made into one or more registers. This
group is known through two differing sets of manuscripts. The other
group consists of miscellaneous letters which are found in different
manuscripts or have been inserted into accounts of councils. In my
translation I have inserted these latter where they would fall chronologically. I have then numbered all the letters consecutively, regardless of their sources. In the introductory note to each letter I have
given its number in the Latin edition of the letters collected and edited
by Julien Havet, upon which my translation is substantially based.

All of the original letters written by Gerbert are lost. He began to
keep copies of his letters regularly only after he became abbot of St.
Columban of Bobbio, when he discovered that Emperor Otto II's
replies to his letters did not correspond to the questions he had asked.

The notebook or registers containing his own copies are also lost.

[39] Lattin, "Eleventh Century MS Munich 14436," *Isis*, XXXVIII (1948), 222-24.
[40] Otloh *Dialogus de tribus questionibus*, PL CXLVI, 60A-62B.
[41] The best evidence of this integration is found in MSS Chartres 497 and 498,
usually called the *Heptateuchon* of Thierry of Chartres. CG XI: *Chartres*, pp.
211-14.

Two contemporary copies were made of the Collection, but unfortunately each was incomplete. One, now lost, seems to have been made by or for Gerbert in 989 for presentation either to the German court or to a powerful German prelate. In 997 Gerbert made a few additions to it. Nothing definite is known of this manuscript (designated as MS P) until the end of the sixteenth century when it appeared in the library of Papire Masson and was used by Papire's brother Jean for publishing the letters in 1611. Before the publication a copy had been sent by Nicolas Le Fèvre to Cardinal Baronius in Italy, who in turn made a copy and returned Le Fèvre's copy to Paris. Baronius's copy survives in MS Vallicelliana G. 94 in Rome (called MS V). Le Fèvre's copy and the original manuscript (P) have disappeared.

The second contemporary copy of Gerbert's letters was undoubtedly made from material collected by Richer, monk of St. Rémy of Rheims and a devoted pupil of Gerbert. Richer assembled accounts of church councils, Gerbert's letters, and similar material to use in preparing the only early biography of Gerbert,[42] which he inserted into his *Historia Francorum*. A copy of this assembled material was made possibly at Rheims, possibly at St. Mesmin of Micy, by a monk Stabilis during Gerbert's papacy or soon after his death in 1003. This manuscript survives as MS Leyden Vossius, quarto, latin No. 54 (referred to as MS L). In the seventeenth century three copies were made of the second half of MS L. Two of them begin with Letter 163 (Havet Letter 155)—MS Berlin Phillipps 1718 and MS Vatican Barberini XXXII (olim 118). The third copy begins with Letter 161 (Havet Letter 153) and is now MS Paris Bibliothèque nationale franç. 6046, fols. 477-507.[43]

Some of the first 151 letters of MS V are missing in MS L. Likewise, certain syllabic shorthand signs or Tironian notes which are reproduced in MS V do not appear in MS L, although occasionally spaces have been left as if for their insertion or their transcription. This is true even for the headings of some letters in MS L. Havet

---

[42] Richer iii.xliii ff.

[43] F. Weigle, "Studien zur Überlieferung der Briefsammlung Gerberts von Reims," DA, X (1953-54), 20, 51ff. Weigle is the first person to study this copy of MS P since Leopold Delisle called attention to it in his *Catalogue des manuscrits français* in 1902.

believed that the letters missing from MS L but present in MS V were written in this shorthand because they were politically compromising. However, such a theory fails to explain why a few Tironian notes still appear in MS V, and Havet did not realize how widespread the knowledge of Tironian notes was, as later research has demonstrated.[44] Havet and Bubnov [45] each independently solved the transcription of most of the Tironian notes in the letters. Although Havet's idea of complete letters entered into a notebook in Tironian notes has been abandoned, the basic idea that Gerbert tried to keep the record of some of his letters secret still persists. According to Lot and Uhlirz, Gerbert kept at least two registers of his letters, and one of them was secret. This latter contained the letters in MS P not found in MS L.[46]

The letters in the Collection did not attract much attention until the latter part of the sixteenth century. Between 1007 and 1028 Hartwich of St. Emmeram of Regensburg copied Letters 8 and 40, perhaps from Gerbert's register at Rheims.[47] A few years later both the charges and countercharges of Bishop Dietrich of Metz and Duke Charles of Lower Lorraine in Letters 39 and 40 were copied into a collection at Worms cathedral.[48] But even earlier, just a short while after the penning of these polemical letters of the controversy in 984, one of Gerbert's students from St. Willibrord of Echternach had copied them from his notebook into what is now MS Paris, Biblio-

---

[44] H. Leclercq, "Notes tironiennes," DACL, XII, Pt. 2 (Paris, 1936), cols. 1669-1708, contains an extensive discussion (with 3 plates), summarizing practically all the different articles on the subject.

[45] Havet, pp. lvii-lxx; Bubnov, I, 262-89, 349-54, 365-66.

[46] F. Lot, "Etude sur le recueil des lettres de Gerbert," BEC, C, (1939), 31f.; M. Uhlirz, *Untersuchungen über Inhalt und Datierung der Briefe Gerberts* (Schriftenreihe der historischen Kommission bei der Bayerischen Akademie der Wissenschaften, No. 2, Göttingen, 1957), p. 12. Both authors believe that the registers consisted of small packages of parchment, each package containing somewhat related material. In this way they account for the fact that so many letters are chronologically out of place.

[47] Lattin, "Eleventh Century MS Munich 14436," *Isis*, XXXVIII (1948), 225, notes 133, 134. Gerbert's registers could have been at St. Rémy of Rheims, many of whose manuscripts were destroyed by fires in 1420 and 1774. An unidentifiable manuscript of the letters was at Cluny in the twelfth century, since a catalogue of the Cluny library, drawn up in the twelfth century, lists Gerbert's letters (No. 289). L. Delisle, *Le Cabinet des manuscrits de la bibliothèque nationale*, II (Paris, 1874), 469.

[48] P. Ewald, "Reise nach Italien im Winter von 1876 auf 1877," NA, III (1878), 321, 328-29; Bubnov I, 153-56.

thèque Nationale lat. 11127, fols. 62r-63v.[49] The scientific information in Letter 161 was copied at the beginning of the eleventh century into MS Paris, BN lat. 8663, fol. 50r, from Fleury, and from this into the twelfth century MS Paris BN lat. 13013 (once St. Germain 989).[50] Either the original draft or a copy of Letter 85, the epitaph of Otto II, appears in MS Rheims 385.[51]

The public first became acquainted with Gerbert's letters in 1587 when twelve of them were published from MS L by Nicolas Vignier,[52] physician and historian of King Henry III of France. More extensive acquaintance came in 1611 with the publication of the letters by Jean Masson from the now lost MS P of his deceased brother Papire.[53] In 1636 André Duchesne reprinted the letters in Masson's edition and added the letters in MS L not used by Masson.[54]

The nineteenth century saw two editions of the letters, that of Alexandre Olleris in 1867 in a volume devoted to all of Gerbert's works,[55] and that of Julien Havet in 1889, the latter being the first and only critical edition.[56] It is based upon the order of the letters in MS V through Letter 160, but upon the text of MS L wherever available. A proposed edition by Nicolaus Bubnov resulted in a 1038-page study, which he published (in Russian) in 1888-90,[57] but the edition of the letters was abandoned because of the unexpected publi-

---

[49] Bubnov I, 153-56; Havet, pp. liv, n. 4; 25, note; G. Lacombe and others, *Aristoteles latinus*, I (Union académique internationale, Corpus philosophorum medii aevi, Rome, 1939), 534, ascribes this manuscript to Echternach. The text of the letters is closer to MS P than to MS L.

[50] Bubnov I, 156-57; Bubnov, *Gerberti opera mathematica*, pp. lvii, lxi, 38-39; F. M. Carey, De scriptura Floriacensi (Unpublished Ph. D. Dissertation, HU 90, Harvard University, 1923), p. 102. Used with kind permission of the author.

[51] Folio 160v. The same writer jotted down the title of an epitaph to King Lothair, but failed to continue with the epitaph itself. CG XXXVIII: *Reims*, I (1904), 507.

[52] *La Bibliothèque historiale* (Paris, 1587), II.

[53] *Epistolae Gerberti primo Remorum, dein Ravennatum archiepiscopi, postea Romani pontificis Silvestri secundi.*, etc. (Paris, 1611), cited herein as Masson edition, or edition Masson.

[54] *Historiae Francorum scriptores*, II (Paris, 1636), 789-844, cited herein as Duchesne edition, or edition Duchesne.

[55] *Oeuvres de Gerbert* (Clermont-Ferrand and Paris, 1867), cited herein as Olleris.

[56] *Lettres de Gerbert (983-997)* (Paris, 1889), cited herein as Havet.

[57] *Sbornik pisem Gerberta kak istoricheskii istochnik (983-997): Kriticheskaia monografiia po rukopisiam.* 2 vols. (St. Petersburg, 1888-90), cited herein as Bubnov.

cation of Havet's edition. A new edition has been announced by the editors of the *Monumenta Germaniae historica* by Dr. Fritz Weigle.

PAPAL PRIVILEGES, LETTERS, AND ACTS

The fragmentary state of early papal registers extends to those of Sylvester II. Although Erich Caspar [58] has suggested that possibly no papal registers were kept between the time of Stephen V (885-891) and Alexander II (1061-75), there are three vague references to a collection (or collections) of Sylvester II's papal documents.[59]

The list or *Regesta* of papal documents by P. Jaffé, revised and enlarged by F. Kaltenbrunner, P. Ewald, and S. Loewenfeld,[60] was the starting point of my research on Sylvester II's privileges, letters, and acts. Thirty-seven authentic and two spurious ones are listed there; Letter 35 is incorrectly included among these papal documents (as JL † 3938) because of the nineteenth-century idea that it was a summons to a military crusade for recovery of Jerusalem.

Sylvester II's documents are known through originals, later copies of the originals, references and insertions in chronicles, and references in both imperial diplomas and documents of later popes. The thirty-one documents by Sylvester for which texts exist have been translated here. They have been placed in chronological order, insofar as possible, and numbered continuously after the letters written prior to his papal reign. The remaining documents, for which texts are not extant, are listed in Appendix C. Indications are that the whole number is more than two and one-half times the number of the authentic documents in the Jaffé-Loewenfeld *Regesta*.

Papyrus was used for papal documents until the year 1057, with

[58] "Studien zum Register Johanns VIII," NA, XXXVI (1910), 101, n. 2.

[59] MS Berlin 612, latin folio 197 (s. XII), fol. 188b, has a notation *Ex privilegiis et epistolis Silvestri pape.* [From the privileges and letters of Pope Sylvester]. V. Rose, *Handschriften-Verzeichnisse der Königlichen Bibliothek zu Berlin*, XIII, Abteilung 2 (Berlin, 1903), 553. J. Pflugk Harttung (*Iter Italicum* [Stuttgart, 1883], p. 131) states that JL 3904 [Letter 240] was copied into MS Vatican 7157 (MS Margarini) from an autograph in the Secret Archive 3308, which was volume VII on German affairs, fol. 118. Masson (p. 79) alludes to a manuscript collection of Gerbert's letters to King Robert II, Emperor Otto III, and other notables, which I interpret to indicate papal letters.

[60] *Regesta pontificum Romanorum ab condita ecclesia ad annum post Christum natum MCXCVIII* (2d ed., Leipzig, 1888), cited as JK, JE, JL. Sylvester II's letters are numbered JL 3900-JL 3940.

few exceptions,[61] and three of Sylvester II's papyrus originals are still extant (Letters 242, 251, 261 [JL 3906, 3918, 3927]). Sylvester participated in the preparation of his documents by making a labarum ☧ before his signature—a practice just previously introduced by Pope Gregory V—and by signing his name to the document in Tironian notes, one of his little conceits. The signatures are the writing of a man very certain of himself, quite accustomed to signing his name and that with considerable dispatch (see facsimile facing p. 364).

If one takes into consideration all of Sylvester's documents they may be grouped into four classifications: (1) judgments (*constituta*) pronounced by synods; (2) opinions or decrees (*decreta*) rendered by him which especially touched points of canon law; (3) privileges granting exemptions, or rights, or confirmations of previous ones; and (4) personal letters which, though bearing on affairs of the papacy, seemed sufficiently personal for Sylvester himself to write (or to dictate), and in which can be observed his compact, impatient, often brusque style. A fifth (unclassified) group consists of three documents in which he recorded his presence at, or his approval of, court proceedings.

Sylvester II's documents, except the personal letters, follow general papal chancery practice. The opening and closing portions (protocol and eschatocol) are formulas. The protocol contains the invocation (if any) by words or by symbolic monogram like a labarum or chrismon, the name of the addressor (*intitulatio*) with a formula of devotion and the name of the addressee (*inscriptio*). In the eschatocol is found the signature of the pope (and of the emperor occasionally), the statement (*scriptum*) of the notary who prepared the document, the general date, and the more specific date and signature of the librarian as he authenticated the pope's signature and delivered the document. Part of Sylvester's conclusion in his own hand consisted of Farewell (*Bene Valete*).

[61] The earliest known use of parchment by the papal chancery was a privilege of Pope John XIII, April 15, 967 (JL 3714), issued at Ravenna, and this was an exception. The second papal parchment document is the judicial decision of a council, presided over by Sylvester II, rendered against Bishop Cono of Perugia, December 3, 1002. It is the only parchment document known to have been issued during Sylvester II's reign. Kehr, *Italia pontificia*, IV, p. 67, No. 4; Ewald, "Zur Diplomatik Silvesters II," NA, IX (1884), 345-46.

The text itself consists of the statement (*arenga*) of the motivation for granting the document; the promulgation or notification; the narration of events preceding the issuance of the privilege (which might include a statement of the sponsorship), the petition, the declaratory statement (*dispositio*) of the grantor (the pope); and the decree. Ordinarily there follows a sanction or threat of punishment, usually containing a threat of excommunication for any infringement of the terms of the document, as well as the positive sanction of inducements or promises of rewards for observing them.

In all of these various parts the papal notaries made use of formulas and scraps of formulas which they had learned from their textbook, the *Liber diurnus* or Daily Book, a collection of appropriate papal documents dating back at least to Pope Gregory I.[62]

SIGNIFICANCE OF THE LETTERS AND PAPAL PRIVILEGES

A great loss of documents, manuscripts ,and other forms of historical evidence has long prevented recognition of the much maligned tenth century as an important creative period. Thus, the survival of a considerable body of letters written by, and to, a central figure— Gerbert—is a matter for rejoicing.

In a measure they help to compensate for some of the losses by their illuminating all facets of tenth-century life as Gerbert and his correspondents write of many things: politics; emperors, kings, nobles, popes, and other ecclesiastics; the confusion between the secular and ecclesiastical obligations of the clergy; agriculture; money; artisans, architects, teachers, musicians; wars and sieges; constant intrigues; dialectic, rhetoric, arithmetic, music, geometry, astronomy, art, medicine, and law; books and libraries; travel; sickness; even love and marriage; and, above all, faith, fealty, fidelity, and friendship.

Most typical of the four latter categories are the nineteen letters written to Archbishop Egbert of Trier (Letters 20, 34, 46, 60-62, 75, 110, 113, 115, 118, 122, 127, 130, 135, 143 [?], 165, 177, and 181). Their political importance is overshadowed by the picture they reveal not only of Gerbert but also of a warm friendship between two noble personalities. Separated from each other by some distance, they kept this friendship flourishing through letters, containing expressions of

[62] Santifaller, "Verwendung des *Liber diurnus*," MIOG, XLIX (1935).

fine attitudes and high ideals—in this tenth century which has seemed to many persons to be lacking in man's finer sentiments.

Although the Collection originated as a measure of self-defense whereby Gerbert might have at hand a ready record of just what he wrote during the trying days at Bobbio, it became a type of autobiography. This is true in spite of the fact that only about half of the letters were sent in Gerbert's own name, for emperor, king, archbishop, bishop, duke, count, and council employed his pen. Moreover, a few of them were epitaphs, some inscriptions on gifts, and four letters which he received. Many of the letters were written under the stress of an urgency that makes them ring true. Hence, they provide the best sort of material for a study of his personality, as not only Gerbert's morality and strength of character are revealed in his own words, but also his weaknesses, temptations, and doubts.

In most cases where he acted as secretary, only the general tenor of the letter was outlined for him. He then wrote it in his own vigorous language, and the contents conform so closely with his own ideas that there is more than a suspicion that the contents, too, originated with him.

This is strikingly revealed in the war of words which Gerbert penned for each side in Letters 39 and 40. Each writer, at Gerbert's instigation, accuses the other of infidelity to the Ottos. Gerbert influenced Bishop Dietrich of Metz, unenthusiastic about Empress Theophanu's guardianship of Otto III, to remind Duke Charles of Lower Lorraine in strong words of the obligations of fealty. The sarcastic irony of his explanation of his own part in the controversy (in Letter 41) indicates that, although ostensibly writing Letter 40 for Charles of Lorraine, actually Charles was only Gerbert's mouthpiece in the latter's effort to clinch Dietrich's transference of allegiance from Duke Henry of Bavaria to Empress Theophanu.

The letters were written in good, if not excellent, Latin. The style is compact, even cryptic, and the vocabulary is mainly classical. Like Cicero, Gerbert was not averse to a well-turned pun, and occasionally he used a *clausula*, or particular rhythmic sentence ending, such as Cicero employed throughout his orations. However, in spite of his literary interests and his access to manuscripts in the libraries of Bobbio and Rheims, Gerbert's vocabulary expanded very little during the twenty years covered by the Collection of letters, and he repeats certain brief phrases many times over. Furthermore, his quotations from classical authors are not unusual, nor as numerous as we might expect. On the other hand, the number of his Biblical citations may appear surprising in view of the fact that so much emphasis has always been laid upon his secular learning.

Turning to his papal letters and privileges as Sylvester II, it is difficult to express a true appreciation of them since we possess the texts of considerably less than half of those known from all sources. However, even in the field of papal diplomatics they are important because of the three precious surviving originals (Letters 242, 251, 261).

Scanty though the number of the extant texts is, still the striking cooperation between emperor and pope, the two "luminaries of the universe," is clearly apparent (Letter 235). Certain details of the struggles of ecclesiastics to free themselves from lay control and of the regular clergy to free themselves from control by the secular clergy, as well as the rapidly increasing process of attaching both directly to the papacy, appear in these papal letters. Incidental to these matters there appears information on the manorial system, which has not yet been utilized in the studies of agrarian organization. The many names and boundaries of localities in the privileges are important for local history studies. Letter 249 (JL 3912) presents a significant change in papal attitude, so that now papal land is to be used to assure military power as a necessary permanent bolster to spiritual power.

Sylvester's determined resolve to exact a higher standard of conduct from churchmen emerges in his condemnation of nepotism and simony and in his numerous summonses of miscreants, lay and ecclesiastical, to Rome to answer for their misdeeds before papal councils. In such cases the formalized style of his notaries seemed inadequate so that we have here more of his personal letters, couched in his direct, unvarnished, biting style (Letters 248, 253, 255-57).

Even on the negative side the papal letters have significance, for they cover the period of the so-called "fateful" year, A.D. 1000,[63] but

[63] See A. A. Vasiliev, "Mediaeval Ideas of the End of the World: West and East," *Byzantion*, XVI (1944), 479-87.

there is not one hint that this year was viewed in a different light from any other period of time.

THE PRESENT TRANSLATION

This is the first complete translation of Gerbert's letters into English, although a few have been translated elsewhere. Two translations have been made into French,[64] but neither followed the best Latin edition of the letters. Bubnov in his *Sbornik pisem Gerberta* translated many of the letters into Russian, some completely, some partially, but there are no translations into other languages except for isolated letters.

As stated above, the present translation follows substantially the Latin edition by Havet. But there are some additions to his collection and some departures from his order which call for explanation. Because of considerations of language, style, content, and attendant circumstances, the first 7 letters are ascribed to Gerbert, even when his name does not appear in connection with them. These have been published in various places, as indicated in connection with the translation of each of these letters.

Then follow 226 letters. Of these, 217 are found in MSS L and V, some in MS L only, some in MS V only, some in both manuscripts. Three other letters (222, 225, 226) of the 226 were present in a now lost manuscript from which, in 1587, they were published by Vignier in his *Bibliothèque historiale*. Using the edition of Julien Havet as the basis of the translation of these 220 letters of the 226, I checked it by collating Havet with MS L, MS V, MS Berlin Phillipps 1718, MS Vatican Barberini XXXII (by a photostat), the Masson and Duchesne editions, Vignier, and the notes of Etienne Baluze on his copy of Masson which is now MS Bibliothèque Nationale, Baluze 129 (by a microfilm).[65]

Four other letters of the 226 are those (Nos. 173, 185, 187, 188) which Gerbert included in his account of the council of St.-Basle-de-Verzy of Rheims of 991 (*Acta concilii sancti Basoli*). In addition I have included Gerbert's dedicatory letter and closing portion to his *De rationali et ratione uti* (Letter 232), and the only known letter

---

[64] By Barse, and by Barthélemy. See Bibliography.
[65] See Bubnov, I, 128-46, 357; Havet, pp. liii-liv.

which was undoubtedly written during the year (998-999) of his occupancy of the archbishopric of Ravenna (Letter 233). The papal letters and privileges begin with Letter 234.

The "Collection," that is, those letters which Gerbert himself, before becoming pope, apparently kept as a collection of letters, begins with the letter here numbered 8, but excluding Letters 173, 185, 187, 188, 232, and 233.

Each letter and papal privilege is preceded by my abstract of its contents and by an indication of the place where written and the date of writing as precisely as I have been able to determine them.

The problem of dating the letters, practically all of which are undated in the form in which we have them, has exercised all persons who have studied them. I have dated most of the letters more exactly than Havet and others; great uncertainty I indicate by a question mark. Each date has been arrived at by my consideration of all of the circumstances surrounding the letter, namely, its position in the manuscripts, the reference to future time in a few of the letters, the speed of transportation of persons, letters, and news, pertinent facts concerning the addressees and persons mentioned in the letters, and events mentioned in the letters as checked by other sources. Some of the papal letters have the dates that were put there at the time of writing and delivery (*data*) of the document, and those whose dates have been lost during the manuscript transmission of the documents I have determined according to the same considerations as in the case of the previous letters. The fact of the close cooperation between Otto III and Sylvester II has materially aided my conclusions as to dates since, in several instances, they issued similar documents to the same recipient at approximately the same time.

Many of the letters written before Gerbert became pope are preceded by a heading, indicating the sender and the receiver, often by the first letter of the name only and occasionally in Tironian notes. Where absent in the manuscripts, I have supplied this information in brackets, indicating doubtful names by question marks. Classical letters began with a simple salutation—the name of the sender, the name of the recipient, and the word *Salutem* (greeting; literally, let me greet). Such a salutation is missing from many of Gerbert's letters, and I have not supplied it in such cases. The classical closing, *Vale*, or *Valete* (Farewell) is usually missing, although in a few cases it is present and sometimes very extended (e.g., Letters 41, 51, 102, 105).

An effort has been made to retain in the translation Gerbert's compact style in order to reproduce its full flavor. Except where the English cognate has acquired a different meaning, a Latin word is usually translated by the same English word wherever it is encountered. Gerbert slips from "we" to "I," and "our" to "my," or vice versa, in the same letter, apparently for emphasis, and I follow him in this.

In the papal letters the location of the printed texts which I used is indicated in the introductory note. Where a copyist mentioned the presence of a seal (*bulla*) on a papal letter, or where it actually exists (see Letters 237 and 261), I have indicated it thus: [BULLA]. In the introductory note for each papal document I also give the number in the Jaffé-Loewenfeld *Regesta* I, thus: JL 3924. I have tried to make the chronology more correct and more precise than in the JL *Regesta*.

LETTERS

LETTERS

1. RHEIMS. July 21 - September, 976?

Adalbero, archbishop of Rheims, and Stephen, deacon of Rome and papal legate, rebuke Thibaud, bishop of Amiens, for securing his office by force, for refusing to attend synods, and hereby excommunicate him

ADALBERO, ARCHBISHOP OF RHEIMS,[1] AND STEPHEN, CARDINAL DEACON OF ROME, TO THIBAUD, BISHOP OF AMIENS

O Thibaud,[2] aged in days and in evil doing, what profit has your absence brought you? Is it only to abuse our patience,[3] you despiser of divine and human laws, that you have called upon the Holy See but have not traveled thence? On July 19th we received from you letters, prepared at Rome as a result of your money and lies, which contain a little more against you than for you.

You would not attend this [present] synod unless the reservation of your honor was agreed to. Since this was not agreed to, you were not present. Why do you hide yourself? Why do you shun the holy synod? You were unwilling to present yourself to the one called for July 3d, and you refuse to be present at the one convoked for September 24th. The reverend "physicians," well acquainted with your ailments, to wit, the tyrannical power by which you have been adorned with a priest's fillet, contrary to the royal wish, and that pseudo-archbishop [4] of yours with his excommunicated bishops, who, by the laying on of his hands, infected you as if by a certain contagion, agreed upon the dishonor [5] as far as you are concerned.

Therefore, because in the council condemning Boniface[6] the judgment of Lord Pope Benedict VII found you incurable, and because his son Stephen, deacon of the Holy Roman Church, was unable to cure you, we are separating you from the Lord's flock; and by authority of the Omnipotent One and of St. Mary and of St. Peter, prince of the apostles, we condemn and excommunicate you, and forbid you access to the threshold of the church until you gain true insight into yourself and make worthy satisfaction.

I, Stephen, deacon of the Holy Roman Church, presided at this judgment in place of Lord Pope Benedict VII and ordered it.

I, Adalbero, archbishop of the holy church of Rheims was present and signed with the rest.

This translation is based on Havet, pp. 234-36, Appendix I (from MS Leyden Voss. Q. 17, s. X, fol. 1, from St. Mesmin de Micy). The style and vocabulary indicate Gerbert's authorship, even though it is not in his Collection.

Synods were usually held on Sunday, or Sunday-Monday, and since July 3d fell on Monday, and September 24th on Sunday in 976, Havet (pp. 234, n. 1, 235, n. 6) suggests 976 as the year. However, Olleris (p. 485), and T. Schieffer (*Die päpstlichen Legaten in Frankreich* [Historische Studien, No. 263, Berlin, 1935] pp. 35f.) insist the date was 975.

1. A canon of Metz cathedral, who succeeded Odelric (962-November 6, 969) as archbishop of Rheims in 969, where he carried on a vigorous reform program in church matters. Richer III.xxiiff.

2. "Thibaud, named bishop of Amiens in 947 by the intruding archbishop of Rheims, Hugh, son of Count Heribert [II] of Vermandois, was excommunicated at the Council of Trier in 948 by Marin, legate of the Holy See, and was chased out. After the death of Bishop Raimbaud in 972, he returned. In 975, Pope Benedict VII excommunicated him; and in the same year this condemnation was announced in the city of Rheims." Olleris, p. 485.

3. Cicero *In Catilinam* II.i.

4. Hugh. See n. 2 above.

5. Havet (p. 235) leaves a space after *convenerunt* [agreed]. However, I could make out the letters *ifā Bene* in the MS so that the text seems to read: *Convenerunt infam[iam?] Bene pro te reverendi medici.*

6. Boniface VII (974, 984-85). At the Council of St. Basle (991) Bishop Arnulf of Orléans referred to him as "a horrible monster, surpassing all mortals in wickedness." Olleris, p. 205; Gregorovius, *History of Rome*, III, 377f., 384f., 396-98.

2. RHEIMS. 978?

Gerbert explains the construction of a hemisphere for making astronomical observations to Constantine, grammaticus *of Fleury*

GERBERT TO CONSTANTINE[1]

In reply to your query about the sphere for demonstrating the celestial circles and constellations,[2] my brother, it is made completely round, divided equally through the middle by the circumference, which has been divided into sixty parts. Place one foot of the compass wherever you determine the beginning of the circumference to be, and place the other foot on that point which includes six of the sixty parts of the aforementioned circumference; and while you are swinging the compass you will include twelve parts. Without changing the first foot, the second is extended to the point on the circumference that includes the eleventh part; and it is rotated so that it embraces twenty-two parts.[3] In the same manner as before the foot is extended to the fifteenth part of the aforementioned line and by this rotation of the compass, half of the sphere having thirty parts is cut. This has thirty parts.

Then, with the compass changed to the other part of the sphere, pay particular attention to the point where you shall place the first foot of the compass so that it will be exactly opposite, and observe the selfsame method for measuring off the circumference and the encircling of the parts. Now there will be only five circles and the middle one equals the line divided into sixty parts.

Therefore, take one of such hemispheres, and, after it has been hollowed out, make a hole at each point on the said line where you place the other foot of the compass for making the circles so that these points on the circumference shall be in the middle of the opening.

Also, make separate holes at the poles of the sphere where you have placed the first foot of the compass so that the middle of those holes will determine the boundary of the aforementioned hemisphere. Now there will be seven openings, in each of which you place tubes half a foot long; the two at the ends will be opposite each other so that you may see through both as if through one.[4]

To prevent the tubes from swerving hither and yon, utilize an iron semicircle measured and perforated in the same proportions as the aforementioned hemisphere and to it fasten the upper ends of the tubes. They differ from organ pipes by being all equal in size in order not to distort the vision of anyone observing the circles of the heavens. Actually, let the semicircle be almost two inches wide and have thirty parts lengthwise, like the whole hemisphere; and use the same measures for dividing it so as to center the tubes [properly] in their [respective] holes.

Accordingly, when our polestar [5] can be observed, place the hemisphere which we have described under the open sky in such a way that, [looking] through the tubes at the extremities, you may perceive the polestar itself by an unobstructed view. If you doubt that this is the polestar, station one tube [6] in such a position that it does not move during the whole night and look toward that star which you believe to be the polestar. If it is the polestar, you will be able to see it the whole of the night; if any other star, it will soon not be visible through the tube because it will have changed its position.

Therefore, having placed the hemisphere in the aforementioned manner so that it is immovable, you will be able to determine the North Pole through the upper and lower first tube, the Arctic Circle through the second, the summer through the third, the equinoctial through the fourth, the winter through the fifth, the Antarctic [Circle] through the sixth. As for the south polestar, because it is under the land, no sky but earth appears to anyone trying to view it through both tubes.

This translation is based on Bubnov, *Gerberti opera mathematica*, pp. 25-28. Included also in Olleris, pp. 479-80.

1. Monk of Fleury (St.-Benoît-sur-Loire, dept. Loiret, diocese of Orléans), elementary teacher (*grammaticus*) and later an advanced teacher (*scholasticus*) there, who became abbot of St.-Mesmin-de-Micy, nearby, about 1004. He was one of Gerbert's most stimulating pupils. F. M. Warren, "Constantine of Fleury, 985-1014," *Transactions of the Connecticut Academy of Arts and Sciences*, XV (1909), 285-92; Manitius, II, 506-09, and Index s. v. Konstantin. F. Weigle, "Studien zur Überlieferung der Briefsammlung Gerberts von Reims," DA, XIV (1958), 158ff.

2. "The calculation of this instrument was so accurate that with its diameter pointed at the pole and its prolonged semicircle turned towards the sky unknown circles were brought to light and stamped deep in the memory." Richer III.li.

3. Hyginus' translation of the *Phainomena* of Aratos of Soli was the source for these distances, as well as for a considerable portion of this letter. Hyginus I.i.6. Olleris (pp. 479, 596) suggests correcting "VI" to "IV," and "XII" to "VIII" parts of the circumference, but he did not know Gerbert's source, nor the fact that 6 parts = 36°, the height of the Pole at Rhodes, was generally used for the Arctic Circle.

Constantine knew the Hyginus work at Fleury where there were two MSS of it—MS Vat. Regin. 1260, s. IX or s. X, and MS Bern 45, s. X. F. M. Carey, "De scriptura floriacensi" (Unpublished Ph. D. dissertation, HU 90, Harvard University, 1923) pp. 134, 56; used by kind permission of the author. In 978, Abbo also used the Hyginus work at Fleury. A. Van de Vyver, "Oeuvres d'Abbon," *Revue Bénédictine*, XLVI (1935), 146.

4. For medieval representations of a person observing the stars through a tube see F. Feldhaus, *Die Technik der Antike und der Mittelalters* (Potsdam, 1931), p. 249, no. 276, and p. 291, no. 306, reproducing MS St. Gall 18, s. X in., p. 43, where the observer wears classical or clerical costume and the tube is supported on acanthus leaves on top of a column; and MS Munich 17405, a. 1241, p. 3 (probably from Tegernsee), where a cleric, seated in a high-backed chair, with his left hands holds an unsupported tube to his left eye. Other medieval illustrations are found in Henri Michel, "Les tubes optiques avant le telescope," *Ciel et terre,* LXX (1954), 175-80.

5. This would have been either δ or ε Ursa Minor, each a very faint star.

6. Bubnov (*Gerberti opera mathematica,* p. 28, n. 1) believes that this was a tube separate from the tubes of the hemisphere. It could have been, but the meaning here is not necessarily that.

3. RHEIMS. 978-980?

Gerbert to Constantine (?) of Fleury, explaining a passage in the Boethius De arithmetica *referring to the changing of sesquiquartal numbers*

[GERBERT TO CONSTANTINE (?)]

This passage, which some persons think is insolvable, is solved thus.[1] Take sesquiquartal superparticular numbers,[2] as 16, 20, 25. If you wish to know how these sesquiquartal numbers are resolved first into sesquitertian, then into sesquialteral, and lastly into three equal terms, arrange them thus: 16, 20, 25. Take the lesser number from the middle and make it the first, i.e., take 16 from 20 and place this 16 first, and the remainder from 20 is 4: place this in second place. From the third term, then, i.e., from 25, take one first term, i.e., 16, and twice the second term, i.e., two 4s, which are 8, and 1 remains. Place this unity as the third term, and the ratios are: 16, 4, 1. You see how sesquiquartas are changed into quadruple ratios and from whence the numbers came.

But this resolution ought not to be done in a confused and disordered manner, i.e., they ought not to be resolved into sesquitertias suddenly, but in orderly fashion.[3] Thus, take these quadruple numbers-16, 4, 1. Reserve them and arrange them thus: 1, 4, 16.[4] Therefore, take away the lesser from the middle, i.e., 1 from 4, and this 1 place first and the 3, which is left from the 4, place second. From the third term, i.e., from 16, take away the one first and two second [terms], i.e., 1 and twice 3, and what is left from 16, i.e., 9, place as a third term and arrange thus: 1, 3, 9.

You see, therefore, how quadruple ratios may be changed into triple, and after these same quadruple ratios have been changed, from what they originated. With this triple ratios, i.e., 1, 3, 9, reversed and arranged thus: 9, 3, 1, if, mindful of the rules of Boethius, you make the first equal to the first, i.e., 9; the second equal to the first and second, i.e., 12; the third to the first and the two seconds and the third, i.e., 16, the resolution of the sesquiquartal superparticular has been accomplished first into a sesquitertian, as Boethius teaches by the rules which he lays down so astutely, not confusedly, but in orderly fashion, just as numbers were procreated from the beginning of number.

If, therefore, you wish to know secondly how these sesquiquartas may be changed to sesquialteras, [take] these triple converted ratios, i.e., 9, 3, 1, and change them about by arranging them thus: 1, 3, 9, and take away the lesser from the middle, i.e., 1 from 3, and place it as the first term and what remains from 3, place as the second term. Thus, from the third, i.e., 9, take away the first, i.e., 1, and two second numbers, i.e., twice the second and what remains from 9, i.e. 4, place as the third term, and these numbers are then arranged thus: 1, 2, 4. Therefore, you see how triple ratios are turned back into duples, whence they were procreated.

If, indeed, these duples are reversed and arranged thus: 4, 2, 1, and if, as above, you make the first equal to the first, i.e., 4; and the second to the first and second, i.e., 6; the third to the first and two seconds and to the third, i.e., 9, they will be 4, 6, 9. The resolution of the sesquiquarta into a sesquialter has been accomplished as Boethius points out, not in one step but in two, not confusedly but methodically.

If you still wish to know how the sesquiquarta may finally be resolved into three equal terms, reverse these converted duples, to wit: 4, 2, 1, and arrange them thus: 1, 2, 4. Therefore take away the lesser from the middle, i.e., 1 from two, and place this 1 as the first term, and the remainder place second, i.e., 1. From the third term, i.e. from 4, take away unity, i.e., 1, and twice the second term, i.e. two unities, and the remainder will be for you one unity, and it will be 1, 1, 1. Therefore, you see how the whole quantity of the sesquiquarta has been changed into three equal terms, i.e., unities: 1, 1, 1, not confusedly but in definite order, just as it was procreated in the beginning. This, therefore, is the true nature of numbers.[5]

This translation is based on Bubnov, *Gerberti opera mathematica*, pp. 32-35. It is included also in Bubnov, I, 318-21. The fact that several other letters of Gerbert concerned with mathematical and scientific matters have some connection with Constantine is the basis for the assumption that he is the addressee.

1. The passage is Boethius *De arithmetica* ii.i. The solution here is practically that of Boethius, which was taken from Nicomachus of Gerasa. See D'Ooge, pp. 230-31. Boethius is wordier than Nicomachus, but he does include some figures, thus:

8	32	128
8	24	72
8	16	32
8	8	8

2. Superparticular numbers are those in the relationship of one and an aliquot part of the number to the antecedent number, such as one and a half (sesquialtera, 3 : 2), one and a third (sesquitertia, 4 : 3), one and a fourth (sesquiquarta, 5 : 4), and so on. Nicomachus i.xix.

3. Boethius *De arithmetica* ii.i.: "If there be a superparticular sesquiquarta, first change it to a sesquitertia, thence to a sesquialtera, and finally to three equal terms." Owing to the lack of an adequate symbolism for fractions Boethius felt compelled to continue and to elaborate a system of ratios (the Latin word for which was *proportio*, since *ratio* meant computation). See D. Smith, *History of Mathematics*. Vol. II. *Special Topics of Elementary Mathematics* (Boston, 1925), 218, 478-80.

4. D'Ooge (p. 231, n. 1) states that Theon of Smyrna gives the rule, taking it from Adrastus (but he uses no numbers for illustration). However, G. Johnson (*The Arithmetical Philosophy of Nicomachus of Gerasa* [Ph. D. Dissertation, University of Pennsylvania; Lancaster, Pa., 1916], p. 30) indicates that Philoponus explains it, using the numbers 1, 4, 16.

5. Bubnov, *Gerberti opera mathematica*, pp. 297-99, publishes the explanations of Nohtger (Notker, bishop of Liége?) and of Abbo of Fleury on this same Boethius passage from MS Munich 3517, s. X, fol. 15v, and MS Cambrai 928 (827), s. IX, fol. 55, which are manuscripts of *De arithmetica*.

4. RHEIMS. 978-80?
Gerbert explains to Constantine of Fleury a passage in Boethius
De musica, *relative to superparticular numbers*

GERBERT, THE TEACHER, TO HIS CONSTANTINE

The theory of superparticular numbers, briefly discussed in the second book [iv-xi] of *De musica*, is expounded more fully and by examples in the second chapter of the fourth book. We shall copy these words here and proceed forthwith to discuss them: "If a superparticular ratio is multiplied by two,[1] the result is neither a superparticular nor a multiple." The ratio is said to be multiplied by two when the ratio is doubled so that as the first ratio is, so is the second, that is, the first term's ratio to the second will be the same as the second term's ratio to the third.

Let there be the superparticular ratio four to six. Because this is one [ratio], let it be multiplied by two. For twice one are two. It is necessary that as four is to six, six is to some other number; this is nine. I say that the ratio of nine to four is neither that of a multiple number to its root, nor that of a number to one of its aliquot parts. But, if the result of such multiplication is neither a multiple number nor a superparticular one, then the result when it is multiplied by two, whether superparticular or any other kind of number, will not be a multiple number.

The result of the first multiplication will be a double sesquiquartal ratio, as nine to four, which is neither multiple, nor superparticular, but multiple superparticular. However, the result is not a multiple number because it was multiplied by two but a superparticular of another sort. But here the question is not one of a multiple nor of any other, but definitely of a superparticular. For it is a multiplied sesquialter ratio.

This translation is based on Bubnov, *Gerberti opera mathematica*, pp. 29-30. Included also in Bubnov, I, 316-17. One of the manuscripts containing this letter is the autograph copy of Thierry of Chartres *Heptateuchon* (MS Chartres 498 [142], s. XII, added in the margin of fol. 114). CG XI (1890), 212. C. Bühler ("A New Manuscript of the Middle English Tract on Proportions," *Speculum*, XXI [1946], 229-33) adds to Bubnov's list of manuscripts: MS British Museum Lansdowne 763, a. 1460, and a fifteenth-century MS owned by Mr. Bühler.

1. Actually, it is made equal to another ratio having the same numerical value ("multiplied by two"), making a proportion (in the more commonly accepted arithmetical meaning). See Chilston's table of proportions (ratios) in S. Meech, "Three Musical Treatises in English from a Fifteenth-Century Manuscript," *Speculum*, X (1935), 266, lines 41-43. Chilston (*ibid.*, pp. 265ff.) defines the same terms of proportions as those in Gerbert's letter.

L. Ellinwood, "Ars musica," *Speculum*, XX (1945), 293, mentions three thirteenth-century writers who deal with musical proportions: Michael Scot (d. c. 1235), *Liber introductorius* (MS Munich lat. 10268, fols. 38v-43r, not published); Bartholomew the Englishman (middle of 13th cent.), *De rerum proprietatibus*, xix; and Vincent of Beauvais (d. 1264), *Speculum doctrinale*, who has four chapters on proportions and consonance. F. Bukofzer, "Speculative Thinking in Mediaeval Music," *Speculum*, XVII (1942), 178-80, emphasizes the influence that such medieval absorption in the problems of numerical proportions exerted on musical form.

5. RHEIMS. 978-80?

Gerbert explains to Constantine of Fleury another passage in Boethius De musica, *relative to superparticular numbers*

GERBERT, THE TEACHER, TO HIS CONSTANTINE

In Chapter 21 of the Second Book of *De musica*, Boethius states as follows:[1] "If from every superparticular, one subtracts a continuous superparticular ratio, that which is left, which is indeed less, is less than half of the ratio which has been subtracted: as in a sesquialtera and sesquitertia. Because the sesquialtera is larger, let us substract the sesquitertia from the sesquialtera. There remains a sesquioctaval ratio, which, when doubled will not make a whole sesquitertian ratio, but is less by the distance that is found in a semitone. But if the doubled sesquioctaval relationship is not a whole sesquitertia, a simple sesquioctave is not a whole half of a sesquitertian ratio."

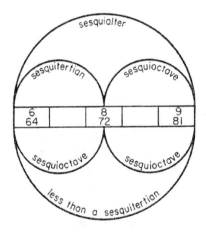

Let there be assumed one and the same number on which the sesquialteral and the sesquitertian ratio is constructed, namely 6, to which 9 is the sesquialter, and 8, indeed, is the sesquitertia. Let these be arranged in this manner: 6, 8, 9. And because these two ratios are continuous superparticulars arranged in three terms: 6, 8, 9, let us take away the first term to which 8 is the sesquitertia; 9 the sesquialtera. There will remain 8 and 9, which are a sesquioctave. But the sesquioctaval ratio is not a half of the smaller ratio, that is the sesquitertian, because when doubled it will not make it, but is less. Therefore, let us double the sesquioctaval ratio, and the three numbers will be arranged in such a way that they do not depart from the ratio 8 to 9, and there will result 8 times 8, and 8 times 9, and 9 times 9, i.e., 64, 72, 81.

I say that the first to the second and the second to the third maintain the sesquioctaval relationship, but the third to the first is less than a sesquitertia, and therefore the sesquioctave is not one half of a sesquitertia. And this will be observed generally in all continuous superparticulars because, if the lesser is subtracted from the larger, that which remains is less than half of the subtracted ratio, because doubled it is not equal to it, as the accompanying diagram demonstrates.

This translation is based on Bubnov, *Gerberti opera mathematica*, pp. 30-31. Included also in Bubnov, I, 317-18. See Letter 4.

1. PL LXIII, 1213C-D, where it is Chapter 20 instead of 21.

6. RHEIMS. 979?

Gerbert refers to the argument over the propriety of studying numbers and promises Constantine a more complete discussion

[GERBERT TO CONSTANTINE]

O Constantine, sweet solace of my labors, we are entrusting your sagacity, which has always flourished in the freest honesty of studies, with a prepublication of these axioms designed for the utmost exercise of the mind. By using them, the way for grasping these ideas immediately is opened to those persons of less comprehension who, because this pattern of thinking has either been neglected or completely unknown, exasperate every one of the skilled masters of the subject, moreover, by their habitual loquacity, replete with fallacies.

For, if, by considering carefully the nature of each statement, they preserved the maxims for observing the rules of health equally derived from the ancients, then they are in nowise to be so vigorously censured for diligently studying their works through arguments and disputations. Thus, when they are about to discuss numbers standing either by themselves or in chance relationship with each other, they will be able to say what are the digits, what also the articles,[1] since the nature of all number revolves only about the change of such relationships.[2]

But for the sake of our aforesaid friendship I shall, if life continues, explain these matters [to you] more clearly, as much as is necessary [for you] to attain fullest understanding.

This translation is based on Bubnov, *Gerberti opera mathematica*, pp. 23-24. Letter 7, dealing with similar material, is supposedly of the year 980, and was written not too long after Letter 6.

1. See Letter 7, n. 6.
2. A reference to the decimal system (without zero or decimal point) as developed on the abacus, with the nine Hindu-Arabic numerals. The "axioms" which Gerbert sent along with this letter do not appear in the only manuscript containing the letter, MS Vatican lat. 3123 (s. XII), fols. 40v-41r. See Letters 7 and 142.

7. RHEIMS. First half of 980
Gerbert sends to Constantine, monk of Fleury, rules for using the abacus and indicates their usefulness

GERBERT, THE TEACHER, TO HIS CONSTANTINE

Only the compulsion of friendship reduces the nearly impossible to the possible. Otherwise, how could we strive to explain the rules of the abacus [1] unless urged by you, O Constantine, sweet solace of my labors? Since it has now been some years [2] since we have had either a book or any practice in this sort of thing, we can offer you only certain rules repeated from memory, sometimes in the same words, sometimes in the self-same sentences. [3]

Do not let any half-educated philosopher [4] think they are contrary to any of the arts or to philosophy. [5]

For, who can say which are digits, which are articles, [6] which the lesser numbers [7] of divisors, if he disdains sitting at the feet of the ancients? Although really still a learner along with me, he pretends that only he has knowledge of it, as Horace says. [8] How can the same number be considered in one case simple, in another composite, [9] now a digit, now an article?

Here in this letter, diligent researcher, you now have the rational method, briefly expressed [10] in words, 'tis true, but extensive in meaning, for the multiplication and division of the columns [of the abacus] with actual numbers resulting from measurements determined by the inclination and erection of the geometrical radius, [11] as well as for comparing with true fidelity the theoretical and actual measurement of the sky and of the earth. [12]

This translation is based on Bubnov, *Gerberti opera mathematica*, pp. 6-8. Included also in Havet, Appendix iii, pp. 238-39.

Gerbert's designation of himself as a teacher indicates the years 972-80, and the reference to the elapse of several five- (or four-) years periods (n. 4 below) since dealing with the abacus points to 978-80. Evidence of interest in this new abacus method of calculating at Fleury appears in Abbo's *Commentary* on the Calculus of Victorius (written 978-82) into which he slipped rules for the abacus. Bubnov, *Gerberti opera mathematica*, pp. 198-203.

1. Richer iii.liv, thus describes Gerbert's abacus: "PREPARATION OF AN ABACUS. In teaching geometry, indeed, he expended no less labor [than in teaching astronomy]. As an introduction to it he caused an abacus, that is, a board of suitable dimensions, to be made by a shield maker. Its length was divided into 27 parts [columns] on which he arranged the symbols, nine in number, signifying all numbers. Likewise, he had made out of horn a thousand characters, which indicated the multiplication or division of each number when shifted about in the 27 parts of the abacus. [He manipulated the characters] with such speed in dividing and multiplying large numbers that, in view of their very great size, they could be shown [seen] rather than be grasped mentally by words. If anyone desires to know this more thoroughly let him read his book which he wrote to Constantine, the *grammaticus*; for there he will find these matters treated completely enough." The "book" consists of Letter 7 and the following text of rules, published in Bubnov, *Gerberti opera mathematica*, pp. 8-22. The "characters" which Richer mentions were the Hindu-Arabic numerals, about which see Lattin, "Origin of Notation," *Isis*, XIX (1933), 181-94; and S. Gandz, "The Origin of the Ghubar Numerals, or the Arabian Abacus and the Articuli," *Isis*, XVI (1931), 393-424.

2. *Lustra*, a period of five years, or, according to the Julian calendar, four years (Pliny *Historia naturalis* ii.xlvii. 47). Hence, Gerbert studied the abacus at Aurillac, or, if *lustra* equaled a four-year period, then it might have been in Spain, 967-70. Lattin, *Peasant Boy*, pp. 45-46, 57-61.

3. Bubnov reconstructed the rules for the abacus (under the title *Anonymous Bubnovianus*) which he suggested approximated those which came down from antiquity and were thus the ones Gerbert studied. Lattin, "Origin of Notation," *Isis*, XIX (1933), 188, 191.

4. This might refer to the teacher Abbo, whose material on the abacus does not reveal much comprehension of its principles; nor does the material of his pupil Byrhtferth of Ramsey, England.

5. "For the ancient Greeks after Pythagoras... arithmetic [*arithmetike*] was primarily a philosophical study, having no necessary connection with practical affairs. Indeed the Greeks gave a separate name to the arithmetic of business, λογιστικη [logistike]; of this division of the science no Greek treatise has been transmitted to us. In general the philosophers and mathematicians of Greece undoubtedly considered it beneath their dignity to treat of this branch which undoubtedly formed a part of the elementary instruction of children. The evidence for the existence of treatises on the fundamental operations is very insecure and vague, resting upon a passage of Diogenes Laertius and a citation by Eutocius." L. C. Karpinski, "Studies in Greek Mathematics," in D'Ooge, p. 3.

B. L. van der Waerden, *Science Awakening* (Groningen, Holland, 1954), pp. 115-16, indicates that Plato distinguishes between practical logistics (calculation, particularly with fractions) and theoretical logistics ("the study of numbers in their mutual ratios"), and between practical arithmetic (counting) and theoretical arithmetic ("the even and the odd").

Furthermore, the use of a mechanical aid, the abacus, caused Gerbert's critics to claim that abacus arithmetic did not belong in a formalized curriculum.

6. Thus, in $8 \times 3 = 24$, the number 2 is an article, the number 4 is a digit. In $8 \times 30 = 240$, the number 2 is an article, and the number 4 is a digit. Cf. Gandz, "The Origin of Ghubar Numerals," *Isis*, XVI (1931), 413, 407ff.

7. *Minuta.* "In divisors, which consist of two or more numbers, as 42, 535 (not, however, 500) the largest number is the largest divisor, all the others (as 2 in 42, 35 in 535) are called the lesser or the lesser ones." Bubnov, *Gerberti opera mathematica*, p. 7, n. 9.

8. Horace *Epistulae* ii.i.87.

9. "A composite number is so named because it can be separated [factored] into those very ones from which it was put together, to wit, into those which measure [factor] the composite number." Boethius *De arithmetica*, i.xv. Cf. Letter 142. Thus, 3 alone is simple, but 3 in 30 is composite.

10. Bernelinus, early in the eleventh century, comments on Gerbert's brevity. "The rules for the abacus, which like some seed plots, were briefly and very intelligently sown by Lord Pope Gerbert." Olleris, p. 357. Cf. Richer (n. 1 above).

11. John Scot Erigena (*De divisione naturae* iii.xxv) defines the radius as a geometrical rod "which, multiplying five paces by cubing them, that is, five times five times five, measures a stade." PL CXXII, 725. Bubnov (*Gerberti opera mathematica*, p. 8, n. 6) interprets Gerbert's words as a possible reference to the astrolabe, because of these words in the *De utilitatibus astrolapsus* ii.xii: "Here is the alidade, i.e., the vertical, which we can call the radius, which is placed above the disc [of the astrolabe] like an extended ruler. At right angles to it are fastened two wings which have two openings corresponding to itself for receiving the rays of the sun and of the fixed stars, or for the knowledge of geometrical measures." Bubnov, p. 123.

R. Gunther, *Astrolabes of the World* (Oxford, 1932), I, 239, Plate II (lower part), no. 101, reproduces an astrolabe in the Galileo Tribuna at Florence, said to have been made by Gerbert. On the back appear, with the zero, somewhat modern numerals for which Gerbert could not have been responsible. The numerals on the front are tenth-century forms, but the list of stars is in Arabic.

12. These were undoubtedly the measurements of Eratosthenes, Macrobius, and Martianus Capella, found in the York Astronomical Encyclopedia (vi.iv-vii). Lattin, "Eleventh Century MS Munich 14436," *Isis*, XXXVIII (1948), 218, n. 96. A monk of St. Andrew of Cambrai, writing in 1133, stated that Gerbert "was so skilled in geometry that he could easily measure the spaces between places both on the earth and in the sky just by looking." MGSS VII, 527.

8. ST. COLUMBAN OF BOBBIO. April - May, 982

Gerbert apologizes to Emperor Otto II for troubling him with the difficulties of administration at the monastery of St. Columban of Bobbio, begs for more explicit orders, and defends himself against charges of treason

[GERBERT TO EMPEROR OTTO]

To Caesar, his ever august Lord Otto, from Gerbert, formerly a free man.[1]

When I ponder on the public affairs of the realms I am terrified to occupy my most serene lord's attention with my own affairs. I pray my lord to indicate clearly to his servant in the usual way by his own letters that the latter is to give evidence of his service. I pray that his letters be less ambiguous, for they are unbecoming the widely recognized seriousness of our Caesar, that we have experienced often. Accordingly, the sign for us that you agree or do not agree will be your notation appended to our letters: "Approved" or "Disapproved." If we know your wishes we intend to accomplish whatever is possible.

Let Lord Bishop Gerbert[2] speak out as to our innocence with respect to Bruning[3] and Isimbard. Let Liutfred and Gerard explain why Rudolph[4] took possession of their benefice.[5] Let not an accusation of high treason[6] be brought against him for whom it has always been a glory to take a stand for Caesar and a dishonor to be against Caesar.

This is Letter 1 in Havet.

In MS L this letter is preceded by the heading: *"Here Begins the Copy of the Letters of Pope Gerbert which He Wrote to Different Persons."* Although Gerbert chose the name of Sylvester upon his elevation to the papacy, he used both names in his signature on papal documents. Changing one's name upon becoming pope was recent, the first instance being that of John XII (955-63) whose name was Octavian. Gerbert's contemporaries continued to think of him as Gerbert because of the great reputation he had earned before being elected pope.

1. As abbot of the monastery of St. Columban of Bobbio Gerbert had sworn an oath of fealty to Emperor Otto II with its concomitant heavy obligations. See Letters 18, n. 6; 28; 33; 166; 229.

2. See Letter 10, n. 1.

3. A Bruning, dative (palatine) judge and notary, appears in a document at Asti, October, 981. C. Cipolla, "Di Brunengo vescovo di Asti e di tre documenti inediti che lo riguardano," *Miscellanea di storia italiana*, XXVIII (1890), 308, 387.

4. A Memorandum of Bobbio property, drawn up about the end of the tenth century (by Gerbert?), lists a Liufred and a Rudolph who held properties from Bobbio, some as a benefice, some through a book-lease. Cipolla, *Codice diplomatico di Bobbio*, I, No. cvii, p. 375, lines 81ff.; p. 377, line 133.

5. Usually this was the land of a church or monastery, once usurped by the crown, then bestowed as a life tenure by the king or other overlord in return for both military protection and partial maintenance of the church or monastery, and military service to the overlord. The tendency was for the benefice to develop into a fief. H. Brunner, *Deutsche Rechtsgeschichte* (Leipzig), I (1887), 211f., II (1892), 250f.; F. L. Ganshof, "Benefice and Vassalage," *Cambridge Historical Journal*, VI (1939), 157ff.

6. Gerbert here calls Otto II's attention to the rather precise and limited definition of treason found in the *Lex Iulia Maiestatis* of Justinian's Digest. For

certain extensions of its meaning see F. S. Lear, "*Crimen laesae maiestatis* in the *Lex romana Wisigothorum*," *Speculum*, IV (1929), 73-87.

9. BOBBIO. May - June, 982

Describes depredations at Bobbio; hints at important news from Germany

LIKEWISE TO THE SAME OTTO

I prefer to carry joyful rather than sad news to the most serene ears of my lord. But, when I see my monks wasting away from hunger and suffering from nakedness, how can I keep silent? This evil might be endurable, however, if, at the same time, the hope for improved conditions here was not also being snatched away. The whole sanctuary of God has been stripped bare by some sort of documents which they call "little books";[1] the money which was collected is nowhere to be found; the storehouses and granaries have been emptied; in the purses[2] there is nothing. What, therefore, am I, a sinner, doing here? If it could be done at the pleasure of my lord, I would prefer to be the only one in need among the French rather than to be begging with so many in need among the Italians.

Renier the Frank,[3] intimate with us, and desirous of your esteem, has entrusted to my confidence many things to be repeated to you about the condition of your realm, not, however, to be entrusted to a messenger, but [even more] not to be inserted in letters unless by your approval.

This is Letter 2 in Havet.

1. *Libelli* (sing., *libellus*), book-leases. The "little book" was originally the letter of the lessee, requesting the lease, and then became the contract between landlord and tenant. Ordinarily the lease was for twenty-nine years or less in order to avoid the prescription by Roman law of thirty years, whereby the leased portion would have passed out of the original property complex. The book-lease holder was obligated to pay a rent and to perform certain services, such as the improvement of the land. Gerbert was protesting the nonfulfillment of these obligations. H. Brunner, *Deutsche Rechtsgeschichte*, I (Leipzig, 1887), 200-212; K. Jordan, "Das Eindringen des Lehnswesen," *Archiv für Urkundenforschung*, XII (1932), 13-16; M. Uhlirz, "Die italienische Kirchenpolitik der Ottonen," MIOG, XLVIII (1934), 225-27; C. E. Boyd, *Tithes and Parishes in Medieval Italy* (Ithaca, N.Y., 1952), pp. 69-71.

2. This confirms the growing realization of a more extensive money economy in the period than previously believed. See further, R. S. Lopez, "An Aristocracy of Money in the Early Middle Ages," *Speculum*, XXVIII (1953), 1-43.

3. Apparently a cleric of the church of Rheims. See Letters 96, 103, 136, 149, 150.

10. BOBBIO. May - June, 982

An appeal for advice to Bishop Gerbert of Tortona, with a description of the stringent economic situation at Bobbio

To Gerbert, Bishop of Tortona [1]

O you from whom we hope for counsel, it is foolish to dissemble the present evil situation, yet hateful to speak of it lest we seem to be influenced by personal hatred. If the abbot [2] is allowed to hand over the immovable property of a monastery to any persons whatsoever under the name of a book-lease, to give away the movable property [3] on the pretext of alms, and to make a monk specifically the heir of whatever, perchance, is left, whither shall a new abbot look after he is consecrated?

Everything is said to have belonged to Petroald,[4] nothing to the abbot, and the result is that nothing is left to us save the buildings and the use of the natural elements, common to all. A letter of my lord [Otto II] orders me to cherish Petroald and to hold what he held. The weight is doubled when his kindred are placed in the same pan of the scale.

Weigh the merits of this affair; consider what I have lost and what I have gained, aside from the favor of my lord. Support the burden of a friend with advice and aid, and write back what ought to be done.

This is Letter 3 in Havet.

1. Bishop of Tortona, 979-88 (DO II 206); chancellor for the whole empire, September 8-October 20, 977 (DO II 163-68); chancellor for Italy, October 5, 977–November 5, 979 (DO II 173, 206). G. Schwartz, *Die Besetzung der Bistümer Reichsitaliens*, p. 127. At the time the letter was written he was with Otto II in southern Italy (DO II 276-77).

2. Probably Peter, abbot in 977 (DO II 322).

3. The *Miracula S. Columbani*, written between 973-83, lament the alienation of Bobbio property. Cipolla, *Codice diplomatico di Bobbio*, I, 294-311; III, 74ff.

4. Petroald, a monk and prior of Bobbio and a member of a prominent family, through some legal maneuvering, but in accordance with Roman law, had been designated heir by Abbot Peter as if Peter owned the property personally rather than by virtue of his office. M. Uhlirz, "Studien zu Gerbert," *Archiv für Urkundenforschung*, XIII (1935), 443, 446-47, 471. Petroald was chosen abbot of Bobbio in 999 after Gerbert's election as pope. See Appendix C, Nos. 13 and 14.

11. BOBBIO. July 15, 982

Gerbert refuses to recognize Boso's claim to Bobbio property and demands the return of some hay

[GERBERT TO BOSO]

Gerbert, a follower of the divine Caesar, sends greetings in Christ to Boso.[1]

Let us avoid superfluous words and let us keep to facts. Neither for money nor for friendship will we give to you the sanctuary [2] of God, nor will we consent if it has already been given to you by anyone else. Restore to St. Columban the hay which your followers took if you do not wish to test what we can do with the favor of our Lord Caesar and with the aid and advice of our friends. By these conditions, [however], we do not intend to disclaim the laws of friendship.

This is Letter 4 in Havet.

1. Undoubtedly the same Boso of Nibbiano (Nebiano), a town north of Bobbio, who repeatedly despoiled the property of St. Martin of Pavia (DO III 304).

2. Probably Bobbio's church of St. Simphorian in Nibbiano, on the river Tidone. M. Uhlirz, "Studien zu Gerbert," *Archiv für Urkundenforschung,* XIII (1935), 464-65.

12. BOBBIO. First half of July, 982

Gerbert demands restitution of Bobbio's property and refuses an interview; adds a reminder of the obligations of allegiance to Otto II

GERBERT TO PETER, BISHOP OF PAVIA [1]

As for the fact that we appear to have the abbey of St. Columban, we have none of the Italians to thank for that. If we have been praised by you in our lord's presence, still we have more often rendered to you not undeserved praises.

You demand interviews yet you do not cease from thefts from our church; you, who ought to compel the complete restoration of what has been distributed, are yourself distributing our possessions to your knights as if they were your own. Steal, pillage, arouse the forces of Italy against us; you have found the opportune time. Our lord is occupied with the strife of war.[2] We shall not keep back the bands of soldiers,³ prepared to aid him, nor shall we rashly take upon ourselves an office which is his.

We shall give attention to the service of our Caesar not only when present before him, but also when absent from him, if we can avail ourselves of peace. But, if not, his presence alone will mitigate our weakness. Since, as the poet says: "Nowhere is faith preserved," ³ and because things neither seen nor heard are invented, we will reveal our purpose to you in no other way than by letter, nor will we receive [word of] yours in any other manner.

This is Letter 5 in Havet.

1. Peter Canepanova, bishop of Pavia, April, 972—end of 983, Otto II's chancellor for Italy, December 980—end of 983 (DO II 238, 317). He became Pope John XIV, November-December, 983, but died in prison, August 20, 984. Schwartz, *Die Besetzung der Bistümer Reichsitaliens*, p. 142. See also Letter 47, n. 2.

2. Otto II was campaigning against the Saracens in southern Italy in July, 982.

3. Virgil *Aeneid* iv.373, copied by Isidore *Etymologiae* ii.xxi.15.

13. BOBBIO. Second half of 982

Gerbert rebukes the dowager Empress Adelaide for requesting grants of land for too many of her followers, especially for Grifo who has not yet arrived at Bobbio

GERBERT TO QUEEN ADELAIDE ¹

To his ever august Lady Adelaide, from Gerbert.

As to benefices and book-leases, we have carried out your wishes in part, and those of our Lord Caesar in whole. I pray my lady to remember what she intimated to her servant—that she was about to ask in behalf of many persons more favors than could be granted. With this understanding we departed from you.² We have not seen Grifo³ nor his messenger. How can we take away tomorrow the land which yesterday we granted to our faithful followers? But, if all the things that everyone orders are done, what are we doing here? And if we give the whole away, what shall we keep? As far as it lies in our power, we shall do something for Grifo, but we will grant no benefice.

This is Letter 6 in Havet.

1. Adelaide was the widow of King Lothair of Italy (d. 950) and of Emperor

Otto I (d. 973). Adelaide controlled more of the crown land of the Lombard kings in northern Italy than Otto II so her power was considerable. Gerbert may have used "queen" instead of "empress" to remind her that her prerogatives were due to the fact that she was queen in Italy, but that the emperor's prerogatives superseded hers. Odilo, *S. Adalheidae imperatricis epitaphium*, MGSS IV, 636-49; F. Steffanides, *Kaiserin Adelheid, Gemahlin Ottos I. des Grossen* (Jahresbericht der Staats-Realschule in Böhmisch-Leipa, XXX; Böhmisch-Leipa, 1893); F. P. Wimmer, *Kaiserin Adelheid Gemahlin Ottos I.* (Dissertation, Erlangen, 1897); Bubnov, II, p. 152, n. 62; M. Uhlirz, "Italienische Kirchenpolitik der Ottonen," MIOG, XLVIII (1934), 212-14, 254-55.

2. Adelaide was at Ravenna December 28, 980 (DO II 238), at the same time as Gerbert (Richer III.lvii-lxvii), and both probably were at Otto's court until Easter, 981, when she accompanied her brother, King Conrad, to Burgundy. She next appears near Otto II on September 30, 982, at Capua (DO II 281).

3. Perhaps the same as the "Griffo, notary of the sacred palace" and "judge of the Lord Emperor" of the years 945 and 967 (DO I 340). A Grifo, a dative judge, appears in a Roman document of September 17, 985. P. Fedele, "Carte del monastero dei SS. Cosma e Damiano in Mica aurea," ASR XXI (1898), 514.

14. BOBBIO. Second half of 982 or first half of 983
Requests Ayrard of Rheims to have a Pliny manuscript corrected, and other manuscripts copied

GERBERT TO AYRARD [1]

Gerbert, formerly a teacher, sends greetings to his Ayrard.

We give assent to your requests, and we advise that you carry out our business as if it were your own. Have Pliny [2] corrected; let us receive Eugraphius; [3] and have copied those books which are at Orbais [4] and at Saint Basle. [5] Do what we ask in order that we may do what you ask.

This is Letter 7 in Havet.

1. Ayrard was one of Gerbert's pupils at Rheims, later abbot of St. Thierry near Rheims, and a different person from the Ayrard in Letter 25.

2. Undoubtedly the *Natural History*, and probably now MS Bamberg Class. 42 (M.V. 10), s. X, containing books XXXII-XXXVII As to Gerbert's high regard for Pliny, see Lattin, "Eleventh Century MS Munich 14436," *Isis*, XXXVIII (1948), 209ff.

3. Actually Pseudo-Eugraphius, author of a *Commentary* on Terence, written at the beginning of the sixth century. M. Schanz, *Geschichte der römischen Literatur*, I, pp. 157ff. Gerbert's Eugraphius manuscript may have been either MS Milan Ambrosian H 75, s. X, or MS Paris BN Lat. 16235, s. X. For further evidence of the presence of a Pseudo-Eugraphius manuscript at Rheims, see C. Erdmann, *Studien zur Briefliteratur Deutschlands* (Leipzig, 1938), pp. 36, 38; and Lattin, "Eleventh Century MS Munich 14436," *Isis*, XXXVIII (1948), 222ff.

4. Monastery in diocese of Soissons, arrondissement of Epernay (Marne).

5. Monastery in diocese of Rheims, today Verzy (Marne).

15. BOBBIO. June 22, 983

Promises to explain in person the failure of Archbishop Adalbero's plans; excuses his not sending keys to the book-chests; requests a copy of Caesar Commentarii de bello gallico; *and announces his discovery of Boethius* De astrologia, *a* Geometria, *and other works*

To Archbishop Adalbero of Rheims

What I failed to accomplish at Mantua [1] in regard to your affairs I can explain to you better by words when present than by letters when absent. I did not know what keys to the books [book-chests] I should send on account of their lack of distinguishing marks. Procure the *Historia* of Julius Caesar [2] from Lord A'dso,[3] abbot of Montier-en-Der, to be copied again for us in order that you may have whichever [manuscripts] are ours at Rheims, and may expect ones that we have since discovered, namely eight volumes: Boethius *De astrologia*,[4] also some beautiful figures of geometry,[5] and others no less worthy of being admired. Only absence from you disquiets our happiness day and night.

This is Letter 8 in Havet.

1. As an ecclesiastical vassal Gerbert probably attended the imperial Diet at Verona between May 7 and June 18, 983 (DO II 291-312; Thietmar iii.xxiv). During a portion of his return journey to Bobbio he probably accompanied the court to Mantua on June 20 (DO II 313) where Adalbero's messenger may have met him.

2. Gerbert, of course, refers to Caesar's *Commentarii de bello gallico*. Although lacking in the catalogue of Adso's books, a work entitled *Historia Julii Caesaris* (the same title which Gerbert gives) is listed in the library catalogue of St. Evre at Toul, drawn up before 1084, where Adso had taught. Becker, *Catalogi bibliothecarum antiqui*, No. 41; No. 68, Item 258.

3. C. 920-992/3, member of a distinguished family in the Jura Mountains, abbot from 967, and the author of several works. Richer iii.lvii; Manitius II, 432-42.

4. This work by Boethius—the correct title probably was *De astronomia*—is lost. He himself (*De arithmetica* i.i) indicates that he planned such a work. Moreover, King Theodoric writes to Boethius as the man who made the astronomy of Ptolemy available for the Italians. Cassiodorus *Variae* I, 45, MGAA XII, 40. P. Courcelle, "Histoire d'un Brouillon Cassiodorien," *Revue des études anciennes*, XLIV (1942), 86, adds an additional early reference to Boethius as an astronomer. In MS Paris Bibliothèque nationale latin 7530, fol. 64v, he found the following note to Cassiodorus's chapter on astronomy (in *Institutiones* II) in an eighth century hand: "Among the Greeks, Ptolemy is famous for this art, among the Latins, indeed, Boethius and others are noted." For Boethius' plan of translation see H. Weissenborn, "Die Boetius-Frage," *Abhandlungen zur Geschichte der Mathematik*, II (1879), 188-92; P. Courcelle, *Les Lettres grecques en occident: De Macrobe à Cassiodore* (Paris, 1943), pp. 260ff.

Whether Gerbert means here eight volumes of a Boethius work on astronomy plus the other works mentioned, or eight volumes altogether, is unclear, because of the confused Latin text and punctuation.

However, in the tenth-century catalogue of the Bobbio library (Olleris, p. 493) is this: *Libros Boetii III de Arithmetica et alterum de Astronomia* (three books of Boethius on arithmetic and another on astronomy). See also Letter 138.

5. Surely a manuscript of excerpts of the writings by the Roman surveyors (*agrimensores*), MS Naples, Bibl. Borbonica V, A, 13, Codex Farnesianus. A later hand added to the upper margin of fol. 17r: "Here begins the book *Liber geometricae artis* edited by Lord Gerbert, Pope and philosopher named also Sylvester the Second," and another hand made corrections on the manuscript. These corrections were embodied in a copy made in 1004 in the Swiss monastery of Luxeuil. Hence, the corrections were certainly due to Gerbert or his circle. Bubnov, *Gerberti opera mathematica*, pp. 99-101 (corrected on pp. 397, 475, 558), 476-79; C. Thulin, *Zur Überlieferungsgeschichte des Corpus Agrimensorum Romanorum* (Göteborg, 1911), pp. 9, 13.

16. BOBBIO. July, 983

Requests the beginning of Demosthenes' Ophthalmicus, *and the end of Cicero* Pro rege Deiotaro

To ABBOT GISALBERT [1]

If you are well, we rejoice. Your needs we consider ours. Pray inform us what needs we are thus lacking. Concerning diseases of the eyes and their remedies Demosthenes [2] the philosopher wrote a book which is inscribed *Ophthalmicus*.[3] If you have it, let us have the beginning of this book, and likewise the end of Cicero *Pro rege Deiotaro*.[4]

Farewell.

This is Letter 9 in Havet.

1. A *Necrology* from St. Savin of Piacenza, begun in the eleventh century, lists one Abbot Giselbert at April 20th, and another at June 12th. H. Bresslau, "Handschriftliches aus Italien," NA, V (1880), 438, 440.

2. Demosthenes Philalethes. He lived at the time of Nero in Rome, Alexandria, or Zeuxis, and wrote in Greek three books on the pulse, a work on children's diseases, and a book on the eyes. Sarton, *Introduction to the History of Science*, I, 260.

3. Apparently, this was the Latin translation made by Vindicianus in the second half of the fourth century. The Bobbio library owned a "Demosthenes I volumen" (Olleris, p. 493). When Gerbert became pope he may have taken a copy of the work to Rome, because the later Simon of Genoa, chaplain of Pope Nicholas IV (1288-92), used a Latin translation of Demosthenes in his work, entitled *Clavis sanationis* (The Key of Health), and this copy was mutilated at the beginning like Gerbert's copy at Bobbio. M. Wellmann, "Demosthenes ΠΕΡΙ ΟΦΘΑΛΜΩΝ", *Hermes*, XXXVIII (1903), 546-74: J. Hirschberg, "Die Brückstücke der Augenheilkunde des Demosthenes," *Archiv für Geschichte der Medizin*, XI (1919), 183-88. See also Letter 138 below.

MacKinney, *Early Medieval Medicine*, pp. 116ff., discusses Gerbert's medical interests.

4. MS Wolfenbüttel Gudianus 335, s. X, containing this work (*Pro rege Deiotaro*) is incomplete, ending at ix. 26 with the word *aetate*, and is perhaps the one Gerbert had. A. C. Clark, ed., *M. Tulli Ciceronis Orationes Pro Milone Pro Marcello Pro Ligario Pro Rege Deiotaro Philippicae* (Oxford, 1908).

17. BOBBIO. July, 983

Reports to Otto II the flight to Bobbio of two monks of Precipiano, and the injuries to their monastery by the bishop of Lodi and the Abbot Neophyte

To Caesar

Two brothers of the monastery of Precipiano,[1] have been received by us as exiles and pilgrims. They report the desolation of their place by the bishop of Lodi [2] and by Abbot Neophyte—a wicked deed. At the same time they insist that they ought not to be subject to any church. We shall trust Your Prudence and Piety, therefore, to decide that neither the church of Lodi shall be deprived of its rights (over the monastery), because of hatred for its pastor, nor the monastery shall be subject to the tyranny of a devastator.[3]

This is Letter 10 in Havet.

Otto II was at Ravenna, July 14-16, and hence could more readily heed complaints of disorder. DO II 314-15.

1. Province of Alessandria, commune of Vignole-Borbera, diocese of Tortona, but placed under the authority of the bishop of Lodi-Vecchio. Havet, p. 8, n. 2.

2. Andrew, November 19, 970/71-1002, suffragan bishop of Milan. DO II 120, 256; Schwartz, *Die Besetzung der Bistümer Reichsitaliens,* p. 119.

3. A document of the year 1006 makes clear this destruction of the monastery of Precipiano. A. Tallone, "Novi, Ligure," in *Enciclopedia italiana* (New ed., Rome, 1935) XXV, 5a.

18. PAVIA. August, 983

Complains bitterly to Otto II about the faithless hangers-on in the palace, and reports their slanderous remarks about Otto and himself; hints at pressure on him to abandon his fidelity to Otto

Likewise to the Same

Why do the mouths and tails of the foxes here flatter my lord? Either let them depart from the palace, or let them present [for judgment] their satellites, who disregard the edicts of Caesar,[1] who plot to kill his messengers, who compare even him to an ass. I keep silent about myself about whom they whisper in a new kind of talk, saying that I am an emissary horse,[2] as if I had a wife and children, because of the part of my household [3] brought from [northern] France. The dispossessed have no sense of shame. O the times, O the customs; where in the world am I living? [4] If I conform to the customs of this region,[5] I [will] be abandoning a most sacred pledge; [6] if I do not conform, I [will] be living in exile. But, rather may I live in exile in the palace with fidelity intact than rule in Latium [7] without fidelity.

This is Letter 11 in Havet.

The words *hic* [here] and *palatium* [palace] indicate Gerbert's presence at the royal palace in Pavia where the Dowager Empress Adelaide was temporarily residing, and where Empress Theophanu may also have been at the time the letter was written.

The incipient plotting against his power, revealed in this letter, suggests that Otto was at some distance from Pavia and Bobbio, i.e., in central or southern Italy. His last known diploma was issued August 27, 983, at Larino (DO II 317).

1. Otto II. The edicts, undoubtedly concerning Bobbio and possibly similar to the regulations issued in 977 (DO II 322), were perhaps promulgated at the Diet of Verona in June, 983 (Letter 15, n. 1, above).

2. Used by the slanderers probably in the meaning of "stud horse."

3. *Familiae* (nom., *familia*), the collection of persons, usually secular, attached to the service of a religious establishment or even of a religious person. By *familia* Gerbert does not mean his consanguineous family. His household at Rheims must have been considerable, since even the portion, transferred to Bobbio, aroused comment there by its size.

4. Cicero *In Catalinam* i.ii; iv.ix.

5. *Patriam* (nom., *patria*) i.e., Lombardy. Gerbert uses *patria* here in the widely accepted sense of administrative district. Many medieval writers use it even more specifically to mean the county as an administrative district. H. Lattin, "Patria," ALMA, VII (1932); H. Koht, "The Dawn of Nationalism in Europe," *American Historical Review*, LII (1947), 266-67.

6. Gerbert's oath of fidelity to Otto II, (Letter, 8, n. 1) was doubtless similar to the oaths sworn by bishops, abbots, counts, and other magnates to Emperor Charles the Bald at Pavia in 876: "Thus, I promise this, my seigneur, that, from this day forth, as long as I shall live, I will be a faithful and obedient helper with as much more and better knowledge and ability as I shall have, and I will render counsel and aid in everything, according to my office, without treachery or deceit and without reference to any person." Odegaard, "Carolingian Oaths of Fidelity," *Speculum*, XVI (1941), 294, n. 4.

7. Gerbert makes a play on the words *palatium* (Otto II's palace or court) and *Latium* (Rome and nearby environs, or Italy).

19. **PAVIA** or **BOBBIO**. August - September, 983
  Describes his enemies' designs on Bobbio's property, and requests advice

To Hugh [1]

To his Hugh, from Gerbert, formerly a teacher.

In proportion to the greatness of my mind [2] my lord has enriched me with very extensive properties. For what part of Italy does not contain blessed Columban's possessions? [3] This, indeed, our Caesar's generous beneficence provided. But fortune decreed otherwise. For, in proportion to the greatness of my mind, she has honored [4] me with enemies everywhere. For what part of Italy does not contain my enemies?

My military strength is unequal to Italy's. The terms of peace are these: if, after being robbed, I am subservient, they will cease from striking. An inflexible man, owning so much as a suit of clothing, they will pursue with swords.[5]

When they are unable to strike with the sword, they assail him with the darts of words. The imperial majesty is despised, not only in me, but also in its very self by their spoliation of God's sanctuary.[6] Because I refuse to comply with the provisions of the book-leases, executed under their special laws, I am called faithless, cruel, tyrannical. The scoundrels compare Caesar himself, the most superior of all men, to an ass.

O most faithful of friends, do not fail to give a friend your aid and counsel. Remember what I have entreated you, that I prefer to be a soldier in Caesar's camp than a king in foreign lands.[7]

This is Letter 12 in Havet.

1. Hugh, a chaplain, who appears in DO II 311 at Verona in June, 983, is probably the same person as the addressee of this letter. Gerbert's use of "his" and "teacher" here indicates that the Hugh of this letter had studied with him at Otto II's court or at Rheims. Apparently Hugh drew up the diploma bestowing the abbey of Bobbio upon Gerbert (n. 2 below). He seems to have become bishop of Würzburg (d. August 29, 990) and acted as a royal representative, or *missus*, at Ravenna in 990. M. Uhlirz, "Studien zu Gerbert," *Archiv für Urkundenforschung*, XI (1930), 403f.; M. Uhlirz, "Italienische Kirchenpolitik der Ottonen," MIOG, XLVIII (1934), 256, n. 5; 257, n. 3.

2. Cicero *Tusculanae disputationes* ii.26. Otto II's lost nomination diploma for Gerbert (n. 1 above) apparently used these words. Schlockwerder, *Untersuchungen zur Chronologie der Briefe Gerberts*, p. 6, n. 1.

3. For the extent of the possessions of the monastery of St. Columban of Bobbio see DO I 412, a confirmation of rights and privileges by Otto I, July 30, 972; the ninth- and tenth-century Memoranda in Cipolla, *Codice diplomatico di Bobbio*, I, No. CVII; and the identification of these possessions by M. Uhlirz, "Studien zu Gerbert," *Archiv für Urkundenforschung*, XIII (1935), 458ff. They extended all over the region between Genoa and Petronio on the Mediterranean seacoast, Genoa and Tortona on the west, Pavia and Piacenza on the north, and Pontremoli, Solignano, and Ancarano on the east.

4. A pun, playing on the word *honoribus* [honors, i.e., possessions] and *honeravit* [honored], since in Latin pronunciation *honeravit* is not distinguishable from *oneravit* [burdened].

5. Or Ms V, *Vestitum districtis persequentur gladiis* [Any man, owning so much as a suit of clothing, they will pursue with drawn swords]. Cf. Bubnov, II, 165, n. 86.

6. As a ruler the emperor has the duty of protecting a vassal (Gerbert), and as a Christian emperor the obligation of protecting the church. Thus, those who injure the church are by extension guilty of lese majesty. See Letters 8 and 221.

7. See Letters 18 and 31.

20. BOBBIO. November, 983

Expresses cordiality; will let Archbishop Egbert decide whether students should be sent to Gerbert in Italy

GERBERT TO EGBERT, [ARCH]BISHOP OF TRIER [1]

We consider your happiness our pride. If you are suffering any inconvenience, we likewise are afflicted with it. You have known the generosity of our Lord Caesar, his efforts [to secure] and his surpassing fondness for excellent men. In the same way, if you are wondering whether you should direct students [2] to us as far away as Italy; on this matter we have an open mind. What you commend we shall commend; what you propose, we shall propose. [3]

This is Letter 13 in Havet.

1. Son of Dietrich II (d. 988), count of West Frisia, and of Countess Hildegard (or Hildegund); brother of Count Arnulf II of Holland. Chancellor of Otto II, June 30, 976—July 30, 977 (DO II 130-63), archbishop of Trier from June 5, 977 —December, 993.

2. Egbert was at Verona May 7, 983.(DO II 291), remained in Italy at least a month (DO II 298), and possibly saw Gerbert.

3. Cf. Cicero *De oratore* ii.75.304.

21. BOBBIO. December 17, 983

Begs Pope John XIV for advice; despairs over ability to maintain himself at Bobbio; suggests Lady Imiza as an intermediary

GERBERT TO POPE JOHN

To His Holiness, Pope John, from Gerbert, abbot in name only of the monastery of Bobbio.

Whither shall I turn,[1] Father of the country? [2] If I call upon the Holy See, I am mocked and without opportunity to go to you on account of the enemy; nor can we freely depart from Italy, even if we wish. To tarry, [however] becomes difficult because neither in the monastery nor outside have I anything left except the pastoral staff [3] and the apostolic benediction.[4]

We love Lady Imiza [5] because she loves you. Let us know through her, pray, either by messengers or by letters, whatever you wish us

to do, while at the same time through her we shall inform you of
anything that concerns you relative to the condition and undertakings
of the kingdoms.

This is Letter 14 in Havet.
Gerbert's words indicate that he is still at Bobbio, although his salutation
reveals that both monks and landholders had rebelled against him. Otto II died
in Rome, December 7, 983. By allowing seven days for the news to reach Bobbio,
and a few days for open rebellion against Gerbert to materialize, one arrives at
the date of the letter.
See Letter 12, and compare the tone of the two letters.
1. Terence *Hecyra* iv.i.1; Cicero *In C. Sallustium Crispum Invectiva* i.1.10.
2. A title of some of the Roman emperors. Cicero had been called *parens
patriae* [parent of the fatherland].
3. Apparently Gerbert had been consecrated abbot of Bobbio in Rome by
Pope Benedict VII. Letter 31. Pastoral staffs were made of wood combined
with bone, ivory, crystal, iron, lead, copper, silver, or gold. C. Cahier and
A. Martin, *Mélanges d'archéologie d'histoire et de littérature*, IV (Paris, 1856),
145-256, and plates.
4. Letters 31 and 167.
5. See Letter 30, n. 1.

22. PAVIA, OR ON THE ROAD TO RHEIMS. January, 984

*Sympathizes with Petroald at Bobbio monks' treatment of him;
grants him permission to act as head of the monastery in place of
himself; reminds him of their agreement*

GERBERT TO MONK PETROALD

Do not let the uncertainty of the times disturb your great intelligence, brother. Those who once proclaimed you lord and father when
you were prosperous [1] now disdain to have you as their fellow servant
and equal. Chance upsets everything.[2] Use our permission in giving
and receiving,[3] as becomes a monk and as you have known how to do.
Do not neglect what we have agreed upon [4] in order that we may
have you more frequently in mind.

This is Letter 15 in Havet.
See Letter 23 which I assume to have been written on the journey north from
Pavia to Rheims. Therefore, the present letter must have been written from the
royal palace at Pavia or during the journey north. If Letter 23 was written at
Rheims, then this letter might have been also, but I doubt it. In my *Peasant
Boy*, pp. 107-8, for the sake of the story I assume Rheims to be the place, and
the date to be after Letter 23.
Empress Theophanu was in Rome when Otto II died. Soon she traveled north
to Pavia where she apparently found Gerbert in the royal palace. Sufficient time

also elapsed before Letter 22 was written for Petroald's complaint to reach Gerbert, probably at Pavia.

1. See Letter 10.

2. Virgil *Eclogae* ix.5.

3. Boethius *De arithmetica, Preface,* i. Petroald is to follow the usual monastic principles of charity, and is to accept no gifts on an arrangement unfavorable to Bobbio. If any of the book-leases (for twenty-nine years) expired, Petroald might be able to renew them on terms more favorable to Bobbio.

4. Undoubtedly, Petroald was to write letters and to send Gerbert reports about Bobbio.

23. ON THE ROAD TO RHEIMS or AT RHEIMS.
January, 984
Deplores the riotous condition of northern Italy since Otto's death; has refused his knights' military aid; will renew his studies, but will go to Rome December 1st

To Gerald, Abbot of Aurillac[1]

Ruined, ruined,[2] my father, is the stability of God's churches. The commonwealth has perished; the sanctuary of God is broken into; the people have become the booty of [His] enemy.[3] O, father, advise me whither I shall turn.[4] My knights,[5] it is true, are prepared to take up arms and to fortify a camp. But what hope is there without the ruler [Otto II] of this land, since we know so well the kind of fidelity, habits, and minds certain Italians have?[6]

To fortune, therefore, we are yielding as we again seek our studies that were interrupted for a time, though [always] kept in mind. We should like our former master Raymond[7] to take part in these studies, if it pleases him.[8] Meanwhile, we shall start for Rome on December 1st.[9]

This is Letter 16 in Havet.

For the place from which this letter was written see introductory note on Letter 22; and Lattin, *Peasant boy*, pp. 103-7.

1. Member of the family of the lords of the village of Saint-Céré, sixth abbot of St. Gerald of Aurillac, a monastery founded in 898 by Count Gerald. Aurillac is the chief town of the *département* of the Cantal, on the banks of the Dordanne river. Abbot Gerald died in 986 (Letter 102).

2. Horace *Odae* iv. 70.

3. Cf. Virgil *Aeneid* ii.5, quoted in Letter 171.

4. Letter 21, n. 1.

5. Letters 51 and 102. Undoubtedly, these loyal knights were the men who held benefices granted by the Ottos, especially by Otto II, by Empress Adelaide, and by Gerbert (Letter 13).

6. See also Letters 42, 47, and 102, relative to Gerbert's distrust of Italians; and

M. Uhlirz, "Studien zu Gerbert," *Archiv für Urkundenforschung*, XIII (1935), 446, n. 1.

7. Member of a noble family of Quercy, from Vaura, and Gerbert's teacher of the trivium at St. Gerald. He succeeded Gerald as abbot in 986 (Letter 102). See also Letters 51, 171, and 196; and Lattin, *Peasant Boy*, pp. 26ff.

8. Gerbert thus invites Raymond to Rheims, probably hoping that he might become one of the teachers at the Rheims cathedral school.

9. This journey, which finally was planned for November 1, 984 (Letter 33), had originally been agreed upon with Empress Theophanu at Pavia after Otto II's death (Letter 45). See also Letter 47, Introductory note. M. Uhlirz, *Untersuchungen über Inhalt und Datierung der Briefe Gerberts*, pp. 9-10, insists that Letters 23 and 33 refer to two different planned journeys, the first in December, 983, the second in November, 984. Accordingly, she dates Letter 23 end of October-November, 983, ignoring the fact that in Letter 23 Gerbert mentions Otto II's death which occurred December 7, 983.

24. RHEIMS. January 22, 984

Reminds Bishop Notker of his oath of fidelity to the Ottos; warns him of the approaching meeting between Henry and King Lothair, even revealing their plans, particularly to attack Lorraine

To NOTKER, BISHOP OF LIÉGE

Are you watchful,[1] O father of the country, for that onetime famed fidelity to the camp of Caesar, or do blind fortune and ignorance of the times oppress you? Do you not perceive that at the same time divine and human laws are being trampled underfoot? Behold, openly deserted is he[2] to whom you have vowed your fidelity on his father's account and to whom you ought to preserve it once vowed.

Secretly now the kings of the Franks are going to the German Breisach on the banks of the Rhine and Henry, called an enemy of the state, meets them there on the 1st of February.[3] See to it, my father, that this is opposed by every means lest they come together against the Lord, and your Christ [Psalms 2 : 2; Acts 4 : 26]. When a crowd rules there is turmoil in the kingdoms. If it is difficult to shut out the whole crowd, choose the more competent part. I, who am indeed very faithful to the master's son because of Otto's great beneficence, think about this continuously. We know the ambitious plans of Henry: an attack by the Franks; and we are not ignorant of their ultimate aim.[4] Do not make a sharer of the kingdom one whom you will be unable to drive out, once he is admitted.[5]

This is Letter 39 in Havet. There has been great disagreement about the date of this letter. In MS V (it is not in MS L) it is among letters of the second half of 984 so that Havet, Bubnov, and others, hesitating to destroy the apparent chronological sequence of the letters in MS V, dated this letter about the 1st of December, 984. However, the tone of the letter and its contents have more meaning if it is dated immediately after Gerbert's arrival in Rheims, January 21, 984. Richer's account of King Lothair's useless expedition to Breisach (n. 3 below) and return (III.xcvii-xcviii), with the added details given by Jean de Bayon (*Chronicon Mediani monasterii*, in R. Parisot, *Origines de la Haute-Lorraine* (Paris, 1909), p. 344, n. 1), when considered in conjunction with Lothair's two captures of Verdun (in May-June, 984, and in February, 985) convince one that Letter 24 deals with events of January-February, 984, and not 985. M. Uhlirz, *Jahrbücher des Deutschen Reiches unter Otto II. und Otto III*, Vol. II: *Otto III*, pp. 25-28; 432-41; J. Böhmer, *Regesta imperii*, Vol. II, Pt. 3: *Die Regesten unter Otto III*, No. 1: *Bis 997* (new ed. M. Uhlirz), Nos. 956 d/1-f/1, k/1, i/2, k/2, y/2, 962g, 967a-c; M. Uhlirz, *Untersuchungen über Inhalt und Datierung der Briefe Gerberts*, pp. 10-12.

1. Virgil *Aeneid* x.228.
2. Otto III. See Letter 45.
3. Duke Henry failed to come to Breisach. Richer III.xcviii.
4. Henry was already plotting to have himself made king, and was willing to surrender control of Lorraine to King Lothair as the price of Lothair's non-interference. Letters 30, 34.
5. Duke Henry of Bavaria. Letter 34.

25. RHEIMS. February or March, 984

The turmoil caused by Counts Heribert and Eudes prevented Archbishop Adalbero from visiting Aurillac, so he asks the condition of affairs at Aurillac and news of Hugh, the count-abbot; he is sending a linen coverlet, and requests the book De multiplicatione et divisione numerorum *by Joseph the Spaniard; and begs Gerald to visit Rheims*

To Abbot Gerald of Aurillac

My father Adalbero, archbishop of Rheims, desires to wish you well. Both the disturbance in the kingdoms[1] and the particular activity of Heribert [III] of Troyes and Count Eudes [I],[2] son of Thibaut, against his church prevented him from going to visit you. He desires to learn the condition of your kingdom[3] and whether Hugh, whom you call count-abbot in your language,[4] has married a wife.

Consider his possessions yours and, lest he should ask a favor from you for nothing, indicate what thing of his you would desire. By this token, he is sending you a fancy linen coverlet just as through your Ayrard[5] he once sent another but a plain one.

Abbot Guarin [6] left with you a little book, *De multiplicatione et divisione numerorum*, written by Joseph the Spaniard,[7] and we both should like a copy of it. If an opportunity of visiting St. Rémy [8] and St. Denis [9] presents itself to you, and if you send a messenger ahead, we will be able to enjoy some conversations with you.

This is Letter 17 in Havet.

1. Germany and Lorraine.

2. Gerbert frequently mentions the cousins Heribert (d. 995) and Eudes (d. 996), usually with disfavor, though Richer (iii.c) calls them "illustrious men, famous for their power."

3. Aquitaine, which in 982 had been entrusted to the administration of King Louis V, Lothair's son, and possibly the Spanish March, which was not actually a kingdom. Richer iii.xcii-xciv.

4. Probably the son of Raymond I (d. 961), count of Rouergue and marquis of Gothia (Havet, p. 14, n. 1); or possibly son of Raymond II, count of Rouergue and marquis of Gothia (Bubnov, II, 204, n. 67). An *abbicomes* (*abbacomes*) was a count to whom the king had given a church or abbey as a benefice, on condition of his protecting the establishment.

5. A monk of Aurillac, and not to be confused with the Ayrard of Letter 14. See also Letter 171.

6. *Warnerius*, who is surely to be identified with Abbot Guarin (Letter 51) who was not only abbot of St.-Michel de Cuxá but also, by virtue of exceptional administrative ability, controlled St. Hilary of Razès, SS. Peter and Paul of Lézat, Notre Dame of Alet, and St. Peter of Mas-Garnier. Guarin was a close friend of the Catalan counts, especially of Miró Bonfill (Letter 33), count of Besalú and bishop of Gerona, from whom Gerbert requests the same arithmetical work.

7. *Hispanus* was the term applied in the Spanish March to Mozarabs, the Latin-Romance-speaking Spaniards once under Arab domination, who fled from Moslem Spain to secure freedom and land in the March, thus becoming colonizers. Rovira III, 24-27. The Mozarabic style of the church of Cuxá of the year 953, revealed by archaeological studies there, proves that Cuxá had close connections with Mozarabs.

Heretofore, writers argued that Joseph's work *De multiplicatione et divisione numerorum* could not refer to the abacus because, they said, the abacus was not used in Spain. However, see Lattin, "Origin of Notation," *Isis*, XIX (1933), 190-92 (Author's note), reprinting the rules for multiplication on the abacus found in the twin Spanish manuscripts Escorial d. I. 2 (from Albelda, a. 976), fol. 12v, and d. I. 1. (from San Millán de la Cogolla, a. 992), fol. 9r. In addition, MS Escorial d. I. 2, fol. 12v contains the earliest appearance of the nine Hindu-Arabic numerals in western Latin Europe.

The name Joseph was not as rare as most writers have stated. In 969, at the very time Gerbert was in Spain, a Joseph signed a document of the monastery of Gerri in the diocese of Urgell. Villanueva, XII, 253. The youngest brother of St. Eulogius (middle of 9th cent.) of Cordoba was named Joseph. He had been allowed to study Arabic as a child, later becoming a *catib* or government secretary. J. Perez de Urbel, *A Saint under Moslem Rule*, trans. by a Benedictine of Stanbrook Abbey (Milwaukee, 1937), p. 71.

8. Monastery two miles from the cathedral of Rheims.

9. Monastery in city of Rheims.

26. RHEIMS. March 18, 984

Reprimands the rebellious monks of Bobbio for abandoning him and attaching themselves to his local enemies; reminds them of the danger of associating themselves with these excommunicated persons

To the Brothers of Bobbio

The Holy Scripture says: Those who make a pretense of seeking God never deserve to find him. You who have professed the Rule of St. Benedict and have cast it aside by deserting your pastor, and who have willingly submitted your necks to tyrants—I am not speaking of all—how will you appear with your tyrant leaders before the tribunal of Christ? I am writing these things not, indeed, for the sake of keeping the office [of abbot], but, by saying what ought to be said in accordance with my pastoral charge, I clear my soul of crime and indict those who do not heed my warning. Consider the apostolic privileges; bear in mind the curses of excommunication that you have shown me. Above all, hearken to what the sacred canons say: "Let him who has joined himself in any way whatsoever with an excommunicate be excommunicated." [1] Observe in how great danger your affairs are. May the Supreme Judge make you acquainted with His precepts, and cause you to fulfill them by deeds.

This is Letter 18 in Havet.

Letters 26-31 were dispatched to Italy probably by the same messenger. Letter 28 mentions "Lenten penance," and Lent in 984 began February 5th, with Easter on March 23d.

1. Apparently, the excommunication in these papal privileges took effect when the abbot pronounced it. Gerbert had already pronounced it against those who defied his authority. See Dionysius Exiguus *Codex canonum ecclesiasticorum*, PL LXVII, 142.

27. RHEIMS. March 18, 984

Consoles Rainard, monk of Bobbio, for the loss of his abbot (Gerbert himself) and advises him to act on his own initiative

To Monk Rainard [1]

Rightly, indeed, brother, you complain about being deprived of your abbot. Monks without an abbot in a monastery—how similar to shepherdless sheep in enclosed valleys as they face the mouths of wolves. I urge and advise you to think and act as best you can according to your knowledge and ability.[2] The explanation for the three different heads over you in one year lies in the deceit and changeableness that is apparent to you.[3] Bewail the future ruin not so much of buildings as of souls; and do not despair of God's mercy.

This is Letter 19 in Havet.

1. Monk of Bobbio, loyal to Gerbert. See Letters 138, 169; and Lattin, *Peasant Boy*, pp. 97-101. Possibly he is the monk *Rainaldus* who signed a document of the later Abbot Petroald, March 18, 1010. Cipolla, *Codice diplomatico di Bobbio*, I, No. cxii.

2. This was a significant concession because the power of the Benedictine abbot over the monks was absolute.

3. An unknown usurper was in control of the abbey, although Gerbert, less than four months earlier, had left Petroald as prior to act as the head for Gerbert.

28. RHEIMS. March 20, 984

Gerbert begs not to be separated from the service of Empress Adelaide, asserting he is faithful to her

GERBERT TO EMPRESS ADELAIDE

Many, indeed, are my sins before God; but against my Lady what, that I am driven from her service? Never have I broken my pledged word, never betrayed her trust. I thought I was practicing piety [1] without avarice. If I have in the least mistaken your desires, improvidence caused this, not intention. And hoping that my Lenten penance, continued now day after day, may sufficiently satisfy [2] you, I am confident that it will.

Up to now the reckless greed of certain poor nobles has prevailed [with you]. Now, let your piety prevail which has always existed where justice was involved. The Divinity, conciliating kingdoms for you and reducing powerful kings to your rule,[3] delights in such action.

My decision is this: the fidelity that I maintained towards the son of my Lady Adelaide I will maintain towards his mother.[4] If absence from you prevents my exhibiting it in your presence, then, at least, while absent I can display it by speaking eloquent praises of you, by wishing the best for you, by praying for God's favor towards you.

This is Letter 20 in Havet.

See Letter 26, introductory note.

1. Gerbert had granted land only on terms favorable to the monastery of St. Columban of Bobbio. See Letter 13.

2. See Letter 26, introductory note.

3. Cicero *De inventione* i.ii. Adelaide was the grandmother of Otto III, the

mother-in-law of King Lothair, and the sister of King Conrad of Burgundy. Her first husband, Lothar, was king of Italy, and her second, Otto I, conquered the next king of Italy, Berengar.

4. Letter 18, n. 6.

29. RHEIMS. March 20, 984
Requests the monk Eceman to speak favorably for him at the imperial court

To Eceman, a Monk of the Court [1]

Perceiving your good will towards me, my brother, I congratulate myself on the friendship of such a man. It is clear that you are constantly faithful, indeed, both towards me and towards those who have entrusted themselves to you. For the household of an admirable woman [Adelaide?] would not otherwise consider you illustrious. Therefore, you will [I hope] assume the burden of a friend by suggesting good words in his behalf. Pray interpret my letters indulgently, and consider my business yours.

This is Letter 21 in Havet.

1. Undoubtedly the confessor of Empress Adelaide. In 987 she founded the monastery of Selz in the diocese of Strassburg and Eceman became abbot. Odilo, *S. Adalheidae imperatricis epitaphium*, MGSS IV, 641; Bubnov, II, 216, n. 101; Havet, p. 17, n. 1.

30. RHEIMS. March 20, 984
Thanks Lady Imiza for her fidelity to him and requests her to approach the Pope in behalf of both of them; sends political information for Empress Theophanu

Gerbert to Lady Imiza [1]

I consider myself fortunate in being accepted as a friend by such a remarkable woman [as you]. The admiration of my French friends, so amazed at her staunch fidelity and long continued constancy, cannot be measured by their numbers. Although Your Prudence does not need reminding, yet, because we feel that you are grieving and suffering severely from our misfortune, we wish the Lord Pope [John XIV] to be approached by messengers and letters, both yours and ours,[2] so that, if we have any patrons and supporters, either individually or in common, we who grieve together may rejoice together, God helping us.

Approach my Lady Theophanu in my name to inform her that the kings of the French are well disposed towards her son [Otto III], and that she should attempt nothing but the destruction of Henry's tyrannical [3] scheme, for he desires to make himself king under the pretext of guardianship.[4]

This is Letter 22 in Havet.

1. Probably she was Irmintrud, nickname "Imiza," daughter of Megingoz, count of Avelgau, Geldern and Zutphen (d. 995), and Gerberga who was a sister of Archbishop Adalbero of Rheims. Hence, Lady Imiza was Adalbero's niece and Gerbert's esteem for her is quite understandable. DO III 32 gives evidence of Count Megingoz's and Countess Gerberga's importance. In addition, Lady Imiza was probably the wife of Count Heribert, brother of the influential Duke Conrad of Swabia. M. Uhlirz, "Studien zu Gerbert," *Archiv für Urkunden-forschung*, XIII (1935), 450, n. 6; M. Uhlirz, *Jahrbücher des Deutschen Reiches unter Otto II und Otto III*, Vol. II: *Otto III*, pp. 78-79, 149; Böhmer, *Regesta imperii*, Vol. II: *Die Regesten Otto III*, Pt. 1 (new ed., M. Uhlirz), Nos. 956r and 989.

2. Letter 31. See Bubnov II, 218, n. 108.

3. Quintilian *Institutiones* i.x.48.

4. Usually the nearest male relative became guardian of a minor. However, Empress Adelaide had acted with the minor Otto II, May 7, 973—June, 974, after the death of Otto I. Thietmar iii.i; Odilo, *S. Adelaidae imperatricis epitaphium*, Chap. VI. Both Duke Henry (the Quarreler) of Bavaria and King Lothair were cousins of Otto II. Henry's father, Duke Henry I, was a brother of Otto I, and Lothair's mother, Queen Gerberga, was a sister of Otto I. According to one plan, Lothair and his son Louis V should assume the guardianship of the three-year-old Otto III.

31. RHEIMS. March 20, 984
Complains to Pope John XIV of the rebellion at Bobbio against himself, the legal abbot; requests a message from him; if the message is not received, plans drastic action

To Lord Pope John [xiv]

The seizure and spoliation of God's holy place, entrusted to me by the Holy Roman and Apostolic Church,[1] weighs heavily upon me as my heart grieves.[2] Moreover, what will henceforth be stable if that is overthrown which was done by the agreement of the prince, the election of the bishops, the wish of the clergy and the people, and, finally, by the consecration of the most distinguished of all men—the Pope;[3] if charters are violated, privileges despised, divine and human laws destroyed? Deign to intimate to the holy bishops with what hope I may undergo the danger of approaching you.

Otherwise, do not wonder if I attach myself to these groups where human but never divine law is the controlling factor. For the human feeling, the first sentiment of mankind assuredly lies in things of action; the divine sentiment, the second of mankind, lies in things of contemplation.[4] This will happen because of my faintheartedness, if your generosity shall cease.

This is Letter 23 in Havet.
1. See Letter 167.
2. Sallust *Oratio in Tullium* i.i.4. MS Rheims 1329 (Cathedral scriptorium), s.XI, fol. 107, contains this work. CG XXXIX: *Reims*, II, 475.
3. Abbots were chosen by the monks after consultation with whatever ruler (king, prince, count) had any claims upon the monastery, and consultation with one or more bishops. Hence, the expression "by the clergy and the people," regularly found in the decree of election of a bishop, but not in that of an abbot, appears out of place. Gerbert's words suggest that, after nomination by Otto II, a papal synod actually chose Gerbert abbot.
4. Gerbert is using the language of the Aristotelian divisions of knowledge or philosophy into inspective, i.e., contemplative or theoretical; and actual, i.e., active or practical (Isidore *Etymologiae* ii.xxiv.9-16). This second division included correcting morals, persuading people, and government. The first division included theoretical knowledge in the mind, which scholars looked upon as the way of achieving knowledge of the Divine, and which, therefore, included the study of theology. Hence, Gerbert suggests that he probably will devote himself to more worldly affairs than trying to instill theoretical knowledge into his Bobbio monks or Rheims clerics.

32. RHEIMS. March 25, 984

Requests a book De astrologia, *translated by the recipient*

To LOBET [1] OF BARCELONA

Although I have no claim on you, still your renown and your courtesy lead me to trust in you, in fact to presume on you. And so, I am asking you to send me the book *De astrologia*, translated by you,[2] and if you desire anything from me in return, ask for it unhesitatingly.

This is Letter 24 in Havet.
1. Undoubtedly the prominent and wealthy archdeacon of the cathedral of Barcelona named Seniofred (Sunyer, Suñer) (d. before June 15, 997, and possibly in 995). Lattin, "Lupitus Barchinonensis," *Speculum*, VII (1932), 58-64. *Lupitus* or *Lubetus* (Lobet) was his nickname, and he appears in many Barcelona documents of this time with both his nickname and his real name.
2. Presumably, Lobet translated this work from the Arabic, and it is important, therefore, as one of the earliest works known to have been translated from Arabic into Latin, especially in the field of science. The earliest such translation in astronomy appears to have been a work *Astrolabii sententiae*, published from early eleventh-century manuscripts by Millàs, *Assaig d'història*, pp. 275ff., which Millàs ascribes to Lobet. A Prologue to a translation from the Arabic of a work on the astrolabe, published by Bubnov, *Gerberti opera mathe-*

matica, pp. 370-75, and by Millàs, pp. 271-75, as "probably" by *Lupitus*-Lobet, was undoubtedly *not* by Lobet, even though the flowery language is characteristic of the Spanish Latinity of the period. A. Van de Vyver, "Les premières traductions latines (Xᵉ-XIᵉ siècles) de traités arabes sur l'astrolabe," *1ᵉʳ Congrès international de géographie historique*, II (1931), *Mémoires*, p. 274, n. 36.

33. RHEIMS. March 25, 984

Excuses himself for not having obeyed Bishop Miró Bonfill's orders; asks for some message to be sent to Rheims until November, or to Rome at Christmas; requests the book De multiplicatione et divisione numerorum *by Joseph the Wise*

To Bishop Bonfill of Gerona [1]

The great reputation of your name,[2] indeed, moves me not only to see and speak with you, but also to comply with your orders.[3] It is only due to the fact that liberty has been denied me that I have so long put off this compliance. Now that I have gained my liberty, though only through sorrow, since my Lord Otto the Caesar no longer lives, it is right for me both to talk with friends and to obey their commands. If you wish to make known anything to us, you can communicate with us at Rheims until November 1st, or at Rome on December 25th,[4] if we are able to avail ourselves of peace. Joseph the Wise published certain sentences *De multiplicatione et divisione numerorum*,[5] and my father Adalbero, archbishop of Rheims, wishes to have these through your efforts.

This is Letter 25 in Havet.

1. Son of the Catalan Count Miró (d. 929) and Countess Ava. His name was Miró with the nickname Bonfill (*Bonusfilius* [good or worthy son]). Villanueva, XIII, 73. He was the first cousin of Count Borrell, Gerbert's early patron, and was the best educated and most prominent prelate of Catalonia. He was count of Besalù, and bishop of Gerona, January, 971—January 22, 984. For bibliography on Gerona see Paul Kehr, "Papsturkunden in Spanien," ABG n. f. XVIII (1926), 135.

2. In 1003, Odo, a successor in the see of Gerona calls him "my very famous predecessor." Villanueva, XV, 268.

3. According to JL 3804, Bishop Miró attended a papal synod in Rome, March 27, 981, when he may have seen Gerbert, and have requested him to return to Spain. As count of Besalù, Miró claimed a certain control over the monastery of Santa Maria de Ripoll where Gerbert had presumably studied in Spain.

4. See Letters 23 and 45 about this proposed journey.

5. See Letter 25, n. 7.

34. RHEIMS. March 26, 984

Archbishop Adalbero tries to arouse Archbishop Egbert against supporting Duke Henry as king of Germany; offers to share Rheims with him

To Egbert, Archbishop of Trier,[1] in the Name of Adalbero

That your state is tottering through the cowardice of certain persons fills us not only with horror but also with shame. We are thus tormented because we are privileged in loving you as well as in being joined by the tie of a common fatherland.[2]

Are there so few kings created that you wish to put a new one ahead of the son[3] of your lord? Because, by chance, he is Greek,[4] as you contend, you wish to institute a coruler according to the custom of the Greeks.[5] Whither has sacred fidelity vanished? Have the benefits bestowed on you by the Ottos escaped from your memory? Bid your great intelligence return; reflect on their generosity, unless you wish to be an everlasting disgrace to your race.

If you protest that soldiers persist in deserting you, seek for some [men] with better ideas. Trust that we shall be your partisans and assistants in such matters. In the disturbance and confusion of all things, who will lighten the load of another? [Gal. 6:2]. Finally, if you are not able to protect the city of Trier while maintaining the dignity of your name, let the city of Rheims be enough for both of us, and we shall be more splendid than Eucharius[6] and Sixtus[7] were formerly. A decision to this effect will take away the ignominy from you, but a decision in the negative will free us.[8]

This is Letter 26 in Havet. It answers one from Egbert that had expressed approval of the recognition of Duke Henry of Bavaria as king at Magdeburg on March 16th by nobles and clerics. Thietmar iv.i. The distance of 380 miles from Magdeburg to Rheims would have required 8-9 days for the news to reach Rheims.

1. See p. 8, and Letter 20, n. 1.

2. Lorraine.

3. Otto III. Egbert, as archbishop, had sworn fealty to Otto III at the time of his coronation, in Aachen, December 25th, but was already violating it by his adherence to Duke Henry.

4. Otto III's mother, Empress Theophanu, was Greek. See Appendix A.

5. During the minorities of the Byzantine coemperors, Basil II and Constantine VIII, first Nicephorus Phocas (963-69) and then John Tzimisces (969-76) had thrust themselves onto the throne while pretending to rule with Basil and Constantine. These latter two were ruling as coemperors at the time of this letter.

6. St. Eucharius (3d cent.) first bishop of Trier.

7. St. Sixtus (290 A.D.) first bishop of Rheims.

8. Adalbero urges Egbert to choose exile to Rheims rather than accept Henry as king; otherwise, Adalbero declares himself to be free from the obligations of friendship with Egbert.

35. RHEIMS. March 27, 984

Gerbert, in the name of Adalbero, attempts to arouse Archbishop Willigis to the dangers of supporting Duke Henry; requests information about persons loyal to Otto III; solicits aid for property of St. Rémy near Mainz

TO WILLIGIS, ARCHBISHOP OF MAINZ,[1] IN THE NAME OF THE SAME

With great constancy must we work, father, in order to maintain a plan of peace and leisure. What else does the disorder of the realms mean than the desolation of the churches? Piety, indeed, and the many kindnesses of the Ottos toward us do not allow us to be turned against the son of Caesar.

At length, we have secured a promise of assistance from our kings [Lothair and Louis V] for him. We are going to establish by common consent a lasting agreement of both parties,[2] if acceptable, and we shall ask nothing from you except an unshaken fidelity to our lord.[3] We utter these things with God as witness, and in complete trust we commit them to your discretion. Will he, who has attempted to kill two Ottos,[4] be willing that a third should survive? Remember that Ciceronian[?] passage: "It is foolish to expect fidelity from those by whom you have been many times deceived."

At the same time, moreover, because not for nothing has the Divinity bestowed on you knowledge and power, indicate to us in safe replies what you approve in these suggestions, and wherein you think contrariwise, as well as what persons favor your ideas and what ones disagree with you. May your advice extend to provision for the property of St. Rémy in your vicinity [5] lest a rapacious robber seize it, or lest Otto,[6] who ought to protect it, should plunder it. In these matters also may we know your wish.

This is Letter 27 in Havet.

1. Born 930 at Schöningen, Brunswick, probably of the lower nobility; chancellor of Otto I in 970 (DO I 404); archbishop of Mainz from 975; primate of Germany. He and Archbishop John of Ravenna crowned Otto III as king, December 25, 983. Mainz was the most important spiritual body of the time in western Europe after the papacy. Böhmer, *Willigis von Mainz*, p. 13; U. Stutz, "Reims und Mainz in der Königswahl des zehnten und zu Begin des elften Jahr-

hunderts," SBB, 1921, pt. 1, pp. 422-23; Johnson, *German Episcopate*, Index, s.v. Willigis, especially pp. 37, n. 48, 194-95, 203-04.

2. Otto III, represented by Willigis, and Lothair, represented by Adalbero. Bubnov, II, 227, n. 133.

3. Otto III. A small portion of the Rheims diocese lay in Upper Lorraine, and several of the dioceses of the archbishopric were located in Lower Lorraine and in Holland, which were all parts of the empire.

4. In 974 and 976 Henry rebelled against Otto II (*Annales Hildesheimenses*, a. 974, 976, MGSS III, 62, 64; Thietmar III.iv-v.vii; K. Uhlirz, *Jahrbücher des deutschen Reiches unter Otto II*, pp. 51f., 77f.) but an attempt against the life of Otto I by Henry is not known. For further background details about Duke Henry (II of Bavaria), leading up to his effort to become king see M. Doeberl, *Entwickelungsgeschichte Bayerns*, Vol. I: *Von den ältesten Zeiten bis zum Westfälischen Frieden* (Munich, 1906), 114-17.

5. In the Mainz diocese St. Rémy of Rheims possessed a priory at Kusel (Rhenish Palatinate) (DO I 156, 286; DO III 28, 122) and property adjoining that of St. Maximin at Nahegau on the Nahe river. In 902 Archbishop Hatto of Mainz made a formal agreement with Archbishop Hervé of Rheims to care for the property of St. Rémy and of the cathedral of Rheims located in his archdiocese. A. Werminghoff, "Reise nach Italien im Jahre 1901," NA, XXVII (1902), 598f.; *Notitia de conventu Hattonis archiepiscopi Moguntini et Hervei archiepiscopi Remensis*, ed. F. Balthgen, MGSS XXX, Pt. 2 (1934), 755-56; Flodoard *Historia Remensis ecclesiae* iv.xiii, MGSS XIII, 576; Sigehard *Miracula S. Maximini*, MGSS IV, 232; Bubnov, II, 228, n. 136. Flodoard III (MGSS XIII, pp. 514-19, 536-44) gives a further idea as to how extensive the possessions of the Rheims churches were. They extended into Aquitaine, Provence, Limoges, and Lyons.

On November 29, 986, Archbishop Willigis fulfilled his obligation to protect Rheims property by requesting from Otto III a diploma in favor of the property of St. Rémy of Rheims at Kusel (and also at Meerssen, northeast of Maastricht); and again on May 9, 993. DO III 28, 122. Böhmer, *Regesta imperii*, Vol. II, Pt. 3: *Regesten unter Otto III* (new ed. M. Uhlirz, Graz-Cologne, 1956), Nos. 985 and 1090.

6. Probably Otto, duke of Franconia, who with his son Conrad was notorious for his frequent altercations with the bishops of Worms. *Vita Burchardi*, Chap. VII, MGSS IV, 835; Bubnov, II, 228, n. 136; Johnson, *German Episcopate*, pp. 60-61. Yet, this may have been Otto, count of Worms and duke of Carinthia, the son of Duke Conrad of Lorraine and the grandson of Emperor Otto I, who disturbed the monastery of Weissenburg (diocese of Speyer) in 985 and distributed some of its landed property among his followers. *Annales Weissemburgenses*, a.985, MGSS III, 70.

36. RHEIMS. May, 984

An appeal for financial assistance sent out in the name of the devastated church of Jerusalem and a reminder of all the church of Jerusalem means to the Christian world

TO THE UNIVERSAL CHURCH [1] IN THE NAME OF THE DEVASTATED CHURCH OF JERUSALEM

From that church which is in Jerusalem to the Universal Church, which commands the scepters of kingdoms.

Since you are flourishing successfully, Immaculate Bride of God, a member[2] of whom I confess myself to be, through you I have the greatest hope of raising up my head, up to now almost exhausted. What! should I despair of you in anything, mistress of all things? If you recognize me as yours, ought anyone of yours to think that the infamous injury[3] inflicted on me does not pertain to himself, and ought he not to abhor it as the most terrible of events?

Behold! the world still regards me as the best part of itself, prostrate though I now am. With me are the oracles of the prophets, the manifestations of the patriarchs; here the clear lights of the world, the apostles,[4] made their appearance; here it [the world] discovered the faith of Christ; with me found its Redeemer. For, although He may be everywhere in His divine nature, yet in His human nature here was He born, did He suffer, was He buried, and from here was He raised up to heaven. But, though the prophet has said: "His sepulcher be glorious" [Isa. 11 : 10], now that the infidels have overthrown the sacred places, the devil strives to render it inglorious. Shine forth, therefore, soldier of Christ, be His standard-bearer and cofighter; and because you are not powerful in arms, assist with counsel and the aid of riches.[5] [Consider] what you are giving, and to whom you give it. Assuredly it is only a little from great wealth, even though [you give it] to that Man who notwithstanding his giving freely all that you have, nevertheless receives not ungratefully. For He multiplies, and He rewards in the future. Through me He blesses you that you may grow by giving, and He forgives sins so that you may live by reigning with Him.

This is Letter 28 in Havet.

1. This letter is apparently a solicitation of alms for the Holy Sepulcher, composed by Gerbert for Abbot Guarin of Cuxá (Letters 25, 51) perhaps, who embarked on a journey to Jerusalem in 985. Rovira, III, 358-60. Pilgrimages to to the Holy Land had never ceased, and research is revealing an increasing number of tenth-century visitors.

At one time this letter was erroneously believed to have been a call by Pope Sylvester II (Gerbert) for an armed crusade (JL 3938).

2. Augustine *De baptismo* ii.ix, PL XLIII, 135.

3. Gerbert must be referring to the capture of the East by the Moslem Arabs three hundred years before, since no more recent event fits this description.

4. Philip. 2 : 15. See the discussion of *luminaria* (lights) in Schramm, *Kaiser, Rom und Renovatio*, I, 85, n. 5; 125, n. 1.

5. II Tim. 2 : 3-4. Christ's soldier is here called upon to furnish only counsel and aid, whereas the medieval soldier or knight (*miles*) was obligated to furnish military service also. Therefore, this letter is not an appeal for an armed crusade.

37. RHEIMS. May, 984
Reprimands Gualo for disregarding synodal decrees and summons him to appear at a synod on June 29

To Gualo [1] and His Followers in the Name of Archbishop Adalbero

Up to now, indeed, we have patiently endured your foolishness. Now, because you consider the synod's decrees of little weight, refusing to come although you have been summoned, and because you place human things ahead of the divine, we again summon you to be heard at the meeting of our brothers that will be held at Vaudancourt [2] on June 29th. Either [3] you come there or you and your protectors, in any frame of mind you choose, may expect a sentence of damnation on that same day.

This is Letter 29 in Havet.
1. Gualo (or Walo) is unknown. He is probably not the same as the "G." of Letter 195, as suggested by Bubnov, II, 138. See Letter 195, n. 6 below.
2. Perhaps Vaudancourt (Gualdonis Cortem) in the commune of Brugny-Vaudancourt (Marne). Havet, p. 24, n. 1, and Bubnov, II, 138.
3. I follow the reading of MS V, *eo aut venite.*

38. RHEIMS. May 21, 984
Count Godfrey, whose inactivity is due to an injured foot, requests Notker to act for him; Adalbero's legate has seen Lothair and secured a favorable answer; Notker is requested to attend a a meeting in early June

To Notker, Bishop of Liége, [1] in the Name of Adalbero

Do not think that my brother Godfrey [2] is not worthy of your friendship, I beseech, my father, because he has not gone to the king [3] as agreed, or because, as agreed, he has not come where you wished. Indeed, excellent intention drove him on but chance in the shape of an injured foot [4] retarded him. May Your Prudence, therefore, transact the business of a friend, represent him in that matter and make promises with confidence, as you know and as is just.

We, indeed, accomplished the business of the child [Otto III], your master, in accordance with your decision and if, by the help of

God, you shall have changed this for a better plan, we will equalize the balance with better effort. We have undertaken your business as if it were our own. He [Gerbert] whom you know to be intimate with us and a most faithful interpreter for you was with his royal majesty [Lothair], as was fitting. What you requested has been secured by firmness without respect for enemies;[5] and, since everything ought not to be entrusted to letters, we wish you to go to the meeting agreed upon,[6] and we shall make them await your presence even to June 11th. The meeting must occur while the time is opportune lest, when you shall have taken yourself away, it may become inopportune.

This is Letter 30 in Havet.

1. A Swabian by birth; member of Otto I's chapel; bishop of Liége, 972-1007, which city he helped make an important cultural center, especially in schools, from which came numerous bishops. *Kurth, Notker de Liége*; Manitius, II, 219-23; Johnson, *German Episcopate*, pp. 121-22.

2. See Letter 54, introductory note and n. 1.

3. Otto III, who, at this time was still detained by Duke Henry.

4. Godfrey had never recovered from the effects of a foot injury from a lance, suffered during an engagement with the troops of Renier and Lambert, sons of Renier Long-Col, and Duke Charles of Lower Lorraine, April 19, 976. Lot, *Derniers Carolingiens*, pp. 82-83.

5. Duke Charles, Archbishop Egbert, and Bishop Dietrich of Metz. Possibly Adalbero viewed Counts Heribert and Eudes as the enemies, since they were King Lothair's advisers. Bubnov, II, 233, n. 140.

6. Apparently, those who were to participate in discussing the guardianship for Otto III included Duke Henry, Empresses Theophanu and Adelaide, King Lothair, possibly Duke Charles, plus their followers. A meeting may have occurred in early June but accomplished little. For the important meeting at Rohr (Rara) on June 29th see introductory note under Letter 45.

39. METZ? May 27, 984

Bishop Dietrich of Metz rails at Duke Charles for his broken oath of fidelity; recounts his treasonable plans and slanderous words; and threatens him with excommunication

THE CONTENTION OF BISHOP DIETRICH OF METZ[1] AGAINST CHARLES[2]

From Dietrich, servant of the servants of God, lover of the emperors, the very watchful protector of their offspring, to Charles, his nephew by blood relationship, but the most shameless violator of fidelity.

You fickle deserter, keeping faith neither in this direction nor in that,[3] the blind love of ruling drove your weak-minded self to neglect a pledge, given under oath before the altar of St. John[4] while the venerable Bishop Notker was present along with yourself and others not nobler than you but surpassing you in fidelity. Good men never violate such a pledge, as you know.

What wonder if you pour forth the disease of your utterly wicked heart against your kinsman [5] since, with bloody hand always very ready for all crime, with a gang of robbers and a band of thieves, you would steal the city of Laon from your brother, the noble king [Lothair] of the French—his city, I repeat, his, never under any circumstances yours; since you would deprive him of his kingdom; [6] since you would bring the imperial sister, sharer of his kingdom, into ill repute and would defile her with your lies? [7] Have you ever had any scruples?

Swell up, grow stout, wax fat, you who, not following the footsteps of your fathers, have wholly forsaken God your Maker. Remember how often my finger restrained your impudent mouth while you were spreading abroad shameful things about the archbishop of Rheims,[8] and more shameful insinuations against the queen by simulating a serpent's hiss. What you did against the bishop of Laon,[9] you yourself know well.

As you are hiding away in a little corner of the kingdom of Lorraine and are boasting with groundless arrogance that you will rule the whole, remember what is held and possessed, with God as the Giver, by our cousin, a woman [10] better than you a man, with her son [Thierry] of noble character; by the vicars of the apostles, shepherds of the sheepfold of the Holy Church whom you with the tooth of a dog attempt to gnaw at night and day; and by other princes besides who owe you no allegiance. By sweeping out empty dreams and clearing your brow, muddled by the delusive cup, you will thus finally be able to judge that what you do is nothing and that through the Divine Will what you plot [11] must come to naught. Enrolled as I am among those vicars, though not on account of merit, and given the office of binding and loosing [Mat. 16 : 19], I intend to defend the Church entrusted to me, unworthy of the pastoral staff though I am. The Church, I repeat, no other than that one redeemed by the blood of the greatest Shepherd that you, despising divine law, with your accomplices strive to lacerate and destroy wherever possible.[12] You scorn the Lord's fearful voice, thundering: "For he that toucheth you, toucheth the apple of my eye" [Zech. 2: 8], and that other voice speaking in the same manner: "He who rejects you, rejects me" [Luke 10 : 16].

Eager to care for your wounds, hitherto I poured oil and wine upon them by mixing soft words, secretly through our followers, with my harsh public censure.

Henceforth, unless you repent, by the sword of the Holy Spirit, entrusted to me, I will cut you off along with your putrescent members, and I will abandon both to the unextinguishable fire to be certain that, just as your home would be with those above if you do not refuse [to reform], so it will be forever with those below if you refuse. When now the bars have been strengthened and the gates of the heavenly Jerusalem have been closed by the Son of the Virgin, Bridegroom of that very city, to the false ones it will be said: "Depart from me, accursed ones, into the everlasting fire which was prepared for the devil and his angels" [Mat. 25 : 41]. It is written: "Woe to thee that spoilest, shalt not thou thyself also be spoiled?" [Isa. 33 : 1]. Beware lest you be discovered in such a robbery that he who is found out is exiled from the eternal inheritance.

May God make foolish the counsel of Achitofel [2 Sam. 15 : 31].

This is Letter 31 in Havet. Possibly Bishop Dietrich wrote this letter himself.

1. A learned bishop (964-September 7, 984) who, though a relative of Otto III (being a cousin of Otto I), favored Henry's guardianship against that of Empress Theophanu. See Johnson, *German Episcopate*, Index, s.v. Dietrich I of Metz.

2. Younger brother of King Lothair, who had been created duke of Lower Lorraine in June, 977, by Otto II, to whom Charles promised to oppose all of King Lothair's designs on Lorraine. Havet, p. 26; Lot, *Derniers Carolingiens*, pp. 91, n. 4.

3. Sallust *Oratio in Tullium* IV.vii.

4. Possibly the altar of Chèvremont (on the Vesdre, Belgium, province of Liége, commune of Vaux-sous-Chèvremont), dedicated to St. John. Havet, p. 26, n. 1; Bubnov, II, 237, n. 151. Kurth (*Notker de Liége*, p. 75, n. 2) states that Chèvremont was not under the control of the bishop of Liége at this date. There was a collegiate church in Liége, dedicated to St. John, which Bishop Notker had established. Lesne V, 359.

The oath was probably given either in 977 when Charles received the duchy of Lorraine (n. 2 above); or in 978, after the death of Duke Frederick (Letter 83) when Charles may have sworn to respect the rights of Frederick's minor son Thierry; or as a preliminary to his coronation as king of France in 978 by Bishop Dietrich. Lot, *Derniers Carolingiens*, pp. 97, 99. A different interpretation is offered by M. Uhlirz, *Jahrbücher des deutschen Reiches unter Otto II. und Otto III*, Vol. II: *Otto III*, p. 29. She insists that Kings Lothair and Louis, Bishop Notker, Duke Charles, Archbishop Egbert, Bishop Dietrich, Count Godfrey,

Archbishop Adalbero, Gerbert, and many others met in the monastery of St. John in Liége and made an agreement to support the rights of succession of Otto III. Each one took an oath to this effect. This meeting, according to Uhlirz, took place at the end of February, 984.

5. Probably Otto III (see Letter 40), although possibly his cousin Beatrice's son, Duke Thierry, is meant.

6. Dietrich apparently proclaimed Charles king in 978 at Laon, capital city of the last Carolingians. Such a proclamation could have had no validity in France. Johnson, *German Episcopate*, p. 210.

7. Charles had accused Queen Emma (half-sister of Otto II) of adultery with Bishop Ascelin of Laon. Richer III.lxvi; Lot, *Derniers Carolingiens*, 91, n. 4.

8. An unknown event, although it may have been reports of Adalbero's assistance to Otto II, especially in 978, rumors of which later resulted in formal accusations of treason against Adalbero on other grounds. Letters 64, 103; and Bubnov, II, 387, n. 61.

9. Adalbero (b. 947), 977-1030, called also Ascelin (the name used in these notes to distinguish him from the numerous other Adalberos of the time); member of a wealthy Lorraine family, probably the nephew of Archbishop Adalbero of Rheims (Letter 131, n. 9); chancellor of King Lothair, 974-77. Manitius, II, 525-31.

10. Duchess Beatrice, daughter of Dietrich's cousin Hadwig and Hugh the Great.

11. Charles planned to seize control of Upper Lorraine.

12. Counts Arnulf of Valenciennes and Godfrey of Verdun had requested Duke Charles to take charge of the affairs of the bishopric of Cambrai during the vacancy of the see after Bishop Tetdo's death in 979. Charles moved into the bishop's palace, bag and baggage, seized all possible episcopal revenues, and even sold ecclesiastical offices to gain still more. *Gesta episcoporum Camera-censium*, I.ci, MGSS VII, 443; Johnson, *German Episcopate*, p. 130.

40. LOWER LORRAINE? or LAON? June 5, 984

Charles makes counteraccusations of Bishop Dietrich's infidelity to Otto III and enumerates Dietrich's other crimes

GERBERT, IN THE NAME OF CHARLES, IN REFUTATION OF DIETRICH

From Charles, if he is anything, only by the grace of God, to Dietrich, archetype of hypocrites, faithless murderer of emperors and their offspring, and, in general, an enemy to the state.

It has befitted my dignity, indeed, to cover up your curses and not to give any weight to what the caprice [1] of a tyrant rather than the judgment of a priest proffered. But, lest silence would imply to your conspirators the making of a confession, I shall touch briefly upon the chief particulars of your crimes, saying the least about the greatest. Grown stout, fat and huge, as you rave that I have, by this pressure of my weight I will deflate you, who are blown up with arrogance like an empty bag, as I hasten some advice to you.

Why do you call our attention to Duchess Beatrice, her son, and the nobles of the kingdom? You do not discern that you have been deceived, wretched one, and that no one will share the punishment for your oath.[2] Not alone, nor in a corner, do I furnish irreproachable fidelity to the son of our Caesar,[3] as you belch forth in your nightly cup of wine. There are with me the princes of Gaul, the kings of France—most illustrious men whatever you may say—and faithful Lorrainers. The son of Caesar concerns them greatly; they do not desire to snatch away his kingdom as you do, nor to set up a coruler.[4]

You have confused divine and human rights and in your babbling about laws you resemble a snail who after withdrawing into his shell believes that he still has horns.[5] Against whom are you directing threats by your pastoral authority, as if you were really a shepherd instead of a greedy wolf, or more correctly, another Judas? If Judas, who betrayed his Lord for thirty pieces of silver, is considered an apostle, then you who, hoping for a reward—a scandalous reward— have deprived your lord, the hereditary king, of his kingdom may be considered a bishop. Little does it matter to you that you have incurred endless punishment from him as from an enemy. Is it by such acts that others have merited the favors of the Ottos?

Finally, it is not in the son's cause alone that you are incontestably proved never to have kept faith with them. For, when you were driving out Lothair, king of the French, whom you call glorious though you especially hate him,[6] and were forcing me to rule, were you maintaining the fidelity promised to them or to me? I repeat, promised to me before the altar that you shamelessly mention.

Really, you know what you did. You forced me to prepare arms against my brother and the sister of your seigneur so that you were stabbing àll our royal race with mutual wounds; and for him you were substituting tyrants under the name of kings, with whom, in defiance of your priestly office, you might dwell in empty palaces.

You think you are injuring me by asserting that I injured those persons whose good opinion of me I prize and whose censure disheartens me. The truth is contrariwise. The enormity of your crimes does not allow you to hide your own shameful acts. And, although you wish to clear yourself by accusing someone else,[7] yet, a paleness forthwith and presently a blush, your sudden silence while speaking, then sudden words incoherent with the preceding words—all reveal even to the incurious a violently tormented conscience. Blush, wretch, and recognize that what you thought you alone knew has come to the notice of all· Do not pollute the innocent with your crimes and do not judge others according to your vilely disgraceful life. Since perjury has so often defiled your hands, cease to violate holy things, and you who enjoin it upon us, first seek the remedy of repentance yourself.

You have uttered public perjury. You have exhausted your own city with plundering. You have depopulated the church, entrusted, as you remind me, to yourself. Certainly, this last is true. Therefore, make restoration to the extent that you have abused the protection of Our Lady [the Church] whom you have humiliated by snatching away her freedom and imposing servitude upon her. And you, though calling yourself the eye of God, have heaped up your table with the luxury of the rich man of the gospel [Luke 16 : 16ff.] by reducing the fatherless and the widow to tears. You have piled up mountains of gold through your similar exactions from unfortunates.

Bewail these conditions privately and publicly, unhappy one. Finally, hear what is intended for you: "For days will come upon thee and surround thee, and shut thee in on every side, and will dash thee to the ground, because thou has not known the time of thy visitation" [Luke 19 : 43-44].

"We have heard of the pride of Moab, he is exceeding proud. His pride and his arrogancy is more than his strength" [Isa. 16 : 6].

This is Letter 32 in Havet.
See Letters 39 and 41.
1. Sallust *Oratio in Tullium* i.i.
2. That is of allegiance to Henry of Bavaria. Dietrich had expected Duchess Beatrice and other Lorraine nobles to support Henry, as he was doing.
3. Caesar was Otto II, and his son was Otto III.
4. See Letter 34, n. 5.
5. Proverbs of Pseudo-Aristotle, the *Paroimiai*, cited also by the nearly contemporary Gunzo of Novara. PL CXXXVI, 1295; more correct in J. H. Baxter, "An Emendation to Gunzo," ALMA, I (1925), 110. See also Manitius, I, 535; II, 810; III, 1063; and C. Selmer, "An unpublished Latin collection of Pseudo-Aristotelian Paroimiai," *Speculum*, XV (1940), 92, n. 2, who incorrectly ascribes this letter to an Egbert.
6. Sallust *Oratio in Tullium* iv.vii.
7. Cicero *De inventione* ii.xxix.

41. RHEIMS. June 9, 984

Gerbert, on his own account, tries to persuade Dietrich to support Otto III; satirically apologizes for Charles's letter; and calls on Dietrich to look to him (Gerbert) for political advice

JUSTIFICATION OF GERBERT FOR THE POLEMIC TRANSCRIBED BY HIMSELF

To the most reverend prelate Lord Dietrich, from Gerbert, one of Caesar's faithful followers.

O ornament of the Roman empire, are we, to say that the onetime father of the state [1] has lost so much reasoning power that the people with their shepherd, like a cowardly flock,[2] is a prize for the enemy? [3] Like three powerful legions bring forward your nobility, your generosity, your sagacity to the support of the house of Israel [the Ottos]. Place the Divinity as leader in command of these lest we who have thought your good fortune our glory henceforth be rendered inglorious by losing the ornament of the empire· And, indeed, we are saying these things, not that you may be in need of a suggestion, but that we may explain our mind's solicitude for you.

This sort of explanation we have recently employed in the polemic of a very bitter enemy who was irritating Your Majesty. There we fear that we incurred the fault of an unfaithful interpreter, since we did not make his speech equal to the impulses of his mind. But, if this [present] effort please you we shall try to do better henceforth, and we shall portray the moods of friends and enemies more carefully to enable you to learn through us with complete confidence what you ought to follow, what to avoid. In this matter we rejoice to have shed light upon you, and darkness on the enemy.

Farewell.

This is Letter 33 in Havet.
1. Dietrich had been the principal adviser of Otto I.
2. Virgil *Georgicon* iv.168.
3. The devil, i.e., Henry of Bavaria.

42. RHEIMS. June 26, 984

Gerbert sends messages to Archbishop Willigis for Archbishop Adalbero, and recommends the trustworthiness of the bearer of

this letter, Ayrard; begs Willigis to support Empress Theophanu;
and through his influence to secure his own (Gerbert's) recall to
the German court

To WILLIGIS, ARCHBISHOP OF MAINZ

Many things we do not trust to letters but do entrust to messengers, just as [now] my father Adalbero, archbishop of Rheims, faithful to you in all respects, has entrusted to his intimate friend, this Abbot Ayrard,[1] much information about the condition and peace of the kingdoms that you should keep to yourself. Furthermore, as to those matters that he made known to you by letter,[2] he invokes God as a witness that [these] things are so. Place faith in this messenger as in himself, therefore, and make such answer as seems good to you; if it is not suitable for the written word, then by the spoken word.

But, O my father, with what words shall I address a grieving person when I grieve for the same reason? Deprived of Caesar, we are the prey of the enemy. We thought that Caesar had survived in the son. O, who has abandoned us, who has taken this other light from us? It was proper that the lamb be entrusted to his mother,[3] not to the wolf.[4] My boundless grief does not allow me even to look after my own affairs. Now my mind is carried quickly to my Italian enemies who completely plundered my possessions.[5] Now, in thought my mind turns to distant places of the earth [6] as if they were better. But, as long as Otto [II] comes back to my mind, and as long as his features remain imprinted in my heart,[7] and as long as his Socratic disputations [8] recur frequently to my mind, the violent impulse is destroyed [9] and the weariness of my journeying [10] among the Gauls is somewhat alleviated.

Advise me, father, for even if I possess no merits in the sight of Your Majesty, my affection has not been absent, nor will I fail in achievement if fortune should smile as formerly. When you will have found an opportune moment either with the empresses or with those persons to whom you may remember to propose it, pray recall me from exile [11] who have been a faithful [12] servant of Caesar and who have committed no crime unless it be that I have been faithful to Caesar. Thus you alone will bear my burden because I have not cared to communicate with my friends the princes until I should try what could be done through him [Willigis] whom I judge most influential.

This is Letter 34 in Havet. It was written a few days before the news reached Rheims that Henry had surrendered Otto III to Empress Theophanu at Rohr on June 29th (Letter 38, n. 6).

1. Letter 14, n. 1.

2. Letter 35, which Willigis either had not answered at all, or had answered in a noncommittal manner.

3. Otto III and Empress Theophanu. This indicates that Otto III had not yet been returned to her (see introductory note above).

4. Duke Henry of Bavaria.

5. At Bobbio. See Letters 9-12, 19, 21, 23, 26, 27, 31, 51.

6. Probably Spain. Letters 33, 51, and Bubnov, II, 189, n. 19, 248, n. 169.

7. Virgil Aeneid iv.4.

8. Richer (iii.lxvii) states that Otto II "in arguing could propound questions skillfully and arrive at credible conclusions," and (iii.lvi) that Otto II "had heard him [Gerbert] dispute not infrequently."

9. Pliny the Younger *Epistulae* ix.26.7, *impetus refringitur* [the violence is destroyed].

10. In Letter 229 Gerbert describes his activities in behalf of the Ottos.

11. See also Letter 45 for a similar request.

12. *Fidelem*, MS V, instead of *fidelium* [of the vassals] in MS L.

43. RHEIMS. June 29, 984

Gives details of Archbishop Adalbero's political activities in behalf of Otto III; Adalbero will soon send suitable gifts and now requests news of Hugh, son of Raymond

To Gerald, Abbot of Aurillac

How intensively Adalbero, archbishop of Rheims, our spiritual father (if I may speak thus), is occupied with public affairs, both his present absence [1] from the city of Rheims and the tardiness of this messenger indicate. The determining cause is business, i.e., the state of the kingdoms. [2] For, while he is receiving hostages [3] from the princes of the kingdom of Lorraine, while he is forcing obedience to the son of the emperor under the tutelage of the king of the French [Lothair], and while he keeps Henry from reigning in Lorraine, he has had nothing worthy of your reputation which he might send. But, if he should feel that it would please you, he will change for a new one the old vestment, woven of gold, [4] which he was hesitant to send but the shortness of the time permitted nothing else; and he will add to it a richly embroidered stole, [5] with other gifts of the same sort. He desires to learn through you the condition of your kingdom [Aquitaine], either what that Hugh, son of Raymond does, [6] or what he plots. Together we ask this question for we regard your opinion very highly.

This is Letter 35 in Havet. Archbishop Adalbero was to have gone to Vaudancourt on June 29th (Letter 37). The present letter was written after his departure and before the news reached Rheims of the meeting at Rohr (Letter 45, introductory note).

1. See introductory note above, and Letter 37.

2. This vocabulary of rhetoric is that of Cicero (*Topica* 25) and Quintilian (iii.xi).

3. The hostages served as surety for the Lorraine nobles' fidelity to King Lothair as guardian of Otto III. Count Godfrey's son Adalbero was one of these hostages. Letter 64.

4. *Vestem auro textam.* Although *vestis* also meant "carpet," "curtain," or "woven hanging" (cf. Letter 150), the close association here with another liturgical garment—the stole—seems to indicate that *vestis* here means "vestment." Richer, iii.xxxvii) uses *vestis* for vestment.

Material described as *auro textus (-a, -um)* could be a woven piece with embroidery done in gold thread, or the thread might be inserted into the threads of a fabric where it might be used for a design or not. Gold and silver thread was often reckoned among the treasures of a church. Lesne, III, 178, 242.

5. *Stola... phrygii operis adjuncta,* which was probably of gold embroidery. "The expressions of... orphrey (auriphrygium) ... applied to precious cloth (*pallia, vela, vestes*) certainly indicates that they were woven and colored according to procedures borrowed from Byzantine workshops, [and] more likely that they came from such workshops." Lesne III, 246, 265-66 (references to stoles with gold). The stole, or *orarium,* a liturgical garment of the clergy, was actually made of a narrow strip of material, usually silk, worn about the neck and hanging down over the chest in front. The gold embroidery might have been on the ends, or possibly there was a fringe of gold thread. The most ancient surviving specimens are not earlier than the eleventh century.

6. See Letter 25, n. 4.

44. RHEIMS. July 2, 984

Archbishop Adalbero requests from Abbot Gui of Ghent news of himself, the return of an oblate, and the possibility of placing others

To Gui, Abbot of Ghent,[1] in the Name of Adalbero

In vain do those who subvert especial parts of religion annex the protection of religion to themselves. Does he defend religion who has no love, or he who neglects his promised fidelity? Your conscience is witness whether you have displayed brotherly conversations to us or made us happy by messengers of any sort in a long period of time. Those who eagerly desire the things of another hold to their own more closely. We have adopted one of your brothers, but you are detaining one of ours who ought to return. At least, answer, therefore, as to what you think about these matters, and whether any of

our boys can be placed with you, and if so, when this ought to
be done.

This is Letter 36 in Havet.
Adalbero had apparently just returned from the meeting at Vaudancourt
(Letter 42).
1. Abbot (980-86) of St. Peter of Ghent, diocese of Tournai, province Rheims.
Annales Blandinienses MGSS V, 25; Havet, p. 35, n. 1; Lot, *Hugues Capet*, App.
xiv, p. 329; E. Duckett, *Saint Dunstan of Canterbury: A Study of Monastic
Reform in the Tenth Century* (N.Y., 1955), pp. 72ff., with bibliography on
p. 73, n. 27; 198. See also Letters 98 and 111.

45. RHEIMS. July 8, 984, or soon after
*Requests Robert to remind Empress Theophanu of himself and
his efforts in her behalf and begs to know whether earlier plans
for himself are to be followed; reiterates Adalbero's fidelity to
Otto III*

To ROBERT OF THE PALACE

I know that you, the remembrance of whom day and night inter-
mingles with my private concerns in my thoughts, think much about
me. Accordingly, pray make my Lady Theophanu mindful of me,
whom I always wish well, and for whom I desire that she rule
auspiciously with her son,[1] whose memory I keep frequently before
me, as is right. Lorraine is witness that by my exhortations[2] I have
aroused as many persons as possible to aid him, as you are aware.

Therefore, let it be your office to ascertain and to write whether
I shall remain in France as a reserve soldier for the camp of Caesar[3]
or, prepared to undergo all danger, I shall go to you; or whether
instead, I shall prepare myself for the journey which you and my
lady know well enough about, as it was decided in the palace at Pavia.[4]
Moreover, do not fail to tell me where and when I shall act, and
your opinion about this matter.

Also, I wish you to know this, that whatever I entrusted to safe
ears in the same palace about his fidelity, piety, and steadfastness
towards the heir of our Caesar and his family that illustrious Archbishop Adalbero fearlessly holds himself ready to carry out according
to his knowledge and ability.[5]

This is Letter 37 in Havet. It was written upon receiving the news that Duke
Henry had finally surrendered Otto III to Empress Theophanu at Rohr (in
Grabfeld, east of Meiningen) on June 29th. (Letter 42, introductory note). The
Annales Quedlinburgenses, a. 985, MG SS III, 66, and Thietmar IV.viii, MG SS III,

report the appearance of a brilliant star at midday as a sign of the great importance of the meeting at Rohr. A formal peace was concluded at Worms about October 20, 984, but Henry's agitations continued until his duchy of Bavaria was restored to him at Frankfort, soon after June 20, 985.

1. Hence, news of the Rohr meeting had reached Rheims.

2. Letters 24, 34, 35, 38, 41, 43, and probably 39 and 40.

3. Otto III. Cf. Terence *Phormio*, 239ff.

4. This proves that Gerbert did not leave Italy until after Theophanu had arrived in Pavia from Rome after Otto's funeral (Letter 85, n. 1), and that Gerbert was justified in believing that he was to continue in the service of the Ottonian family whom he admired and loved. Lattin, *Peasant Boy*, p. 101.

5. Compare the bishop's oath of fidelity to Charles the Bald in 872, *Quantum sciero et potuero* [As much as I shall know and be able]. Odegaard, "Carolingian Oaths," *Speculum*, XVI, 294, n. 3.

46. RHEIMS. August-October, 984

Acknowledges news received through Gerbert (?), especially of the changed attitude of an important man (Charles ?)

To EGBERT, ARCHBISHOP OF TRIER,[1] IN THE NAME OF ADALBERO

Dangerous times do not allow one to commit all the things to letters that can be entrusted to very trusty messengers. We derived great pleasure and enjoyment from the news conveyed to us through our G.[2] about the condition of God's churches, and of the kingdoms, and through what man[3] these things could be carried out. If we have feared him as a tyrant, now we wonder at him, full of faithfulness and wisdom. Carry out your promises to us concerning him. What you are demanding from us relative to him and to yourself had already been carried out both with the utmost silence as to your secrets and with the most zealous activity on our part.

This is Letter 38 in Havet.

1. See Letter 20, n. 1.

2. Probably Gerbert. However, Bubnov, II, 260, n. 198, suggests the monk Gausbert (Letter 62) or the Rheims archdeacon Gerann. Archbishop Adalbero, though, could scarcely call Gausbert "our G."

3. This seems to apply more logically to Duke Charles of Lower Lorraine than to Duke Henry of Bavaria (so Havet, p. 36, n. 6). Letter 143 shows Egbert's partisanship for Charles. Bubnov, II, 260, n. 198, and M. Uhlirz, *Untersuchungen über Inhalt und Datierung der Briefe Gerberts*, p. 32, insist the man was Henry.

47. RHEIMS. November 15, 984

Requests news of Rome, of the Saracens, and of the Byzantines, and manuscripts of Suetonius, Symmachus, and others

To STEPHEN, DEACON OF THE ROMAN CHURCH[1]

The unsettled conditions of the state, my brother, forced me to seek France again. All Italy seems Rome to me. The world shudders at the conduct of the Romans.[2] What is the situation in Rome now? Who are the popes and masters of affairs? [3] What sort of death did he suffer, that special friend [4] of mine to whom I entrusted you? Do not hesitate to convey this information to your well-wishers as well as news of your own particular concerns.

Through Count Gui [5] of Soissons pray send back to me, indeed, and to my Archbishop Adalbero, Suetonius Tranquillus [6] and Quintus Aurelius [7] with the other manuscripts that you know, separately but without argument as to which belongs to whom. In addition, we beg you to inform us what gifts worthy of yourself we can make ready to send to you.

Also, the news that you know to be accurate about the empire of the Greeks, the kingdom of the Africans,[8] and the efforts of the Italians,[9] you ought not to conceal from us, your friends. The weightiness of ideas [in this letter] suffices more than verbosity.

This is Letter 40 in Havet. It was written after Gerbert had received news of the death of Pope John XIV (Letter 12, n. 1, and n. 2 below). Lot, *Derniers Carolingiens*, pp. 141-142, and M. Uhlirz, *Jahrbücher des Deutschen Reiches unter Otto II. und Otto III*, Vol. II: *Otto III*, p. 59, think that Gerbert's first sentence means that he actually began the journey planned for November 1, 984 (Letter 33), but that he turned back—before he reached Italy (Lot), or after he reached Pavia (Uhlirz).

1. Since Gerbert addresses Stephen (probably not the same person as in Letter 1) as "brother" he may have been a monk, possibly of Bobbio. As abbot there, Gerbert possessed authority to allow a monk to leave. Stephen's knowledge of manuscripts suggests intellectual contact with an important library, such as the one in Bobbio. He may have been a papal secretary, for a Stephen appears as a secretary in papal documents of the time (JL 3828ff.). See also Letter 78.

2. Early in 984 Pope Boniface VII (974, 984-85) had returned from exile in Constantinople, usurped the position of Pope John XIV, and imprisoned him in Castel Sant' Angelo, where he died August 20, 984. In the council of St. Basle (991), Bishop Arnulf of Orléans describes Boniface VII thus: "There succeeded in Rome the horrible monster Boniface, surpassing all mortals in wickedness, stained with the blood of his predecessor." Olleris, pp. 205-6.

3. A Roman faction of considerable size supported the imperial Ottonian family, but many Romans rallied around the family called (incorrectly) Crescentius, now led by John, the patricius.

4. Surely Pope John XIV.

5. Cousin of Bishop Bruno of Langres (Letter 155, n. 1) and of Count Heribert III of Troyes (Letter 25); *Acta concilii S. Basoli*, in Olleris, p. 178; Lot, *Hugues Capet*, p. 18, n. 3 (correcting his *Derniers Carolingiens*, p. 255); Latouche, II, 194, n. 2. Undoubtedly Gui carried this letter to Rome, and left Soissons and Rheims in time to reach Rome by Christmas, 984.

6. Roman historian, A.D. 75-150.

7. Quintus Aurelius Symmachus, Roman noble and man of letters, A.D. 345-405. His letters are printed in MGAA VI. See also P. Courcelle, *Les Lettres grecques en occident de Macrobe à Cassiodore* (Paris, 1943), pp. 4-6; 127; 238, n. 6. Gerbert apparently desired several works by each author, or more than one copy of each, and indicated this by using the plural of each author's name.

8. The Saracen empire of the Fatimites, in control of Africa and a few places in southern Italy.

9. It was important to the unification of Italy under German imperial rule to have the Italian princes themselves sever their connections with both Byzantium and the Saracens.

48. RHEIMS. December 10-12, 984
Godfrey's messenger was purposely left ignorant of the news; Adalbero himself will soon learn more from Egbert

To Notker Bishop of Liége in the Name of Adalbero

As promised, my brother [Godfrey] directed a messenger to you, but one lacking all knowledge of the present business [1] lest he should seem to be lying or to be stupid. We, who shall be able to talk with the archbishop of Trier [Egbert] on December 18th, will take care to indicate more fully to Your Prudence as soon as possible what we shall learn more fully.

This is Letter 42 in Havet.
1. Numerous obstacles prevented the consecration of Adalbero, son of Godfrey, as bishop of Verdun (Letters 53, introductory note; 70; 86).

49. VERDUN? December 22, 984
In the name of Count Godfrey, Gerbert informs Notker, bishop of Liége, of the approaching ordination of Godfrey's son Adalbero

To the Same in the Name of Godfrey [1]

According to the promises of the archbishop of Trier [Egbert] we are to see the ordination of our Adalbero on January 3d in the place where he shall have previously decreed. On December 28th we shall send in advance the guide for your journey, and we shall make known what more definite facts we have learned. We consider it doubtful that my brother [2] will come thither.

This is Letter 43 in Havet.
1. Probably Gerbert himself had accompanied Archbishop Adalbero to the interview with Archbishop Egbert (Letter 48). Adalbero then returned to Rheims, but Gerbert carried the news of the conference to Godfrey, who then employed him to write this letter to Notker.
2. Archbishop Adalbero of Rheims.

50. RHEIMS. January 2-7, 985
Discusses the honorable and the useful; especially desires to be an eloquent orator, and is building up a library for that purpose; appends a list of books which he desires copied, and promises parchment and money for the copyists

To Ebrard[1] Abbot of Tours

Since you hold the constant memory of me among things worthy of honor, as I have heard from a great many messengers, and since you bear me great friendship because of our relationship,[2] I think I shall be blest by virtue of your good opinion of me, if only I am the sort of man who, in the judgment of so great a man, is found worthy to be loved. But, because I am not the sort of man who, with Panetius, sometimes separates the honorable from the useful, but rather with Tully would add the former to everything useful,[3] so I wish that this most honorable and sacred friendship may not be without its usefulness to both parties. Since philosophy does not separate ways of conduct[4] and ways of speaking, I have always added the fondness for speaking well to the fondness for living well, although by itself it may be more excellent to live well than to speak well, and if one be freed from the cares of governing, the former is enough without the latter. But to us, busied in affairs of state, both are necessary. For speaking effectively to persuade and restraining the minds of angry persons from violence by smooth speech are both of the greatest usefulness. For this activity, which must be prepared beforehand, I am diligently forming a library.

And, just as a short time ago in Rome[5] and in other parts of Italy, in Germany also, and in Lorraine, I used large sums of money to pay copyists and to acquire copies of authors, permit me to beg that this be done likewise in your locality and through your efforts so that I may be aided by the kindness and zeal of friends who are my compatriots. The writers whom we wish to have copied we shall indicate at the end of this letter.[6] Not unmindful, moreover, of your kindnesses, we shall send parchments for the copyists and the necessary funds in conformity with your instructions. Finally, lest speaking further, we should abuse the laws of letter writing, the reason for so much labor is to acquire a serene disregard of bad fortune. Not nature alone, as appears to many, commands us to this disregard, but a carefully elaborated system of philosophy. Equally in leisure and in work we both teach what we know, and learn what we do not know.[7]

This is Letter 44 in Havet.

1. Abbot of St. Julien of Tours, 976-91.

2. *Affinitatis jure.* This could mean that they were related, perhaps distantly. Farther down, Gerbert calls Ebrard a "compatriot."

3. Cicero *De officiis* iii.iii. Cicero's work is a rather free compilation of Panetius (B.C. 185-110) *Peri ton kathekontos*, essentially a work of Stoic philosophy. W. Schmid, *Geschichte der griechischen Literatur*, II (6th ed., Berlin, 1920), 345.

4. Observe the similar idea in Cassiodorus *Institutiones* ii.iii.7, copied by Isodore, *Etymologiae* ii.xxiv.1.4-6.

5. Cf. Letter 47.

6. Unfortunately, Gerbert neglected to transcribe the list in his memorandum notebook. Undoubtedly, Gerbert expected Ebrard to have copies made of manuscripts not only at St. Julien, but especially at St. Martin, which possessed the largest and most important collection in Tours. Lesne, IV, 560-65.

7. Cicero *De senectute* ix.29. For other use in the early middle ages see L. Wallach, "Charlemagne's *De litteris colendis* and Alcuin: A Diplomatic-Historical Study," *Speculum*, XXVI (1951), 291, notes d, g; 292, note v.

51. RHEIMS. January 2-7, 985

Explains his philosophical attitude towards bad fortune, and outlines what he must have done to remain at Bobbio; he invites Raymond to visit Rheims; his own plans are uncertain, because Empress Theophanu has need of him

GERBERT TO MONK RAYMOND [1]

By how great love we are bound to you is known to the Latins and foreigners, partakers of the fruits of our labor. They earnestly desire your presence, since, in fact, it is public knowledge that for no other's sake would we, filled with cares, tarry in a place of study.

For these cares philosophy alone has been found the only remedy. From the study of it, indeed, we have very often received many advantageous things; for instance, in these turbulent times, we have resisted the force of fortune violently raging not only against others but also against us. And, indeed, since the condition of the state in Italy was such that we had to submit shamefully to the yoke of the tyrants, if we professed innocence, or if we attempted to exert our strength, it meant that a following must be secured, camps fortified, thefts, fires, and murders made use of. Therefore, we have chosen the certain leisure of studies rather than the uncertain business of wars.

However, while we follow the footsteps of philosophy, since we do not overtake it, we have not yet curbed all the impulses of a disturbed mind. Now we are turning back to those things which we left. Now, influenced by the encouragement of our friend Abbot Guarin [2] we consider approaching the princes of Spain. [3] On the other hand, at present we are turned away from these earlier undertakings by the sacred [4] letters of Lady Theophanu, ever august empress, always to be loved, always to be cherished.

In such changeableness of things, of sorrow, fear, joy, desire, his son Gerbert particularly asks the opinion of his most trusted Father Gerald, [5] whom these events do not touch, as to what course should be followed.

Farewell. Farewell, Father Gerald, farewell, Brother Ayrard [6], farewell, Holy Order, my foster father, and my teacher; in his holy prayers may he remember me and also my Father Adalbero, archbishop of Rheims, entirely devoted to him.

This is Letter 45 in Havet.
1. Of Aurillac. See Letter 23, n.8, and in the text, Gerbert's invitation to Raymond to come to Rheims.
2. See Letter 25, n.6.
3. Probably Count Borrell. Introduction, p. 3.
4. Byzantine protocol required the term "sacred" for whatever pertained to the emperor. Gerbert must have received some word from Theophanu (Letter 45).
5. Letters 23 and 52.
6. Not the same person as in Letter 14. This Ayrard appears in Letters 25, 102, and 171, in addition to this letter.

52. RHEIMS. January 2-7, 985
Congratulates himself on acquaintance with Abbot Gerald and always values his advice

To Abbot Gerald [1]

I do not know whether the Divinity has granted anything better to mortals than friends, if only they are the ones who seem suitably sought out and suitably kept. Fortunate day, fortunate hour, in which we were permitted to know the man, the recollection of whose name has deflected all annoyances from us. Indeed, if I should enjoy his presence occasionally, not without cause would I think myself more blessed. In order to accomplish this I had established for myself a not unworthy abode [2] in Italy.

But blind fortune,[3] pressing down with its mists, enwraps the world, and I know not whether it will cast me down or direct me on, tending as I am now in this direction, now in that. But the features of my friend remain fixed in my heart.[4] I mean him who is my lord and father—Gerald—whose counsel we will transform into deeds.

This is Letter 46 in Havet.

1. Of Aurillac (Letter 23, n. 1).

2. The location of Bobbio and of its several xenodochia on or near highways to Rome from France might have offered such an opportunity. Monks from Aurillac made annual journeys to Rome to offer payments to St. Peter for his protection. M. Uhlirz, "Studien zu Gerbert," *Archiv für Urkundenforschung*, XIII (1935), 465; Lattin, *Peasant Boy*, p. 172.

3. For a discussion of "fortune" see H. R. Patch, *Tradition of Boethius* (N.Y., 1935).

4. Virgil *Aeneid* iv.4. See also Letter 42.

53. RHEIMS. February 15, 985

Informs Bishop Adalbero of an agreement made with Duke Hugh on behalf of the followers of his father Godfrey; urges him to use influence to have the pact renewed between Hugh and the Ottos

To Adalbero, Bishop of Verdun [1]

Do not look at the number of lines of this letter: weigh carefully the many ideas in the few lines. These dangerous times have extinguished our freedom of saying clearly exactly what we mean.

Seizing an opportunity, by means of faithful legates we reached an agreement on behalf of Godfrey's men [2] with him whom fortune has placed in command of the French in fact, if not in name.[3] We assured him that you will use your influence to have the agreement renewed that was formerly made between our Otto the Caesar [4] and him, with his son [Robert], in whom alone he delights, joined in the alliance. Through Siegfried's son, whom he highly esteemed, we persuaded Caesar himself as he was dying to seek its accomplishment.[5] For, in this alliance seemed safety in common for us and for the son of Caesar.

You will, I hope, write back quickly whether you wish to promote this arrangement that has been started, or to abandon it. Also, whether we may with safety be leisurely in this business, although it is generally dangerous. It is not easy to say what efforts or what attacks have ceased on account of this [alliance].

This is Letter 41 in Havet. It was written at the time of King Lothair's second siege of Verdun (January 12-March 1, 985) when the successful Lorraine resistance either had or would convince Archbishop Egbert to consecrate Adalbero. M. Uhlirz, *Untersuchungen über Inhalt und Datierung der Briefe Gerberts*, pp. 44-45. At the time of this letter Bishop-elect Adalbero was somewhere away from Verdun trying to secure aid for the beleaguered city within which his father, Count Godfrey, and other relatives were resisting the attack of the French.

1. In early November, 984, after the recapture of Verdun by Count Godfrey and Duke Thierry (Letter 54, introductory note), Otto III nominated Godfrey's son Adalbero to the bishopric of Verdun. This had become vacant because Thierry's brother Adalbero, who was the second successor to Bishop Wicfrid (d. August 31, 983), had been nominated to the bishopric of Metz on October 16th to succeed Bishop Dietrich (d. September 7, 984). Constantine *Vita Adalberonis II Mettensis*, MGSS IV, 660. At this time Adalbero, son of Godfrey, was a cleric of his uncle's church of Rheims, one of the hostages sent earlier (Letter 43). Godfrey secured his brother's permission for his son to leave Rheims, presumably with King Lothair's assent (Letter 64). However, Archbishop Egbert, still favoring King Lothair and resisting Empress Theophanu's guardianship over Otto III, refused to consecrate Adalbero, son of Godfrey, even though he first promised to do so (Letter 49), but did consecrate to the bishopric of Metz Adalbero, brother of Thierry (and son of Beatrice), December 20, 984. Not until after August 25, 985, when Egbert definitely accepted Theophanu's guardianship (DO III 19) was Godfrey's son Adalbero consecrated by Egbert, December, 985, or January, 986. He died in Italy, April 18, 990 or 991. *Gesta episcoporum Virdunensium*, Chap. VI, MGSS IV, 47; Bubnov, II, 274, n. 218; Parisot, *Origines de la Haute-Lorraine*, pp. 338, n. 1, 339, n. 3, 340, n. 1, 348, n. 2; Böhmer, *Regesta imperii*, Vol. II, Pt. 3: *Regesten Otto III*, No. 1: *Bis 997* (new ed., M. Uhlirz), Nos. 958a, 962c,d,h, 968f, 969c, 973a.

2. The text of the editions of both Masson and Duchesne, *pro parte virorum Godefridi*, against that of MS V. This letter is not in MS L.

3. Duke Hugh Capet, who became king of France in 987. See also Letter 55.

4. Richer III.lxxxiv. Easter, 981, in Rome, Hugh Capet had entered into a pact with Otto II.

5. Siegfried II, count of Luxemburg, and a cousin of Archbishop Adalbero and Count Godfrey, and of Duke Thierry of Upper Lorraine. He was one of Otto II's important vassals in western Germany, and in Otto II's military summons of 983 (?) he was listed to supply thirty knights. M. Uhlirz, "Die ersten Grafen von Luxemburg," DA, XII (1956), 36ff. Siegfried must have carried a letter from Gerbert at Bobbio south to Otto II in Rome, a letter missing from Gerbert's collection. The present letter implies that Gerbert knew that Otto II was dying, apparently of malaria that killed so many Germans in Italy in the Middle Ages. Anna Celli-Fraentzel, "Quellen zur Geschichte der Malaria in Italien und ihrer Bedeutung für die deutschen Kaiserzüge des Mittelalters," *Quellen und Studien zur Geschichte der Naturwissenschaften und der Medizin*, IV (1935), 341-425.

54. RHEIMS? April 5, 985

For Godfrey, Gerbert exhorts his sons Adalbero and Hermann to maintain fidelity to Theophanu and not to surrender anything to the Franks

To the Brothers Adalbero, Nominated Bishop of Verdun, and
Hermann

Fortunate ones, who have an example of paternal courage which
can be imitated, your father[1] makes the following request of you
lest some unexpected event hinder you. The fealty which you have
promised to the son [Otto III] of Caesar keep inviolate: guard all
strongholds from the enemy. Finally, you should surrender to the
Franks neither Scarponne nor Hattos fort,[2] nor any of those places
which he left to you, though you may be tempted by the vain hope
of securing his liberty and that of his son Frederick, or by the fear of
their being tortured. Because you are free the enemy feel that they
have not captured Godfrey completely. Prepare assistance everywhere; show yourselves, like your father in everything as liberators
of your fatherland. Your great-souled father gave these injunctions
to his noble sons on March 31st. He wished me, most faithful to him
and to his followers, to become his interpreter.

This is Letter 47 in Havet.
King Lothair with an army went to Breisach on the Rhine to meet Duke
Henry (Letter 24), but Henry failed to appear. Lothair's army was attacked by
the Lorrainers on its return. After consulting with Counts Heribert and Eudes
(Letter 25) Lothair captured Verdun in early June as a springboard for capturing
all of Lorraine. Leaving Queen Emma in charge, he returned to Laon where his
troops disbanded. Then, the Lorraine nobles combined to recapture the city of
Verdun. Quickly Lothair reassembled his army, hastened to Verdun, and recaptured it by a surprise attack, taking many prisoners, including Count Godfrey
and his son Frederick. Two other sons, Adalbero and Hermann, the addressees
of this letter, avoided capture, as did the Countess Mathilda, their mother.
Letters 24, introductory note, 57; Richer III.xcviii-cviii.
   1. Count Godfrey, who was imprisoned by Counts Heribert and Eudes in a
castle on the Marne (Letters 57, 58).
   2. Scarponne, dept. of Meurthe-Moselle, commune of Dieulouard; and Hattonchâtel, dept. of the Meuse. Havet, p. 45, n. 3.

55. RHEIMS. April 6, 985
   Suggests an alliance to be arranged between Duke Hugh Capet,
   his son Robert, and Otto III

[To the Brothers Adalbero and Hermann (?)]

We are completing this secret and anonymous letter in a few words:
Lothair is king of France in name only; Hugh not in name, it is true,
but in deed and fact. If with us you had sought his friendship, and

had allied his son [Robert] with the son [Otto III] of Caesar, you would not just now feel the kings of the French to be enemies.[1]

This is Letter 48 in Havet.
1. See Letter 58.

56. RHEIMS. April 6, 985
Urges Notker to maintain his loyalty to Count Godfrey and his fidelity to Empress Theophanu. Archbishop Adalbero is greatly oppressed by King Lothair and has no freedom of expression

To NOTKER BISHOP OF LIÉGE

The present times add lustre to your name, times in which the honesty of few is praised, the dishonesty of many is openly asserted. Your friend Godfrey now is watching to see which of his friends loved him rather than his possessions, and which would be faithful to his wife[1] and children, if death should seize him. And, because so great a man thinks very highly of you, this alone can be an indication of how much excellence shines forth in you.

Those who love him and those who are his men he urges and advises to preserve [their] fidelity to his Lady Theophanu and to her son, not to be overwhelmed by the power of the enemy, not to be frightened by any event: the happy day will come which will separate the betrayers of the fatherland, and will decorate the zealous liberators with offerings and rewards. By no means should you believe Adalbero, archbishop of Rheims, and most loyal to you, to be an accomplice of these deeds,[2] for he himself is oppressed by great tyranny, as his letters[3] to you archbishops testify. In those letters he wrote none of the things which he wished, but he proferred what the tyrant[4] wrenched from him.

This is Letter 49 in Havet.
1. Countess Mathilda (Letter 57). Their children were Godfrey, Gozelo, Adalbero (bishop-elect of Verdun), Frederick, and Hermann.
2. Probably refers to Adalbero's furnishing soldiers as a vassal for the Verdun expedition (Letter 63).
3. These letters are not extant, nor is it clear whether Gerbert wrote them for Archbishop Adalbero.
4. King Lothair. Archbishop Adalbero was his chancellor.

57. RHEIMS. April 6, 985

*Advises Countess Mathilda on behalf of Count Godfrey to remain
cheerful, to maintain fidelity to Empress Theophanu and Otto III,
to make no agreement with the French, and not to abandon the
defense of their forts*

To COUNTESS MATHILDA [1]

Let my Lady Mathilda cease all complaining: your very illustrious
husband Godfrey, outstanding among those of his rank, and formi-
dable to the victors themselves, advises this. Make your mind joyful
because a sorrowful spirit dries up the bones [Prov. 17 : 22] and
confuses the judgment. You with your sons preserve an unstained
fidelity to Lady Theophanu, ever august empress, and to her ever
august son; make no agreement with the enemy, the French; repulse
the kings of the French; so keep and so defend all the forts [2] that the
latter may not think you have abandoned any part of your followers
in these forts, neither because of the hope of freeing your husband,
indeed, nor because of the fear of his death or that of your son
Frederick. These words that I have faithfully conveyed to you he
entrusted to my confidence near the river Marne on March 31st.

This is Letter 50 in Havet.
1. See Letter 56, n. 1; and Olleris, p. 511.
2. Scarponne and Hattonchâtel (Letter 54, n. 2).

58. RHEIMS. April 6, 985

*Informs Count Siegfried of conversations with his captured
relatives. Gerbert can pass on to them words from Siegfried or
from Lady Theophanu; urges an alliance with Hugh Capet*

To SIEGFRIED [II],[1] SON OF THE COUNT

We who are filled with very great love for your now exiled kins-
men talked with them at the river Marne [2] on March 31st, and through
a letter we are confiding [3] the information sought by our Lady
Theophanu concerning their fidelity. Furthermore, because we are
able to talk with them through the kindness of Eudes and Heribert [4]
in whose custody they are kept, inform us, please, by letter whatever
either you or our lady wish us to transmit to them. In addition, we
entrust the following to your confidence, that if you link Hugh to

you in friendship you will be able easily to avoid all attacks of the French.[5]

This is Letter 51 in Havet.
1. See Letter 53, n. 5.
2. See Letter 54, n. 1.
3. Letter 59.
4. Letter 54, n. 1.
5. See Letters 53 and 55.

59. RHEIMS. April 6, 985

Informs Empress Theophanu of his activities in behalf of the captive Lorraine nobles; suggests that she secure more harmony among the German princes; reveals that Archbishop Adalbero and he are suspected of treason by King Lothair, and are in great disfavor

To Empress Lady Theophanu [1]

Not without purpose did the Divinity oppose my desire to go to you according to your command.[2] For, on March 31st, while speaking with the captive counts, Godfrey and his uncle Siegfried, in the midst of the troops of the enemy I was found to be the only one of your followers to whom they could with confidence commit their opinions concerning the condition of your empire.

And so, in accordance with what I learned from them I wrote letters to their wives, children and friends, urging them to persist in their fidelity to you, to be frightened by no invasion of the enemy, and, with their [3] example in mind, if fortune would have it so, to elect exile because of maintaining fidelity to you rather than to hold the ground of their fatherland with perfidy.

Especially dear to me are these men to whom it is a heavier burden to be unable to carry out your business than to seem to be abandoned to captivity by the enemy. Moreover, because the disagreement of princes is the ruin of kingdom, harmony among your princes seems to us to be the remedy for such great evils. "A threefold cord," indeed, "is with difficulty broken asunder" [Eccles. 4 : 12].

Also, you know that the kings of the French look upon us in an unfavorable light [4] because we do not agree with them about fidelity to you, and likewise because we enjoy great familiarity with Adalbero, archbishop of Rheims, whom they, while railing at him for a like reason, consider faithless to themselves.

What you wish us to do in all these matters, and where and when we can go to your presence, if any road through the enemy [5] shall be open, indicate to us more definitely, since we are ready to obey you through all contingencies. Matters have reached this point, that it is no longer a question of his [Adalbero's] expulsion, which would be an endurable evil, but they are contending about his life and blood.[6] The same is true of myself, as if I were arousing him against the policies of the kings.[7] Finally, the burden of oppression is such, and such is the jealousy of your name, that in no letters to you dare he indicate his miseries. But, if this feeling shall have grown stronger in the tyrants, and an opportunity of fleeing to you shall have opened for him, it will not be in vain, will it, that he who planned all possible support to you and your son anticipates better treatment from you—in fact, has certain hope of it.

This is Letter 52 in Havet.
1. See Appendix A.
2. See Letter 51. Perhaps Theophanu had written from Mühlhausen (on the Unstrut river in Thuringia), where she stayed on February 6th (DO III 9), requesting Gerbert to meet her at Grone, a castle near the Weser in Saxony, where she was on March 28th (DO III 11).
3. The captive Lorraine nobles.
4. Virgil *Aeneid* IV. 372.
5. To have reached Theophanu, Gerbert would have gone northeast (n. 2 above). King Lothair was in control of Verdun to the east, and, apparently, could count on loyal vassals to the north and northeast of Rheims. Otherwise, Gerbert would scarcely have wondered where he might find a safe road. The German court moved frequently and to find it without delay was not always easy.
6. See Letter 64.
7. Gerbert was still abbot of Bobbio, and therefore a vassal of the Ottos.

60. RHEIMS. April 7, 985

Wrote a previous letter under compulsion; refuses to excommunicate his nephew Adalbero; will uphold ecclesiastical law even against the king; begs for advice

To the Archbishop of Trier [1] in the Name of Adalbero

I do not wish to conceal the fact that it was only at the command of my lord [King Lothair] that I sent a former letter [2] to you to whom I owe everything. And because my nephew [Adalbero] was prepared to promise and to keep the fealty which you have promised to my lord,[3] he obtained from us that permission which is required by the authority of the fathers.[4] But, by what sort of agreement[5] his fidelity will have been debased is indiscoverable by our mind. Therefore, how shall we either summon, or excommunicate this Adalbero, or ask others to do this? Because we are not capable of this course of action according to law, we ourselves are neither taking it nor are we urging others to do so lest we seem to drag ourselves to the precipice or those deserving well at our hands.

And, because the King of Heaven says: "Render unto Caesar the things that are Caesar's, and unto God the things that are God's" [Mat. 22 : 21; Mark 12 : 17; Luke 20 : 25], we shall render to our kings [Lothair and Louis] an undefiled fidelity, an undefiled obedience by our service; we shall deviate in nothing, and yet we shall make the share owed to the Lord the first consideration. But, because few persons at this time have any thought for the things which are the Lord's, if we are accused of treachery or of any fault whatsoever when we ardently love the law of the Lord, the result is that, placed between the hammer and the anvil, so to speak, there is little hope of escaping without loss of soul and body.

If, therefore, you possess a heart of kindness [Col. 3 : 12], if we have always cherished you as a brother or rather as a father, assume the burden of a friend by giving counsel and aid so that we who in times of prosperity wished you well shall not despair of your help in time of adversity. But these words we speak, which ought to be kept secret, we entrust not to the man but to the good faith of a great priest. We offer the Lord as witness, doubly calling upon the Terrible Avenger, if these things are betrayed with resulting injury to us.

This is Letter 54 in Havet.

For date of this letter see the introductory notes to Letters 61 and 63.

1. Egbert.

2. Not in this collection, and now lost. It was apparently sent from Rheims where Lothair's spies were more to be feared. The frankness of Letters 60 and 61, in contrast, argues for their having been sent from Verdun.

3. King Lothair. See Letter 64.

4. Dionysius Exiguus *Codex canonum ecclesiasticorum*, Chap. xv, PL LXVII, 143. According to Letter 64 Lothair had consented to the granting of this permission to Adalbero to return to Verdun.

5. Egbert argued that the oath which Adalbero would swear (or had sworn) to Otto III would contravene the pledge already made to King Lothair as Otto's

proposed guardian. Archbishop Adalbero argued that his nephew's pledge to Lothair was made to him as guardian so that any additional oath to Otto was, in effect, as if made to Lothair.

61. RHEIMS. April 18, 985

Archbishop Adalbero disclaims having the same attitude as his relatives towards Duke Henry; offers some philosophical words; suggests that Egbert learn more news of the Germans and requests information about the conference at Duisburg

LIKEWISE TO THE SAME

Although your letters have freed us from a multitude of cares nevertheless other anxieties trouble us. For, here we are congratulating ourselves on the constancy of your love, on your fidelity, and on your loyalty towards us. But who has twisted your power of discernment on this point that you should suppose us to be of the same mind as our relatives? I know no reason to hate Lord Henry;[1] I know why I love him: but what is the outward reward of this love? To be sure, the Divinity makes some things necessary; but blind fortune is heard in others. In brief, overwhelmed by such a heavy burden of cares, we think the following words to have been said not poetically but wisely: "What cannot be cured must be endured,"[2] and: "If you cannot do what you wish to do, then wish to do what you can."[3] Among the promises we have this: May the power of the wicked be broken, and may God prove this [Ps. 36 : 17].

One matter requires an explanation: Why am I who was once the most trustworthy interpreter of the royal mind and of yours being deprived of this office; and why through others rather than through you do I find out many things? And as I continually acknowledge, because I owe everything to you, I fear for you in the same measure as for myself. Indeed, in a different way is it said to both of us: Whoever stands, let him take heed lest he fall [I Cor. 10 : 12].

Accordingly, we must take counsel together. In order to accomplish this, pray make me the sharer of everything that your conference devises at Duisburg.[4] Also, inquire diligently and let us know what the royal power demands of the Duchess Beatrice [5] and of your nobles, if, as the rumor is, this is [now] concealed from your knowledge; and also what is in your mind about this matter. For the rest, we entertain the best thoughts of you, as we said in the beginning, and in the same trustfulness with which we have committed our thoughts to you, we have received yours.

This is Letter 55 in Havet
Otto III, Theophanu, and Archbishop Willigis were at Duisburg on April 29th (DO III 12), which was probably the conference date. Hence, Adalbero wrote a few days before Egbert's departure by the 27th. See also introductory note to Letter 63.

1. Of Bavaria, who was still seeking to share in the ruling of Germany.
2. Horace *Odae* xxiv.19-20.
3. Terence *Andria* ii.i.5-6. See also Letter 182.
4. See introductory note above.
5. See Letter 68. Beatrice's son Thierry was a prisoner of King Lothair so that the reference may be to Lothair's demands as conditions for his release.

62. VERDUN. May 3, 985

Adalbero plans to return the monk Gausbert to Trier on May 18th and requests an escort for him from Mouzon

LIKEWISE TO THE SAME

Just as we have never tried to hold the monk Gausbert [1] against your wishes so it is our intention to lead him back as far as Mouzon [2] on the first day of Rogations.[3] And, because we have used him for such a long time, we shall not be unmindful of this great kindness at your hands. If, therefore, you object to his remaining longer with us, let your men receive him there since we shall be unable to travel farther, not only on account of the abundance of the enemy, but also because of the crafty activity of those opposed to us.

This is Letter 56 in Havet.
Letter 75 mentions that Archbishop Adalbero's order respecting the monk G. was sent from Verdun. Letter 65 gives news of Rheims and Compiègne and mentions May 11th and May 15th so that Archbishop Adalbero must have returned to Rheims from Verdun by May 15th, and undoubtedly by May 11th (see also Letter 64). He sent the order about Gausbert to Rheims, and then departed for there within a few days, at the latest by May 7th.

1. Probably a monk of Mettlach in the diocese of Trier. See Letter 75. Whether he is the same person mentioned in Letter 71 is not clear. Bubnov, II, 335, n. 44. Possibly Gausbert had been used by Archbishop Adalbero for artistic work.
2. On the Roman road from Rheims to Trier. Letter 96, n. 4; Havet, p. 54, n. 2. The frequency with which messengers traveled between Rheims and Trier, as evidenced in Gerbert's letters, attests the fact that this Roman road was still in good condition.
3. Rogation Days are the first three days of the fifth week after Easter. In 985, Easter fell on April 12th so the first day of Rogation was May 18th.

63. VERDUN. May 3, 985

Criticises the lack of identifying marks on King Lothair's letter and argues against the destruction of the wall around the monastery of St. Paul of Verdun; the soldiers refuse to prolong their period of guarding Verdun

To King Lothair in the Name of Adalbero [1]

A letter in your name but with unknown seal and unknown signature,[2] and known to be yours only through the messenger whom we recognized, brought great distress to us. For the writer orders the wall around the monastery of St. Paul [3] to be leveled completely as if it were a hostile fortification, although we know the place to be rather an enclosure of a courtyard than the citadel of any fortification. Hence, that act ought not to be enjoined upon a priest that even a tyrant would fear to do, especially since there are very many who delight in such an act, if the doing gives so much pleasure. Moreover, the fact that nature made many more suitable places around the city for easier fortification, if it so pleased an enemy, proves that this place is not suitable for an enemy.

Besides, you know that we look out for your safety and fidelity, and always respect and obey your wishes with the divinely inspired respect already shown. But what you commanded about prolonging the period of guarding the city the soldiers will not listen to, and they are sorry that they promised since their need and want has reached its limit.[4]

This is Letter 53 in Havet.

1. The sender, designated only as "A." in the manuscripts, must have been Adalbero of Rheims, not his nephew Adalbero, bishop-elect of Verdun. Lothair would hardly have entrusted the guarding of Verdun to the son of his captured enemy Godfrey (Letter 54). Furthermore, Lothair was trying to bring pressure upon Adalbero of Verdun through Archbishop Egbert of Trier, who suggests excommunication (Letter 60). The criticism of the changed details on Lothair's letter bespeaks Archbishop Adalbero of Rheims, who was Lothair's chancellor and hence very familiar with such epistolary practice; as does his complaint about his weary troops. Havet, p. 49, n. 1; and Bubnov, II, 302, n. 21 on p. 303.

2. *Impressione ignota* [unknown seal]. Probably a strip of parchment had been cut at the bottom from right almost to the left edge, then the letter was folded and the strip was wound around the letter. Upon this wax was placed and in this wax Lothair impressed his seal which was new to Adalbero, although he was chancellor. Poole, *Studies in Chronology* (Oxford, 1934), pp. 93-94. *Signis incognitis* [unknown signature]. Usually the signers of documents completed the signatures begun by notaries. Ordinary letters were not usually signed, but this letter was sent as an official document.

3. The political importance of this monastery, founded in 973 by Bishop Wicfrid (DO II 22a) next to the merchants' quarter outside the city wall of Verdun, is shown by Otto III's diploma, DO III 3 (October 20, 984 at Worms), confirming its extensive possessions and permitting it to elect its own abbot. Thus, Otto III and the empresses hurled defiance at King Lothair by showing that Verdun was within German jurisdiction. Count Godfrey and other Lorrainers had recaptured Verdun from Lothair about the end of September, 984. Richer III.ciii.

4. Lothair was plagued by the limited service characteristic of feudal armies. Soldiers were supposed to live off the land, but apparently Verdun had little to offer Lothair's troops. Lothair did not release all of his troops after his return to Laon, as stated by Richer III.cviii.

64. RHEIMS. May 8, 985

Archbishop Adalbero defends himself from a charge of treachery for having granted his nephew Adalbero permission to leave Rheims

THE ACCUSATION AGAINST ADALBERO [1]

I am accused of engaging in the crime of treachery and infidelity against the royal majesty [King Lothair] for the alleged reasons that I granted my nephew [Adalbero], as a cleric of my church, permission to leave; and that he [then] went to the [imperial] palace, and, as the gift of another king [Otto III], has received a bishopric [Verdun] in his kingdom, which my seigneur King Lothair, had brought back [2] under his authority, and that I afterwards conferred the ecclesiastical grades upon him without the permission and authority of my seigneur.

DEFENSE

At a time when my seigneur, King Lothair, neither held the Lorraine realm, nor had regained possession of it, with difficulty I obtained the son of my brother through my pledged word that I would return him to the latter and his followers without objection, if occasion should at any time demand it.[3] However, when it was brought about that my lord seigneur would be guardian of the emperor's son, and since hostages had been given for this very reason, my brother demanded his son back again by frequent messengers. Rebuking me as a violator of my pledge for accepting him when it was too late, he says that many persons are throwing his affairs into confusion, and that this state of things is ruining him. At the same time he calls upon the terrible Judge of the last judgment as the avenger of scorned fidelity and kinship.

Because my seigneur had said nothing to me about regaining possession of the kingdom [Lorraine], but only about his guardianship,[4] nor had he forbidden the giving of permission [to leave] to a cleric, but rather because, above all, he had kindly consented to it, as I learned from my messengers, I gave him leave, provided he was willing to carry out these things which his father had promised. In order that he might very honestly preserve that in behalf of which hostages were given, I exacted a pledge which he has offered up till now, and even now, as we believe, is [still] offering.[5]

I conferred the grade of deacon and priest on him lest, when emancipated from us, he should be transferred to another by receiving grades from him, and lest our church should suffer blame for having raised the subdeacon from his own office to the episcopal rank; and also because these grades confer neither provinces, nor cities, nor villas, which belong to kingdoms, but rather those things which belong to the kingdom of Heaven, that is,[6] to war on vices and to cultivate virtues.

In so far as the crime of treachery and infidelity has been alleged against me, I have, as I think, shown both that I particularly kept faith and maintained fidelity, especially to my seigneur.

This is Letter 57 in Havet.

1. Apparently Gerbert drew up this defense for Archbishop Adalbero to be offered to the assembly of the French on May 11th at Compiègne. However, Adalbero received news of the dispersal of the meeting (Letter 65) before he could reach Compiègne. Bubnov, II, 313, n. 25, doubts that Lothair had begun any formal case against Archbishop Adalbero. Cf. Lot, *Derniers Carolingiens*, p. 156, n. 1; and Parisot, *Origines de la Haute-Lorraine*, p. 356, n. 1. In 987, Louis V formally accused Adalbero of treachery, but based his accusation on other acts. Richer iv.ii-vii.

2. Lorraine, once part of the Carolingian domain (fisc), became a separate kingdom under Lothair, son of Louis the Pious, but was always claimed by the Carolingians by hereditary right. See Letters 54ff.; and Lot, *Derniers Carolingiens*, p. 156.

3. Young Adalbero was apparently one of the hostages given by the Lorrainers as guarantee of their acceptance of King Lothair as Otto III's guardian (Letter 43).

4. Gerbert puns here on *revocatione* [a taking back], a word from Cicero *De oratore* iii.liv, and *advocatione* [legal assistance or guardianship].

5. See Letter 60.

6. *Id est*, from the edition by Duchesne against *idem* in MS V and Masson.

65. RHEIMS. May 17, 985

Has learned of King Lothair's and Duke Henry's plans through Henry's stupid messenger; reports that the French nobles scattered at the report of Duke Hugh's troops; urges Adalbero of Metz to hold out against King Lothair; suggests recapture of Verdun

To the Bishop of Metz [1]

On May 15th the suspicious actions of Henry's [2] messenger made clear what the king [Lothair] is doing and planning for the present. For on his return he revealed by his curious questioning that he had in his mind something other than he allowed to show in his face. Duke Hugh [Capet] is said to have collected six hundred knights. This report suddenly dissolved and scattered the meeting of the French at Compiègne held May 11th. [3]

Of yours, there were present Duke Charles [4] and Count Renier; [5] of ours, Heribert of Troyes. But Eudes was kept away by a more pressing preoccupation. In addition, Gibuin [6] was present and Bishop Adalbero of Laon. After the son of his brother Bardo had been given as a hostage of peace, his brother Gozelo [7] escaped on this condition, that they would do what Siegfried and Godfrey seem about to do. [8] What can this be? What the French hope for, but in vain, as we know for certain.

In any event, this much is certain, you should not be willing to turn over the land you now hold by virtue of counsel, aid, and troops to our enemies who cannot furnish such counsel and aid. I endure with a restless and disturbed mind the fact that without any effort a few thieves hold the city of Verdun, unless perhaps this [attack] is being postponed for a more comprehensive plan of destroying them by a sudden overthrow from an unexpected point.

This is Letter 58 in Havet. Gerbert wrote it perhaps in his own name.
1. Adalbero, son of Duchess Beatrice and Duke Frederick.
2. Of Bavaria. He was still negotiating with King Lothair.
3. See Letter 64, introductory note.
4. Of Lower Lorraine. Although a brother of King Lothair, Charles was a vassal of the German king.
5. See Letter 67, n. 3.
6. Nephew of Gibuin, bishop of Châlons-sur-Marne, and later himself bishop of the same place (991?-1004). Probably he was a son of a Eudes and grandson of Count Hugh Beaumont of Dijon (d.c. 955). Havet, p. 164, n. 6; Lot, *Derniers Carolingiens*, p. 332, n. 5; Lot, *Hugues Capet*, p. 116, n. 3.
7. The brothers Gozelo and Bardo (Richer iii.ciii) were brothers of Bishop

Ascelin (Adalbero) of Laon, all of them sons of Count Renier of Bastogne. Parisot, *Origines de la Haute Lorraine*, p. 350, and Table I. They were also nephews of Archbishop Adalbero and Count Godfrey. At this time Gozelo was count of Bastogne.

8. The French hoped that these counts would make some concessions to secure their release. Apparently Siegfried did so, but Godfrey refused. Letter 67.

66. RHEIMS. May 28, 985

Urges Archbishop Adalbero to remain for the conference, to cultivate Hugh's friendship; Hugh wishes Abbot Ayrard to help reform St. Germain-des-Prés

To Archbishop Adalbero [1]

Advice has been sought as you wished, and your tarrying until the conference that has been planned is generally praised. Hugh's friendship ought to be actively sought after, and every effort should be exerted lest we fail to make the most of this friendship which has been well begun. For this, indeed, is discernment.

By some sort of agreement your brother Godfrey and Renier [2] told my messenger Gobther, whom I had sent to Tours, that you would be here [3] so that if Eudes should send any messenger to you, you would be able both to talk to him and to carry out his suggestions.

As for the rest, Duke Hugh, finding an opportunity arising from the disagreement of the bishop of Paris and Abbot Walter, [4] asks your Abbot Ayrard [5] among others to come to him, and we are confident that he can be persuaded to do so. When the conference has broken up, dispel all delays and restore yourself to the city and to your people.

This is Letter 60 in Havet.

1. Apparently Adalbero was in Verdun (Letter 70).

2. Undoubtedly, the same person mentioned in Letters 9, 96, 103, 136, 149, and 150.

3. Godfrey was imprisoned either at Chateau Thierry on the Marne, where roads from Verdun and from Rheims (going to Tours) crossed, or he may have been moved to Tours, which was in Count Eudes' domain. Lot, *Hugues Capet*, Appendix xi.

4. Abbot of St. Germain-des-Prés, of which Hugh Capet had been lay abbot. Newman, *Domaine royal*, p. 207, citing *Gallia christiana*, VII, col. 432. The bishop of Paris was Elisiard. Havet, p. 59, n. 6; Bubnov, II, 325, n. 40.

5. Abbot of St. Thierry near Rheims (Letter 14, n. 1).

67. RHEIMS. June 28, 985

*Complains that the recipient has too many secretaries; warns of
a plot against Otto III; King Lothair and Duke Hugh are reconciled; excessive demands are made on Count Godfrey; peace
is being arranged between Heribert, Eudes, and Archbishop
Adalbero; requests news of meeting at Frankfort*

[GERBERT TO DUCHESS BEATRICE?]

Secret information certainly ought not to be entrusted to many
persons; but not without cause do we assume that letters written to
us in different handwritings have been handled by different persons.

The silence of your friend Adalbero [1] indicates his condition, and
at the same time that of the churches of the Lord, and of the French
court. As far as I am able I shall touch upon this briefly.

I am not unmindful of those persons faithful to Caesar. A plot
either has been formed or is being formed against the son of Caesar
and against you not only by the princes, among whom Duke Charles
now openly appears, but also by such knights as it is possible to entice
by hope or fear. Through the adroitness of certain persons Duke
Hugh was finally reconciled with the king and queen on June 18th
in order to create the impression that such a great man's name is
promoting the plot—a very unlikely thing, and at this time we think
he will not do so.

Count Siegfried returned to his own followers. If Count Godfrey
would return Mons with Hainaut [2] to Renier,[3] if he would deprive
himself and his son of the county and the bishopric of Verdun, and
besides, if he would swear an undivided allegiance to the kings of the
French, perhaps, after hostages had been exchanged, he might be
allowed to return [home]. The fate of Duke Thierry [4] depends upon
Duke Hugh.

A tentative peace,[5] agreed upon to eventuate in a permanent one,
now at length reconciles Eudes, Heribert and Archbishop Adalbero
who is faithful to you. In this affair of yours and theirs, in whose
name it was proposed, nothing which is inimical to your safety and
to theirs can be agreed upon. A secret and stealthy expedition is
suddenly planned against some of your vassals. What you will have
done at Frankfort [6] pray do not conceal from us who rejoice in your
welfare.

This is Letter 59 in Havet. It mentions the Frankfort meeting as in the immediate future, and the meeting was held June 26-July 2, 985 (DO III 14, 15) when Otto III, Empress Theophanu, and Archbishop Willigis and others were at Frankfort. During this time Duke Henry made complete submission to Otto III and Theophanu and thus received back his duchy of Bavaria. *Annales Quedlinburgenses*, a. 985, MGSS III, 67; Thietmar iv.viii. Duchess Beatrice played some part in this peace (Letter 70). Other addressees are possible for this letter —Bishop Notker, Archbishop Willigis, or even Empress Theophanu.

1. Of Rheims. See the same expression in Letter 70 to Duchess Beatrice. Actually, she was Adalbero's aunt by marriage, the wife of his uncle Frederick.

2. "Hainaut, an old division, whose territory is today divided between the Belgian province of the same name [of which Mons is the capital] and the [French] Department of the North." Havet, p. 58, n. 4. See also Johnson, *German Episcopate*, pp. 113-15, 117, 125.

3. Renier IV, son of Renier III (Longcol), count of Hainaut. In 958, Otto I deprived Renier III of his domains. Richer iii.vi-x. In 960, 973, and 976 Renier IV and Lambert, the sons of Renier III, attempted to regain these possessions, some of which (Hainaut and Mons) were bestowed on Count Godfrey of Verdun. King Lothair's support of Renier IV's demands on Godfrey must have resulted from Renier's aid during Lothair's captures of Verdun. Parisot, *Origines de la Haute Lorraine*, p. 304, n. 4. Godfrey refused the conditions proposed in the present letter, and Renier IV regained Hainaut only in 998, probably after Godfrey's death. Havet, p. 58, n. 5; Holtzmann, *Geschichte der sächsischen Kaiserzeit*, pp. 178, 254, 266-69, 296, 300, 418-19. Renier IV married Hadwig, daughter of Hugh Capet. M. Uhlirz, *Jahrbücher des deutschen Reiches unter Otto II. und Otto III*, Vol. II: *Otto III*, p. 52, n. 51.

4. Son of Duchess Beatrice, and nephew of Hugh Capet.

5. Virgil *Aeneid* xii.133. See Letter 25, referring to the conflict between Archbishop Adalbero and Counts Eudes and Heribert.

6. See introductory note, above.

68. RHEIMS. July 6, 985

Archbishop Adalbero has no further news; wishes Duchess Beatrice well, and requests that she recommend him to Hugh Capet; reports that monk Meingus left Corbie for Laon

To DUCHESS BEATRICE IN THE NAME OF ADALBERO

About those matters concerning which you ask for more definite information, we know nothing more than we either told you when present with you, or than you received through our messenger. Furthermore, we hope that, saving the royal honor, affairs are progressing well with you, your children, your friends, and if this is so, we congratulate you.

Consider our business yours: without hesitation acquaint Duke Hugh with our steadfast mind and constant fidelity. What we are asking of you, furthermore, we shall return in the form of service to you. Also, we are especially grateful because through you we have been informed of many happenings. We have heard that the monk Meingus,[1] who for a long time was searched for at the request of Abbot Rainard,[2] left Corbie[3] and went to Rouen. In this matter, if opportunity offers, we shall try to follow out your wish, as in all things.

This is Letter 61 in Havet.
1. See Letter 74. Bubnov, II, 327; 328, n. 41, suggests that his name was Maingaud and that he became abbot of Corbie in 987.
2. See Letter 74.
3. Monastery of Corbie (dept. Somme). Lot, *Derniers Carolingiens*, pp. 117, 224.

69. RHEIMS. July 14, 985
Congratulates Duchess Beatrice upon her successes; requests news of the failure of the meeting of noblewomen at Metz

To THE SAME

We offer you our congratulations, certainly well deserved because events are happening according to your wish, and because through you we frequently gain information unknown to us. Especially do we value the fact that we are experiencing your sincere affection toward us.

But what event so changed the planned conference of noblewomen[1] that Duke Henry is coming alone?[2] If you know, pray answer our query, with complete confidence in us, as to whether this results from someone else's treachery, and what princes are about to come thither.

This is Letter 62 in Havet. Probably it was written in Archbishop Adalbero's name to Duchess Beatrice.
1. Empresses Theophanu and Adelaide, Duchess Beatrice, Queen Emma, and perhaps Adelaide, wife of Hugh Capet, planned to meet at Metz. See Letter 72.
2. Originally, Henry's wife, Duchess Gisela, was to participate in the conference, but now she had been excluded.

70. RHEIMS. July 14, 985
Praises Beatrice for the part in bringing peace; hints at possible treachery of Archbishop Egbert as back of his refusal to consecrate Adalbero of Verdun; asks Beatrice to find out

[GERBERT] TO THE SAME DUCHESS BEATRICE

I seem to see your excellent judgment in the peace effected among the nobles,[1] and in the well-managed public affairs, that you have changed for the better. One important matter, however, disturbs many persons, namely, the fact that the archbishop of Trier is deferring the consecration[2] with such effort. Either he desired to transfer himself with the duke[3] and the kingdom of Lorraine to the French and to conceal it from you, a possibility which the conference to be held at Verdun[4] makes appear likely, or he wishes to contrive greater schemes than this. The ordination of his nephew[5] your friend Adalbero is ordered to nullify. Is it the king [Lothair] or the primate of Trier [who orders this]? From any point of view this affair seems to show the hand of the archbishop [Egbert]. Therefore, alert your caution and search out whither these important matters are tending; and consider whether you can trust Duke Henry to keep faith with you.

This is Letter 63 in Havet.
1. The Peace of Frankfort, July, 985. Letter 67, introductory note.
2. Of Adalbero as bishop of Verdun. See Letters 48 and 49.
3. Undoubtedly Charles. Letter 67; Bubnov, II, 332, n. 43; M. Uhlirz, *Untersuchungen über Inhalt und Datierung der Briefe Gerberts*, p. 61, n. 68.
4. Cf. Letter 66.
5. Archbishop Adalbero had ordained Adalbero a deacon and a priest (Letter 64) in order that his nephew might qualify for a bishopric.

71. RHEIMS. July 14, 985
Rebukes Abbot Nithard for demanding the immediate return of the monk Gausbert

[ARCHBISHOP ADALBERO] TO ABBOT NITHARD [1]

The good of the greatest number, indeed, must always be borne in mind, and public advantage must be put ahead of private. Suddenly, with no consideration for the shortness of the time, you force Brother Gausbert[2] to return with everything belonging to him. Do you not feel the great rumblings of the earth caused by civil war?[3] We, who seem to be masters of the situation and princes, have, in fact, only a few escorts and our frequent journeys have exhausted the horses.

You have said that he is unwilling to return to the tedium of the monastery. If this is so, how are you going to hold him after he has been returned? It follows, therefore, that we are learning in this matter whether the convenience of the few or of the many is more precious in your eyes.

This is Letter 64 in Havet. The reference to the sender as a prince who possesses numerous escorts indicates Archbishop Adalbero.

1. Abbot (from 978) of Mettlach on the Sarre in the diocese of Trier. Havet, p. 62, n. 4; Bubnov, II, 335, n. 44.

2. *Gan.* in MS V, *Gaut.* in the editions by Masson and by Duchesne. This letter is not in MS L. See Letters 62 and 75.

3. Cf. Letter 67.

---

72. RHEIMS. July 17, 985

Archbishop Adalbero promises to secure restitution of the property of Notker's followers; requests Notker's participation in the conference of noblewomen and information about its progress

To Bishop Notker in the Name of Archbishop Adalbero

In transacting affairs with a perspicacious person one does not need to struggle with a long speech. The property, seized from your followers by force, will be restored; trust in the reliability of a friend who makes the promise. If this is not enough, let these persons, for whom we are asking the restoration of their possessions, accept a hostage; nor should this be postponed because of the necessity of an immediate meeting. And because we think so highly of you we are informing you that, while we are dictating these lines, we have received hostages from a besieged castle which must be surrendered on the morrow.

A conference of noblewomen is to be held at Metz, and we hope that you will take as much part in it as possible. If the meeting is abandoned while being formed,[1] we are anxious to learn through you the reason for it. Those details that we ought to learn privately, private occasions will make known to us.

This is Letter 66 in Havet.

1. See Letter 69. This particular meeting did not materialize.

73. RHEIMS. August 20, 985
The messenger's slowness caused cancellation of bishops' meeting; will welcome Notker; Walter's soldiers should cease overrunning Wazo's estates

TO NOTKER BISHOP OF LIÉGE IN THE NAME OF ADALBERO

The fact that the bishops' meeting,[1] about which notice had been given, did not take place is to be charged to the slowness in conveying the letter. These matters will be discussed upon your arrival and later, if it shall seem advisable, together we will consider them more fully in private.

Furthermore, because my brother considers that he and his followers belong to you, and ascribes much of his hope of safety[2] to you, you ought to prevent Walter's[3] soldiery from overrunning the estates of his vassal Wazo. By doing this you will both avoid evil rumor, and will appear not to have failed in your official duties.

This is Letter 65 in Havet.
1. Perhaps a meeting planned to discuss the postponed consecration of Adalbero of Verdun, but not the same as those mentioned in Letters 66 and 70.
2. Godfrey was still a prisoner. See Letter 78.
3. Possibly the lord (Gautier) of Cambrai. Havet, p. 63, n. 6.

74. RHEIMS. August 20, 985
The monk Meingus is being returned to Abbot Rainard; suggests mild treatment of this wandering brother

TO ABBOT RAINARD [1]

Although it is not concealed from Your Intelligence that the art of arts is the guidance of souls, yet, since you are so occupied with public affairs, it has seemed not useless to remind you of this. Brother Meingus, now perplexed and dubious, whom by your sweet speech and fatherly kindness you influenced to come from across the sea,[2] we have persuaded, by such words as we were able, to cast himself upon your mercy with which he is acquainted.

It will, therefore, be the part of a learned man to give honeyed doses according to the manner of a good physician lest, when the bitter antidotes are administered, the patient, made fearful by the first taste, should begin to tremble for his safety. Receive him in this manner, if acceptable to you. Even if not acceptable, still permit it with the calm mind with which he wishes to return lest we, by chance, should be playing the part of a betrayer.

75. RHEIMS. August 20, 985
Apologizes for Gausbert's not returning before; requests kindness for him, especially a chance to pursue his studies

To Egbert, Archbishop of Trier

The failure to carry out our order sent from the city of Verdun concerning the return of Brother Gausbert [1] resulted from the more acute anxiety caused by the present times, while necessity forces us to do what we do not wish and takes away the opportunity to do what we do wish. Now, at length, not to seem ungrateful to those deserving kindness from us, we are returning him to Your Clemency, assuming we are able. We ask only this of your customary good will, that you exhibit kindness to him on account of our recommendation, and, if it can be done in your peace, [2] let him not lack the studies to which he has arranged to devote fuller attention.

76. RHEIMS. February, 986
Begs Abbot Mayeul to investigate the case of the intruder abbot at Fleury and to render an opinion

To Abbot Mayeul [1]

Even if watchful care over your own flock constantly occupies you, yet it is a work of greater charity, if you occasionally minister to the disease of another flock. An intruder, [2] so the report is, has seized the highest position among the monks of the monastery of Fleury, dedicated to the veneration of Father Benedict. If you keep silent, who will speak? If this remains uncorrected, what wicked person will not have similar aspirations? We, for our part, are saying these things from a zeal for divine love, and in order that, if he appear worthy, after your investigation he may be received, but if unworthy, that he may be deprived of the society of all abbots and of the monastic order as the penalty of his condemnation. Your opinion, sent to us by letter, we shall especially welcome.

This is Letter 69 in Havet.

1. St. Mayeul, abbot of Cluny, 964-94. Gerbert undoubtedly was acquainted with Mayeul through their simultaneous visits at the courts of Otto I (in 971 and 972) and of Otto II (in December, 980, and the early part of 981). See L. Bourdon, "Les voyages de saint Mayeul en Italie," *Mélanges d'archéologie et d'histoire*, XLIII (1926), 75-76, 87.

2. Oylbold (d. 988). He succeeded Amalbert (d. 985) through the sponsorship of the lay nobility and against the desires of most of the Fleury monks. See Letters 87, 92-94, 97, 148, 151; and Lot, *Hugues Capet*, p. 13, n. 5. Although Archbishop Adalbero and Gerbert strongly opposed Oylbold, Abbo, the later abbot of Fleury, esteemed him highly. Aimo *Vita S. Abbonis*, PL CXXXIX, 392f.

77. RHEIMS. February 20, 986

Urges Abbot Gerald to pray for the churches and for him; impossible for Gerbert to visit St. Gerald of Aurillac; King Louis, being unstable, probably will not aid Count Borrell; Gerbert's organs in Italy will be sent to Gerald when there is peace; invites Gerald to visit Rheims

GERBERT TO ABBOT GERALD

O thou most pleasing to God,[1] do you see the world on fire with wars, and yet not raise your hands to the Almighty in behalf of the condition of God's churches? You desire us to make the salvation-bringing journey—a pilgrimage of love—to the abode of the blessed Gerald. Would that the Divinity might favor this wish, but how difficult this is to do is easily understood, unless your merits may obtain it.

With reference to King Louis,[2] you ask what sort of person he is considered, and whether he is about to conduct the armies of the French as aid to Borrell.[3] It is unnecessary to ask the first question of us, because, as Sallust says: "It is necessary that all men who take counsel about doubtful matters should be free from wrath, animosity, and compassion."[4] Considering the other question according to its nature, equally whether it is to be or not to be, our opinion seems rather to incline to the negative.

To continue, the organs [5] and those things that you have directed to be sent to you are being kept in Italy but are to be brought before your eyes when peace has been made in the kingdoms.[6] Those things which are ours of right look upon as your own.

Show to your longing sons [7] the longed-for presence of the devout father, or else come because of St. Remi,[8] apostle of the French, so that what we find impossible to accomplish may be supplied by what is possible for you.

This is Letter 70 in Havet. It is Gerbert's reply to a letter from Abbot Gerald (see n. 3).

1. Claudian *De tertio consulatu Honorii*, 96.

2. Louis V (967-87), son of Lothair and Emma, was associated on the throne with his father Lothair from June 8, 979. He became king alone after Lothair's death on March 2, 986 (Letters 78 and 82). See also Richer iii.xcii-xcv, as to Louis' character.

3. Count of Barcelona, Ausona-Vich, Gerona, and Urgel, called also marquis of Gothia (JL 3888) and duke of Hither Spain (Richer iii.xliii). Kehr, "Papsttum und der katalanische Prinzipat," ABB, 1926, p. 13; A. Lambert, "Barcelone (Comtes de)," DHGE, VI, 727-28.

On one of their annual campaigns against Christian Spain, the Saracens, led by Muhammed ibn-abi-'Amir (al-Manṣūr), captured Barcelona, July 6, 985, after a five-day siege. They sacked and burned the city, capturing many prisoners, and then advanced to the monastery of Sant Cugat del Vallés, eight miles from Barcelona. Here they pillaged and murdered, one victim being Abbot John.

As soon as Count Borrell, Gerbert's first patron, was able to take the initiative, the Saracens withdrew, and the people and the monks began the rehabilitation of Barcelona and Sant Cugat. The monk Odo was elected abbot, and soon after December 5, 985, he traveled north to King Lothair to secure a new charter of confirmation of property rights, because the previous ones had perished in the Saracen assault, particularly an important one granted by Louis IV, father of Lothair. Probably Borrell had requested Odo also to appeal for military aid. About February 15, 986, in Compiègne, Lothair issued a diploma to Odo, confirming the property rights of Sant Cugat. Marca, *Marca hispanica*, col. 937. Apparently, Odo's route passed through Aurillac where Abbot Gerald had entrusted him with a letter to Gerbert at Rheims. See F. Fita, "Destrucción de Barcelona por Almanzor 6 Julio 985," BAH, VII (1885), 189-92; and Letter 261, a similar confirmation of property rights for Sant Cugat issued in 1002 by Gerbert as pope to this same Abbot Odo. A document in the Cartulary of Sant Cugat, dated March 31, 1031, states that Count Borrell was present with Abbot Odo before King Lothair. Màs, IV, No. CCCLXXXI. Letter 120 contradicts this.

4. Sallust *Oratio in Catilinam*, 51.

5. See Letters 102, 105, 171; H. Bittermann, "The Organ in the Early Middle Ages," *Speculum*, IV (1929), 390-410; and W. Apel, "Early History of the Organ," *Speculum*, XXIII (1948), 191-216.

6. Gerbert feared to return to Bobbio without German military support. Apparently, he anticipated that Empress Theophanu would go to Italy to re-establish effective German control as soon as she had reached an agreement with King Lothair about Lorraine, as Otto II had done at Margut-sur-Chiers in July,

980, before he undertook his Italian expedition. Richer III.lxxviii-lxxx; Lot, *Derniers Carolingiens,* pp. 118-19. As to the unsettled Italian situation in the second half of 985, as well as Theophanu's strengthening of Germany's eastern border, see M. Uhlirz, *Jahrbücher des Deutschen Reiches unter Otto II. und Otto III,* Vol. II: *Otto III,* 58-61, 63-65. Empress Adelaide had already hastened to Pavia during or immediately after the Frankfort meeting, June 20-July 2, 985 (p. 58f.).

7. Gerbert and probably Archbishop Adalbero, although possibly Aurillac monks were sojourning in Rheims. Letter 25.

8. .The abbey church of St. Rémy of Rheims contains the tomb of St. Remi.

78. RHEIMS. March 2, 986

All Lorraine nobles except Count Godfrey have escaped; requests Stephen to send the manuscripts and the bill for same

To Stephen, Deacon of the City of Rome, Dated March Second

We who have been occupied with the funeral ceremonies of Lord Lothair,[1] the king, are answering a few of the many questions you asked us. All the Lorrainers captured a short time ago [2] have escaped, except Count Godfrey for whom better things are anticipated shortly. Make answer as to what events are happening with you and your associates, and through this messenger send back the books copied for us through your efforts,[3] with the reckoning of the expense.

This is Letter 71 in Havet.

This is the only letter which carries the specific date. The form, *data VI non[ae] Martias,* is the same as that of papal privileges where it appears at the end.

1. Died March 2, 986, at Laon. Letters 80-82; Richer III.cx; Prayer Book of Queen Emma, quoted in Olleris, p. 523. A description of his tomb and its fate is found in J. Chardron, "Le premier pape français, Gerbert, archevêque de Reims," *Revue de Champagne et de Brie,* XV (1883), 185, n. 2. See MacKinney, "Tenth-Century Medicine," *Bulletin of the Institute of the History of Medicine,* II (1934), 370, for a translation of Richer's account of Lothair's final illness, and Mac-Kinney's commentary on it.

2. See Letter 67.

3. See Letter 47.

79. RHEIMS. March 7, 986

Urges Abbot Nithard to retrieve his treasure since Gerbert expects to leave Rheims

To Abbot Nithard of Mettlach [1]

Political disturbances [2] account for the fact that we do not occasionally enjoy your presence. You think you alone bear burdens but you do not know what the overwhelming trials of others are.

But, since men are tossed about by an uncertain fate, and since, as you know, a certain position seeks me out, uncertain though I am, why do you lay up a treasure for a bad turn of fortune by leaving it with me for so long a time? And, inasmuch as I, a trustworthy man, am addressing a trustworthy man, make haste. For, either the imperial court will summon me quickly, or, more quickly, Spain, which has been neglected for a long time, will seek me again.[3]

This is Letter 72 in Havet. The date is based upon its position in MS L and MS V between Letters 78 and 80, and upon the assumption that Abbot Odo of Sant Cugat (Letter 77, n. 3) had suggested to Gerbert that he return to Spain. However, it might have been written at some other time, such as next after Letter 51, or after 125-26.

1. See Letter 71, n. 1.

2. The reference is obscure if applying to the period just preceding King Lothair's death on March 2d, but if this letter was written after Letter 126, then the times were dangerous, owing to Duke Charles's rebellion.

3. See Letters 33, 51, and 77, n. 3.

80. RHEIMS. March 10, 986

Expresses affection for Egbert and appreciation for the latter's affection and prayers for him; Queen Emma has taken him into her favor

To Egbert, Archbishop of Trier, in the Name of Archbishop Adalbero

Although I know that no benefits resulting from my prayers can correspond to your merits, yet my spirit glows with love, and what it cannot gain by a deed, it attempts by affection. We have experienced the privilege of your love toward us very often through letters, very often through messengers, very often through deeds. The fact that you offered holy prayers to God on our behalf and that you poured these forth not in vain is evidenced by the kindness of the august lady,[1] shown to us on March second, the day on which Lothair, the most illustrious king of the French and brightest star, was taken from the world. He whom you have thought lacking the royal favor [2] is deprived of no intimacy with the court.

This is Letter 73 in Havet. Egbert had received news of Lothair's death, but not news that Adalbero was being taken into favor at the French court. Therefore, Egbert's letter was written about March 4th or 5th, and this reply was sent soon after its receipt on the 7th or 8th.
1. Queen Emma, widow of King Lothair. See Letter 81.
2. Archbishop Adalbero himself, who had been in disfavor. Letter 60.

81. LAON. End of April, 986

Queen Emma begging her mother Adelaide for advice asks her to arrange a meeting at Remiremont on May 18th; the French vassals have sworn fealty to her and to King Louis; Emma begs for prayers for King Lothair

To Her Mother, in the Name of Queen Emma [1]

To the ever august Empress Lady Adelaide, from Emma, formerly queen, now bereaved of the light of the French.

The time of my joy, the time of my charm has disappeared, O my lady, and O sweet mother, while he in whose blossoming I blossomed, in whose ruling I ruled, has made me, hitherto a wife, everlastingly a widow. O bitter day, the second of March, which snatched my husband from my side, precipitating me into such miseries. Let an affectionate mother sense the distress and grief of a daughter full of sorrows. Inwardly, I would not wish to be, but that the Divinity has left my mother as a comfort. O when shall I see her, when speak with her?

Our advisers,[2] indeed, wish my son [Louis V] and me to meet you and King Conrad [3] in the neighborhood of Remiremont [4] where the kingdoms adjoin, on May 18th. But this delay is a thousand years to me.

You know that meanwhile the princes of the French have sworn their oaths of fealty both to me [5] and to my son. In this and in the remaining matters we shall use your judgment as to what should be followed and what should be avoided in order that you shall be called the mother not only of Emma the queen, but of all kingdoms. Besides, remember your words, that you cherished my husband on my account and that he loved you on my account. May these sweet emotions profit his soul, and what you are unable to offer in worldly things, make up for spiritually, I beg, through the holy fathers—bishops, abbots, monks—and any of the very devout servants of God.

This is Letter 74 in Havet. Laon was the principal residence of the last Carolingians.

1. Daughter of Empress Adelaide and her first husband, King Lothar of Italy. Emma married King Lothair of France in 965. *Continuator Reginonis*, a. 965, MGSS VI; Letter 28, n. 3.

2. Probably Archbishop Adalbero and Gerbert.

3. King of Arles or Burgundy (937-93), brother of Empress Adelaide. Conrad married Mathilda, sister of King Lothair of France.

4. Remiremont (Vosges), on the Moselle in Lorraine, near the kingdom of Burgundy.

5. This indicates that Queen Emma intended to act with her nineteen-year-old son Louis in the government. Letter 131, n. 4. Emma was not powerful enough to carry out her plan. Letter 100.

82. RHEIMS. End of April, 986

EPITAPH OF KING LOTHAIR [1]

> The dukes met for the funeral of him—
>
> O Lothair, Caesar, sprung from the Caesars—
>
>   whom every good man loved;
>
> The memorials of grief thou spread before us
>
>   in the second light of terrifying Mars,[2]
>
> Because thou wert seen clad in purple.[3]

This is Letter 75 in Havet. The epitaph appears to have been inserted in Gerbert's Collection at the date of its composition. The following epitaphs (Letters 83-85) were then included, although they memorialized friends who had died earlier. Possibly he later wrote some that are not included in the Collection, such as those for Archbishop Adalbero and Abbot Adso of Montier-en-Der.

1. See Letters 78 and 81.

2. A frightening representation of the month of March (*Mars*) appears in some of the illustrations (miniatures and sculptures) of the Labors of the Months, where, armed with a spear, he is shown as a hornblower with wild, flame-like hair, as in MS BM Lansdowne 383, s. XII, described by Meyer Schapiro, "[Review of] J. C. Webster, Labors of the months (Northwestern University Studies in Humanities, No. 4 ... 1938)," *Speculum*, XVI (1941), 135.

3. Virgil *Georgicon* III.17; Horace *Ars poetica* 228. See Richer III.cx.

83. RHEIMS? April - May, 986?

EPITAPH OF DUKE FREDERICK [1]

> The desire of the French [2] brought the name
>
>   of Frederick here.
>
> From the blood of kings [3] have the dukes, his
>
>   forefathers, produced him

Their peer in position and merits; the last

    sleep consumed him

When the lofty home of Mercury was open

    to you, O Phoebus.[4]

This is Letter 76 in Havet.

1. Duke of Upper Lorraine, husband of Beatrice (Letter 39, n. 10), and father of Bishop Adalbero II of Metz (Letter 65) and Duke Thierry (Letter 39, notes 4 and 5).

2. Note 4 below.

3. He was a descendant of Louis II the Stammerer (877-79) through the female line.

4. According to Parisot, *Origines de la Haute Lorraine*, p. 319, n. 8, several necrologies give the date of Frederick's death as May 18th. Gerbert's epitaph for him confirms this. The planet Mercury has two "homes"—Gemini and Virgo —and Gemini, its day "home", is in the northern or upper part of the zodiac, hence its "lofty home." The sun entered Gemini on May 16th, a date poetically accurate enough to stand for May 18th, especially since Gerbert does not say that Frederick died *on* the day the sun entered Mercury's home. Since the French caused Frederick's death it must have occurred during a French attack on Lorraine or Germany in the spring. Such an attack occurred in May-June, 978, when King Lothair chased Otto II from Aachen. Perhaps Frederick attacked Lothair at the beginning of his invasion. On the homes of the planets see Robert the Englishman in L. Thorndike, *The Sphere of Sacrobosco and Its Commentators* (Chicago, 1949), pp. 169-70, 221. As to Lothair's invasion see Richer III.lxviii-lxxi; Lot, *Derniers Carolingiens*, pp. 93ff.; K. Uhlirz, *Jahrbücher des Deutschen Reiches unter Otto II. und Otto III*, Vol. I: *Otto II*, pp. 105-9.

84. RHEIMS? April - May, 986?

Epitaph of the Teacher Adalbert [1]

O thou exalted among noble men, skilled in the

    science of reasoning,

Belgic [2] land named thee Adalbert. Fate not suffering

    thee to live longer [3]

Carried thee away in the flower of youth

When Apollo had produced the return of the bissextile

    of February.[4]

This is Letter 77 in Havet.

1. Trithemius (*Chronicon Hirsau*, I, 100) states that Adalbert, first *scholasticus* of St. Vincent of Metz, founded in 968, was thoroughly versed in all knowledge. He was perhaps the person mentioned in this epitaph. Adalbert of Metz wrote several works: a Chronicle of the bishops of Metz, and probably an abridgment of Gregory I's *Moralia on Job* called *Speculum*. Emile-Auguste Begin, *Histoire des sciences, des lettres, des arts et de la civilisation dans le Pays-Messin, depuis les Gaulois jusqu'à nos jours* (Metz, 1829), pp. 220-21; *Biographie nationale de*

Belgique, I (Brussels, 1866), 36. He may, however, have been a monk at St. Arnulf of Metz. On the intellectual interests of these two monasteries see Lesne IV, 657-60.

2. Lorraine, his native region.

3. Lucan *Pharsalia* I. 70ff.

4. The bissextile was the extra day of leap year, inserted between February 24th and 25th, and was so called from the Roman custom of having two February twenty-fourths, i.e., two days called the sixth day before the kalends (the first) of March—*VI kalendas martii* being equivalent to February 24th, and bis *VI kalendas martii,* our February 25th. Adalbert probably died February 25, 984. Undoubtedly he had been a pupil of Gerbert's in the 970s.

85. RHEIMS? April - May, 986?
EPITAPH OF OTTO [II], THE CAESAR

> The enemy [1] brought here him who was known as the
>> master and father of his people,
> At whose command [2] the princes trembled;
> Thee, O Otto, divine ornament, most illustrious Caesar
> The seventh light of December snatched from us,
>> undeserving of this.

This is Letter 78 in Havet. MS Reims 385, s. IX, fol. 160v, also contains this epitaph written in a later hand than the body of the manuscript. Was this Gerbert's first draft jotted down on a blank part of this manuscript? Whoever wrote this down planned to put down the "epitaph of King Lothair," but neglected to write more than the title.

1. Probably not a specific enemy, but Satan. Otto II had died in Rome on the 7th of December, 983. In the Vatican Grottoes, i.e., the Crypt of St. Peter's, a chapel, named the Chapel of Otto II, contains, at the left side, the sarcophagus tomb of Otto II and, at the right, that of his cousin Pope Gregory V. Opposite the entrance stands an altar above which is a mosaic depicting a seated Christ, with right hand raised in benediction. St. Paul with a staff is at Christ's right, and St. Peter, holding three keys in his left hand, is at His left. This mosaic came from Otto II's tomb.

2. *Cujus ad imperium.* The same expression was used in a brief poem inserted into a Rheims Evangeliary (MS Epernay 1) of the time (816-35) of Archbishop Ebo, fol. 2. "Manuscrit d'Hincmar à Epernay," *La Chronique de Champagne,* I (1837), 211.

86. RHEIMS. April - May, 986
Upbraids the city of Verdun for not receiving their duly elected bishop, Adalbero; for acknowledging the French king; and for plowing up land around altars; appeals to the good citizens separately

A SPEECH REBUKING THE CITY OF VERDUN

What remedy will you find for your ills, cursed city of Verdun?

You have split apart the unity of God's holy church. You have torn
asunder the very holy society of mankind. For, what else is this that
you have done when you obstinately persist in not acknowledging
your pastor,[1] who was elected by the wish of the hereditary king
[Otto III] with the consent and favor of the archdiocesan bishops,
and above all was given the episcopal benediction[2], and when you
without wholeness of body are striving to graft yourself like a
mutilated and deformed branch of the olive tree onto the wild olive
tree [Romans 11 : 17]? [3]

You do not acknowledge your pastor because you plot to deprive
your king of his kingdom. You have no right to create new kings
and princes by submitting to unaccustomed yokes.[4]

Shocking is your sin, wicked city. No battering ram broke your
walls; hunger did not overcome the soldiers; no sort of weapon
pierced them.[5] God's sanctuary it was that seduced you. This
sanctuary of God you have invaded and now possess. You have
become a den of thieves [Jer. 7 : 11; Mat. 21 : 13]. The enemies of
the human race, your friends, unmindful of virgins and of holy
marriage, unmindful of kinship and rank, even on holy days and in
holy places, have made of you a dreadful brothel. The altars of God
have been kicked over and have been dug up by hoes.[6] The resources
of the religious and the poor were laid open to plunder [7] and fire.
Return, return, [Song of Songs 6 : 13] O city, to the peace of the
churches and the unity of the kingdoms, you who are driving out
virtues and welcoming vices.[8]

TO THE GOOD CITIZENS

You who are the better part, if any are of God, return and be
separated as sheep from goats. We know the vanguard of the sinful
city, we know the followers among the ranks, whom we have patiently
endured up to this time though they should be struck down by the
divine sword. Since the sentence of condemnation has been promulgated [9] in accordance with divine laws, with the common consent of
all good men we are striking these men, now burdened by blindness
of mind and stupefied by the darkness of death.

This is Letter 79 in Havet.
1. Adalbero, son of Count Godfrey.

2. See Letter 53, n. 1, concerning Adalbero's consecration.

3. The biblical words are reversed here to mean that the Verdun church (the cultivated olive branch) was trying to break away from the universal church (the cultivated olive tree) in order to attach itself to an uncertain group (the wild olive tree) which could not nourish it.

4. Cf. Letter 70.

5. Gerbert and Adalbero deliberately ignore the strong resistance of the Verdun citizens to Lothair's prolonged siege of Verdun, from the middle of January to the middle of March, 985. Technically, Gerbert is correct. Previous to the siege of Verdun, Count Godfrey and the other leaders ordered their soldiers to stock the city with food, seized in the neighborhood, and they also requisitioned supplies from the merchants. With remarkable speed the Verduners had manufactured arms and had prepared defenses *within* the walls, but the final French attack was made by means of soldiers in a movable tower on wheels *outside* the walls. The Verdun soldiers attempted a defense in a similar but inferior tower and were defeated. See Richer (iii.civ-cvii) for a lively account of these events. Gerbert's letter indicates that the French were utilizing that favorite instrumentality of conquerors to win over the common people— a new land policy favoring those less fortunate, and here at the expense of the church.

6. The citizenry of Verdun resented the location of various altars because land convenient to their homes was thereby removed from cultivation. The altars themselves occupied only small bits of ground, but the surrounding land or property complex belonging to altars was often extensive. This land the citizenry seized by putting it under cultivation.

7. This indicates the importance of altars for ecclesiastical revenues.

8. Cicero *Tusculanae disputationes* v. 2.

9. Probably by Archbishop Egbert, since Verdun was in his archdiocese.

87. RHEIMS. June 1-15, 986

Agrees that a certain ecclesiastical irregularity is disgraceful; suggests that Ebrard write Abbot Mayeul

To Abbot Ebrard of Tours [1]

Not without cause are you disturbed and affrighted by the fact that where religious perfection ought to be the rule, criminal behavior is the highest point.[2] But who will be the instigator of this correction when all the prominent men of your order remain silent? We, indeed, have written a few words about these matters to the venerable Abbot Mayeul,[3] because we know him to be wise in comprehending many ideas expressed in a few words. For so great an undertaking and, speaking more exactly, to punish such great audacity, we have designated him as leader. Whichever one of us shall learn his decision shall inform the other without delay.

This is Letter 80 in Havet.

1. See Letter 50, n. 1.

2. A play on the words *summa* [peak] and *summum* [highest]. This letter is undoubtedly concerned with the question of Oylbold, deemed an intruder abbot at Fleury (Letters 76, 92-94).

3. Letter 76.

88. RHEIMS. June 18, 986
Urges Adso to come to Rheims by July 1st, and to bring along manuscripts

To Abbot Adso of Montier-en-Der [1]

End all delay,[2] my father, and depart from Ur of the Chaldees [3] either June 29th or 30th. Old friends, and especially those whose fidelity has long been tested, must comply. Our Adalbero, father of his country, always faithful to you, and now especially faithful and impatient of delays, desires your presence. It is not right to make known to an absent one those things which we wish to say to him when present. Let the volumes of books, very precious to you and to us, attend upon your journey.

This is Letter 81 in Havet.

1. Letter 15, n. 3.
2. Virgil *Aeneid* ix.13.
3. Genesis 11 : 31; 12 : 1. See also Letter 228. Havet, p. 74, n. 7, suggests that the emphasis is on the idea of a promised land. Bubnov, II, 372, n. 40, believes the words designate "hellish regions" or a "very disagreeable place," i.e., Montier-en-Der.

89. RHEIMS. August 1, 986
Expresses his pleasure over the fidelity of some of the Bobbio monks; hopes to be with them soon again; urges them to pray

[Gerbert to His Monks and Vassals at Bobbio]

Gerbert, if he is anything by the grace of God, sends hearty greetings to his beloved sons of Bobbio of both orders.[1]

You have done a worthy act and one thoroughly in accord with your name in seeking and visiting your father. You have thereby shown yourselves to be true sons. Thus, both for your attentiveness and for your constant fidelity towards me, I who am now absent from you feel duly grateful, and soon, God willing, present among you, I shall show it. Although I, 'tis true, am now almost in the harbor,[2] yet, indeed, I am disturbed that you are tossed about by the wicked waves. But we know God is all powerful, and we have confidence that, moved by the prayer of the poor, He will straightway bear aid to the afflicted.

This is Letter 82 in Havet. The same messenger carried Letters 89-91 to Italy.
1. Both monks and lay vassals of Bobbio. See Letter 23 which mentions Gerbert's faithful vassals at Bobbio, and Letters 22, 26, and 169 to faithful Bobbio monks.
2. Now that Margrave Hugh and Duke Cono exhibited concern about Bobbio (Letters 90 and 91), and apparently requested Empress Theophanu's presence in Italy, Gerbert was convinced that he would soon return to Bobbio. Letter 79 (reference to the recall by the imperial court); Böhmer, *Regesta imperii*, Vol. II, Pt. 3: *Regesten unter Otto III*, No. 1: *Bis 997* (new ed., M. Uhlirz), Nos. 986a, 986c. Uhlirz dates Letters 89-91 at Cologne, December 20, 986.

90. RHEIMS. August 1, 986
Expresses gratitude for Margrave Hugh's interest in him; begs him to aid Bobbio

To MARGRAVE HUGH [1]

Not without reason do we hold you in the highest esteem, exalting you and your followers with vows and praises, for you, though so busy, deem it worth while to have remembered me.[2] This we value especially, therefore and hence with the utmost confidence in you, we pray the more earnestly that your memory of us may not be destroyed. We are pouring forth such prayers as we, absent, are able that you may relieve the present exhausted circumstances of St. Columban [Bobbio].

This is Letter 83 in Havet.
1. Hugh, son of Hubert and husband of Juditt, margrave of Tuscany, 970-1001, and one of the chief supporters of the rule of the Ottos in Italy. He seems to have been a friend of Guarin of Cuxá. Letters 25, n. 6; 52.
2. Through the Bobbio monks (Letter 89) Gerbert must have received messages from Margrave Hugh, either oral or written.

91. RHEIMS. August 1, 986
Recommends himself to Margrave Cono of Ivrea; will be zealous to promote his fortune

To THE ITALIAN MARGRAVE CONO [1]

Although we do not deserve your favor by any merits of service, yet the virtue and nobility of your family and of yourself influence us to think well of you, and to hope for better things. And if humble persons can be of aid in very important matters our zeal for your honor will not be lacking as we participate in deliberations at a suitable place and time, where we will speak words in your favor in order that our mediocrity can rest under your wings [Ruth 2 :12; Ps. 17 : 8, 36 : 7, 57 : 1, 61 : 4, 63 : 7, 91 : 4] when fortune shall have smiled on you.[2]

This is Letter 84 in Havet.
1. Cono is a nickname for Conrad. He was the only son of King Berengar II (d. 966) of Italy to accept the Ottonian overlordship in northern Italy. Thus, the margravate of Ivrea (in the extreme northwest of Italy) was restored to him. Probably he is the same person as the "Cono" in Letter 211, and thus had become duke or count of Spoleto and administrator of Camerino before August, 996.
2. These words point to disturbed conditions in northern Italy, in spite of Empress Adelaide's presence in Pavia in 985-86.

92. RHEIMS. August 3-5, 986
Reports to Constantine Mayeul's decision about the intruder abbot; urges him to come to Rheims on August 17th with news and with manuscripts of Cicero

To CONSTANTINE THE TEACHER [1]

Discreetly and cleverly that well-known man of God [2] decided that the intruder [3] ought to be condemned, but he pointed out that the affair was outside his jurisdiction. He argued cautiously and prudently that that man was disreputable before he had received the insignia of office, that his patrons were impious, and that his bad name would be worse if he were deprived of the fellowship of the holy.

Therefore, hasten your journey and return to us on August 17th in order that we may be more fully informed in these matters, and, likewise, that you may rejoice in our censure of the intruder. May he who has thought you the filth in our nostrils feel that it was said of himself,[4] and may he shudder to find you redolent with the perfume of incense. Let the Tullian works accompany your journey,[5] both *De re publica* [6] and *In Verrem*, as well as the many *Orationes* which he, the father of Roman eloquence, wrote in the defense of many.

This is Letter 86 in Havet. The journey of Richer to Chartres in 991 (Richer iv.1) required four days so that at least another day would have been required to reach Fleury, near Orléans. Since Gerbert wished to see Constantine in Rheims on the 17th he must have written him from ten to fourteen days earlier than the 17th.

1. Letter 2, n. 1. Constantine was now the teacher at Fleury during the absence of Abbo in England.

2. Abbot Mayeul (Letters 76, 93).

3. Oylbold (Letter 76, n. 2).

4. Terence *Heauton Timorumenos* Prologue 30.

5. Martial xiv.clxxxviii.

6. Surely Gerbert is requesting Macrobius *Commentarii in Ciceronis Somnium Scipionis*, and the *Somnium Scipionis* itself which formed Book VI of Cicero *De re publica*. Gerbert's description of Cicero copies Macrobius ii.v.7. The only known manuscript of Cicero *De re publica* is a palimpsest now in the Vatican Library, that belonged to the Bobbio library in Gerbert's time. He gives no evidence of having read this underwriting, which is still legible.

93. RHEIMS. August 3-5, 986

Praises Mayeul's reprimand, but says it is too gentle; urges complete disassociation from the intruder

To Abbot Mayeul [1] in the Name of Archbishop Adalbero

Excellent, indeed, your exhortation against the intruder.[2] But, since it was written: And those thing Jesus began to do and teach,[3] why do you allege different jurisdictions, different regions of the heavens, in order to have intercourse with him whom you have decided is a criminal, when others have no communication with him?

The holy fathers opposed heresies, nor did they think that it was no concern of theirs to hear of anything evilly done anywhere. One Catholic Church there is, indeed, spread over the whole earth. These are your own words, nay rather, the words of the Holy Spirit through you: "He to whom this ambitious audacity does not become abominable will not be faithful to Christ." [4] You, therefore, abominate the intruder.

Let him feel that you do not favor him, that you have no intercourse with him, and that he is being beset not only by you and those clergy of your order but also, if it can be brought about, by the curses of the Roman pontiff. And because you have become acquainted with the affair as it [actually] was, and familiarized with it, have adjudged it according to the dignity of your name, we and all of our associates, like very faithful followers, will follow such a leader, and never without your order communicate with this intruder, proved wicked by so honorable a person.

This is Letter 87 in Havet.
1. See Letter 76, n. 1.
2. Oylbold of Fleury. Letters 76, 87, 92, 97.˙
3. Acts 1 : 1. The emphasis is on the fact that Jesus performed deeds as well as taught by words.
4. See Letter 97.

94. RHEIMS. August 20, 986

In replying to Ebrard's letter, Gerbert seeks a definite opinion about the intruder at Fleury; plans to have him removed from monastic society

To ABBOT EBRARD OF TOURS [1]

What weightiness of character is yours, how blameless the acts of your life,[2] how pure your eloquence, your letters have clearly shown. And so your devotion to piety and strictness, as well as that man [Mayeul] filled with God's Spirit, towards whom we maintain great fidelity, have influenced us to agree with your opinion. Thus, by the judgment[3] of such noted fathers, we shall be driving away that wicked one [Oylbold] from our society and that of our associates; and whoever shall try to say what ought not to be said against the decisions of the revered Father Mayeul and of the worshipful Father Ebrard we shall consider as an enemy. And, if, by a propitious Divinity, we shall secure the favor of the princes,[4] we shall add to these effective measures [still] more effective ones.

This is Letter 88 in Havet.
1. See Letters 50, n. 1; 87; and 97.
2. Horace *Odae* xx.1.
3. Bubnov, II, 383, n. 54, suggests that Ebrard wrote to the abbots of Rheims who met as a group, and that this present letter is a reply to him. They discussed the action they hoped to take against Oylbold, but decided to seek more definite and stronger condemnation from Mayeul and Ebrard, and then they will act as indicated in this letter.
4. Probably Count Eudes of Blois, since Fleury and Tours were in his territory, and Duke Hugh Capet, since Fleury was under his protection. Newman, *Domaine royal*, pp. 202, 205 (No. 5).

95. RHEIMS. September 15, 986

Not everyone agrees that Archbishop Adalbero's absence from Rheims is advisable; urges him to advise Count Godfrey to deal with Counts Eudes and Heribert

To ARCHBISHOP ADALBERO

The impossibility of ascertaining from popular opinion the best course of action characterizes troublous times. According to the opinion of many what you are doing is best. Many more think it better for you to remain in the city to hinder the small wicked band of thieves[1] not only by your presence but also by the number of your soldiers. They think that you ought to advise your brother [Godfrey] to listen to what Eudes and Heribert[2] wish since unexpectedly they are asking for an interview. Even if they are not to be trusted, perchance we might make use of them. Certainly, while they are fearful, their danger will extort from them what their trustworthiness would not.

This is Letter 93 in Havet.
1. Apparently some undisciplined troops of Louis V took advantage of Adalbero's absence in Lorraine, where he was accompanied by his own troops, to attack Rheims. See Letter 96.
2. Counts of Blois and Troyes, who still held Godfrey captive. Letter 96.

96. RHEIMS. October 5, 986
Renier has returned, urging Adalbero to meet the counts and Count Godfrey; plots are brewing so Adalbero should hasten his return

To the Same

On September 24th Renier[1] returned to Rheims from the mission, and he is about to undertake your business. His opinion is this, that if you wish to learn surely about your brother's fate, and this opinion must be told to no mortal but to you, meet your brother and the counts [Eudes and Heribert] on [October] 29th at Hautvillers.[2] Do not allow your nephew Herilo[3] nor any close relatives of your family to go away again.

A great undertaking is seriously being prepared. Fortify Mouzon and Mézières[4] on all sides with a large number of soldiers. Duke Conrad is plotting on behalf of his Otto,[5] but we shall find an easy remedy for this. The bishop of Laon [Ascelin] at the advice of Eudes and Heribert, who look with favor upon him, has gone to the duke [Hugh] in that place called Dourdan.[6]

Return, and let there be no delay.

This is Letter 94 in Havet. Its date is between Renier's return and the proposed meeting with Counts Eudes and Heribert. The Latin text does not give the month of this meeting, and so, presumably, it is the same month as that in which the letter was written. Otherwise, even the recipient, Archbishop Adalbero, would have been uncertain as to the month.

1. See Letter 103, n. 5.

2. MS V gives only *IIII kal.* (fourth day of the kalends) (see introductory note above). This letter is not in MS L. If the meeting was held it did not result in Count Godfrey's release from captivity. See Letter 103.

Hautvillers (dept. Marne) was an abbey in the diocese of Rheims, near Epernay, possibly in the district where Godfrey was imprisoned. See Letters 54, 57-59, 67, 95.

3. Diminuitive of the name Hermann, Count Godfrey's youngest son (and later count of Eenam).

4. Mouzon (dept. Ardennes), on an island formed by the Meuse River, southeast of Sedan; Mézières (dept. Ardennes), on a narrow isthmus of the Meuse River, twin city of Charleville, 50 miles northeast of Rheims. Both places were in Upper Lorraine. Their military importance is shown in Letter 103.

5. Cono (Conrad) was duke of Swabia, 983-97 (middle). (DO III 2, 4, 11, 32, 38, 61), and a loyal and powerful supporter of Otto III. M. Uhlirz, *Jahrbücher des deutschen Reiches unter Otto II. und Otto III*, Vol. II: *Otto III*, Index, s.v. "Konrad."

Otto was probably Count Otto of Worms. See Letter 35, n. 6; Uhlirz, p. 73.

6. Dept. Seine-et-Oise, arrondissement Rambouillet, part of the patrimony of Hugh Capet. Newman, *Domaine royal*, p. 135, lists it as a Capetian possession first under King Louis VI.

97. RHEIMS. October 10, 986

The abbots of Rheims, citing Abbot Mayeul's and Abbot Ebrard's letters, urge the monks of Fleury to separate themselves from their intruder abbot

To the Brothers of Fleury in the Name of the Abbots of Rheims [1]

Not without cause do we profess to be of one fraternity with you since your good fortune lifts our spirits up, and likewise in the estimation of noted men your misfortune humbles us. The wanton, detestable audacity of certain persons defiles this most holy association and chaste friendship while a faction places as father over you that man [2] whom the real fathers do not fear to condemn. And, since there is one Catholic Church and one society of all the faithful we have decided not to deviate from the opinions of those in the Church of God who, like the brightest stars, shine forth in everlasting eternity. Is not the venerable Father Mayeul [3] a very bright star? Or is not Father Ebrard [4] a gleaming star?

The former in a letter, sent recently to our venerable Father, Archbishop Adalbero, since his opinion was asked, states among other things, relative to the removal of your father: "The person, indeed, had already for some time been known to us for his infamous life, but was thought to be beyond hope of correction by a judgment of this sort." Likewise, in the same letter: "Therefore, as far as we are concerned, we have striven to encourage neighbors and companions in religion. If they are unable to eradicate this sin, they will brand him with infamy as one who should be deprived of the society of the blessed, nor will anyone be a faithful follower of Christ to whom this ambitious audacity does not become abominable.[5] We cannot approve of the things that have been done. What may happen we do not know."

The other declares and, at the same time referring to us, says: "No less does it burden us that that headship of the cloister which we believe stands at the height of religion while it functions under you,[6] yet, disagreeing with you, dares to judge us to be in error." And further: "For who dares to approve one puffed up by deceitful ambition since Father Benedict says 'all exaltation to be a kind of pride'?"[7] Likewise, at the end of the same letter: "If it does not seem foolish to you we will censure his appeal to us by shutting him out forever. Let the princes act and judge as they please. The favor or fear of worldly power will not turn us, the poor of Christ, from this opinion."

Hearken to these things, O companions and fellow servants of God. Ye sheep of Christ, separate yourselves from him who is not a shepherd, but a wolf, a destroyer of sheep. Let him claim for himself the kings, dukes, and princes of the world—he who by their favor alone has made himself the leader of the monks. Nor has he who out of humility ought to have refused it blushed at thrusting himself into this place. Let it suffice that up to the present we have gone astray through ignorance.[8] Let him who is condemned by the judgment of such fathers be deprived of our society. Then let him be united to us only when he has been reconciled by the sentence of those by whose judgment he is now deprived of communion with us.

This is Letter 95 in Havet.

1. This refers to the abbots of the diocese only, not of the whole archbishopric of Rheims, and may have included only those abbots in the immediate vicinity of the city of Rheims.

2. Oylbold. Letters 76, 87, 92-94, 151.

3. Abbot of Cluny. Letter 76.

4. Abbot of St. Julien of Tours. Letters 50, 87.

5. Letter 93.

6. The expression appears an exaggeration since Archbishop Adalbero exercised no jurisdiction over Fleury, nor did the abbots of Rheims have any control over Fleury. The implication here was that abbots assembled as a group possessed an authority over any other abbot. However, this was contrary to the Benedictine organization and to canon law. Their only authority was moral, expressed in their censure which, however, possessed no legal validity.

7. St. Benedict *Regula* vii. PL LXVI, 371.

8. Not all the abbots originally agreed to the censure.

98. RHEIMS. October 15, 986

Offers sympathy for the death of Abbot Gui, and his services in choosing a new abbot. Requests return of his books and the new manuscript being copied by Claudian

TO THE BROTHERS OF GHENT [1]

You who have adopted [2] me as your brother have caused us to feel your bereavement deeply. For, by his honorable services that man of venerable memory [3] kept us continually mindful of him. Therefore act, and quickly seek out a father worthy of yourselves lest the flock of the Master be restless without a shepherd. If need be, use our assistance, both advice and aid according to our abilities and knowledge.

Send back our books quickly. And, if you can send also the one that was to be copied by Claudian [4] it will be an act most worthy of you and of your kindness.

This is Letter 96 in Havet. Possibly it was written in Adalbero's name.

1. Letters 44, 111.

2. Gerbert (or Adalbero?) had thus been made a member of the confraternity of St. Peter of Ghent, though not of its actual monastery. He was thereby entitled to hospitality, aid, and comfort from the monastery, and especially to their prayers both in life and death. For his part, he was obligated to pray for the members of the monastery. Such spiritual associations between monasteries became customary by the end of the seventh century and soon thereafter individuals welcomed adoption into such confraternities. Gerbert's deep conviction of the efficacy of prayer was probably his strongest spiritual belief. U. Berlière, "Les fraternités monastiques et leur rôle juridique," Académie royale de Belgique, Classe des lettres—*Mémoires.* 2e sér., XI (1920), 4-19; J. Duhr, "La Confrérie dans la vie de l'Eglise," *Revue d'histoire ecclésiastique*, XXXV (1939), 436-78; W. Levison, *England and the Continent* (Oxford, 1946), pp. 101-2.

3. Abbot Gui (Letter 44).

4. Letter 111. Although these two letters indicate the existence of an important scriptorium at St. Peter of Ghent (Blandigny), only a portion of one manuscript, contemporary with Gerbert's time, has survived, a Vegetius in MS

Escorial L III 33. From an earlier period there are still extant a Glossary, an Antiphonary, a Collection of Canons, a Life of St. Amand, and a Martianus Capella. Lesne IV, 250-51, 653-54.

99. RHEIMS. December 15, 986

Offers his fidelity to Empress Theophanu; requests the return of some possessions to the monastery of St. Rémy; begs for information about the proposed peace with King Louis

To EMPRESS THEOPHANU IN THE NAME OF ADALBERO

If up to this moment I have honored you as my sovereign because of the merits of your most excellent august husband, ever to be remembered, now then, your own particular favors and those of your son cause our devotion to continue without interruption and greatly increase our fidelity towards you and yours. Among its especial treasures our church cherishes a gage of your affection toward us.[1] Therefore, if it is possible, may the blessed Remi experience[2] the favor of so great a lady, by receiving back his lost possessions[3] both on account of his merits and of our services rendered to you, if they are pleasing to you. Let us experience your already well established favor to the further extent that you regard it as fitting to inform us by messenger, or better, by letter, about the peace and the conditions of the peace to be made with our king [Louis V],[4] since we are prepared, as far as is right, to exhibit the most sincere fidelity in everything. So, indeed, we shall be better able to take counsel for the welfare of both of us.

This is Letter 85 in Havet. Archbishop Adalbero's thanks are apparently for the diploma for St. Rémy of Rheims, issued by Otto III, November, 29, 986. See Letter 35, n. 5; and M. Uhlirz, *Untersuchungen über Inhalt und Datierung der Briefe Gerberts*, pp. 73f.

1. See introductory note above.

2. An intense feeling for the joys and sorrows of a saint was woven into the fabric of the medieval mind. Gifts were made, not to the building which carried his name but to the saint himself.

3. M. Uhlirz *Untersuchungen* (see introductory note, above), p. 73, states that this refers to other property whose administration had been forcibly seized from St. Rémy of Rheims, or the Rheims cathedral.

4. Peace plans would concern Lorraine, and hence Archbishop Adalbero could anticipate the release of his brother Godfrey. The plans did not materialize. See Letter 103; and M. Uhlirz, *Jahrbücher des Deutschen Reiches unter Otto II. und Otto III*, Vol. II: *Otto III*, pp. 75-77, 79-81.

100. RHEIMS. January 2, 987
Queen Emma appeals to her mother, Empress Adelaide, for advice and aid to counteract the enmity of her own son, Louis V; suggests an alliance between the German princes, herself, and Counts Eudes and Heribert; and urges her to become more friendly with Empress Theophanu

To Her Mother in the Name of Queen Emma [1]

My sorrow has been increased, O my lady, O sweet name of mother. When I lost my husband there was hope for me in my son. He has become my enemy. My once dearest friends have withdrawn from me. They have fabricated the wickedest things against the bishop of Laon,[2] to my disgrace and that of my whole family. They persecute him and are trying to deprive him of his own office in order to brand me forever with everlasting disgrace, and thus furnish an excellent pretext for depriving me of my royal office.

Dear mother, be near to your daughter so full of sorrows. My enemies exult that I have not a brother, relative, nor friend left who can bring me aid. May my dear lady give ear to this: let your daughter-in-law [3] return to favor; may you soften her heart towards me. Would that I might be permitted to love her son [Otto III] since I look upon mine as an enemy. Join the princes of your kingdom to me; my alliance will profit them. Those very powerful counts, Eudes and Heribert, will join me in making plans with you. If possible, free yourself from cares in order that we may enjoy an interview together; if not, bring your customary wisdom to bear on this matter: prepare attacks against the French from an unexpected direction in order to blunt their menacing attack against us.[4] Meanwhile, indicate either by letter or by a very trustworthy messenger what we should do.

This is Letter 97 in Havet.

1. Queen Emma, no longer exercising royal power with her son, Louis V, and fearful of him, sought refuge in Rheims.

2. Ascelin. Letter 39, notes 7 and 9.

3. Empress Theophanu. Intermittent periods of unfriendliness existed between Theophanu and Adelaide. However, Adelaide was at the German court at the end of October, 986 (DO III 27, at Grone), and at Andernach, January 18, 987 (JL 3863). Perhaps she presented Emma's plea to the princes assembled at Andernach.

4. *Nos* according to the editions of Masson and of Duchesne, against *vos* [you] in MS V. This Letter is not in MS L.

101. RHEIMS. January 2, 987
Bishop Ascelin reminds the other bishops that his exclusion from his diocese is due to royal caprice, not to conviction for proved crimes; warns them against performing episcopal functions there

To the Bishops in the Name of the Bishop of Laon [1]

Although through the opposition of certain men [2] I have, for the present, been excluded from my own see by the royal power, yet I have not been deprived of the episcopal office. Nor do falsely alleged crimes condemn him whom a conscience, guiltless in this direction, does not torment. I pray, therefore, that my flock may feel the absence of its shepherd. Let me feel that you mourn my lot.

Likewise, I advise, I ask, I beg, I implore, and I conjure you through the terrible name of the ever-living Lord that you do not give holy unction to my church in any way through any person, nor perform the episcopal benediction and the rites of the mass in my diocese, because it is written: What you do not wish done to yourself, do not do to another [Tobias 4 : 16; Mat. 7 : 12; Luke 6 : 31]. But, if you despise divine and human laws and do not hearken to my warnings, then know that you will certainly be summoned to the larger hearing of ecclesiastical law as well as incur divine vengeance.

This is Letter 98 in Havet.
1. Ascelin (Adalbero). He, like Queen Emma (Letter 100, n. 1), had sought refuge in Rheims.
2. Duke Charles was undoubtedly among them.

102. RHEIMS. January 24-31, 987
Congratulates Raymond upon his election as abbot of Aurillac; is wearied by the turmoil of the life at Rheims; expects to lead an army into Saxony March 25th, and perhaps to Italy in the autumn if not used against King Louis; is uncertain about the organs in Italy; Otto III led a successful campaign against the Wends

To Raymond, Abbot of Aurillac [1]

Bereft of my illustrious Father Gerald [2] I do not seem to survive as a whole man. Since you, though, best beloved, agreeably to my wishes, have been made father, as your son I am reborn a whole man anew.

Not only do I rejoice at your honor, but Father Adalbero rejoices, while from his heart he offers himself and his possessions to you, and all the more sincerely, the more you shine with the light of religion and learning.

On account of my love for him, which he so well merits, I have spent almost three continuous years in France.[3] While I endure here the wrath of kings,[4] the disturbances of the people, and the disquiet of discordant kingdoms, I am so wearied that I am almost sorry I undertook the care of the pastoral office.[5] Furthermore, because my Lady Theophanu, ever august empress, orders me to depart into Saxony with her on March 25th, and because I have ordered[6] certain of my monks and knights from Italy to assemble there, I do not now know what to write for certain about the organs[7] located in Italy and about sending a monk there who shall learn and practice on them, especially since without the presence of my Lady Theophanu I dare not rely on the trustworthiness of my knights because they are Italians.[8]

Nor am I certain whether I shall lead the army[9] into Italy before autumn, or whether we shall delay in Germany in order to prepare as many troops as possible against Louis, king of the French, unless he shall have quieted down.[10] Events will soon show what sort he is and what should be thought of him, a person most disturbing to his friends but not very disturbing to his destructive enemies.

After peace[11] had been established between the leaders and the princes, the most illustrious offspring of Otto, the Caesar, of divine memory, last summer led the legions[12] of soldiers against the Sarmatians, called Wends in that language, and there, by his presence and by the strength of his soldiery, he captured, destroyed, and laid waste forty-six well fortified cities.

Adalbero, archbishop of Rheims, greets you, Ayrard,[13] and likewise all the associates of the cloister, and I, very devoted to you in everything, join him.

Again and again farewell.

This is Letter 91 in Havet.

1. Letters 23, n. 7; 51.

2. Letter 23, n. 1.

3. *Francia*, i.e., northern France, the region of the West Franks. Gerbert means three years since his arrival from Bobbio at the end of January, 984.

4. See Letter 59.

5. See also Letter 31.

6. Gerbert's letter containing this order does not appear in this Collection, and is not extant. The Germans did campaign against the Slavs east of the Elbe in 987. *Annales Hildesheimenses*, a. 987, MGSS III, 67.

7. Letter 77, n. 5.

8. Thietmar (vii.iii) mentions the mutual hatred of Italians and Germans, and adds that both in Rome and in Lombardy treason always prevails.

9. Cicero *De inventione* i.xvii, quoted by Cassiodorus *Institutiones* ii.ii.7.

10. See Letter 103.

11. Peace of Frankfort, July 2, 985. Letter 67, introductory note.

12. *Annales Hildesheimenses*, a. 986, MGSS III, 67. German armies were not organized as legions.

13. Letter 25, n. 5.

103. RHEIMS. February 15, 987

Gives details of King Louis's attack upon Rheims, and his ultimatum to Archbishop Adalbero; pleads for aid from Empress Theophanu; he is being accused of treason; Gerbert and Renier will meet her in Cologne; hopes to secure release of Count Godfrey

To Empress Theophanu and Her Son in the Name of Adalbero

In what full measure the wrath and fury of the king [Louis V] have burst forth against us is evidenced by his sudden and unexpected attack,[1] barely repulsed without great slaughter on both sides. Those who were trusted go-betweens ordered [us] to destroy the citadels belonging to us under your rule,[2] to take an oath conforming to their desire, or to withdraw from the city and the kingdom. They spoke of the divine august Otto's kindness, exhibited to us in bygone years, and of our intimacy and obedience to him.[3] The situation, at present, menaces our very safety.

We beg you to bring definite aid to us, therefore, at this uncertain time, permitting no false hope to delude us who never have hesitated in maintaining our fidelity to you.

At a meeting of the French, planned for March 27th, we are to be accused of the crime of treason [4] because we gave the bishop of Verdun permission to leave [Rheims]; and, to make the matter impossible, they are requiring us to bring him back [here]. If this should happen, Gerbert and Renier,[5] faithful to you and to us, will not be able to meet you at Nijmwegen as you desired, but they will meet you at Cologne whither they are about to go soon, as quickly as

Your Clemency may provide a suitable escort for them for the journey.

On February 28th we expect to talk with Counts Eudes and Heribert and, moreover, after receiving hostages, we shall attend to the matter of restoring my brother [Godfrey] to your service.

By what dangers we are oppressed on account of the fidelity that we have maintained toward you and always will we have indicated in a few words. We look forward with a firm faith to saving aid from you, and we beseech you that this [letter] may be kept from the enemy lest they be fired with fiercer anger against us.

This is Letter 89 in Havet.
Empress Theophanu was at Andernach (on the Rhine, northeast of Coblenz) on January 18th (DO III 32), and at Nijmwegen (in the northwest extremity of Lower Lorraine, now The Netherlands) on February 27th (DO III 33). Adalbero knew her immediate plans, perhaps through the monk Adelard of St.-Rémy who secured a diploma from Otto III at Duisburg, November 29, 986 (DO III 28), so this letter was undoubtedly written just in time to reach her before she departed for Nijmwegen, probably on the 21st. Hence, the date of the letter probably was February 15th.
1. Richer (iv.iii-v) gives the details.
2. Probably Mouzon and Mézières (Letter 96). Church possessions by no means followed national boundaries.
3. During Otto II's rapid campaign in northern France in 978 (Letter 83, n. 4) Archbishop Adalbero welcomed Otto to Rheims, even furnishing him guides. Richer iii.lxxiv; iv.ii.
4. See Letter 64 which is a defense against such a charge, made previously by King Lothair.
5. Probably the same person mentioned in Letters 9, 66, 96, 136, 149, and 150, but not the Vidame Renier of Rheims as stated by Bubnov (II, 143, n. 29; 389, n. 68) since at the present time Louis V held Vidame Renier as a hostage from Archbishop Adalbero. Richer iv.iv.

104. RHEIMS. February, 987?
DISTICH ON A CHALICE [1]

Flee hence, hunger and thirst; [2] hasten, ye faithful.

Adalbero the priest divides these treasures among the people.

VERSE FOR GIFTS

Virgin Mary, [3] your priest Adalbero offers a gift to you.

This is Letter 90 in Havet.
1. See Lesne, III, 223-25, regarding chalices.
2. Possibly an indication that communion in both bread and wine was given to the faithful at this period. Havet, p. 82, n. 1.
3. Rheims cathedral was dedicated to the Virgin Mary.

105. RHEIMS. March 1, 987
*Force, not law and right, prevail in France and Italy; describes
a rhetorical chart he constructed; recommends Constantine of
Fleury for teaching rhetoric, music and organ-playing*

To Monk Bernard [1]

You ask, dearest brother, what things and what sort of things I am
doing and whether they are advantageous or disadvantageous. I doubt
whether I can comply with this division in a few words because, to
one examining these matters more profoundly, there seem to be no
happenings, or if there are any, they carry with them mainly dis-
advantages. First of all, as to what is being done in public affairs,
there is rashness at present. Certainly, divine and human laws are
there confused because of the enormous avarice of wicked men, and
that alone that passion and force extort, is deemed right, after the
manner of wild beasts.

In private affairs, however, I discover that although oppressed by
no misfortune I have abandoned friends in adversity. I leave to others'
judgment whether it be worth remembering that I departed from Italy
in order not to be forced, in any manner whatsoever, to bargain
with the enemies of God and of the son of my seigneur, Otto [II] of
divine memory; or that, meanwhile, I offer to noble scholars the
pleasing fruits of the liberal disciplines to feed upon.

Furthermore, when autumn was over, out of love for them I
constructed a certain table of the rhetorical art, arranged on twenty-
six sheets of parchment fastened together in the shape of an oblong,[2]
made of two sheets by thirteen sheets— a work truly wonderful for
the ignorant, and useful for the studious for comprehending the
fleeting and very obscure [3] materials of the rhetoricians and for fixing
them in the mind.

Therefore, if anyone of you is moved by an interest in such things,
as well as in the learning of music [4] and the playing of organs [5] I will
see to it that what I am unable to finish myself will be completed by
Constantine of Fleury, if I may know the definite wish of Lord Abbot
Raymond to whom I owe everything. For the former is an excellent
teacher, especially learned, and very closely joined to me in friendship.

Farewell, sweetest brother; always enjoy my love which is equal to
thine, and consider my goods to be for both of us.

This is Letter 92 in Havet.

1. Monk of Aurillac, and later, apparently, abbot of St. Martin of Tulle (Corrèze), near Aurillac. Olleris, p. 526; and Havet, p. 84, n. 2.

2. Neither this chart nor any probable copies have survived.

3. Boethius, *De arithmetica*, Praefatio.

4. *Musica*, i.e., theoretical music, the second study in the quadrivium.

5. *Vel in his quae fiunt ex organis*, literally, "and in these things that are made out of organs." This strongly suggests the new technique—finger action—for playing the organ that developed at this time, perhaps originating with Gerbert. Previously the whole hand was used to pull the keys. W. Apel, "The Early History of the Organ," *Speculum*, XXIII (1948), 215-16; and Letters 77, 102, 171.

106. RHEIMS. March 15, 987

Archbishop Adalbero will answer Bishop Hervé's letters in person at the approaching conference; appreciates the attention he is giving to Adalbero's affairs

TO [THE BISHOP OF] BEAUVAIS [1] IN THE NAME OF ARCHBISHOP ADALBERO

We consider it unnecessary at present to answer your letters since, according to our small ability, we shall be able to satisfy you more accurately concerning each matter at the conference which has been announced.[2] We value especially the fact that out of love for us you are neglecting your own affairs and are giving our business careful attention, and we are treasuring it in our memory and mind. You, who will be rewarded, would furnish us no less benefits if faithless fortune should turn about.

This is Letter 99 in Havet.

1. Hervé, 987-97. Gams, *Series episcoporum*, p. 511. See also Letters 195 and 203.

2. Probably the meeting of March 27, 987. Letter 103; Bubnov, II, 412, n. 101.

107. RHEIMS. April 22, 987

Gerbert's long and hasty journey prevented his stopping in Cologne; he enjoyed meeting Folmar; a preliminary peace meeting was held at Compiègne without the knowledge of Empress Theophanu, who desires Everger to learn the conditions; Adalbero and he will attend the meeting of the French

TO ARCHBISHOP EVERGER OF COLOGNE [1]

Burdened by the number of cares incident to a hasty mission as well as worn out by the great length of the journey,[2] we were not able, to our great sorrow, to have the desired meeting with you. But we were refreshed by the presence of the worthy man Folmar,[3] in [the choice of] whom your wisdom is shown, while now we are making use of this servant to fulfill satisfactorily the master's wish even though he was not instructed. Not only because of this fact but also because of our Lord Adalbero's great affection for you, we have been occupied, therefore, in service for you.

Above all, he wished you to share the information which we here relate. On March 29th, at the palace at Compiègne the duchess Lady Beatrice arranged that King Louis, Queen Emma, and Duke Hugh should meet the empress Lady Adelaide and Duke Conrad[4] on May 25th at Montfaucon[5] for the purpose of negotiating a peace. But, because this arrangement was made without the knowledge of the ever august empress Lady Theophanu, we, realizing that there might be a trick concealed in this, advised that peace should be made rather through her and that beforehand she should learn through you what the conditions of peace would be. This has been approved, and the companions for your journey have been designated. On May 18th we must go to a conference[6] of the French, and there, if our lord [Archbishop Adalbero] shall have made peace with the king, he will work hard for the peace of the kingdoms. It is enough to have suggested a few things to Your Great Intelligence.

Furthermore, as to the land that is being forcefully taken from you in our region,[7] we advise silence for the present; afterwards we shall point out what you ought then to do.

This is Letter 101 in Havet.

1. Archbishop of Cologne, 985-June 10, 999. A. Goldschmidt, *German Illumination* (New York, 1928), II, Plate 80, reproduces a miniature showing Everger, from MS Cologne 143, fols. 3r-4, a *Lectionary* which Everger gave to Cologne cathedral. See also Letter 112 and Lesne, IV, 284-86, 696.

2. Gerbert hastened to Saxony only after the March 29th conference mentioned below, perhaps to Allstedt, and probably met his contingent of knights and monks from Bobbio (Letter 102). The dangerous political situation impelled him to return hurriedly to France instead of remaining to lead his military force against the Wends.

3. Parisot, *Origines de la Haute Lorraine*, p. 370. and M. Uhlirz, *Untersuchungen über Inhalt und Datierung der Briefe Gerberts*, p. 85, n. 53, suggest he was a lay vassal of Everger, a count of Bliesgau, Lunéville, and Amance, later father-in-law of Duke Thierry of Upper Lorraine. This identification with a lay vassal seems to be confirmed by Gerbert's use of the word *spectabilis* (worthy) which appears in Justinian's Digest as a title of high officials.

Or he might have been the Folmar who became abbot of St. Maximin of Trier at the end of October, 987. A. Goerz, I, 313, No. 1096; Bubnov, II, 416, n. 109.

4. Duke of Swabia. Letter 96, n. 5; Havet, p. 94, n. 2; Bubnov II, 413, n. 105.

5. Montfaucon-d'Argonne (Meuse), near Verdun, a Benedictine abbey of the diocese of Rheims.

6. Perhaps at Compiègne where Louis V died on May 21st or 22d, after being injured while hunting near Senlis. Richer IV.v. This conference had been postponed from March 27th (Letter 103).

7. Letter 112.

108. NEAR LIÉGE? June 10, 987
Warns Archbishop Adalbero to beware of treachery in dealing with Counts Eudes and Heribert

To Archbishop Adalbero

Consider whether you ought to look forward to conferences with Eudes and Heribert with no misgivings, or with caution lest new plans filled with new treacheries be prepared against you from all sides, especially because of the present siege of Chèvremont.[1] Be mindful of the fate of Wicfrid, bishop of Verdun,[2] on the occasion of the assault on the fortress of Luxemburg.

This is Letter 102 in Havet. Between the dates of Letters 107 and 108 King Louis V had died without an heir, and Duke Hugh Capet had been chosen, but not crowned, king (See introduction, p. 9). Gerbert writes this letter as he is returning from an interview with Empress Theophanu relative to the French kingship.

1. The captors of the castle of Chèvremont had devastated the contiguous countryside, which was visible from the city of Liége. The inhabitants of Chèvremont appealed to Bishop Notker, who not only captured but also destroyed the castle. Anselm *Gesta episcoporum Leodicensium,* MGSS VII, 203; Bubnov II, 426, n. 125; Johnson, *German Episcopate,* pp. 123-25.

2. 962-August 31, 983. The soldiers of Count Siegfried I of Luxembourg (Archbishop Adalbero's uncle) surprised and captured Wicfrid at Vandressel (dept. Meuse), and the count held him prisoner. *Gesta episcoporum Virdunensis continuatio,* iii, MGSS IV, 46.

109. RHEIMS. June 20 or 21, 987
Count Godfrey was released from prison only after the exaction of harsh conditions; prays Empress Theophanu to prevent the execution of these promises; warns her of a plot to capture her at Chèvremont; will carry out her desires indicated through Gerbert

To the Empress Lady Theophanu in the Name of Archbishop Adalbero

A certain light seemed to shine to your honor on June 17th when my brother [Godfrey] was freed from the darkness of the infernal regions. But one must work diligently lest by the blind fire of desire Counts Eudes and Heribert should contaminate this light. Therefore, pray hear with kindness the just and honest petitions of my brother, not only because of his own worth but also because of your kindness to me. By a careful plan you will nullify the unjust promises that the tyrant [1] unreasonably extorted, destructive to the Church of God and bringing shame to your kingdom.

You will not, will you, forever alienate from the church the villages belonging to the bishop of Verdun which Count Godfrey reluctantly gave as a pledge for his ransom, an agreement acquiesced in by his son Bishop Adalbero? You will not, will you, allow the forts in those places to be destroyed at the wish of those who now are bringing together secret troops of chosen soldiers in order to make an attack on you if you should be at Chèvremont? [2] For they pretend that they are invading the town of Juvigny [3] because Duke Thierry [4] assailed the town of Stenay as if taking vengeance on the queen, [5] but they will commit this crime if they feel that you have [only] a small band [of soldiers] with you. Since I have a mind solicitous for you in every detail, I have related these facts, and am about to carry out faithfully whatever desires you have indicated through Gerbert, most faithful to you and requesting that this task be given to him, namely, that he be your truest interpreter.

This is Letter 103 in Havet. Adalbero had just received news of Count Godfrey's release from prison on June 17, 987. Gerbert and Empress Theophanu had already discussed the return of Verdun to the German kingdom as the price of her support of Hugh Capet. Here Archbishop Adalbero urges her to include the cancellation of Godfrey's pledge to Count Heribert (n. 2 below) in her demands.

1. Count Heribert? His possessions, such as Vertus and Vitry, were closer to Verdun than those of Count Eudes of Blois. See Lot, *Hugues Capet*, p. 194. The fact that Heribert was taking property from the church justified the epithet "tyrant."

2. See Letter 108.

3. Juvigny-sur-Loison (dept. Meuse), possibly belonging to Empress Theophanu. Lot, *Hugues Capet*, p. 497. On p. 195, Lot suggests that Heribert and Eudes were feigning the attack in order to capture Theophanu.

4. Of Upper Lorraine.

5. Dowager Queen Emma was the only queen at the time of this letter. Stenay (dept. Meuse) in Lower Lorraine, close to the borders of France, apparently belonged to Queen Emma.

110. RHEIMS. August 1, 987

Comments of Archbishop Adalbero on the materials he is sending Egbert to complete an artistic object

To Archbishop Egbert in the Name of Archbishop Adalbero

We are sending materials designed for the intended work.[1] A brother for a brother, a sister for a sister,[2] will complete the admirable shape which will be a feast for both the mind and the eyes. Your exceptional and famous talent will ennoble our mean material not only through the addition of glass[3] but also by the skillful design of a fine artist.

This is Letter 104 in Havet.

1. Apparently a cross which had been made at Rheims, but which an artist at Trier was to decorate (n. 3 below) according to an artistic design of his own. See Letters 113 and 134. On artistic activity in Trier at this time see A. Haseloff, *Das Psalter Erzbischof Egberts von Trier in Cividale* (Trier, 1900), p. 145; A. Goldschmidt, *German Illumination* (New York, 1928), II, 4ff.; and Lesne III, 183f.

2. Egbert for Adalbero, the church of Trier for the church of Rheims. "From ancient times it has been clear that these two churches have been especially linked together and are said to be sisters." *De rebus Treverensis Libellus*, MGSS XIV, 102. See also Letter 177.

3. Either enamel or small bits of cut glass. The setting of the latter in gold was a particular accomplishment of Trier artists. O. von Falke, "Die Klosterkunst des 10. und 11. Jahrhunderts," *Illustrierte Geschichte des Kunstwerkes*, Vol. I (Berlin, 1907), Chap. VIII.

See Richer III.xxii-xxiii, as to Adalbero's restoration of Rheims cathedral about the year 976, and the additions of objects of artistic beauty, among which was a portable altar with golden crosses.

111. RHEIMS. August 15, 987

Archbishop Adalbero reprimands the monks of St. Peter of Ghent for not forwarding his manuscripts

To the Brothers of Ghent in the Name of Archbishop Adalbero

How long will you abuse our patience,[1] whom once we believed to be the most faithful of friends? You, though prepared to practice robbery, make a pretense of love with your words. Why do you shatter our sacred association? Of your own accord you offered us certain manuscripts but, contrary to divine and human laws, you are retaining those that are rightfully ours and our church's.[2] Either friendship will be renewed by the restitution of the books with that one added[3] or the illegal retention of those entrusted to your care will be justly and deservedly punished.

This is Letter 105 in Havet.

1. Cicero *In Catilinam* i.i.1.

2. Frequently a monastery or church, desiring to borrow one or more manuscripts, would send one or more of its own manuscripts to the lender as security.

3. Letter 98. The additional manuscript was probably the one copied by Claudian.

112. RHEIMS. September 1, 987

Verdun has been peaceably restored to the German kingdom. Attention is now being given to restoration of the property of the church of Cologne; urges the excommunication of Dudo and Count Sigibert; requests recent news of Empress Theophanu and of the Saxon army's expedition

To ARCHBISHOP EVERGER [1]

How much good the firmly established peace between our kings [2] has bestowed or is about to bestow upon the state, the witness is the city of Verdun restored [3] as a whole to your realm without slaughter and bloodshed, without hostages, without money. Cologne will [also] be a witness by the restoration of its long withheld property.[4] Assuredly, this would have been carried out more quickly except for the fact that recently the more pressing business of the kingdoms in bringing about peace detained us longer, due to the perverse habits of certain of our men.

And so, having found an opportune time, we are now giving attention to your service. We urge that Dudo [5] and Count Sigibert, violators of the property of your church, be excommunicated without delay. Let your friend Adalbero, archbishop of Rheims, be advised in brotherly fashion as to Dudo, and Gui,[6] bishop of Soissons, as to Sigibert, in order that they may not allow sons of their churches to injure you with impunity, and that they may excommunicate those excommunicated by you until those persons who have attempted to possess the sanctuary of the Lord for themselves [Ps. 82 : 13] obtain indulgence from you by a suitable reparation.

What our ever august empress, Lady Theophanu, is to do in public affairs in the future, or in what places she will stop, and whether the army of the Saxons has returned as victor from the usual enemy,[7] we ask to be told in full faith, prepared as we are to hear of your adversity or that of your followers with sad countenance, or to receive and make known your prosperity with most joyful spirit.

This is Letter 100 in Havet. The reference to the Slavic campaign indicates a date at the end of the summer.
1. See Letter 107.
2. Otto III and Hugh Capet (Letters 108, introductory note; 109, introductory note).
3. Introduction, p. 10; Letters 53ff.; 109, introductory note.
4. Property of unknown location in the dioceses of Rheims and Soissons.
5. See Letter 145. Dudo was a vassal knight of Count Heribert III of Troyes, and became a vassal of Duke Charles of Lower Lorraine. In August, 989, by Dudo's connivance the city of Rheims was betrayed into Charles's hands. *Acta concilii S. Basoli*, Chap. XI, in Olleris, p. 181; Richer IV,lxii; Lot, *Derniers Carolingiens*, pp. 235, n. 3; 234; 407.
6. December, 972-995. Gams, *Series episcoporum*, p. 633. See also Letters 174, 195.
7. The Wends. *Annales Hildesheimenses*, a. 987, MGSS III, 67.

113. **RHEIMS.** October 1, 987
Announces a journey to worship St. O., and requests the send-ing of the completed cross to Verdun on November 1st

To EGBERT, ARCHBISHOP OF TRIER

The fact that we do not enjoy your long hoped for counsel we bear with an insufficiently patient mind. We are still insisting on this and are striving to prevail over tumultuous events. According to report a synod has been convoked in the region of the Rhine, but the rather serious ailments of our bishops and also the royal affairs both are postponing this synod which we likewise desired.

In order not to grow stiff from leisure, however, we intend, at present, to seek the favors of St. O.[1] Thence we are arranging our return through your region in order to correct our long continued separation by such a meeting. And, because our route lies through Verdun,[2] on November 1st, send thither, if possible, the cross, im-proved as we hope, by your skill; and let this be a pledge of our friendship. Thus, my indissoluble love will be increased from day to day [3] whenever this work of art meets my eyes.

This is Letter 106 in Havet.
1. *Beati O.* Probably St. Otmar, abbot of St. Gall (d. 759), whose translation was October 25th (*L'Art de verifier les dates*, II [Paris, 1818], 89), or October 28th (Giry, *Manuel de diplomatique*, p. 303), although his feast was celebrated November 16th.

2. Apparently Adalbero planned to traverse the Roman road from Rheims to Verdun, Metz, Savern, and Strasbourg, listed by the Itinerary of Antonine (2d-4th cent.), and used by Charlemagne. To go to St. Gall, Adalbero would then have continued on another Roman road to Augst near Basel, and on to Windisch. Havet, p. 98, n. 3; Holland, *Traffic Ways*, p. 36.

3. I follow the punctuation of MS V, against that of MS L.

114. COMPIÈGNE? October 3, 987
King Hugh Capet demands an oath of allegiance from Archbishop Siguin

To Archbishop Siguin [1] in the Name of King Hugh

Wishing to misuse the royal power towards no one, we are managing all the affairs of state in accordance with the advice and opinion of faithful followers, and we judge that you are most worthy to be one of them. Accordingly, with sincere and kindly affection, we advise that before November 1st you pledge that fidelity [2] which others have pledged to us on account of the peace and harmony of the Sacred Church of God and of all Christian people.

Lest, by chance, through the persuasion of certain wicked persons, you hear that you ought to act less diligently (and this we hope not), you should bear in mind the harsher censure of the lord pope,[3] and of the bishops your compatriots; and remember that our clemency, well known to everyone, may change to just zeal for correcting delicts by our royal power.

This is Letter 107 in Havet. Hugh Capet's palace was at Compiègne, where he issued a diploma on September 26, 987. Lot, *Hugues Capet*, p. 231, n. 1; Newman, *Domaine royal*, p. 103.

1. Archbishop of Sens, January, 977-October 17, 999. He was the only important French prelate who, continuing to adhere to the Carolingians and the hereditary principle, refused to recognize Hugh Capet as king of the French. He did not attend Hugh's coronation. Richer iv.xii; A. Fliche, "Séguin archevêque de Sens primat des Gaules et de Germanie 977-999," *Bulletin de la société archéologique de Sens*, XXIV (1909), 149-206, especially 171-81; A. Fliche, "Les Sources de l'historiographie Senonaise au XIe siècle," *Bulletin de la société archéologique de Sens*, XXIV (1909), 19-62. Cf. Lot, *Hugues Capet*, pp. 41-42.

2. On oaths of fidelity see Odegaard, "Carolingian Oaths," *Speculum*, XVI (1941), 284ff.

3. Hugh here recognizes the coercive power that the papacy had long claimed and that had been employed in 948 even against a layman, Hugh's own father—Hugh the Great. In 942, Pope Stephen VIII threatened the French nobility, rebelling against Louis IV, with excommunication. In 947, Agapetus II anathematized Louis IV's enemies and urged his supporters to remain faithful. Flodoard *Annales*, ed. P. Lauer (Paris, 1905), a. 942, 947, 948; Flodoard *Historia*

ecclesiae Remensis iv.xxxvii (MGSS XIII, 590); Richer ii.xxvii, xcv-xcvi; JL 3618, 3619, 3620, 3638, 3639; Lot, *Hugues Capet,* pp. 140-41.

115. ON THE ROAD TO TRIER. October 18, 987
Archbishop Adalbero's journey has been interrupted by floods so he plans to seek Trier

To the Same Archbishop Egbert

Every sort of difficult happening having hindered us from the journey that we had begun,[1] we feel that a haven of safety ought to be sought. For, continual torrents are in possession of the slopes of the mountains.[2] Ever flowing waters so clothe the fields that, with villages and their inhabitants submerged and the herds destroyed, they bring terror of a renewal of the Flood. The hope for better weather has been shattered by the physicists.[3] Accordingly, we are fleeing to you just as Noah to the Ark, and with every effort we are trying to visit Trier whither we are about to bring the marks of veneration to honor St. Peter,[4] prince of the apostles, [an act] which the force of circumstances made impossible in the case of St. O[tmar?].

This is Letter 109 in Havet. The *Annales Colonienses,* a. 987 (MGSS I, 99), corroborate Adalbero's information about this flooding of the Rhine and Moselle valleys. Prevented from continuing on to the shrine of St. O., Adalbero thought it safer to go to Trier than to try to return to Rheims and so sent this letter on ahead of him, perhaps from Metz. His vivid description indicates that he was an eyewitness to the floods. Apparently, Gerbert accompanied him, acting as usual as his secretary.

1. I follow here MS V instead of MS L.
2. Though following the upland and thus avoiding the longer river crossings of the valleys, these roads could not escape a devastating flood.
3. *A phisicis,* i.e., those who deal with the science of nature—in this case, meteorology—or natural philosophy. Clagett, "Some General Aspects of Physics in the Middle Ages," *Isis,* XXXIX (1948), 29-30.
4. The cathedral of Trier was dedicated to St. Peter. Havet, p. 100, n. 5.

116. RHEIMS. November 15, 987
Circular letter summoning the bishops of the Rheims diocese to a meeting

To the Suffragan [Bishops of Rheims]

Since we are about to discuss many matters relative to the state of the churches of God and many questions of public and private affairs,[1] we affectionately invite you with your brother bishops of our diocese [to attend a synod] not so much for the sake of our office and benefit as for yours. The place of speaking, Mont-Notre-Dame of Tardenois.[2] The time, December 17th.

Farewell.

This is Letter 110 in Havet.

1. The public affairs probably included the attitude of Archbishop Siguin; the private affairs, the case of the priest Hidilo (Letter 118).

2. "Mont-Notre-Dame (Aisne) in the ancient district of Tardenois (Longnon, *Études sur les pagi*, II, 99) and in the ancient diocese of Soissons, near the boundaries of those of Rheims and of Laon." Havet, p. 101, n. 1. Here was held an important council in 972.

117. RHEIMS. December 1, 987

Archbishop Adalbero congratulates the abbot of Marmoutier on the restoration of the cell of St. Martin; sends greetings from Osulf

ARCHBISHOP ADALBERO TO THE ABBOT OF MARMOUTIER [1]

The season changes,[2] and the good land, long barren through no fault of its own, brings forth marvelous flowers and fruits. For, behold, the little cell [3] of the blessed Martin revives the host of monks, long dead up to now. The goodness of Martin is observable in his disciples, and we rejoice to have received an alumnus of this blessed conversion, Osulf [4] by name, an exemplar, one might say, of his life and habits. We send his holy love to be joined with your compassion in order that he who struggles in single strife with the ancient enemy may come forth victor, protected by the shield of your prayers. Also, through your merits lighten our burdens for us, weighed down as we are by our sins.

This is Letter 189 in Havet. Mayeul undertook the restoration of the monastery of Marmoutier near Tours after Hugh Capet's coronation (July 3, 987) by re-introducing monks there in place of the secular clerics who occupied the monastery.

1. Mayeul of Cluny (Letter 76). Guilbert (Guislebert) succeeded him at an unknown date. Havet, p. 175, n. 1. Marmoutier belonged to King Hugh and his forbears (although it is not recorded by Newman, *Domaine royal*) and Hugh ceded it to Count Eudes I of Blois. Lot, *Hugues Capet*, pp. 177-78; 188, n. 3.

2. Horace Odae IV.vii.3.

3. *Cellula*. This should mean a dependent "cell" or "priory," such as the near-by St.-Martin-du-Val. However, only children up to ten years of age were taught in the latter place, whereas Osulf was an adult. Lesne, V, 146.

4. Letter 144, n. 3.

118. RHEIMS. December 20, 987
Requests Egbert to free the priest Hidilo from the ban of ex-communication until the hearing of his case; requests the sending of a Sacramentary in addition to his books

To Egbert in the Name of Adalbero

Although we intend to reciprocate your favors in due time, yet a holy bond of friendship assumes that these very favors will be multiplied. Therefore, pray permit Hidilo, my brother's priest, to be free from the ban of excommunication until after his case has been discussed in the next synod which will either return him innocent or will release us from a wrongful request.

Furthermore, permit the person chosen to carry back our books to bring with him a Sacramentary very handsomely decorated in gold. For this we shall, indeed, write back as quickly as possible some words which will please you, and to the same bearer we shall entrust a volume in no way inferior.

This is Letter 108 in Havet.

119. RHEIMS. January 10, 988
King Hugh requests a Byzantine princess as the bride for his son, King Robert

[To Emperors Basil and Constantine in the Name of King Hugh]

To the Orthodox Emperors, Basil and Constantine,[1] from Hugh, by the grace of God, king of the French.

Not only the nobility of your race but also the glory of your great deeds urges and compels us to love you. You seem, indeed, to be such preeminent persons that nothing in human affairs can be valued more highly than your friendship. We are seeking this most holy friendship and most fitting alliance in such a way that we are asking in it neither kingdoms nor your resources; but this arrangement will make yours whatever is rightfully ours. Of great use, will be this union with us if it pleases you, and great fruits will it bear. For, with us in opposition neither a Gaul nor a German [2] will harass the territory of the Roman empire.[3] To carry out these advantageous plans on a permanent basis we therefore seek with especial desire a daughter of the holy empire,[4] because we have an only son, himself a king,[5] for whose marriage we can furnish no one equal to him, because of his kinship with the neighboring kings.

If these requests shall have pleased your most serene ears, inform us either by [sacred?] imperial letters [6] or by trusty messengers, in order that through our own ambassadors, worthy of the majesty of your rank, there may be completed by acts what shall have been set forth in letters.[7]

This is Letter 111 in Havet. It was written immediately after Robert's consecration at Orléans on December 30, 987. There is no reason to suppose with Havet (p. 102, n. 2) and Vasiliev ("Hugh Capet of France and Byzantium," *Dumbarton Oaks Papers*, VI, 227-51) that this letter was merely a creation of Gerbert's wishful thinking and without royal sanction, or that it was never sent. P. Schramm, "Kaiser, Basileus und Papst," *Historische Zeitschrift*, CXXIX (1924), 445. Hugh Capet must have been impressed by Otto I's persistence and success in securing a Byzantine princess, Theophanu, for Otto II, and by her ability at ruling exhibited after the death of her husband. Hugh probably met her in Rome in 981 (Richer III.lxxxiv), and Gerbert's high regard for her certainly influenced Hugh.

1. Sons of Romanos II and Theophanu (not the German empress). See Appendix A.

2. Subjects of Otto III on both sides of the Rhine.

3. Since there was no Roman emperor in the West at this time, Gerbert could use this term without reservation.

4. At this time there were four available Byzantine princesses who were *porphyrogennetae* [literally, "born in the purple marble room" of the palace]: Anna (b. 963), daughter of Romanos II and Theophanu, who married Vladimir, prince of Kiev, in the early autumn of 989; and the three daughters of Constantine VIII and Helen, named Eudoxia, Zoë (born in 978 or 980, and later betrothed to Otto III), and Theodora. The latter two became empresses of Byzantium. Michel Psellos, *Chronographie, ou Histoire d'un siècle de Byzance (967-1077)*, ed. and trans. E. Renauld, I (Paris, 1926), 23ff.

At least seven earlier precedents of attempts at Byzantine-Western marriages are known from 765 on: the effort of Emperor Constantine V (Copronymus, 741-75) to secure the betrothal of his son and Guisla, daughter of Pippin (H. Pirenne, *Mohammed and Charlemagne* [1939], p. 227); plans for the marriage of Charlemagne's daughter, Rotrud (Hruotut) to Constantine VI (*Annales Laurissenses maiores*, MGSS I, 32; Duckett, *Alcuin*, pp. 79, 93, 101, 137f., 184f.); the attempt to marry a Byzantine princess to Louis II, son of Lothar I, in return for German assistance in Asia Minor; the betrothal of Hadwig, daughter of Duke Henry I of Bavaria and niece of Otto I, with a Byzantine prince; the marriage of Bertha, daughter of King Hugh of Italy to Romanos II in 944; and the carefully formulated but unsuccessful plans of the Roman Prince Alberic (d. 955) to secure a Byzantine princess as a bride. B. A. Mystakidis, *Byzantinisch-deutsche Beziehungen zur Zeit der Ottonen* (Stuttgart, 1891), pp. 6, n. 6; 9; 17; 18, n. 2; L. Bréhier, "Albéric. 5," DHGE, I, 1406.

5. See introductory note to this letter. Robert was born probably in 970.

6. MS V has *aut sacris imperialibus*, while the Duchesne edition has *scriptis imperialibus* [imperial writings], but correct Byzantine usage required *scriptis sacris imperialibus*, as suggested in the translation above. The letter is lacking in MS L.

7. *In chartis,* meaning "on papyrus." W. Wattenbach, *Das Schriftwesen im Mittelalter* (3d ed., Leipzig, 1896), pp. 98, 107. The Byzantine imperial chancery, like that of the papacy, used papyrus in the tenth century.

120. RHEIMS? or COMPIÈGNE? January 15, 988

King Hugh intends to lead troops to aid Count Borrell against the Saracens and requests an oath of fidelity from him, first through legates, then in person

To MARQUIS BORRELL IN THE NAME OF KING HUGH

Because the surpassing mercy of God has bestowed upon us the peaceful kingdom of the French we have decided to relieve your distress [1] forthwith in accordance with the counsel and aid of all of our vassals. If you wish to maintain the fidelity so often offered through intermediaries to our predecessors and to us,[2] therefore, as soon as you have learned that our army has spread through Acquitaine, hasten to us with a few soldiers in order to confirm the fidelity already promised, and to point out the necessary roads to our army so that, upon approaching your region, we be not perchance, misled by a useless hope of rendering aid to you. If you choose to be there, and to obey us rather than the Ishmaelites,[3] until Easter [4] direct emissaries to us, who will both delight us by evidence of your fidelity and be able to inform you of our approach.

This is Letter 112 in Havet. According to Richer iv.xii, King Hugh convinced Archbishop Adalbero of the necessity for Robert's coronation during his lifetime by producing a letter from Count Borrell of Barcelona, requesting aid against the Saracens. The present letter must have been sent at least two months before April 8th (n. 4 below) because the trip from Compiègne to Barcelona (a distance of 600 miles) would have required twenty-five or more days each way at the usual rate of speed of twenty-five miles a day.

1. See Letter 77.

2. Richer iv.xii lists the *Hispani* (i.e., Catalans) among the followers who swore allegiance to King Hugh at Noyon on June 1, 987 (more likely on July 3d, the date of the coronation).

3. The Moslem Umayyads of Cordoba, whose ostensible ruler was Hishām II al-Mu'ayyad (976-1009), but whose real ruler was his able finance minister al-Mansūr. See Letter 77, n. 3. In 971 and in 974 Borrell, through ambassadors who conveyed noteworthy gifts to al-Hakam, had sought peace and friendship from this earlier Cordobese ruler, and, according to Arabic sources, even acknowledged his dependency on the caliph. Hugh's letter seems to confirm the Arabic sources. J. Millàs Vallicrosa, "Els textos d'Historiadors musulmans Referents a la Catalunya," *Quaderns d'estudi,* XIV (1912), 157-58; A. Ballesteros y Beretta, *Historia de España,* II (Barcelona, 1920), 53.

4. April 8, 988.

121. RHEIMS. May 3, 988

Archbishop Adalbero requests Bishop Rothard of Cambrai to excommunicate Bal., whom he himself has recently excommunicated

To Rothard [1] of Cambrai in the Name of Archbishop Adalbero

After receiving this letter, excommunicate Bal.[2] for having wickedly deserted his wife, since we have recently excommunicated him. By complying you may correct what has been negligently deferred too long. It will avail him nothing to have gone to Rome where he could deceive the lord pope [3] with lies, since Paul says if any one, even an angel, shall have told anything unto you other than that which has been told, let him be anathema [Gal. 1 : 8-9]. Therefore, act with us as a defender of divine laws, since you rejoice in being a sharer of the priestly dignity.

This is Letter 113 in Havet.

1. Bishop of Cambrai, 976-95, a suffragan bishop of the Rheims archbishopric. Letters 186, 195; *Gesta episcoporum Cameracensium* i.ciii, MGSS VII, 444; Johnson, *German Episcopate*, pp. 120-21, 130; Lesne III, 116.

2. Unknown. Probably Bal. = Baldinus = Baldwin (Baudoin).

3. John XV, 985-96. In May, 988, he granted privileges to Lyndulph, bishop of Noyon, Tournai and Flanders (JL 3829), which may have been the occasion when "Bal.", who was from the same section, was in Rome. In such case, the date of this letter would be May, while Bal. was still in Rome, or June, soon after his return.

122. RHEIMS. May 20, 988

Rejoices over Archbishop's Egbert's recovery, but will still send medical information if needed; is disturbed over events in Flanders

To Archbishop Egbert of Trier in the Name of Adalbero

Your illness had dejected us, but your recovery comforts us. Moreover, we have increased our prayers as much as we are able, and shall continue to do so; and if the art of medicine [1] can supplement our efforts, we shall send this information as quickly as possible.

We are somewhat disturbed, now, because you informed us so tardily about what has been happening to you, especially regarding the cause of your brother and your nephew.[2] Scarcely had we finished reading your letter when we received our messenger from the palace,[3] confirming the news that by royal gift Arnulf's son had received all of Arnulf's possessions.[4] In this matter nothing cheers us except the fact that we know that the knights strongly disagree with him.[5] Later we shall elaborate both on this matter and about those concerning which we shall learn your wish.

This is Letter 114 in Havet.

1. In the Aristotelian division of knowledge (the classification that Gerbert followed), medicine was a subdivision under physics, itself a division of theoretical philosophy. Gerbert accepts medicine as an "art," and therefore as valid a study as the seven liberal arts. (To many persons it was one of the "adulterine" branches of knowledge.) Furthermore, Gerbert divided medicine into theoretical and practical, as he tried to do with the quadrivium (Letter 7), a common tradition among the Arabs, but frowned upon in most of the Latin tradition. M. Clagett, "Some General Aspects of Physics in the Middle Ages," *Isis*, XXXIX (1948), 30-31.

2. Arnulf, younger brother of Egbert, succeeded his father Count Theoderich II of Holland who died May 6, 988. P. Juffermans, "La Vie de Saint Adalbert par Ruopert, moine de Mettlach," ALMA, V (1930), 52. Arnulf's son was Theoderich who became Theoderich III in 993. Theoderich II was a vassal not only of the German king, but also of the French king for Ghent and certain districts on or near the Scheldt river—Waes, Axel, Hulst, Assene de Bocholt. The controversy revolved around these lands. See n. 4 below.

3. King Hugh's palace was at Compiègne.

4. M. Uhlirz, *Jahrbücher des Deutschen Reiches unter Otto II. und Otto III*, Vol. II: *Otto III*, pp. 455-57, believes that this passage means that King Hugh invested Arnulf II's (of Holland) minor son Theoderich with his grandfather's (Theoderich II, n. 2 above) fiefs near Ghent in an effort to detach them from the German crown completely. In support of this she calls attention to the fact that the German court hurried from Frankfort to the disputed districts, and is found at Braine-le-Comte on May 20th. DO III 44.

However, Gerbert's Latin, *omnia quae fuissent Ar. filium ejus regio dono accepisse firmaret*, if correct, produces other interpretations. Count Arnulf II of Flanders died March 30, 988, and was immediately succeeded by his minor son Baldwin whom King Hugh invested with "all the fiefs that had been Arnulf's." The pluperfect (subjunctive) verb form *fuissent* suggests that this Arnulf was not now living. Furthermore, Uhlirz's interpretation makes Gerbert's words exaggerated, since she admits that the minor Theoderich was receiving only part of the property left by Theoderich II, not *all*, as Gerbert says. But whether Gerbert means here the counts of Holland only or the counts of Holland and the counts of Flanders, the land in controversy was undoubtedly in the Scheldt region.

There is a third possible explanation here and this is strengthened by Gerbert's reference to the dissatisfaction of the vassal knights. Very soon after the death of Count Arnulf II of Flanders his widow Susanna married King Robert II, because King Hugh was eager to gain a firm control over Flanders, and to secure access to the sea. Hugh may have invested Robert with Arnulf's possessions, only to meet resistance from Flemish vassals who acknowledged the rights of Arnulf and Susanna's minor son Baldwin. Even in this case, Egbert's brother Arnulf could dispute the lordship of Ghent and the Scheldt region.

5. They had become unwilling vassals.

123. RHEIMS. June 8, 988

Gerbert fears Duke Charles's soldiers, and requests trustworthy guides to conduct him to Charles; reminds him of their conversation at Ingelheim; warns him against mistreating Bishop Ascelin and Queen Emma

To Charles [1]

If our service can contribute anything to Your Excellency, we especially rejoice. The reason that we are not now on our way to you in accordance with your command is attributable to the terror instilled by your knights, running hither and thither. Moreover, if hereafter you desire our presence, send those persons whose fidelity we dare to believe in and such guides for the journey as we can rely on. In order to assure yourself that my words are sincere call to mind our conversation in the palace of Ingelheim,[2] and our advice to you, and observe whether what I promised you relative to the long sought for peace between the kings[3] has been accomplished. Meanwhile, I strongly advise you to treat the queen and the bishop[4] very mildly, as befits your dignity, and by no means to allow their incarceration within walls.

This is Letter 115 in Havet. It was written between Duke Charles's capture of Laon and King Hugh's first siege attempting to regain it. Lot, *Hugues Capet*, pp. 6, n. 2; 7-8.

1. Introduction, pp. 10-12; Richer iv.xv-xvii.

2. Probably in July, 987, after Hugh's coronation. Theophanu was then nearby, being at Frankfort August 7, 987 (DO III 38). Gerbert may have carried Letter 111 and the materials for the artistic work to Egbert at Trier on his way to Ingelheim, since Trier was on his route. This was, then, Gerbert's third journey to Germany within a few months. Bubnov, II, 506, n. 19.

M. Uhlirz, *Untersuchungen über Inhalt und Datierung der Briefe Gerberts*, pp. 98-99, believes Gerbert and Duke Charles met at Ingelheim at Easter (April 8), 988. However, the fulfillment of the promise of peace between Germany and France occurred in 987 with the return of Verdun to Germany (Letter 112). Uhlirz seems to interpret Gerbert's words about the "long sought for peace" to mean that it was not accomplished!

According to Richer (iv.xiv), Duke Charles sought to regain the Carolingian family property, appropriated by Hugh Capet upon his accession to the throne. Gerbert acknowledged the validity of Charles's claims, and at Ingelheim advised patience by pointing out what he had helped to accomplish with respect to peace after several years of effort.

3. Otto III and King Hugh. See Letter 112, n. 2.

4. Emma and Ascelin. See Letters 39, notes 7 and 9; 128; 137; 140.

124. RHEIMS. June 15, 988

In spite of the royal favor he enjoys, Gerbert hints at some change; is sending money for the manuscript

To Abbot Romulf [1]

Although we are faring well through the Divinity's goodness, we hope that we may fare [even] better. We enjoy the favor and kindness of princes, as we have always enjoyed them, and now are anticipating that a dream of ours will become a reality [2] in its own good time. Where we shall most probably be in the future is uncertain, due to the uncertain times.

Through the cleric whom you sent we have sent [you] two *solidi* for our work [3] because you have written that it would be considerable in amount, but the size of the volume we canot guess. We will send more, if you request, until you shall say, "It is enough," because the work has been completed.

This is Letter 116 in Havet.

1. The Romulf of Letters 175 and 179 is undoubtedly the same person, and identical with the Abbot Romulf at the council of St. Basle in 991 (Olleris, p. 189). Possibly he was the abbot of St.-Rémy of Sens, or of St.-Pierre-le-Vif if the same as the Rainard mentioned in some writings. Lot, *Hugues Capet*, p. 39; Latouche ed. of Richer, Vol. II, p. 254, n. 3.

2. See Letters 125 and 126.

3. Probably a manuscript containing a work, or works, by Cicero. See Letter 175.

125. RHEIMS. June 21, 988

Archbishop Adalbero requests a bishopric for Gerbert

To Empress Theophanu to Be Sent in Behalf of a Bishopric [1]

Always, indeed, we desire to watch out for your best interests, rejoicing, in fact, in being thus mindful of them by devoting everything to your service. Because of this obvious affection and love on our part we therefore presume to seek from Your Munificence the favor that we know was once vouchsafed to us through trusty messengers, to wit, that, if any church at all on the border of the kingdoms [2] be lacking a pastor, no other be established in it except one whom we with impartial judgment have represented to you as suitable in all ways to your best welfare.

And because we have a man, the Abbot Gerbert, known to all the brother bishops of this province,[3] who, driven from Italy though he was, continues perseverant[4] in his unfeigned fidelity, we pray, in whatever ways we are able, that he be placed over this church. To us, indeed, he is a true son; to you, in truth, in everything a most humble servant. Although his absence may greatly grieve us, yet we set the common good above private satisfaction.

Your desire in these matters we most earnestly request to learn as quickly as possible through your sacred rescripts.[5]

This is Letter 117 in Havet.

1. There is some question as to whether Letters 125 and 126 were actually sent, although Letter 125, at least, probably was.

2. Germany, France, and Lorraine. The bishop of Verdun was in very poor health (Letter 182, introductory note). Bubnov, II, 516, n. 30, suggests the bishopric of Speyer.

3. Of Rheims, namely, Amiens, Arras, Beauvais, Cambrai, Châlons, Laon, Noyon, Senlis, Soissons, Thérouanne, and Tournai. Cambrai was the only bishopric of the Rheims province that lay on the borders of the kingdoms, but Rothard (Letter 121) was bishop there.

4. *Perstantem*, as in the editions of Masson and Duchesne. MS V has *praestantem* [outstanding]. In MS L this letter ends after "driven from Italy."

5. An example of Gerbert's Byzantinism. The *rescripta*, or rescripts, were the formal answers of the Roman emperor to petitions. Cf. Letter 119, n. 6.

126. RHEIMS. June 21, 988

Letter of consolation prepared for Archbishop Adalbero to send to a bishopric bereaved of its bishop, and warning them to care for the bishop's property

To Be Sent to the Clergy and People[1]

The grievous death of your father, who was also our very beloved brother, has caused us much sorrow and anguish. Now, therefore, you must address God with your whole innermost feelings that He may restore a father to you and a suitable brother to us. Meanwhile, take watchful care that the property of the deceased bishop, both movable and immovable, be kept for the new one according to divine and human laws lest, if carelessness shall have prevailed, which God forbid, not only royal censure but also the heavier divine judgment may be applied to the negligent persons.

This is Letter 118 in Havet.

1. See Letter 125.

127. **RHEIMS.** June 25, 988
Rejoices at Egbert's restored health; expresses the appreciation
of all for the work on the cross

[To Archbishop Egbert in the Name of Archbishop Adalbero]

Because you have been restored from sickness, just so have you diminished our long sadness. We rejoice indeed when you rejoice. Sorrowful are we when you sorrow. So, the holy bond, being of one heart and mind, endures. Nor are we alone in feeling your sweet affection for us. They also are sensible of it who gaze with great delight upon the work of the cross[1] elaborated by you in our name, a token of friendship that aspires to be an eternal one.

This is Letter 126 in Havet.
1. See Letters 110, 113.

128. **LAON.** July 25, 988
Queen Emma begs Empress Theophanu to take action against
Duke Charles

[To Empress Theophanu in the Name of Queen Emma]

May Your Compassion come to the aid of an afflicted one who has been made captive by robbers.[1] Once I had race, rank, and royal name. Now, as if without race or rank, reduced to a captive slave of the cruelest of enemies, I am affronted with every insult. But how would that wicked Charles listen to my voice since he disdains to hear yours? You have, indeed, held me worthy of your memory, and have ordered what you wish done about me.

Because he has occupied the royal city [Laon], here he thinks it unbecoming his name to obey anyone. I do not wish to enlarge upon the particulars of his overconfidence by which he foolishly promises kingdoms to himself. Only this I ask, that his rashness be not dulled against me, a woman, until it has been blunted against men.

This is Letter 119 in Havet. The date of this letter is determined by the length of time required for the events leading up to it to take place. Attempting to recapture Laon from Duke Charles, King Hugh began the siege of Laon soon after June 4, 988. When news of this reached Empress Theophanu, she directed a command to Duke Charles, her vassal, to negotiate with Hugh, and a request to Hugh to end the siege of Laon and negotiate with Charles. Hugh complied by sending an emissary to Charles, probably Gerbert, who conversed with Queen Emma, then a prisoner of Charles. This letter (128) followed, and was written either at Emma's side or upon Gerbert's return to Hugh's camp, from written or mental notes. Letter 129, written immediately after Letter 128, was dispatched to Theophanu by the same messenger. Bubnov, II, 517, n. 31; Lot, *Hugues Capet,* pp. 7-8.

1. Dowager Queen Emma had been captured by Duke Charles and his troops. Letter 123, n. 4.

129. **KING HUGH'S MILITARY CAMP OUTSIDE LAON.** July 25, 988
Duke Charles refuses to negotiate; King Hugh requests an interview with Empress Theophanu for his wife, Queen Adelaide

TO THE AUGUST LADY THEOPHANU IN THE NAME OF KING HUGH

Perceiving your kindness and friendliness toward us and wishing to maintain this very dependable bond and sacred friendship, we agreed, in accordance with your desire, to receive hostages from Charles and to raise the siege. This Charles, however, contemptuous of emissaries and of your command, neither assents to these propositions, nor releases the queen [Emma], nor accepts any hostages from the bishop [Ascelin]. But here [in this letter] he can observe what his obstinacy profits him.

Furthermore, since we wish to establish your friendship with us on a permanent basis, we have decided that Adelaide,[1] the companion and sharer of our realm, is to meet you on August 22nd at the village of Stenay.[2] The agreements you both reach as to what is good and equitable we promise to preserve between your son and ourselves forever, without fraud or treachery.

This is Letter 120 in Havet. See Letter 128, introductory note.

1. Wife of King Hugh Capet, and sister of Duke William IV (Fièrebrace) of Aquitaine. Lot, *Derniers Carolingiens,* pp. 358-60; Lot, *Hugues Capet,* p. 182, n. 3. See also Letter 221. (Queen Adelaide should not be confused with Empress Adelaide of Germany).

2. See Letter 109, n. 5. The German court was at Meersberg at the time of the proposed meeting. Letter 140, n. 3; Böhmer, *Regesta imperii,* Vol. II, Pt. 3: *Otto III,* No. 1: *Bis 997* (new ed. M. Uhlirz, Graz-Cologne, 1956), Nos. 1003*l,* 1004.

130. RHEIMS. August 7, 988

Relates the true account of the burning of King Hugh's siege machines; new ones will be ready by August 25th; urges continuation of Egbert's prayers

To Archbishop Egbert of Trier in the Name of Adalbero

Rumors are not to be trusted without question, as you have often experienced and are now experiencing. For we still possess all the property of the bishopric [of Rheims] as before.

There was nothing else in such a tale except that, after noon, while the king's soldiers were deep in wine and sleep, the townspeople [1] with their whole strength made a sally; and while our men were resisting and repelling them, these very ragamuffins burned the camps. This fire consumed all the siege apparatus,[2] damage that must be repaired many times over by August 25th.

Furthermore, we return heartfelt thanks to you because you are maintaining your interest in us with such especial affection, and we hope that you continue to do so with your holy supplications. We pray that you will prolong these activities, because of a vow and desire, even to the end.

This is Letter 121 in Havet.
1. Of besieged Laon. See Appendix B as to the difficulty of capturing Laon.
2. Richer iv.xxiii; Sigebert of Gembloux, MGSS VI, 353. For a good account of early siege machines, with attention to the early medieval period, see O. Spaulding, H. Nickerson, and J. Wright, *Warfare: A Study of Military Methods from the Earliest Times* (N.Y., 1925), pp. 314ff.

131. RHEIMS. August 20, 988

Archbishop Adalbero explains his antagonism toward Duke Charles, but offers to discuss the matter through a mediator

[To Duke Charles in the Name of Archbishop Adalbero]

Why do you, who count me among your most faithless enemies, seek advice from me? Why call me father when you wish to take my life? After all, I have not deserved this. But I have always avoided the treacherous plans of wicked men—I am not speaking of you—and continue to do so.

Because you say I should remember, let you yourself remember what I discussed with you respecting your safety when first you approached us,[1] and what advice I gave about approaching the primates of the realm. For who was I that I alone should set a king over the French? These affairs are public matters, not private. You think I hate the royal family;[2] I call my Redeemer to witness that I do not hate it. You ask what particularly you should do. Since this is difficult to answer, I neither know well enough what to reply nor, if I do know, do I dare say.

You demand my friendship. Would that that day were at hand in which one might honorably interest himself in services to you. For, albeit you have invaded the sanctuary of God;[3] you have seized the queen[4] to whom, as we know, you had sworn an oath of allegiance; you have transferred the bishop of Laon[5] to prison; you have disregarded the excommunications of the bishops,[6]—I do not mention my seigneur [King Hugh], against whom you have undertaken an affair beyond reason—yet I am not unmindful of your service to me when you removed me from the weapons of the enemy.[7]

In order that you might put them to the test, I might say more, both as to which of your followers especially deceive you and as to which are using you to promote their own interests, but this is not the time. For, I am already fearful for having said the above, and this same fear prevented me from answering your former letters.

Because we consider it wisely written: "Nowhere is there good faith,"[8] we can discuss plans for these matters, consider them and communicate them in whatever way possible, [only] if, after hostages are given, my nephew, the bishop of Laon,[9] can come to us. To entrust such things to him is right, and without him we neither can nor ought to carry on such affairs.

This is Letter 122 in Havet.

1. Richer (iv.ix-x) recounts their conversation pertaining to Charles's claim to succeed Louis V on the throne.

2. The Carolingian.

3. The cathedral of Laon.

4. Emma. See Letter 81 as to Charles's oath; and Letters 128 and 129.

5. Ascelin. Letters 128 and 129. Contrary to Gerbert's request in Letter 123, Ascelin was actually incarcerated (Richer iv.xx describes his later dramatic escape from prison), but Charles kept Queen Emma merely under surveillance in Laon.

6. The council of Compiègne, June 4, 988, probably pronounced this. Letters 163, 201, n. 6; *Acta concilii S. Basoli*, Chaps. v, xiv, xxvi; Lot, *Hugues Capet*, p. 7, n. 3.

7. The danger to Adalbero might have occurred during Louis V's attack on

Rheims in 987 (Letter 103). Bubnov (II, 528, n. 51; and 524, n. 45) believes this occurred during the events described in Letter 130.

8. Virgil. Aeneid iv.373.

9. Tironian notes in MS V, but a blank space in MS L. Bubnov, I, 266 (which reproduces the Tironian notes), 271, 351-52; II, 528, 529, n. 53, interprets these as in my translation, against Havet, p. 112, who transcribes them as *nepos meus episcopus Verdunensis* (my nephew, the bishop of Verdun). Havet's interpretation requires that Adalbero of Verdun be a prisoner of Duke Charles at the time of this letter. Thus, without proof, Lot, *Derniers Carolingiens*, pp. 214, 228-29, states that Adalbero of Verdun had been given to Counts Heribert and Eudes as a hostage for the release of his father Count Godfrey, but this is a mistranslation of Letter 109. In the most recent study of Gerbert's letters, F. Weigle, "Studien zur Überlieferung der Briefsammlung Gerberts von Reims," DA, XIV (1958), 187, transcribes the Tironian notes here as *Laudunensis* (Laon), and argues that the known facts of the situation confirm his opinion, and that Bishop Ascelin was Archbishop Adalbero's nephew.

132. RHEIMS. August 20, 988

Gerbert requests a section missing in the second edition of Boethius Commentarius in librum Aristotelis

To THIETMAR OF MAINZ [1]

Since the labor of the siege against Charles has exhausted me and violent fevers [2] have been harassing me I am unable, sweetest brother, to display my genuine affection for you. This much I indicate: command, and we will obey. And let it be characteristic of our friendship to desire the same things and to be adverse to the same things.[3] Moreover, because, amid the burdensome anxieties of cares, philosophy alone can be a certain relief, may your industry supply whatever parts of it we have incomplete.

For the present, now, write back as much as is lacking in our copy in the first volume of the second edition of Boethius *In libro Peri Hermenias*,[4] that is, from the place where is written: "In truth, I am not speaking a verb when I say, 'He does not run, and he does not work,' for it [a verb], indeed, implies time, and it is always the time of something," up to that place where it said: "These, indeed, called verbs according to themselves, are nouns, and mean something." After receiving this, that is, the missing part of the *Commentarius*, we shall be not unmindful of your kindness, nor shall we abandon our mental pledge to execute your desires as far as our strength permits.

This is Letter 123 in Havet. Since Letter 133 mentions September 4, 988 as still a few days in the future, Letters 131-37 were written prior to that date.

The siege of Laon, begun by King Hugh soon after June 4, 988 (Letter 128, introductory note) was abandoned in its second month, about August 5th-10th. Lot, *Hugues Capet*, p. 7, n. 4. Gerbert's illness (n. 2 below) probably occurred July 25-August 13, 988. This letter was written when he had scarcely recovered from the illness, probably close to August 20th. See Letters 136 and 170.

1. Possibly Gerbert visited with Thietmar during a journey to Ingelheim (Letter 123) or to Saxony (Letter 107).

2. See the introductory note above, and Letters 136 and 170. The heat and drought of the summer of 988, from July 15th to August 13th, is mentioned in various German annals (MGSS I, 99; III, 67, 68, 94; IV, 12; V, 5; XVII, 741; XX, 789; and Goerz, *Mittelrheinische Regesten*, I, 314 (No. 1105), though not recorded by Richer for France. Gerbert was probably suffering from dysentery.

3. Sallust *In Catilinam* 20.

4. Gerbert quotes from Boethius's more difficult six-book *Commentarius in librum Aristotelis Periermenias*, PL LXIV, 428D, 429C. Richer (III.xlvi) mentions the *Periermenias* (i.e., *De interpretatione*) among the texts that Gerbert used for teaching dialectic. Lattin, "Eleventh Century MS Munich 14436," *Isis*, XXXVIII (1948), 222-24.

133. RHEIMS. August 21, 988
Archbishop Adalbero requests his brother Count Godfrey to come to Rheims to discuss their promises to Counts Eudes and Heribert

To Count Godfrey in the Name of Archbishop Adalbero

Although I realize that you are sufficiently occupied with your own affairs, yet the common danger ought to disturb you more. You know what agreements we have made with Counts Eudes and Heribert[1] and why we have given hostages. They are insisting on and demanding the promised friendship. Thus, on September 4th, I must, accordingly, give an answer to their messengers as to your wishes and mine. You know the habits, inclinations, plots, and deceits of those among whom I live. Hence, turn back as far as Bouillon[2] so that I may talk with you about those matters that I am unable to entrust to anyone. For these are important affairs, and pertain especially to you. Because I am unable to leave my city without great danger, let Count Manasses,[3] if acceptable to you, come to you to escort you safely to us.

Farewell, and send word back very quickly as to what you think.

This is Letter 129 in Havet. The recipient, Count Godfrey, had traveled from Verdun to Hainaut, apparently to look after his property there (Letter 66).

1. Letter 109. See also Letter 136; and Lot, *Hugues Capet*, p. 174, n. 4.

2. Near the boundary of the Rheims diocese; now in Luxembourg province,

Belgium. Had Godfrey been at Verdun he would not have gone about fifty miles out of his way to reach Rheims via Bouillon. Introductory note, above.

3. Manasses I, count of Rethel (twenty-four miles northeast of Rheims) a vassal of the Rheims archbishopric. He is mentioned twice in the *Acta concilii S. Basoli* (Olleris, pp. 179, 182). Havet, p. 117, n. 2; Bubnov, II, 542, n. 73; 625, n. 86.

134. RHEIMS. August 25, 988

Archbishop Adalbero reports to King Hugh that his incompleted palace is being overrun with troops; requests Hugh to postpone arrival and to send back architect A

ARCHBISHOP A[DALBERO] TO THE KING [1]

After my old palaces were torn apart, even to their foundations, the restored palace that you began to have built for me has now been almost swallowed up by the deluge of your [2] [troops]. We are making haste, indeed, and so by using additional workers at our own expense we are making remarkable progress in the construction of a building of such size, lest, at your arrival, we be forced to move to beds in the outskirts of the town. Grant still fifteen day's time for this enormous task, and send back your architect A. [3] to complete the things begun, but not at my expense. And so, look for us with all the troops to break through the fortress [4] and uproot the mountain from its very foundations, if this is your desire.

This is Letter 124 in Havet.

1. MS L has only "A." plus a space, while MS V has Tironian notes. Havet, p. 113, and Bubnov, I, 260, 271, 351; II, 533, n. 59. Havet does not transcribe the last note, which he says is doubtful, but Bubnov transcribes it as "R." I think it may be "Regi," and that it indicates King Hugh. However, M. Uhlirz, *Untersuchungen über der Inhalt und Datierung der Briefe Gerberts*, p. 104, insists that a military man, subject to Archbishop Adalbero, sent the letter, namely the Vicedom Renier of Rheims, mentioned by Richer (iv.iv and xcix).

2. *Diluvio vestri.* For a similar use of *vestri* to mean your troops, or your followers, see Letter 143, n. 1. Bubnov, II, 533, n. 59, believes that *diluvio vestri* is a mistake for *diluvio Viduli*, i.e., "by the flooding of the Vesle" river, because Rheims is located on the Vesle (*Vidulus*) river.

3. Probably a layman, although Ayrard, abbot of St. Rémy of Rheims in 1005, was noted as a builder. As to variations in the meaning of *architectus*, the word used here by Gerbert, see N. Pevsner, "The Term 'Architect' in the Middle Ages," *Speculum*, XVII.(1942), 549-62. What was being built may have included a war machine like the one described by Richer (ii.x). See Appendix B.

4. Laon. See Appendix B.

135. RHEIMS. August 25, 988

Archbishop Adalbero requests troops from Archbishop Egbert
to be led by Gozelo(?) or by another

To Egbert of Trier in the Name of Archbishop Adalbero

Though nature joins many to us by kinship, many by affection, no friendship has sweeter fruit than that which rests upon love. For, whose favors have we at any time felt either more discriminating or more agreeable than yours? Briefly, in such turbulent times in our land when we continually suffer from the treachery of our knights, continually do we turn our eyes to you as a sure hope, feeling that not in vain do we seek reassurance. And, unwilling either to burden or to weary you except in extreme necessity, we pray you to send my nephew [?] Goze[lo] [?] [1]—or someone else...[2] if you so decide— with a force of soldiers on September 20th to assist us in order both that our frightened deserters may return and that the enemy may melt away because of the fresh and unexpected troops.

This is Letter 125 in Havet.

1. Tironian notes are in MS V, whose transcription and therefore translation are doubtful. Havet, p. 114, transcribes one note as "B." and omits the other, without identifying the person. Bubnov, I, 267, copies the first Tironian note incorrectly, and in Vol. II, 535, transcribes the two as Berard, the vassal mentioned in Letter 140. Actually, the two notes seem to stand for Goz-E-[lo], i.e., Archbishop Adalbero's nephew Gozelo who was count of Bastogne, and thus within Egbert's jurisdiction. Cf. Letters 65 and 143.

2. MS V and B have here an untranscribable Tironian note. MS L has nothing.

136. RHEIMS. August 26, 988

The inactivity of Renier and Gerbert has been due to the illness
of each; requests Bishop Gibuin to deal with Count Heribert in
his stead

To Bishop Gibuin [1] [in the Name of Archbishop Adalbero]

Though striving and struggling,[2] we are doing what we do not wish and are unable to carry out our desires. Thus, Renier [3] and Gerbert, whom you indicated should be sent to you, have been unable to comply with your command because the former was exhausted due to his usual poor health, and the latter, indeed, by an unaccustomed ill health that ended in great fatigue.[4]

Renier has now improved in health, however, and he will follow your command as quickly as possible. For a long time he has intended to render obedience to Count Heribert. Because you know with what great secrecy and trust we have committed our secrets [to you] we beg that you deal with Count Heribert in place of ourselves and our messengers, for we intend to carry out whatever you may learn from more competent advice. When the conference is ended we beseech that you deign to confer with us on what you heard, told, and found out, for we will employ your wise counsel in everything.

This is Letter 127 in Havet.
1. Died 991. See Letter 65, n. 6. He was probably related to Count Heribert. Bubnov, II, 358.
2. Terence *Heauton Timorumenos* ii.2.11.
3. Letter 103, n. 5.
4. See Letter 132.

137. LAON. August 30, 988
Queen Emma reminds her mother, Empress Adelaide, of the oppression she is suffering; begs her to demand her release by Duke Charles

[TO EMPRESS ADELAIDE IN THE NAME OF QUEEN EMMA]

With what difficulties my Lady Emma is beset and by what anguish she is oppressed that letter, long since[1] sent to the Empress Lady Theophanu, is witness. We have sent[2] a copy to you to acquaint you with what has been done, and how useless it was, and in order that you may investigate the cause of the treachery, if, indeed, it is treachery. Certainly, it is clear that until now you have been a most illustrious lady, the mother of kingdoms,[3] and we believed you wished to come to our assistance[4] in dangers, wherever they befell, not to mention that I am your daughter, once beloved by you. Whether the possibility has been snatched away or not, it does not succor your sorrowing daughter. Nevertheless, we urge you through influential legates to ascertain from Charles whether he is willing to return her to you, or to entrust her to another. He seems, indeed, to retain her with such an obstinate mind so as not to appear to have seized her without cause.

This is Letter 128 in Havet. At this time the recipient, Empress Adelaide, was not with the German court at Meersberg on Lake Constance (DO III 46, August 27, 988). See n. 4 below; and Bubnov, II, 539, n. 72.

1. Letter 128, sent near the end of July, 988. Hence, Gerbert's words exaggerate somewhat, but do indicate the urgency of the situation.

2. *Misimus,* but the present tense *mittimus* (we are sending) would be more accurate because Gerbert sent to Empress Adelaide a copy of Letter 128 *with* Letter 136.

3. See Letter 81.

4. Since Empress Adelaide was in a place from where she could send troops to Laon, but was not with the German court, she was undoubtedly in Burgundy with her brother, King Conrad. Probably this appeal to the far away Adelaide resulted from Empress Theophanu's failure to agree to a meeting with King Hugh's wife Adelaide at Stenay, proposed for August 22nd. See Letter 129.

138. RHEIMS. September 7, 988

Informs Rainard of Bobbio of his work for their monastery, and urges patience; requests copies of M. Manlius Boethius (?) De astrologia, Victorinus (?) De rhetorica, and Demosthenes Opthalmicus; suggests a go-between for their letters

To Monk Rainard [1]

Do not think, sweetest brother, that the fact that I have for so long been deprived of the presence of my brothers is due to any fault of mine. After I left you,[2] according to my ability I carried on the cause of my Father Columban [3] in numerous journeys. The ambition for kingdoms, the cruel and deplorable times, have turned right into wrong. No one receives recompense for his fidelity as a matter of right. But, since I know that everything rests on the decision of God who changes at the same time the hearts and the kingdoms of the sons of men, I patiently await the outcome of events. I both advise and urge you, brother, to do the same thing.

Meanwhile, from you I most urgently ask one favor, which you may accomplish without danger or injury to yourself and which will bind me especially close to you in friendship. You know with what zeal I am everywhere collecting copies of books. You know also how many copyists there are here and there in the cities and countryside of Italy. Act, therefore, and without confiding in anyone, have copied for me at your expense M. Manlius *De astrologia,*[4] Victorius [Victorinus?] *De rhetorica,*[5] and Demosthenes *Opt[h]almicus.*[6]

I promise you, brother, and you may be sure of it, that this faithful service and this praiseworthy obedience I will hold in sacred silence. Whatever you may ask for I shall repay abundantly according to [the requests in] your letters, and at whatever time you may command. Indicate this much: to whom we shall direct both your recompense and our letters, and make us happy more often by letters from yourself. Do not fear that what you have entrusted to our confidence will come to anyone else's knowledge.

This is Letter 130 in Havet.

1. See Letters 27, n. 1; 169.
2. In December, 983.
3. The monastery of St. Columban of Bobbio.
4. Probably Anicius Manlius Torquatus Severinus Boethius, i.e., Boethius. Richer (III.xlvi) also uses the form *Manlius* to designate Boethius. See also Letter 15, n. 4. Certain authors argue that here Gerbert refers to the poem *Astronomicon* by the Augustan age poet Marcus Manilius, which was chiefly astrological. The earliest manuscript of the *Astronomicon* is of the middle of the eleventh century. A. E. Housman, *M. Manilii Astronomicon* (Cambridge, 1937), I.vii.82.
5. Probably the commentary of C. Marius Victorinus Afer on Cicero *De inventione*. The Bobbio catalogue lists nos. 384-6, 387, *Libros Boetii III de Arithmetica et alterum de Astronomia. Librum M. Victoris de Rhetorica* [Three books of Boethius *On Arithmetic* and another *On Astronomy*. The book of M. Victor *On Rhetoric*]. No. 399 is the work of Demosthenes, which Gerbert also requests. Hence, Gerbert probably had with him at Rheims a copy of the Bobbio library catalogue. A fragment of a Boethius *De arithmetica* from Bobbio exists in MS Turin Theca F. IV., between Nos. iii and iv, probably of the sixth or seventh century. The *De astrologia* is not there. Giuseppe Ottino, *Codi Bobbiesi nella Biblioteca nazionale di Torino* (Torino, 1890), p. 23.
6. Letter 16, n. 3.

139. RHEIMS. September 10, 988
Bishop Adalbero has arrived with news of the recipient's proposed arrival with troops; begs him to be at Rheims on September 20th

[To Count Gozelo (?) [1] in the Name of Archbishop Adalbero]

Because we continually enjoy such kindness as befits your worthy name we rejoice greatly, not only because it is useful to us, but also because it adds to your honor. We are just now happy in the presence of our nephew Adalbero, bishop of Verdun,[2] who has promised that you will be present with troops at the place and time agreed upon. Accordingly, may you, to whom I bear an affection similar to that for him, show your generous self to the city of Rheims on September 20th. Pray conceal this fact and the monk who is the bearer of this letter, and keep the matter under cover in order that your approach to us may be secret and unexpected.

This is Letter 131 in Havet.

1. See Letter 135, n. 1. Bubnov, II, 545, 546, n. 77, and M. Uhlirz, *Untersuchungen über Inhalt und Datierung der Briefe Gerberts*, pp. 109-10, insist that the recipient of this letter was Archbishop Egbert of Trier, especially because of the tone of the letter. In spite of Bubnov, the words "to whom I bear an affection similar to that for him [Adalbero of Verdun]" do seem to indicate another relative of Archbishop Adalbero's. In view of Letter 135 this should be Count Gozelo, his nephew.

2. These words seem to indicate that Bishop Adalbero of Verdun was not the nephew of Archbishop Adalbero mentioned in Letter 131. Perhaps Bishop Adalbero had now come to Rheims in place of Count Godfrey. See Letter 133.

140. RHEIMS. September 15, 988

Reminds the recipient to be cautious of his actions with reference to Duke Charles; seeks information about the failure of the royal conference; requests justice for his vassal Gueinric

[To Archbishop Egbert (?) [1] in the Name of Archbishop Adalbero]

Not only did the other affair indicate how greatly your foreseeing mind has been occupied with advising and persuading men, but Charles's declining fortunes [2] have rendered this even more apparent. But, if you have been striving to drive him from your province as an enemy, you ought to be mindful of your friends Queen Emma and Bishop Ascelin; if, on the other hand, you are elevating him to the throne as a friend, still do not forget them, and remember that among treacherous men the [remembrance of past] evil deeds is not eradicated by services [to them]. Therefore, indicate which of these actions you can improve upon; also why the conference, appointed for discussing peace between the royal persons, [3] was disregarded, and whether peaceable relations, at least, will exist between them in the future.

Meanwhile, if we are at all deserving of your kindness, we seek and pray especially that no precedent be cited against our knight Gueinric in favor of Berard. [4] Indeed, the land in litigation with the church belongs to them in common, to be sure, and Berard, for his part, wishes that the chapel be granted to him according to the law pertaining to a new work. But, this cannot be done justly unless an equal division is made.

Farewell, and if it pleases you, give back our manuscript by a trusty messenger.

This is Letter 132 in Havet.

1. The identity of the recipient is uncertain. Gerbert refers to his "province," and, if used correctly, this should designate an ecclesiastical province or arch-bishopric. Hence, the recipient would be either Archbishop Egbert of Trier or Archbishop Everger of Cologne. However, Bishop Notker had been with the German court since the middle of August (DO III 45), and was thus more familiar with recent developments at court.

2. *Exitus viarum.* Letter 157 has the same expression. Apparently, a decree of exile had been issued against Charles.

3. Empress Theophanu and Queen Adelaide at Stenay (Letter 129). On August 22, 988, the date suggested for the meeting, Empress Theophanu was in Meers-berg on the north shore of Lake Constance, having reached there August 20th, apparently on her way to Italy. DO III 46; and M. Uhlirz, *Jahrbücher des Deutschen Reiches: Otto III*, p. 103.

4. Cf. Letter 164. Berard was claiming a chapel, which was part of the new construction, as indemnity for the injury to his property rights by the church (probably that of the recipient of this letter) that had carried out the con-struction. Adalbero claimed that his knight Gueinric, as co-owner of the land with Berard, was entitled to half of the rights in the chapel, apparently relying upon Justinian's *Digest* xxxix. 1 (ed. Mommsen, p. 635), that pertains to the erection of buildings with a disregard for the rights of servitude of a neighboring proprietor. Adalbero is citing Roman law against the provisions of canon law as found in the Council of Chalcedon of 451, Chap. XXII, which restricted private ownership of chapels. This latter provision was continually disregarded, and, in fact, a Roman synod of 826 had practically recognized the existence of proprietary churches (MG *Capitularia*, I, 374f.; MG *Concilia*, I, 576f.). See W. Levison, *England and the Continent* (Oxford, 1946), pp. 27-33.

141. RHEIMS. September 15, 988

Desires to take counsel with the recipient and requests his presence for the ordination of Eudes, bishop-elect of Senlis

To Bishop Gibuin [1]

With misgivings, indeed, have we been deprived of your presence for so long a time, and we are reserving many things to be executed according to your advice. You know to how few persons the affairs of state can be entrusted with confidence. Therefore, we hope, we advise, we pray that because of your affectionate kindness you will be present at Rheims on September 22d not only for the extensive plans, so properly to be entrusted to you, but also for holding the ordination of Eudes, the bishop-designate of Senlis. [2]

This is Letter 133 in Havet.

1. Tironian notes in MS V, but a space left for heading in MS L. Bubnov, I, 266, 271, transcribes these as "Ildrico," i.e., Hildricus, another name for Herveus (he says) or Hervé, bishop of Beauvais. However, in Letters 195 and 203 Gerbert uses the abbreviation "Ill." to designate Hervé. The Tironian notes in Letter 141 are sufficiently similar to those in the heading of Letter 136 to justify the

same transcription "To Bishop Gibuin," as given by Havet, p. 120. As to Bishop Gibuin see also Letter 65, n. 6.

2. Eudes' predecessor, Constantine, died July 16, 988. Havet, p. 120, n. 3.

142. RHEIMS. September 30, 988

Offers explanations for comprehending abacus arithmetic; preoccupation with public affairs prevented sending a sphere; desires Statius Achilleidos

TO REMI, MONK OF TRIER [1]

You adequately comprehended, indeed, how the tenth [2] number measures itself. For one times one is one. But every number, does not therefore measure itself because it is equal to itself, as you have written. On the contrary, although one times four is four, four does not therefore measure four, but rather two. For twice two are four.[3]

Moreover, the letter i [4] which you have found written down under the ten times figure signifies ten unities, which, separated into six and four, make a sesquialter ratio.[5] The same may be observed in the ratio three to two where unity is a difference.

We have sent no sphere [6] to you, neither have we any at present; nor is it an object of small work to one so occupied in civil causes. If, therefore, you are eager to have this that involves so much work, send to us a carefully written volume of Statius *Achilleidos* [7] in order that, unable to have the sphere gratis because of my excuse of its difficult construction, you may be able to wrest it from us as your reward.

This is Letter 134 in Havet.

1. Remi, succeeding Hezzelo, became abbot of Mettlach (see Letter 71, n. 1) during the lifetime of Archbishop Egbert of Trier (d. 993). He was described as a man "in the shrine of whose heart wisdom had built for itself a peaceful home." Like Gerbert he became a noted teacher whose pupils became teachers, bishops, and abbots. He was especially famous for his religious musical compositions, but wrote also an *Excerptio Prisciani super octo partes Donati*, and *Regulae de divisionibus abaci*. *Ex miraculis S. Liutwini*, ed. H. V. Sauerland, MGSS XV, 2, p. 1266. See also Letters 156, 160, 170; and Bubnov, II, 551, n. 84.

2. *Denario*. In this letter Gerbert attempts to correlate a portion of Boethian arithmetic with abacus arithmetic. As a mnemonic device, the columns of the abacus were labeled C D S C D S C D S, etc., from the Latin words *centies* ["the hundred times" number], *decies* ["the ten times" number], and *singularis* ["the one, "or" single" number], and they were discussed from right to left, each set of three columns being connected by an arc placed above it. Thus, a figure 1 placed under D in the first group at the right equals ten, in the next group to the left equals ten thousand, in the next to the left, ten million. We

today use commas to aid the eye. The number 1 was thought of as unity, no matter in what column it appeared, and therefore its factor was itself. (Sometimes the first right-hand column of the three was labeled M, from *monos*, the Greek for "the one," or "single" number.)

3. Two numbers which measure another number are factors of that number. Boethius *De arithmetica* i.xiv, "A number measures another number as much as, compared to another by one, two, three, or any number soever, it approaches the limit of the compared number."

4. Although the abacists and algorists used various forms of the Hindu-Arabic numerals for the numerals two through nine, many of them used a letter "i" for the numeral one, even in the first printed arithmetic. See E. Waters, "A Thirteenth Century Algorism in French Verse; with introduction by L. C. Karpinski," *Isis*, XI (1928), 59; D. Smith, *A Source Book in Mathematics* (New York, 1929), pp. 3, 9.

5. Any property which X has, 1(0) also has. See Letters 3-5 as to these ratios.

6. See Letters 156, 160, 170.

7. See also Letter 156, n. 2. Richer (iii.xlvii) mentions that Gerbert used the poet P. Papinius (Surculus or Sursulus) Statius (c.A.D. 40-95/96) in his teaching, but Richer does not specify the particular works used. Statius' popularity is attested by the forty-nine extant manuscript copies of the *Achilleidos* and the one hundred and twenty of the *Thebaidos* written before 1300. H. Buttenwieser, "Popular Authors of the Middle Ages: The Testimony of the Manuscripts," *Speculum*, XVII (1942), 52.

143. RHEIMS. October 1, 988

Rejoices that the recipient has ceased traveling; is preparing gifts, and equipping soldiers; needs reinforcements because of the intended renewal of siege of Laon on October 18th; requests he send B. and G.

To the Archbishop [Egbert (?) in the Name of Archbishop Adalbero]

Just as the news of your foreign travels brought sorrow to us, so the changed rumor that you have delayed your journey made us almost happy. We were anxious not only because of the absence of your troops,[1] to be sure, but also because the honors did not correspond to the merits[2] of so great a person.

Therefore, we are exerting ourselves, and what the shortness of time did not permit us to accomplish we have assigned to this breathing spell and are preparing gifts at the same time as [equipping] troops.[3] Yes! troops! For you know among whom we live and how we are harassed by the monstrous treachery of certain persons, and what kind of a so-called truce interrupted the siege of the city of Laon, which must be renewed on October 18th.[4]

Just as we have urged you, therefore, we continue to urge, both for the comfort produced by reinforcements of soldiers, should we need them, and for the aid of our captured brother Ascelin, that B[ardo] and G[ozelo],[5] because of your exhortation, shall in these critical moments show themselves more worthy to be his brothers.

This is Letter 135 in Havet.

1. *Vestri.* See Letter 134, n. 2, for a similar use.

2. *Meriti* in MSS L and V, but *meritis* in the editions of Masson and Duchesne, which offers better sense.

3. *Munera iuxta vires... vires dicimus* in MS V, which could mean "gifts according to our abilities," but the repetition of *vires* seems rather to indicate troops, for which Adalbero kept begging frantically. MS L has *munera justa vires,* which does not make sense.

4. MS V has *X Kal. Novemb.* [the tenth kalends of November], i.e., October 23d.

5. See Letter 65. Gerbert here contrasts the fact that Bishop Ascelin was only a *frater* [brother ecclesiastic] of Egbert and Adalbero of Rheims, whereas he was a *germanus* [brother by blood] of B. and G.

144. RHEIMS. October 1, 988

Archbishop Adalbero encourages the recipient to bear trouble and suggests an exchange of news through their representatives celebrating the feast of St. Denis at Paris

[To Abbot Mayeul (?) [1] in the Name of Archbishop Adalbero]

Do not bear God's very just reproof with heavy and inimical spirit, sweetest brother. In fact, the Divinity, forsooth, does not deem the wicked worthy of his whip, reserving them to be punished by everlasting torments. Learn to serve constancy in adversity, and, if you cannot imitate Job and the ancient priests of our order, at least have as a model a layman of our time, a man related to you—Count Godfrey.[2]

Indeed, we will not be unmindful of your safety, nor will we leave untried anything that ought to be done for you. Therefore, let Osulf [?] [3] know everything about yourself in order that he may completely inform our messenger who will be present at Paris for the feast of the blessed Denis [4] so that, if there is pressing danger [5] in the future, or if there is not, plans for the one or the other contingency may be remade.

Farewell and good luck, but hearken to this one admonition, that you do not dash yourself headlong so that it would have been better to have perished in some other way rather than to have left everlasting disgrace to yourself and your posterity after your death.

Again farewell, and be especially wary of Robert of Paris [6] as of a treacherous impostor.

This is Letter 136 in Havet.

1. Although the general tone suggests Bishop Ascelin of Laon as recipient, why should Adalbero wish to communicate with Ascelin via the roundabout method of messengers who were to meet in Paris? The common interest of Archbishop Adalbero and the recipient in St. Denis suggests that each had a special interest in his worship. For Adalbero, this is easily explained by the presence of the monastery of St. Denis in Rheims. The monastery of St. Denis near Paris together with that of Fleury (St. Benoît-sur-Loire) shared rights over the monastery of Marmoutier near Tours. Mayeul was abbot of Marmoutier for a short time, being succeeded by Guilbert (Guislebert) by 989. Bubnov, II, 2, pp. 814, n. 77, 815. Perhaps some difficulty accompanying Mayeul's cessation from his office of abbot occasioned this letter. Letters 117, 153, and 194 evidence the interest of the archbishop of Rheims in both St. Denis of Paris and in Marmoutier.

2. Brother of Archbishop Adalbero. What the relationship by marriage (*affinem*) was between Godfrey and the recipient is unknown. Ascelin (n. 1 above) was his nephew, a blood relative.

3. Havet, p. 123, and Bubnov II, 555, n. 88, transcribe these three Tironian notes as "Anselm," because an Anselm is mentioned in Letters 149 and 157. However, the notes might be "Osulfus," who is mentioned in Letter 117 to Mayeul.

4. Tuesday, October 9, 988.

5. *Obsidio*, which regularly means "siege." If Ascelin of Laon was the recipient, then it should be so translated.

6. Tironian notes, transcribed by Havet, p. 123, as "Robert of Micy." However, the difficulties experienced with this man occurred after the year 1000, whereas Robert II was abbot of St. Denis at this very time, and was to be ousted very soon. Letter 153; Havet, p. 129, n. 1; Bubnov, II, 570, n. 109; Warren, "Constantine of Fleury," *Transactions of the Connecticut Academy*, XV, 290.

145. RHEIMS. October 18-31, 988

Unable to carry out his promise due to his troops' absence; requests he send Count Sigibert about Attigny, and with troops

[TO ARCHBISHOP EVERGER (?) [1] IN THE NAME OF ARCHBISHOP ADALBERO]

Because of the absence of our knights [2] the thing you desired was not fully effectuated. However, we have vowed to do it; so upon their return, we will accomplish what we can. Moreover, if you hope for continuous peace with the peasants at Attigny, [3] have Count Sigibert [4] come to us as quickly as possible in order that we may prepare suitable plans against Dudo, and, at the same time, that a large group of your soldiers may bring suitable assistance to us in addition to what we shall indicate through him. We are entrusting this information to safe ears because of the multifarious ambuscades of enemies.

This is Letter 137 in Havet. On October 18th the siege of Laon was renewed (Letter 143), but was abandoned again within a short time (Richer IV.xix). This letter was written during the siege. For an opposite view, see Bubnov, II, 556.

1. The contents of this letter and the references to Count Sigibert and Dudo, who are mentioned in Letter 112 to Everger, suggest that Everger was the recipient.

2. They were taking part in the siege of Laon.

3. *Atineti* (arrondissement Vouziers, dept. Ardennes), near the Roman road from Rheims to Trier. In the tenth century it formed part of the royal domain of the Carolingians who owned a palace there. As successor in the kingship Hugh Capet, in 987, probably claimed ownership of Attigny as part of the Carolingian fisc. Letter 145 indicates that Duke Charles, seeking to regain the Carolingian patrimony and to displace King Hugh, entrusted to his vassal Dudo (Letter 112, n. 5) the task of fomenting resistance to the authority of both Hugh and a foreign archbishop—Everger. Flodoard *Annales*, ed. P. Lauer, p. 132; Richer III.lxxiv; Havet, p. 123, n. 7; Newman, *Domaine royal*, pp. 92, 93, 123, 126.

4. Tironian notes. Sigibert (Letter 112) was probably Siegfried, count of Luxembourg (Letter 58).

146. COMPIÈGNE? or RHEIMS? December 1, 988
King Hugh requests Empress Theophanu to meet him to complete an alliance

[To EMPRESS THEOPHANU IN THE NAME OF KING HUGH]

We rejoice in the improvement in the state of your health,[1] and no less at your desire to be informed of ours. Through God's favor we, indeed, are well, and we hope the best for you.

We do not plan to violate knowingly an alliance [2] upon which we have entered, nor to return injury for the injury received at the hands of your vassals.[3] So, from January 1st to the beginning of Lent [4] we are prepared to meet you at the borders of our France, of Burgundy, and of the Lorraine kingdom [5] on whatever definite day you will designate and at a place described by its name, in order that the peace and harmony of the kingdoms and of the churches of God may not be destroyed through any fault of ours.

This is Letter 138 in Havet.

1. Theophanu's ill health caused her to abandon her Italian journey (Letter 140, n. 3), and she remained in Constance two months or more (DO III 47-49, October 12-21, 988). Letter 146 was probably sent to her at Cologne where she celebrated Christmas with the court (DO III 51, December 28, 988).

2. See Letter 129.

3. Duke Charles and his troops, if, as assumed, the letter is to Theophanu.

4. February 13, 989.

5. Such a place would have been in the northeastern part of the bishopric of Langres, near the headwaters of the Meuse. From Cologne this would have required a seven days' journey, and from Hugh's palace at Compiègne at least six. The meeting did not occur.

147. RHEIMS. December 5, 988

Archbishop Adalbero, citing the Bible, urges the recipient to pursue an honorable course by following the bishop's injunctions

[IN THE NAME OF ARCHBISHOP ADALBERO]

To a learned man [1] who holds fast to an unswerving faith, which few possess today, two sayings of Christ will both reveal our advice and make a satisfactory answer to the question you asked. Thus, we say, "Render to Caesar the things that are Caesar's, and to God the things that are God's," [Mat. 22 : 21], and, "Let the dead bury their dead" [Luke 9 : 60].

When you have comprehended these words, act with honor in accordance with the bishop's [2] legitimate orders. Henceforth, avoid anyone's offers made against what is right. This is the not dishonorable way.

The sons of darkness, the sons of Belial [2 Cor. 6 : 14-15], use their own time. We are the sons of light, the sons of peace, who do not place hope in man, withering as if grass [Isa. 51 : 12], since with patience we await that saying of the prophet: I have seen a wicked man highly exalted, and lifted up like the cedars of Lebanon, and I passed by, and lo he was not, and I sought him, and his place was not found [Ps. 36 : 35, 36; 93 : 12].

This is Letter 139 in Havet.

1. The intended recipient is uncertain, but it was probably Arnulf (later archbishop of Rheims), at this time a cleric of the church of Laon, and a partisan of his uncle Duke Charles, who controlled Laon. Schlockwerder, *Untersuchungen zur Chronologie der Briefe Gerberts*, pp. 24-25, interprets this letter as a demand that Arnulf release his bishop, Ascelin, from captivity. Bubnov, II, 570ff., suggests that Abbot Robert II of St. Denis near Paris was the intended recipient. He was forced out of office at the end of 988. Letters 144, n. 1, and 153.

2. Ascelin of Laon, if the recipient was Arnulf; Lisiard of Paris, if the recipient was Abbot Robert II. Bubnov, II, 570, n. 109; Lot, *Hugues Capet*, p. 7, n. 4.

148. FLEURY. December 5, 988

Constantine of Fleury requests Gerbert's influence with King Hugh and Queen Adelaide to compel the return of his stolen house furnishings

CONSTANTINE TO GERBERT

If you will now offer in small matters that kindness that you exhibited in vain in important affairs,[1] you may anticipate no small praise and no few results. Indeed, you did labor to free us from the enemy,[2] but you were scorned. Now that the Lord has delivered us from the mouth of the lion [2 Tim. 4 : 17], apply your usual energy to compel by the command of your lord and lady[3] that violent robber[4] to return at least our household goods. We seek neither gold nor quantities of silver but only what it is shameful to lack, namely coverlets, hangings,[5] and such like. At the same time we ask that our fidelity be not measured by his fidelity since he never promised anything that he deemed unalterable.

This is Letter 143 in Havet, one of the four letters appearing in the collection which were received by Gerbert, not written by him. The others were 225, 226, 230. Letter 148 was probably received about December 10th.

1. See Letter 92.
2. Oylbold, the intruder abbot.
3. King Hugh and Queen Adelaide. See Letter 151, n. 3.
4. Probably Arnulf, lord of Yèvre, nephew of Bishop Arnulf of Orléans, to whom King Hugh forced Abbot Abbo and the monks of Fleury to make exorbitant payments in return for Arnulf's service in Hugh's army. The death of Fleury's abbot, Oylbold, offered Arnulf the opportunity to seize the monastery possessions on the pretext of some payment due him. Lot, *Hugues Capet*, pp. 233-34.
5. *Aulea, tapetis.* For an account of contemporary fabrication of such textile articles in this same Loire valley see *Historia sancti Florentii Salmurensis,* in *Chronique des églises d'Anjou,* ed. by Marchegay and Mabille (Société d'histoire de la France Publications; Paris, 1869); W. G. Thomson, *A History of Tapestry from the Earliest Times until the Present Day* (London, 1906), pp. 44-46, 55; Lesne, III, 241ff.

149. RHEIMS. December 5, 988

Archbishop Adalbero(?) expresses his joy to Bishop Ascelin(?) of Laon over the latter's escape from captivity, and suggests a conference in order to ascertain the political situation

[TO BISHOP ASCELIN (?) IN THE NAME OF ARCHBISHOP ADALBERO (?)]

We are powerless to render thanks worthy of the kindness of our

Liberator.[1] From the heart do we rejoice that our members[2] whom, in your person, the infernal one seemed to have swallowed, have been snatched from his jaws through Christ the Victor. We advise that you learn from conference with us the true state of affairs at this moment—what you should seek after, and what avoid—before you mingle in the meetings of the princes[3] of our kingdom. At the same time, also, indicate by letter through a trusty messenger whether the departure of Anselm[4] and Renier[5] to Count Eudes seems to you safe at present, and where they should meet each other.

This is Letter 140 in Havet.

1. Bishop Ascelin had just escaped from his prison tower at Laon in dramatic fashion (Richer iv.xx; Bubnov, II, 560). Cf., however, Havet, p. 125, n. 5, who believes Ascelin was the writer and Archbishop Adalbero the recipient.

2. Parts of the body of the Church, the bride of Christ. Ascelin, as bishop, was one such part or member, since he represented the Church. Letter 36 contains a similar use of *membrum* [member].

3. Kings Hugh and Robert, and their followers.

4. Letters 144, n. 3; and 157.

5. Letters 9, 96, 103, and 150.

150. **RHEIMS.** December 9, 988

Archbishop Adalbero (?) advises Bishop Ascelin (?) not to go to King Hugh immediately; accepts Senlis as the meeting place for their legates

To the Same Person

After further consultation no safer plan has been devised by all of us than that for the present you should refrain from a meeting with your seigneur,[1] if this can be accomplished honorably. If this is an impossibility, however, then it seems best to touch upon the high points of the more important matters, but you should explain nothing unless it is clearly useful. Right now Renier,[2] most faithful of all good men, will await your messenger at Senlis[3] on the fifth day of this week[4] either to depart for Chartres,[5] if you desire, or to return to Compiègne[6] if you so indicate.

This is Letter 141 in Havet. The recipient (Ascelin?), according to the end of this letter, was in Compiègne. The letter was written on Sunday (n. 4 below).

1. King Hugh. Apparently he was at some other royal residence than Senlis (n. 3) or Compiègne (n. 6), possibly at Chelles.

2. See Letter 149, n. 5.

3. Senlis (dept. Oise), one of the Capetian royal residences, at least in the time of Robert II. Newman, *Domaine royal*, p. 108.

4. *Feria V*, i.e., Thursday. The reference to a specific day in the same week is unusual in Gerbert's letters, and indicates that some letters were being sent back and forth rapidly.

5. Dept. Eure-et-Loire, residence of Count Eudes.

6. A Capetian royal residence. Newman, *Domaine royal*, p. 103.

151. RHEIMS. December 11, 988

Archbishop Adalbero and Gerbert congratulate Constantine of Fleury on being rid of the intruding abbot; suggest a quick election of a worthy man; invite Constantine to Rheims

ARCHBISHOP ADALBERO, FOR OURSELF, AND GERBERT, TEACHER AND ABBOT, TO THE TEACHER CONSTANTINE [1]

We congratulate you, sweetest brother, that the intruder [2] and enemy of the monastic religion has been released from human affairs, with resulting benefit to many persons. Act, therefore, and if you now have someone worthy of election as father [3] by yourself and your brothers, let him be present with us [4] at the approaching feast of St. Remi [5] as evidence of your hard work, so that our affection, alienated somewhat from the monks of Fleury in spite of your efforts, may be fully regained through your efforts. But, if all these proposals cannot be carried out, still let us enjoy your presence regardless of whether we have ever offered you anything pleasing to you, [6] or whether you deem it worth while that we can offer what can please you.

This is Letter 142 in Havet.

1. Letter 92, n. 1.

2. Oylbold. Letter 93, n. 2.

3. Abbo, teacher at Fleury, who had recently returned from a two years' sojourn in England, had already, at the date of this letter, been elected abbot of Fleury. However, it would not have required over a month for the news of Abbo's election to reach Rheims. Hence, I presume that the election occurred about December 7th. Fleury was a royal Capetian abbey, and therefore King Hugh confirmed Abbo's election. On November 13, 1004, Abbo was murdered after being abbot for sixteen years. Aimon *Vita Abbonis*, PL CXXXIX, 393, 406B-412C; Aimoin *Miracula S. Benedicti*, PL CXXXIX, 825; Bubnov II, 565, n. 105; Newman, *Domaine royal*, pp. 202, 205.

4. *Habeamus eum et nos praesentem tua opera.*

5. The translation of St. Remi was celebrated at Rheims on January 13th, although his feast day was October 1st. The reference here is to the translation.

6. An indication that Constantine had studied with Gerbert.

152. RHEIMS. December 23, 988

*Gerbert (?) urges Archbishop Willigis (?) to carry through
the suggestions in the king's letter*

[GERBERT (?) TO ARCHBISHOP WILLIGIS (?)]

We advise, we beg, we beseech you to undertake the accomplishment of the suggestions contained in the letter written in the king's
name [1] that we have sent to you. Do this, pray, not only because
of your kindly feeling toward us, but also for the sake of the peace
of God's church, which the princes [2] will bring about by making
peace with each other. If, by chance, we are [now] deprived of your
desirable presence, [3] do not regard us, who are among those faithful
to you, as faithless and untrustworthy.

This is Letter 144 in Havet. M. Uhlirz, *Untersuchungen über Inhalt und
Datierung der Briefe Gerberts*, pp. 118-19, seems correct in considering Gerbert
the sender (in his own name) of this letter and Archbishop Willigis of Mainz
as the receiver. This is contrary to Havet, p. 128, n. 3; Bubnov, II, 569; and Lot,
Derniers Carolingiens, p. 234, n. 2, all of whom believed the letter was written
in Archbishop Adalbero's name to Archbishop Egbert of Trier, or to Bishop
Notker of Liége, or even to Bishop Adalbero of Metz.

1. Letter 146 in King Hugh's name to Empress Theophanu. This deals with
the same subject as Letter 152—the establishment of peace between the two
monarchs.

2. King Hugh and Empress Theophanu.

3. The words have been interpreted by Havet, Bubnov, and Lot (introductory
note, above) to mean the anticipated arrival in Rheims of the recipient of Letter
154. However, Gerbert seems rather to be reminding Willigis that he belonged
at the German court, and that, though not there, he was still active in behalf of
the Ottos.

153. RHEIMS. December 28, 988

*Archbishop Adalbero refuses to interfere in the affairs of the
troubled monastery of St. Denis near Paris*

[To KING HUGH,[1] IN THE NAME OF ARCHBISHOP ADALBERO]

Although the whole Catholic Church is one and the same, yet a
certain manner is prescribed to each of her priests as to whither he
should extend himself and where he should delimit his activity. Thus,
because of that fidelity which we maintain and always shall maintain
towards you, we are stating these three points for consideration in
the matter of Abbot Robert: [2] First, that it is not within our jurisdiction [3] to place a scythe in a foreign harvest, although we thank

you many times over for deeming us worthy of the undeserved honor; second, that this monastery of St. Denis is of such veneration and dignity that no official there ought to be deposed or imposed without the solemn assent and consent of that province's interested ecclesiastics; third, we recommend that Your Clemency delay any action, and together with very religious and learned men we will try to ascertain what procedure may be more honorable and useful.

This is Letter 145 in Havet.
1. The use of "Your Clemency" in the letter indicates King Hugh.
2. Of St. Denis. Letter 144, n. 6.
3. St. Denis was in the diocese of Paris and the archbishopric of Sens.

154. RHEIMS. December 30, 988
Archbishop Adalbero complains to Bishop Adalbero of Metz (?) about his failure to come to Rheims; is sending a copy of his last letter

[To Bishop Adalbero (?) in the Name of Archbishop Adalbero]

On December 23d, through Ri.,[1] named the same as his father, we sent to Your Fraternity [2] a letter received from the king, relating the news that your approach to Rheims and that of my brother [Godfrey] was hoped for on December 28th, and that the royal messengers were about to meet you on the way. They came, as agreed, but they did not find you. Straightway now we are sending a copy of our earlier letter.[3]

This is Letter 146 in Havet. The use of "Your Fraternity" in addressing the recipient indicates that he was a bishop. The short interval between the dispatch of the earlier letter and the anticipated arrival on December 28th indicates that he lived no more distant than three days' rapid journey. Adalbero's reference to "my brother" with no mention of any relationship with the recipient excludes Bishop Adalbero of Verdun. Cologne (230 miles from Rheims), Trier (175 miles via Verdun), and Liége (151 miles) were too distant to be reached in three days. This leaves Metz (134 miles) and Châlons-sur-Marne (27 miles). Verdun is on the road from Metz to Rheims. Bishop Adalbero of Metz was King Hugh's nephew so that Hugh might reasonably have invited him to a conference in France.
1. A Richard was a canon of Rheims cathedral at this time. In 1002 or 1004 he became abbot of St. Vannes (Vitonus) of Verdun (d. 1046). *Gesta episcoporum Virdunensium*, Chaps. 6, 8-9, MGSS IV, 47-49, Manitius, II, 356f., 362ff.
2. See introductory note.
3. This letter is not extant.

155. LAON. January 10, 989

Queen Emma asks an unnamed priest (Bishop Bruno?) to prevent the loss of one of her castles; requests him to bring money from her treasury

[To Bishop Bruno (?) in the Name of Queen Emma]

Harsh times are these, O priest [1] of God, when most sacred fidelity everywhere has become a rarity. But be you mindful of it, for you have always promised it to me, and I prefer to believe that you feel obligated to maintain it. May my captivity [among] this band of thieves stir you. I speak before one [2] who knows. I, that Emma, one time queen of the French, who commanded so many thousands, now neither have domestic companions in whose company I might go to the conferences with the esteemed Duke Henry,[3] nor may I enjoy your presence that I have longed for in order that I might secure your encouraging counsel.

Therefore, I pray you to see to it that our cause is postponed, not settled until we have exchanged words. We refer to the castle of Dijon.[4] And do not permit your brother [5] to be called a traitor whose fidelity thus far has satisfied us respecting its sincerity.

Meanwhile, because Ad.[6] the bailiff of our possessions, as you know, has not returned, nor have we heard what has happened to him, lest you return empty-handed, carry back in your chests the money we have so long awaited. You will receive reward and gratitude in return for your kindnesses which merit these both on this account and for your many previous services.

This is Letter 147 in Havet. Duke Charles still held Queen Emma in captivity at Laon. Letters 123, 137, 140. A few days must have elapsed after Letter 154 during which Gerbert could have reached Laon and made arrangements to see Emma. Havet, p. 130, n. 3, believes that Emma is now at liberty, but Letter 155 does not read that way.

1. Probably Bruno, son of Renaud, count of Roucy, and Albrade, half-sister of King Lothair. He was a canon of the Rheims cathedral and perhaps its librarian until the beginning of 981 when he was consecrated bishop of Langres. He died January 31, 1016. See Letter 180, n. 1; PL CXXXIX, 1531-34; Lot, *Derniers Carolingiens,* p. 115.

2. Gerbert. He was thus writing from Emma's dictation.

3. Brother of Hugh Capet, and duke of Burgundy, 965-1002. Lot, *Hugues Capet,* pp. 197, 228, 411, n. 1, 416ff.

4. Côte-d'Or dept., diocese of Langres.

5. Count Gilbert of Roucy (Aisne), if the addressee is Bishop Bruno.

6. This is Havet's transcription (p. 130) of a poorly made Tironian note.

Bubnov, II, 578, n. 5, admits he can offer no better transcription. M. Uhlirz, *Untersuchungen über Inhalt und Datierung der Briefe Gerberts*, p. 120, expands this doubtful note to mean Bishop Adalbero of Laon (Ascelin). It seems more likely that the bailiff was a layman. Uhlirz also suggests that the money was to be used by Emma to pay a ransom to Duke Charles for herself. This seems probable.

156. RHEIMS. January 15, 989

Gerbert scolds Remi of Trier for sending an incomplete copy of Statius Achilleidos, *but nevertheless has begun the sphere for him*

To Monk Remi [1]

Your good will, beloved brother, was overburdened by the work on the *Achilleidos* [2] which, indeed, you began well, but left incomplete [just] because your copy was incomplete. Since we are not unmindful of your kindness we have begun to make the sphere [3]—a most difficult piece of work—which is now both being polished in the lathe [4] and skillfully covered with horsehide. [5] So, if you are weary from the excessive anxiety of anticipation, you may expect it, divided by plain red color, [6] about March 1st. If, however, you are willing to wait for it to be equipped with a horizon [7] and to be marked with many beautiful colors, [8] do not shudder over the fact that it will require a year's work. As for giving and receiving among our followers, how true the saying that he who owes nothing, need return nothing.

This is Letter 148 in Havet.

1. See Letters 142, 160, 170.

2. By Statius. See Letter 142, n. 7. This work has come down incomplete. Although Remi's exemplar and the copy made for Gerbert are lost, the Trier Stadtbibliothek owned, under No. XCIb, s. XI, a copy of the *Achilleidos* which very likely was related to Remi's manuscript. F. X. Kraus, "Ueber Trier'sche Handschriften in der kaiserlichen Bibliothek zu Paris," *Serapeum*, XXIV (1863), 51, n. 2.

3. For further details about Gerbert's astronomical instruments see Letter 2; Richer III.1 (solid sphere), li (semicircular observing instrument), lii (planetarium), liii (armillary sphere for observations); Lattin, *Peasant Boy*, pp. 123-30; Lattin, "Symposium on the Tenth Century. Astronomy: Our Views and Theirs," *Medievalia et Humanistica*, IX (1955), 13-17.

4. Wood was a convenient material for globes used for studying or teaching since corrections could be more easily made upon it. Achilles Tatios (3d cent.?) and Leontios Mechanicus (9th cent.) both mention wooden globes. Leontios states that the wooden ones were smeared with plaster of paris or wax in order to prevent cracking. E. Maass, *Commentariorum in Aratum reliquiae* (Berlin, 1898),

p. 598; A. Schlachter and F. Gisinger, "Der Globus, seine Entstehung und Verwendung in der Antike nach den literarischen Quellen und den Darstellungen in
der Kunst," *Stoicheia*, VIII (1927), 33. Virgil, Pliny, and Vitruvius mention a
lathe.

5. Note Tycho Brahe's use of a similar material, parchment, in 1576, to keep
perfect the sphericity of his globe. J. L. E. Dreyer, *Tycho Brahe: A Picture of
Scientific Life and Work in the Sixteenth Century* (Edinburg, 1890), pp. 99-100.

6. The text, *simplici fuco interstinctam*, is reminiscent of Pliny *Natural history*
xxxvii.xi.54, *candor interstinctus coloribus* [the white part divided by colors],
and Martianus Capella *De nuptiis Philologiae et Mercurii* viii.825 Leontios
(n. 4 above) marked his circles on the globe with colors. A. Schlachter and
F. Gisinger, "Der Globus," *Stoicheia*, VIII (1927), 37.

7. The year's time necessary for completion suggests that Gerbert planned to
determine the horizon at Trier and to mark graduations on the horizon, which
was undoubtedly a metal ring within which the globe could be turned. Martianus viii.816; Richer iii.l; *Liber de astrolabio* iv, in Bubnov, *Gerberti opera
mathematica*, p. 128; and Lattin, "Use of a Sphere by Macrobius," *Isis*, XXXIX
(1948), 168.

8. The globe itself was undoubtedly painted a dark color—blue—to represent
the firmament at night. For locating the constellations Gerbert probably followed
Hyginus's Latin translation of the Phainomena of Aratos of Soli (*Hyginus* i.vi,
ii-iv), although he may have used the more accurate account of Martianus
viii.827.

157. RHEIMS. January 15, 989
*Archbishop Adalbero (?) asks Bishop Ascelin (?) about his
activities and requests his advice on the election of a bishop
and attendance at a meeting at Chelles*

[To Bishop Ascelin (?) in the Name of Archbishop Adalbero (?)]

With great difficulty, indeed, do we endure your absence,[1] but
greater anxiety burdens us, due to our ignorance of those events
occurring near you. For, assuredly, we ought not to be unacquainted
with the successes and disappointments of him whose affection we
share. Hasten, therefore, to make plain by letter what general or
private business you presently will have accomplished, what you are
doing, and what you arrange to do soon. At the same time indicate
what you wish us to do in the election of the bishop[2] to be held on
February 12th.

On this day, or rather on the preceding one, we shall be expecting
your replies, informing us how Anselm[3] succeeded with the counts[4]
and why we have not yet seen his messenger; whether we should
approach the king or the counts first; whether we ought to defer
our journey to the conference announced for Chelles;[5] whether you

will come thither, and with whose assistance. In complete confidence entrust these and similar matters to those having the fullest confidence in you.

This is Letter 149 in Havet. It may have been written in Gerbert's own name.
1. This Letter appears most intelligible if Bishop Ascelin of Laon was the addressee, especially if considered in conjunction with Letters 149 and 150. Havet, p. 131, n. 4, and Lot, *Hugues Capet*, pp. 13-14, believe that Gerbert, absent from Rheims, wrote Letter 157 to Archbishop Adalbero.
2. Liudulf, bishop of Noyon, died November 5, 988. Havet, p. 132, n. 1. Ratbod (or Rabeuf) succeeded him. Letter 195, n. 3.
3. Letter 149.
4. Eudes and Heribert.
5. Dept. Seine-et-Marne, arrondissement Meaux, canton Lagny, a Capetian royal residence, according to Havet, p. 132, n. 4, and Lot, *Hugues Capet*, p. 14, n. 2, but not listed among Hugh's residences by Newman, *Domaine royal*, pp. 102-4. The journey from Rheims to Chelles would have required about two days. Richer (IV.l) describes his own journey over almost the same route in 991.

158. RHEIMS. February 20, 989

Gerbert thanks Archbishop Willigis (?) for his offer of some position, but will do nothing until the archbishop of Rheims is elected

[GERBERT TO ARCHBISHOP WILLIGIS (?)]

Not through our own merits are we in a position to be replying to your spontaneous kindness. For what have we done now which is worthy of Roderick's mission? We are doubtful only of this: how to interpret its purpose lest we place the convenience [1] of some king or bishop ahead of your convenience and that of your seigneur.[2] Forsooth, it is not sufficiently clear whether you are ordering us to abandon all that we possess and to go to you and your possessions or whether, by a certain manner of speaking, you wish to relieve us greatly from the impact of savage fortune by a comforting hope.

King Hugh and the neighboring bishops and those who border on the see of Rheims offer much, but we have received nothing definite thus far, nor do we plan to do anything without consulting you. Because of this esteem [for you] we have postponed going to the king lest by chance, strongly attracted by him, we might appear to have shunned your commands that we must prefer to all mortal ones because of the sweet affection of my dear Father Adalbero whom, in some ways, it is appropriate to see in you.[3]

We have entrusted to Roderick other matters which were on our mind and which we wished to be done with regard to ourself, and they should be diligently pursued.

This is Letter 150 in Havet. The content of the letter indicates an influential German prelate, and its formality indicates the most powerful one—Archbishop Willigis.

1. Archbishop Adalbero of Rheims died January 23, 989. Gerbert appeared to be the favored candidate to succeed him. Introduction, pp. 10-11.

2. Otto III.

3. This might be interpreted to mean Archbishop Egbert because of his close friendship with Archbishop Adalbero. However, Gerbert's words seem rather to mean that just as Adalbero was the most important ecclesiastic in France so the recipient was the most important one in Germany, and that each had certain claims on Gerbert's services.

159. RHEIMS. March 1, 989
Gerbert refuses to divulge information on public affairs or to give advice about kidney stones to a person unknown to him

[GERBERT TO AN UNKNOWN]

Gerbert greets the person writing under the name of Reverend Father Adalbero, bishop of Verdun.

If you—whoever you are who alleges friendship—are inquiring about my condition, may I answer by your leave that, although I am among hostile persons, according to reliable opinion I am following the example of a strong man,[1] though not equaling him. I am not detailing public affairs because I do not know to whom I am writing.

On the other hand, I might describe more fully the particulars of the illness of a brother [2] suffering from stone [3] if I were able to glance at the findings of earlier authorities. Therefore, content yourself with a small dose of the antidote *philanthropos* [4] and with the instructions which accompany it, and blame only yourself if by not following the regimen [5] you turn what was designed for health into something harmful. Do not ask me to discuss what is the province of physicians, especially because I have always avoided the practice of medicine even though I have striven for a knowledge of it.

This is Letter 151 in Havet.

1. Apparently Count Godfrey who had refused to capitulate to his enemies (Letters 54-59). Gerbert was refusing to capitulate to those who wished him to withdraw his candidacy for the archbishopric of Reims.

2. A cleric, not the bishop of Verdun as suggested by Havet (p. 133, n. 3), since Gerbert could not have addressed a bishop as brother at this time.

3. *Morbo calculi*, undoubtedly kidney stone, since these stones can be seen. MacKinney, *Medieval Medicine*, p. 116, translates this as "gallstones," which would be an uncommon meaning.

4. "The ancients called antidotes not only counterpoisons but general medicine for internal use. (Galen, *De antidotis*, I.1, ed. Kühn, p. 1.) On *philanthropos* see Pliny *Historia naturalis* xxiv.cxvi and clxxvi; xxvii.xv.32; *Dioscorides* III.civ; Galen xi.834." Havet, p. 133, n. 5.

5. MS L, *dicta*, followed in the translation. MS V, *dietam* [diet], followed by Bubnov, II, 597, n. 41, and MacKinney, *Medieval Medicine*, p. 116. If the illness was caused by gallstones instead of kidney stones, "diet" would be the more proper word.

160. RHEIMS. March 7, 989
   Reproves Remi of Trier for persisting in his request for a
   sphere during such disturbed times

[GERBERT TO REMI, MONK OF TRIER]

Gerbert sends greetings to Brother Remi.[1]

My Father Adalbero of divine memory was both the equipoise and the force in all causes dependent upon the eternal,[2] and now that he has been changed into the original elements one might think that the world is slipping into primordial chaos. Thus, during this great disturbance and, I might add, confusion, you, forgetting to observe proper manners, have inconsiderately taken into account [only] what you hope for, what you seek. In a crisis of this sort, when the state itself has been abandoned, must recourse be made to the comments of philosophers which at this time are not necessities?

I keep silent about myself for whom a thousand deaths were planned both because Father Adalbero with the assent of the whole clergy, of all the bishops, and of certain knights had designated me as his successor; and because the opposition[3] maintained that I was the author of everything that displeased them.

For only a wooden sphere[4] must we abandon friends who like me had enjoyed the friendship of blessed Father Adalbero? Hence, endure the delays imposed by necessity, awaiting more opportune times in which we can revive the studies, now already ceasing for us.

This is Letter 152 in Havet.
1. See Letters 142 and 156.

2. Gerbert was fond of employing the metaphor of the balance. Does it suggest any technological use of it by him? Here the meaning is that in all important matters Adalbero exhibited a judicial temperament capable of balancing the equities, and that his decisions were of such weight as to always turn the scale.

3. Arnulf and his supporters. Introduction, p. 11.

4. Letter 156.

161. RHEIMS. March 10, 989
Gives information for the construction of a horologium

GERBERT TO BROTHER ADAM

Gerbert sends greetings to Brother Adam.[1]

Since my Father Adalbero has taken his place among the immortal souls,[2] heavy cares so weighed me down that I have almost forgotten all studies. As my mind began to remember you, in order not to grow inwardly lazy from leisure and to satisfy an absent friend with something, I wrote down certain sentences, collected from the subtleties of astronomy, to wit, on the drawing near and withdrawing of the sun, and am sending them to you as a token of my friendship. I collected these not according to the theory of the persons who believe that these movements are equal in each month,[3] but I have followed the opinion of those who describe them as altogether unequal.

So, Martianus in his Astronomy thinks that the increases of the hours [of sunlight] occur as follows: "One must know," he says, "that the day increases from the shortest day so that in the first month [4] it increases a twelfth of that time which is added in summer. In the second month, a sixth. In the third, a fourth, and in the fourth month, another fourth. In the fifth, a sixth. In the sixth, a twelfth." [5]

Thus, in conformity with this theory I have sketched the charts (*horologia*) for two climates [6] with ascertained measurements by assigning a definite number of hours to each of the months. One is [the *horologium*] of the Hellespont where the longest day is of fifteen equinoctial hours.[7] The other [*horologium*] is for those persons who have eighteen equinoctial hours in their longest day.[8]

Moreover, I have done this in such a way that you can place the proper *horologia* under every climate according to the scheme of these when you know the length of the solstitial days from the waterclock.[9] This, indeed, is easy to do if flowing water, caught separately for the night and for the day at the time of the solstice, totals the amount of the whole sum, which equals twenty-four parts.

THE HOROLOGIUM FOR THOSE WHOSE LONGEST DAY IS OF EIGHTEEN EQUINOCTIAL HOURS

June and July	Day 18 Hours	Night 6 Hours
May and August	Day 17 Hours	Night 7 Hours
April and September	Day 15 Hours	Night 9 Hours
March and October	Day 12 Hours	Night 12 Hours
February and November	Day 9 Hours	Night 15 Hours
January and December	Day 6 Hours	Night 18 Hours

LIKEWISE THE HOROLOGIUM FOR THE HELLESPONT WHERE THE LONGEST DAY IS OF FIFTEEN EQUINOCTIAL HOURS

January and December	Day 9 Hours	Night 15 Hours
February and November	Day 10½ Hours	Night 13½ Hours
March and October	Day 12 Hours	Night 12 Hours
April and September	Day 13½ Hours	Night 10½ Hours
May and August	Day 14½ Hours	Night 9½ Hours
June and July	Day 15 Hours	Night 9 Hours

This is Letter 153 in Havet.

1. On MS Rheims 129 (E. 349), s. X, which came from the cathedral, is a note in a contemporary hand: "Adam, priest and canon, gave this to St. Mary of Rheims," and above it is his signature. CG XXXVIII: *Reims*, I, 120. Since one of the tables at the end of this letter is for a place where the longest day is eighteen hours, it may be inferred that Adam lived north of Rheims.

2. *Intelligibilia*, i.e., things which could be understood by the mind, in contrast to *sensibilia*, things which could be perceived and felt. Gerbert certainly learned the word from Boethius who, in *In Porphyrium Dialogi a Victorino translati: Dialogus Primus* (PL LXIV, 11C), used it to designate the species in the sublunary world which was originally characterized by purity of substance, thereby partaking of the divine, such as human souls, which, however, became contaminated by their connection with the body and thus degenerated from pure divinity or *intellectibilia* (a word which Boethius tells us he coined). See Latouche ed. of Richer, Vol. II, p. 73, n. 2. *Intelligibilia* were also discussed by Chalcidius (3d cent.). *Platonis Timaeus Commentatore Chalcidio*, ed. Wrobel (Leipzig, 1876), Chap. CCCII. Gerbert knew the Chalcidius work.

3. The ninth-century author of the *De mundi coelestis constitutione* (About the Composition of the Celestial World), PL XC, 883D-884A, gives the reckoning of the computists. They calculated the increase of daylight as the same amount in each month throughout one climate, although differing in amounts between each of the climates. The author ends by noting that the philosophers, "who examine nature itself," do not agree with the purely theoretical figures of the computists.

4. Of winter, i.e., December 21-January 20. There was no agreement as to the

exact day of the solstices or of the equinoxes. Some claimed they were the fifteenth day, some the twelfth, some the eighth, of the kalends. MS British Museum Old Royal 15 B IX, fols. 76r and v, written about the year 1055, gives two methods, differing from Gerbert's, for finding the solstices and equinoxes. Millàs, *Assaig d'història*, pp. 325-26, prints this material, which describes the use both of an astrolabe and of a stylus with marked-off circles and the stylus's shadow.

5. Martianus ascribes the unequal increases of daylight during the first half of the year to the fact, as he says, that the zodiac curves more in Cancer and Capricorn and intersects the celestial equator almost at right angles. The knowledge of the increase of the hours of daylight has been traced to Babylonian astronomical tables of the third, second, and first centuries B.C. Cleomedes *De motu* I.vi, and Plutarch *De animae procreatione* discuss it. O. Neugebauer, "On Two Astronomical Passages in Plutarch's *De animae procreatione in Timaeo*," *American Journal of Philology*, LXIII (1942), 458f.; and his "Cleomedes and the Meridian of Lysimachia," *American Journal of Philology*, LXII (1941), 344-45.

6. *Climata*, i.e., regions lying on either side of our parallels of latitude, but of unequal width and thus extending in a somewhat north and south direction, whose parts had the same angle of inclination of the sun's rays with respect to the horizon. The usual number was seven, although Martianus mentions eight. See Honigmann, *Die sieben Klimata* (Heidelberg, 1929), especially pp. 51ff, on Martianus.

7. Martianus, VIII.877, states that the days (longest and shortest) are named for the names of the climates: Meroës, 13 hrs-11 hrs.; Syene, 14-11; Alexandria, 14-10 plus 1/30; Rhodes, 14-9; Rome, 15-9; Hellespont, 15-8; Borysthenes, 16-8; Riphaeon, 16-8. (The manuscripts of Martianus are corrupt, hence the obvious errors.) Gerbert corrects Martianus on the length of the shortest day in the climate of the Hellespont. At VI.595 (ed. Dick, p. 295), Martianus has a different reckoning.

In antiquity and the middle ages two systems of dividing the day were used. The commoner system, especially favored by an agricultural civilization, was to divide the total amount of daylight into equal parts so that the length of the hour varied from day to day, being long at the summer solstice and short at the winter. In the other system, called the equinoctial, the daylight at the equinox was divided equally and this length of time formed the basis of the length of the hour throughout the year. Although double hours were used, corresponding to the twelve divisions of the zodiac, Gerbert used twenty-four single hours, as is shown here.

8. Martianus does not give a climate with a longest day of 18 hours. At VI.595, he gives 17 for Britain, and for the island of Thule one-half year, day, and one-half, night. Reference to 18 hours of daylight in Britain is found in the *De mundi coelestis constitutione*, PL XC, 883D; John Scot Erigena, *Annotationes in Marcianum*, ed. Lutz (Cambridge, 1939), p. 140 at 296, 5; Bridfert's gloss to Bede *De natura rerum* x, PL XC, 205C; and Pseudo-Anatolius (C. W. Jones, *Bedae Pseudepigrapha: Scientific Writings Falsely Attributed to Bede* [Ithaca, N. Y., 1939], p. 69).

9. A description of such a use of the clepsydra, or waterclock, is found in Macrobius *Commentarii in Somnium Scipionis* I.xxi. 12ff.; and in John Scot Erigena (taken from Macrobius), *Annotationes in Marcianum*, p. 139 at 295,5. Even the sixteenth-century Tycho Brahe resorted to the waterclock, although using mercury instead of water, because he discovered that mechanical clocks still varied considerably even during short intervals of time.

162. VERDUN. April 15, 989

A nephew of Archbishop Adalbero (Count Frederick?) assures
King Hugh of his interest in the kingdom of the French; warns
him to consider carefully his choice for archbishop of Rheims

[To King Hugh in the Name of Count Frederick (?)]

Although many of our compatriots [1] mistrust you, Your Mightiness,[2] for a great many reasons, yet, because of my uncle's [3] tender devotion to you and because we are confident of your affection, we continually hope for more favorable circumstances for you, as we both love and strive for peace in public and private affairs. Nor do we intend to separate ourselves from your assistance [4] unless we suffer a repulse.

Therefore, to guard your safety we are offering advice relative to the condition of the church of Rheims, which is the head of the kingdom of the French. Do not think of putting in charge in that place a deceitful, ignorant good-for-nothing [5] who is unfaithful to you, since all the members follow the head.[6] Let it suffice that by so many postponements [7] and open craftiness [8] you have deceived your cruelest enemies. You should not wish to entrust your safety to the advice of those who have decided to advise nothing except with the assent of your enemies.

We have suggested a few ideas to you in order to indicate in some way the one [Gerbert] whom we hold dear.

This is Letter 154 in Havet. Shortly before Arnulf's election as archbishop of Rheims (Letter 163) Gerbert visited Trier (Letter 170) to seek among the Lorraine nobles and clerics endorsement of his own candidacy for the archbishopric of Rheims. Count Frederick, son of Count Godfrey, apparently complied and allowed Gerbert to write Letter 162 in his name to King Hugh. Cf. notes 1 and 8 below.

1. *Conprovincialium* (nominative, *conprovinciales*), i.e., Lorrainers. Gerbert uses this word to mean not only suffragan bishops as in Letter 116, but also persons of the same district, compatriots, as in Letter 50 and here.

2. King Hugh Capet.

3. Archbishop Adalbero. He and Gerbert were principally responsible for the election of Hugh Capet as King. Richer iv.vii-xii.

4. *Solatio.* This probably means military aid, as in Letters 135 and 143.

5. Arnulf, nephew of Duke Charles.

6. Boethius *Brevis fidei Christianae complexio,* PL LXIV, 1337C-1338A, *cujus caput Christus ascendit in coelos, ut necessario caput suum membra sequerentur* [whose head, Christ, ascended to Heaven so that the members would of necessity follow their head]. Manitius (II, 714, n. 3) calls this a proverb, found later also in Anselm of Besate.

7. Letter 163, "The period of vacancy allowed by canon law has elapsed."

8. According to Letter 201 (p. 237) Bishopp Ascelin alone had reconciled King Hugh and Arnulf, while Richer (iv.xxv) mentions the persons in Hugh's entourage at Paris who promoted Arnulf's candidacy. Ascelin demanded that he be allowed to resume his episcopal functions at Laon without molestation by Duke Charles. Arnulf promised this. Hugh demanded that Duke Charles surrender Laon. Arnulf promised this also. Gerbert's words here imply that Hugh hoped to trick Charles into surrender and did not really intend to nominate Arnulf archbishop of Rheims.

163. RHEIMS. April 28, 989
Notice of the election of Arnulf as archbishop of Rheims

THE ELECTION OF ARNULF[1] AS ARCHBISHOP OF RHEIMS PUBLISHED BY GERBERT

The sons[2] of the archdiocese of Rheims greet the Holy and Universal Catholic Church.

Since our Father Adalbero of divine memory has left behind his corporeal sensations, we have lost the shining light of a pastor and have become the prey of the enemy. Accordingly, while we struggle we are trying to repair the ruin [caused by the death] of so great a man. The period of vacancy allowed by canon law has elapsed, and the law has been broken in which it is forbidden to allow any see to be vacant for a space of more than thirty days.[3] Now, because the Divine Light finally revealed itself, and by its illumination indicated whither we should follow, after antichrist was overthrown and simonaical heresy was condemned, we, the diocesan bishops of the province of Rheims, with all the clergy of different classes, with the acclamation of the people, and with the consent of our orthodox kings, have elected as our head a man distinguished for piety, exceptional in fidelity, wonderful in steadfastness, prudent in advice, suited to the administration of affairs,[4] in whom these qualities, since they shine so brightly, are an indication that others cannot be absent.

We speak of Arnulf, son of King Lothair, cleansed [of sin] by the mystic sacraments of the purifying Church, our Mother, even though his noble blood stained him by a certain contagion resulting from being enmeshed in an anathema.[5] This man we say is a son of the church of Rheims,[6] and, to speak more truly, of Rheims itself. This city, indeed, is the Rheims territory, the Rheims diocese. And it was not so divided by St. Remi that it could be alienated. Truly, that man of God, seeking unity and disliking schism, made the division so that it might hold together like a part in the whole. And, realizing what and how great the future might be, he blessed his natal soil by virtue of his priestly office.

Therefore, we are electing this Arnulf, a native of this place, educated here, free from simonaical heresy, removed from tyrannical faction, giving to each his deserved rights but not dissipating the sanctuary of God. May deceit and fraud be absent from our election, and may the sons of Belial not think it their concern. May the sons of peace and concord make it enduring and real forever by confirming it, corroborating it, and subscribing to it.[7]

This is Letter 155 in Havet.

1. Son of King Lothair and of a sister of a Count Raoul, who was a vassal of Duke Charles. Richer iv.xxvi; Lot, *Derniers Carolingiens*, p. 108, n. 2. Arnulf had acted as Lothair's vice-chancellor. L. Halphen et F. Lot, *Recueil des actes de Lothaire et de Louis V, rois de France (954-987)* (Paris, 1908), *passim*.

2. The suffragan bishops of the Rheims diocese.

3. This must be a copyist's error for *ter XXX* (3 x 30) days. Cf. Havet, p. 138, n. 2.

4. Similar phrases are found in all documents of notification of election of bishops and abbots. See Letter 191. Compare with these the derogatory remarks about Arnulf in Letter 162, and in the Council of St. Basle.

5. On June 4, 988, at the command of King Hugh a council of bishops had promulgated an anathema against Duke Charles and his accomplices, among whom was Charles's nephew Arnulf. Lot, *Hugues Capet*, p. 7, n. 3.

6. Since Laon is in the Rheims archdiocese, Arnulf could be called a son of both churches. Letter 201, p. 237, shows that at the time of Charles's capture of Laon Arnulf was a cleric there under Bishop Ascelin.

7. Richer iv.xxvi-xxxiii. Arnulf's consecration occurred in the monastery of St. Rémy, then about two miles from Rheims. See Letter 168 as to Arnulf's effort to secure the pallium from Pope John XV.

164. RHEIMS. June 5, 989
Archbishop Arnulf requests Archbishop Egbert to settle the dispute between two of their vassals

In the Name of Arnulf [Arch]bishop of Rheims[1]

Even if up to the present our public or private actions have not merited your attention, still our mind has not been inattentive to this matter, especially as to how we might exhibit our eagerness to match and hold your affection. On this account, therefore, we patiently bear the actions of your aged knight Gerard, whereby, invading the benefice of our faithful Gueinric,[2] he inflicts violence upon it. So, we beg you to order him to quiet down. If, by chance, he shall have concealed anything, let him learn by experience that each of his admonishers has most justifiably become his enemy.

This is Letter 156 in Havet.
1. Heading in the edition of Duchesne, and in MS Berlin Philips 1718, but lacking in MS L.
2. See Letter 140. Gerard probably refers to Berard.

165. RHEIMS. July 5, 989
*Archbishop Arnulf seeks to establish with Archbishop Egbert
a friendship similar to Adalbero's*

To EGBERT, ARCHBISHOP OF TRIER, IN THE NAME OF THE SAME PERSON

Since I am acquainted with your good-will, or rather piety, that you always exhibited towards my predecessor, Adalbero of blessed remembrance, I shall judge myself even more fortunate if I can make it my permanent possession. Thus, we rejoice that out of your overflowing kindness you have made a beginning;[1] and [so] we hope to enjoy an indissoluble mutual affection. Furthermore, because the tumult of discordant kingdoms and the newness of our consecration hinder us from deciding and carrying out our intentions, we are delegating the management of our acts to the stability of Your Prudence. At the same time also we ask, that you write definitely, if it is possible, where and when we can meet together after your return from the palace.[2]

For the present, let us be certain whether you have learned anything new; afterwards, you ought to inform us more clearly as to what you yourself have learned more clearly. A forceful argument that our sacred friendship and close association will last forever rests upon the fact that we are using the same advisers always used by my predecessor as negotiators[3] in business and in leisure.

This is Letter 157 in Havet.
1. Undoubtedly, a reference to Egbert's good wishes extended to Arnulf upon his consecration as archbishop, as well as a reference to Egbert's favorable reply to Letter 164 respecting the dispute between their respective vassals, Gerard and Gueinric.
2. Of Otto III, probably at Ingelheim. On April 5th Otto III and Theophanu were at Quedlinburg (DO III 53 and 54); on July 4th at Kirchberg, near Jena (DO III 55); from July 23d to 30th at Ingelheim (DO III 56 and 57).
3. Gerbert and Renier (Letter 136) were certainly two of these advisers.

166. RHEIMS. June, 989
   Gerbert requests a German prelate (Archbishop Willigis?) to
   remind Empress Theophanu of his services to her

[GERBERT TO ARCHBISHOP WILLIGIS (?) [1]]

I am well aware that you understand the emotions of my mind, and on this account I love and embrace you and yours. I am indeed mindful of the very proper warning given me whereby you kept me from the fellowship of certain princes [2] for a sufficiently long time, and indicated what you wished. Therefore, through the venerable name of my Father Adalbero, through the unbroken fidelity with which I have always cherished him and his, I pray you that I be not forced to forget those men whom I have always especially cherished out of love for him while neglecting my own concerns.

Pray remind my Lady Theophanu of the fidelity that I have always maintained towards herself and her son. Do not allow me to become the prize of her enemies whom I reduced to disgrace and scorn on her behalf whenever I was able.

Further, for a common end [3] I pray, I ask, I beseech, that you be not displeased by the service of him whom thus far your command, your honor, and your power have pleased. Act with your accustomed generosity lest, when the noblest arts flee because honesty is absent, I become a partisan of Catiline, although now both in business and in leisure I am the diligent follower of the precepts of Marcus Tullius [Cicero].

This is Letter 158 in Havet.
1. Willigis, archbishop of Mainz, the most powerful German ecclesiastic. As chancellor, he was frequently with the German court. The tone of this letter is exactly that which Gerbert would have used to such a person. Cf. Letters 35, 42, 152, and 158 to Willigis.
2. Dukes Henry of Bavaria and Charles of Lower Lorraine.
3. Cf. Letter 152.

167. RHEIMS. End of August, 989
   Gerbert suggests to a German prelate (Notker of Liége?) that
   he merits some reward for his devotion to the Ottos

[GERBERT TO BISHOP NOTKER (?)]

It is not foreign to your kindness and sacred priesthood to advise those seeking advice. To no mortal have I at any time sworn an oath except to Otto, Caesar of divine memory. I believed that its validity extended to my Lady Theophanu and to her august son Otto, since, forsooth, I understood it to be in a certain way three oaths in one.[1] Therefore, how long do you judge that this fidelity ought to be preserved?

Although despoiled of the great wealth bestowed on me by imperial gift and confirmed by papal blessing,[2] I have received, I may add, not even a little villa for the fidelity which I have maintained and will maintain. Besides, although placed among your worst enemies, I have succumbed to none of their favors although ample ones have been proferred.[3] Advise and offer solace to me, I implore you, if not because of my own merits, then because of your ever praised kindnesses towards all men.

This is Letter 159 in Havet.
1. Cf. Letter 28 where Gerbert extends the same oath to include Empress Adelaide.
2. The monastery of St. Columban of Bobbio.
3. Letter 158, "King Hugh and the neighboring bishops ... offer much." However, the real enemy was Duke Charles, who may have made further overtures to Gerbert. See Letter 123.

168. RHEIMS. October 25, 989
Gerbert requests an important German (Bishop Notker?) to secure the pallium for Archbishop Arnulf from Pope John XV

[GERBERT TO BISHOP NOTKER (?)]

The prohibition of my lord [1] thwarted my anticipated pleasure in the journey to Rome which your [2] company and future conversation with Lady Theophanu [3] would have made more complete. Therefore, act in my stead, as the friend of a friend,[4] in order that we may obtain the pallium [5] from the lord pope through you, and retain the favor of our lady, secured through you. We shall be in her service at Easter,[6] God willing, for there will be no one who can prevent us from fidelity and service to her and her son.

This is Letter 160 in Havet.
1. *Senioris mei prohibitio*. This was Archbishop Arnulf, not King Hugh. See Letter 107, where Gerbert uses the word *senior* in writing of Archbishop Adalbero.
2. In 989 Bishop Notker of Liége with his friend and pupil Heriger, later abbot of Lobbes (Laubach) (990-1007), journeyed to Rome where he secured a

papal privilege for the monastery of Lobbes (JL 3837, February 1, 990). He met Theophanu in Rome. *Annales Laubienses*, a. 989, MGSS IV, 18; *Gesta abbatum Lobbiensium*, MGSS XXI, 309; Kurth, *Notker de Liège*, I, 87f.; Manitius, II, 220, 222-23; M. Uhlirz, "Italienischen Kirchenpolitik der Ottonen," MIOG, XLVIII (1934), 256.

3. Theophanu celebrated Christmas, 989, in Rome, which she brought back under German control. DO III Theophanu No. 1, January 2, 990; *Annales Hildesheimenses*, a. 989, MGSS III, 68; Böhmer, *Regesta imperii*, Vol. II, Pt. 3: *Regesten unter Otto III*, No. 1: *Bis 997*, new ed., M. Uhlirz (Graz-Cologne, 1956), Nos. 1017 l, n, o, p, 1019b, h.

4. Notker was Gerbert's friend, and Gerbert was Archbishop Arnulf's Thus, Gerbert, not Arnulf himself, planned to travel to Rome to request a pallium for Arnulf. Later Notker became Gerbert's enemy. Letter 202.

5. A narrow band of white wool worn about the neck by the pope, his vicars, and archbishops on special occasions. A newly elected archbishop would petition the pope to confer the pallium on him, either personally in Rome or through a legate, as here. He was required to send the pope a Profession of Faith, similar to Gerbert's *Professio fidei* in Letter 192 or to the *Promissio fidei episcopi* in the *Liber diurnus*, No. lxxiii.

Richer (iv.xxxi) states that soon after his consecration as archbishop Arnulf received a pallium from the pope. This letter shows that Bishop Notker brought it from Rome, at the end of March, 990, or in May, if Notker returned to Germany with Empress Theophanu. In 999, after Arnulf's restoration to his see, following his deposition in 991, Gerbert, become Pope Sylvester II, confirms to Arnulf his right to wear the pallium on special occasions. Letter 244.

6. April 20, 990. Gerbert expected to meet Empress Theophanu in Italy (Letter 171), probably at Pavia where she celebrated Easter. With German control reestablished in Italy Gerbert hoped to resume his position as abbot of Bobbio. Bubnov, II, 621, n. 82; M. Uhlirz, *Jahrbücher des Deutschen Reiches unter Otto II. und Otto III*, Vol. II: *Otto III* (Berlin, 1955), pp. 122-23, 131, 463.

169. RHEIMS. October 25, 989

Gerbert sends a copy of his previous letter to Rainard, monk of Bobbio, and grants him permission to change monasteries

To RAINARD, MONK OF BOBBIO

A certain Tetbald, monk of Bobbio as he himself said, came to us last summer,[1] and through him we sent to you our letters, to which your letters do not make satisfactory answer. Accordingly, we are again sending a copy of the earlier letter,[2] and we offer the following advice to your request: If it pleases you to serve in another monastery under the Rule of Father Benedict, your spiritual abbot, use my permission; nor will the change be prejudicial to you when made for the sake of religion and at the command of your [actual] abbot.[3] In other respects, as in giving and receiving,[4] we are partly loosening, partly tightening, the reins of our permission. In this way a distinction may be preserved in order that you may give and may receive what legally and without offense to divine laws must be given and received, but do not think my permission extends to the giving of anything to a tyrant full of wicked desires, or of receiving anything from such.

This is Letter 161 in Havet. The present letter was probably carried by the same messenger as Letter 168.
1. Summer, 989.
2. Letter 138.
3. Gerbert continued to be the legal abbot of Bobbio until 999 when Petroald (Letters 10 and 22) was chosen abbot (DO III 335).
4. See Letter 22.

170. RHEIMS. December 10, 989
Gerbert describes the desolation of Rheims after its capture by Duke Charles

To Remi, Monk of Trier

Your request,[1] sweetest brother, so often repeated, indicates sufficiently well on what billows we are tossed. You know, you know what shipwrecks we suffered after we left you.[2] Indeed, as a result of the very burdensome labors of the summer and after, we contracted those illnesses whereby pestilential autumn[3] almost wrested our life away.

Violent fortune, taking back everything she had bestowed, added to this misery through those brigands who laid waste the city of Rheims.[4] Now we bewail the captivity of our friends,[5] and we meditate with sleepless worry whether we must change our home. On this account our district sorrows, on that, it mourns. Fear and trembling encompass the walls. Want presses hard upon the citizenry. The clergy of both orders groan over the future desolation.

Therefore, let it be your service to lift your hands to the Omnipotent One in our behalf, and if the Divinity lessens the punishment of this sinner, we will not be unmindful of your kindness in everything.

This is Letter 162 in Havet.
1. Remi had requested a celestial globe. Letters 142, 156, 160.
2. Gerbert's visit to Trier occurred probably April 12, 989. See Letter 162, introductory note. Gerbert liked similes and metaphors based upon the sea, and the "shipwreck" undoubtedly refers to his disappointment over not being chosen archbishop of Rheims.
3. A prevalent idea that "pestilential" autumn produced virulent disease is

attributable to Aurelius Cornelius Celsus (c.A.D. 14-37), *De medicina*, ed. C. Daremberg (Leipzig, 1859-91), I.i.-iii. "Therefore spring is the healthiest season: and next after this is winter: summer is more dangerous. Autumn is by far the most dangerous." Richer gives evidence of the general acceptance of this notion (I.lxv, II.xcix, III.xiv, translated by MacKinney, "Tenth Century Medicine," *Bulletin of the Institute of the History of Medicine*, II, 365, 368, 370); and also Bruno of Querfurt (*Vita quinque fratrum*, MGSS XV, 718, line 26). One tenth century manuscript of Celsus exists—MS Vatican Latin 5951—written in different hands. On Celsus see Sarton, *Introduction to the History of Science*, I, 240, who, however, incorrectly states that Celsus "was lost during the middle ages."

Gerbert had also been very ill previously in the summer of 988 (Letters 132 and 136).

4. Duke Charles captured Rheims through the treachery of Archbishop Arnulf, the knight Dudo (Letters 112 and 145, n. 3), and the Rheims priest Adalger. Richer IV.xxxiii-xxxv; *Acta concilii S. Basoli*, Chaps. XIV, LV; Lot, *Derniers Carolingiens*, pp. 252-57.

5. Introduction, pp. 11-12.

171. RHEIMS. January 10, 990

Gerbert describes the deplorable state of affairs incident upon Duke Charles's capture of Rheims

GERBERT TO RAYMOND [1]

To the Very Reverend Father Lord Raymond, from Gerbert his son.

You wish to know, dearest father, in what port I am steering the ship with the pilot [2] gone, and what the situation is in the kingdom of the French. After I had decided not to withdraw from the protection and counsel of my blessed Father Adalbero, I was so suddenly deprived of him that I was terrified to survive, since, indeed, we were of one heart and soul [Acts 4 : 32]; nor could his enemies believe that he had been borne away when they saw that I lived. With [pointing] fingers they singled me out for the ill will of Charles, then as now harassing our land, as the one who deposes and consecrates.

Therefore, since I was involved in affairs of state, I fell with the state, just as in the betrayal [3] of our city I was the greatest part of the booty. [4] This event has completely postponed my journey to Italy [5] where are kept both the organs [6] and the best part of my household paraphernalia. For we have not been able to withstand the headlong rush of fortune nor has the Divinity thus far revealed in what port He wishes me to stay. Thus, as for me and my lot—they expect to rejoice at the outcome of my present fate. I shall work as hard as I am able, and I shall not omit anything necessary until I shall enjoy my hoped-for home and shall return thanks to God in Zion.[7]

Farewell, most loving father. Farewell, Brother Ayrard.[8] Farewell, most holy fraternity, subordinate to you. In your quiet moments be mindful of me together with my Father Adalbero.

This is Letter 163 in Havet.
1. Gerbert's teacher at St. Gerald of Aurillac, now abbot. Letters 23, 51, 102, 105, 196.
2. Archbishop Adalbero.
3. See Letter 170.
4. Virgil *Aeneid* II.5.
5. See Letter 168, n. 6.
6. Letters 77, 102, 105.
7. I.e., Bobbio. Bubnov, II, 637-38.
8. Letters 25, n. 5; 51, 102.

172. RHEIMS. January 15, 990
Gerbert reminds Bishop Ascelin of Laon (?) that he is about
to be deprived of his bishopric, and urges action

GERBERT TO THE VENERABLE A[SCELIN?], THUS FAR A BISHOP

Have you given yourself over to sloth and to trust in uncertain chance to such an extent that you do not see the swords hanging over your neck, nor feel the battering rams and arbors[1] striking at your very foundations? Call to mind, I beseech, O sweet and happy friend of yore, what was done under the rule of my Father Adalbero. The own brother[2] of the divine, august Lothair, the heir of the kingdom, was expelled therefrom. His rivals[3] were made kings, temporary kings according to the opinion of many persons.

By what right was the lawful heir disinherited? By what right deprived of the kingdom? And, because he has returned to his paternal home, what decrees of the Roman pontiffs have forbidden infants to be baptized? What sacred canons have removed innocent priests from the altars?[4] Abraham argued the case with God whether in Sodom the righteous should perish with the wicked [Genesis 18 : 23-33]. Do you, pastor, not hesitate to sentence the wicked at the same time as the blameless?

But why do I mention these details, since I know the indictment, full of crimes and laden with evil deeds, which has been written down against you by the priests of God. Chosen are the judges by whose sentence it will profit you nothing to be absent, if you be absent. But if you are present, you will cease to be a bishop. Someone has been found who will receive your office.

Hasten, therefore, while time remains, and do not place your hopes on the Loire [5] nor the Seine; [6] they will profit you nothing. Mindful as I am, indeed, of the factions and the conspiracies, of the lawyer and the legal advisers, since I trust in your silence, I am compelled to tell you these things because of our old friendship in order to rouse you from your lethargy. Make it your business to seek more thoroughly for a remedy, you who seem to have fallen into an insensibility like epilepsy.[7]

This is Letter 164 in Havet. The contents of the letter seem to apply most to Ascelin, who had finally escaped from Laon after his incarceration by Duke Charles (Letter 149, n. 1). Apparently Ascelin had returned to his see in safety as promised, after Arnulf's election as archbishop of Rheims (Letter 163). See Letter 162, n. 8.

1. Siege engines, words which would be painful reminders to Ascelin of the sieges of Laon.

2. Duke Charles. Gerbert here indulges in certain subtleties. In case the letter fell into the hands of Charles or his partisans, the words would sound favorable to Charles. However, Gerbert intended to convey the idea to Ascelin that Archbishop Adalbero had distrusted Charles and thought him not fit for kingship and so Ascelin should likewise mistrust him.

3. Kings Hugh and Robert.

4. Letter 172 indicates the effectiveness of Ascelin's interdict (Letter 101).

5. Count Eudes of Blois and Chartres, situated in the Loire valley. See Letters 149 and 157 for Ascelin's relations with him.

6. Kings Hugh and Robert had a palace in Paris, and their strongest control was exerted in the valley of the Seine. Gerbert means that neither Eudes nor Hugh could capture Laon and drive Charles out, but it could be read to mean an invitation to join Charles's partisans and so the words would appear harmless to prying eyes.

7. *Comitialem morbum.* This should be added to the diseases known to Richer and Gerbert discussed by MacKinney, "Tenth Century Medicine," *Bulletin of the Institute of the History of Medicine*, II, 374-75. Gerbert could have read of it in Pliny *Historia naturalis* xx.xi.14; xxviii.vii.23; xxxii.iv.14; xxxii.ix.37. See Letter 14 as to the probability that Gerbert owned a copy of Pliny.

173. LAON. January 20, 990

Anathema promulgated through Gerbert's pen against the violators of the church of Rheims

ARCHBISHOP ARNULF TO THE ROBBERS OF RHEIMS

Arnulf, archbishop by the grace of God, warns the robbers of Rheims.

What do you wish for yourselves, wicked band of pillagers of

Rheims? Do not the tears of the orphan and widow move you? Are you not [moved] also by their Advocate, God Himself, and whether you like it or not, Himself the Witness, the Judge, and the Harsh Avenger, Whose judgment you cannot escape?

Behold what you have perpetrated before His very eyes: you have not blushed at the holy chastity of virgins; you have left naked matrons, whom even barbarians respected; you have not respected the orphan nor the ward. It is a trifle to you that you have approached the temple of the Mother of God, revered by all mankind. You have smashed its atrium, you have polluted it, you have violated it. Whatever your eyes beheld there, you desired. Whatever your hand could touch, you seized.

And we, indeed, who are exceeding divine and human justice by [our] mercy, do not condone your actions in carrying off food and drink,[1] but we are not making any [special] demands because of the wicked times. We do, however, demand the return of everything remaining that with your polluted hands you appropriated and still retain. Return it, therefore, or receive the sentence of damnation against the invaders of ecclesiastical property as set forth by the sacred canons and launched against you, which must be repeated over and over again:

ANATHEMA AGAINST THE THIEVES

By the authority of God, the Father, and of the Son, and of the Holy Spirit, with the perpetual Virgin, Blessed Mary, intervening and aiding, and also by the authority and power handed down to the Apostles and to us, we excommunicate, anathematize, curse, damn, and separate you from the churches of the Holy Church, our Mother, you authors of the robberies at Rheims—principals, assistants, evildoers, alienators of their very own property from the owners themselves under the sham of a sale. May the eyes of you who coveted be dimmed; may the hands which looted wither; may every part of the body which aided you become weak. May you always labor, nor ever find repose; may you be deprived of the fruits of your labor; may you dread and tremble at the appearance of an enemy, whether he pursues you or not, until you disappear by wasting away. Let it be your fate to be with Judas, betrayer of the Lord, in the land of death and darkness, until your hearts are changed to complete repentance.

Let this be the manner of your full repentance that you completely restore to their owners everything which you absconded with illegally, except food and drink; that you who did not revere the holy church of Rheims humble yourselves before the church of Rheims as a punishment. Nor shall these curses for your crimes cease from persecuting you as long as you continue in the sin of invading another's property.

Translation based on the text in the *Acta concilii S. Basoli*, Chap. xii (Olleris, pp. 182-83). This anathema was written a short time before Letter 174. The bishops who were meeting in successive sessions at Senlis during the end of the year 989 and the first half of 990 adopted this anathema and promulgated a similar one with some additions (Letter 185). See also Letter 186.

1. See Letter 186.

174. RHEIMS or LAON? February 1, 990
Archbishop Arnulf sends a copy of the anathema against the captors of Rheims to one of his suffragan bishops (Gui of Soissons?)

[TO BISHOP GUI OF SOISSONS (?),[1] IN THE NAME OF ARCHBISHOP ARNULF]

With boundless thanks we are repaying you for your immeasurable good will and even more for your pious affection toward us. Your expression of sympathy surely indicates how highly you esteem us. Therefore, we are announcing what we shall endeavor to do in the future, not only about those matters which we discuss with the fewest persons possible, but also about the anathema,[2] already promulgated against the plunderers of the city of Rheims. A copy of this we are sending to you in order that you may learn from it both what our temper is and that we shall undertake greater matters that we are reserving for the proper time. All things have their season [Eccl. 3 : 1].

We are saying things that must be kept quiet, we are silent about things that should be said; we do what we do not wish, we are unable to do what we wish because everything is so full of disorder, or rather confusion, and hoped-for happenings do not occur with the same frequency as those we wish to avoid. For, if a reasonable opportunity had presented itself we would long since have sought conferences with you. By great plans and with great energy we might have revived the royal name that had almost perished among the French, but, because of the wicked times, because of the hostile remarks of very abandoned men, we are acting secretly since we dare not act openly. The day will come, I repeat, it will come, and is at hand when each one of us shall be judged—our thoughts, our words, our deeds.

Meanwhile, recognize the limits prescribed for you; you should wish neither to delimit the greater affairs of the kingdom without the knowledge of your metropolitan nor to issue a hasty judgment on matters of whose purpose you are ignorant. Conserve your prudence and your strength; then you will present for us the stoutest of hearts to the enemy when you see the victorious signs borne ahead with us as the leader.

This is Letter 165 in Havet. Archbishop Arnulf remained a prisoner of his uncle, Duke Charles, until he swore an oath of fidelity to him. Letter 177. If Arnulf did not return to Rheims until March, 990, as suggested by Lot, (*Hugues Capet*, p. 262) then Gerbert must have contrived to visit him at Laon since he wrote this for Arnulf.

1. Letter 112, n. 6. At the council of St. Basle in 991, Bishop Eudes of Senlis testified (Olleris, p. 182): "At that very time [i.e., early in 990, at a meeting of the council of Senlis] we received from the hands of the venerable Bishop Gui a certain document [Letter 173] written by him [Arnulf] in which there was seen to contain [because of its omissions] both the confession of his [evil] deed and his own damnation." Soissons was in the region where Charles was consolidating his position. Bubnov, II, 643, 645, n. 120.

2. Letter 173.

175. RHEIMS. March 1, 990
Thanks Abbot Romulf of Sens for sending Cicero's works; requests more; invites him to Rheims

To ROMULF, ABBOT OF SENS [1]

By your gifts [2] you have fulfilled the double role of one who gives and one who receives. For, in our opinion, nothing in human affairs is preferable to a knowledge of the most distinguished men which, assuredly, is unfolded in the numerous volumes of their works.

Continue as you have begun and offer the waters of Cicero to one who thirsts. Into the midst of the cares that enveloped us after the betrayal [3] of the city, Marcus Tully so obtrudes himself that in the eyes of men we are considered happy, but, in our judgment, unhappy. Worldly things we sought, we found, we did; and, as I may add, we were made a leader of the criminal elements.

Do something, father, in order that the Divinity, excluded from the multitude of sinners, may return because changed by your prayers. Let It visit us and live with us; and let us, who sorrow at the absence of blessed Father Adalbero, rejoice in your presence, if this be possible.

This is Letter 167 in Havet.
1. Letters 124, n. 1; and 179.
2. Of manuscripts.
3. Thus, Gerbert now knew the real facts about the capture of Rheims by Duke Charles in September, 989.

176. RHEIMS. March 18, 990
Gerbert reveals his agitation over the situation at Rheims, and begs a friend (Bishop Bruno?) to visit him

[GERBERT TO BISHOP BRUNO (?)]

We have entered upon the restless sea, we are shipwrecked, and we groan. Never do safe shores, never does a haven appear. In you we seek tranquillity. You certainly possess it because what you once had when you bestowed some upon another still remains with you to bestow again. Therefore, with all the affection of our love we beseech you to be at Rheims on March 31st, if we have deserved anything [from you] according to the laws of friendship. or are [even] thought to deserve anything.

This is Letter 166 in Havet. Bubnov, (II, 650, n. 7) suggests that Romulf, abbot of Sens, was the intended recipient because of Gerbert's invitation to the latter in Letter 175. However, the tone of the two letters is so different that the friend must be sought elsewhere. Probably he was Bruno, bishop of Langres (Letter 155, n. 1) with whom Gerbert actually did confer during the following two months (Letter 180). Bishop Bruno had been made a prisoner when Duke Charles captured Rheims, but by giving a hostage he had now secured his freedom. Lot, *Hugues Capet*, p. 264.

177. RHEIMS. March 30, 990
Archbishop Arnulf of Rheims asks Archbishop Egbert's advice as to whether King Hugh or Duke Charles has the claim on his loyalty

To EGBERT, ARCHBISHOP OF TRIER [IN THE NAME OF ARCHBISHOP ARNULF [1]]

A sword, saintly father, reaches even to my life; on all sides the swords of enemies touch us. On the one hand we are urged on by fealty promised to the kings of the French.[2] On the other hand, since we were delivered up[3] to the power of Prince Charles, who was recovering the kingdom for himself, we are forced to change lords or become an exile. This one hope remains: that a foreknowing Divinity united [the two of] us by a certain relationship[4] and brought it to pass that we bear one another's burdens [Gal. 6 : 2]. Hence, we flee to you as to a sure protection, as to the altar of prudence, as to the interpreter of divine and human laws. The words of advice offered to your sons[5] will be like heavenly oracles [1 Peter 4 : 11].

This is Letter 168 in Havet.

1. Arnulf had been allowed to return to Rheims from his captivity at Laon after swearing some sort of oath to his uncle, Duke Charles. Letter 181 refers to this Letter 177.

2. Letter 201, p. 237.

3. *Addictus.* There is a subtlety in Gerbert's use of this world which is not apparent in the translation. An *addictus* in Rome was a bondman who differed from a slave especially because he could become free again by canceling the amount paid for his bond, even against his own lord (*dominus*). Ordinarily Gerbert uses the word *senior* [seigneur, or lord] in discussing the feudal relationship, but here he uses the more general term *dominus* [lord, or master]. He is thus trying to say for Arnulf that the bond between Arnulf and King Hugh and between Arnulf and Duke Charles were two different things: the first, towards Hugh, was his fealty (*fides*), his feudal oath; the second, towards Charles, was the bondman (*addictus*) relationship, a condition inflicted upon him willy-nilly, which he must accept until he could free himself from it at a more favorable time, just as the bondman, or *addictus*, could free himself from his bond. Harper's *Latin Dictionary* (1907), s.v. *addictus.*

4. *Germanitate* (nom., *germanitas*), usually indicating the blood relationship of brothers, but used here to show the close relationship of the churches of Rheims and Trier (Letter 111, n. 2).

5. Gerbert includes himself.

178. **RHEIMS. April, 990**
Gerbert informs monk R(uopert?) that he has no medicines to send him for an abscessed liver

[GERBERT TO RUOPERT?]

Gerbert greets his beloved R[uopert?].[1]

Your request is indeed a large order, dearest brother, but nothing not due your merits. For what is so desirable that your goodwill may not deserve it? what so insignificant that these times may permit it to be bestowed on friends? Since you lack a physician and we the materials for healing, we have refrained from describing the remedies which the most skilled physicians judge to be useful for an infected liver. This disease you incorrectly call *postuma*, whereas we call it *apostema*,[2] [abscess]; and Cornelius Celsus says it was called ηπατικον[3] by the Greeks.

This is Letter 169 in Havet.
1. Ruopert, a monk of Mettlach near Trier, and two other Mettlach monks had studied with Gerbert. *Miracula s. Liutwini*, MGSS XV, 1264; Manitius, II, 425-26; P. J. A. Juffermans, "La vie de Saint Adalbert par Ruopert, moine de Mettlach," ALMA, V (1930), 52. Although the "R." might stand for "Remi," the tone of this letter differs from the tone of the letters to Remi (Letters 142, 156, 160, 170).
2. Celsus *De medicina* i.i.1, "Abscesses of the body that the Greeks call *apostemata*."
3. Celsus De medicina viii.xv, "The disease of another organ, i.e., the liver, is as often chronic as it is acute: the Greeks call this ηπατικον."

179. RHEIMS. April 30, 990
   Gerbert hints at escaping from Rheims; begs for prayers; post-pones the meeting already planned

To Romulf, Abbot of Sens[1]

Since we have given equal consideration to the useful and to the honest,[2] we believe that in a brief space of time we shall be relieved of the tremendous weight of cares. This must be accomplished by making use of your pure love as manifested by your contemplating the Divinity as you have begun to do. And so we must enjoy each other's affection in a more suitable place.

This is Letter 170 in Havet.
1. See Letters 124 and 175.
2. Cicero *De officiis* iii.iii. See Letter 50, n. 3.

180. SENLIS. May, 990
   Kings Hugh and Robert request Bishop Bruno of Langres to attend a court at Senlis

To Bruno, Bishop of Langres[1]

The serene *augusti*, our lords, have now for some time been wishing for your desirable presence in order to take counsel with you. There-fore, I advise and request that for the sake of the welfare of the whole state you hasten your journey as soon as possible. And I, who hearkened to you at Roucy [2] in behalf of my own welfare, deserve to be heard now at Senlis [3] in behalf of the freedom of all good men.

This is Letter 171 in Havet.

1. See Letter 155, n. 1; *Acta concilii S. Basoli*, Olleris, pp. 178-79; and Lot, *Hugues Capet*, pp. 13, n. 2, 15, n. 4, 18, 21, 40, 45-46, 69, 77, 78, 261, 263-64.

2. Dept. Aisne, about twenty-five miles from Rheims and from Laon. Bishop Bruno's brother, Count Gilbert, owned a castle here.

3. Senlis (dept. Oise), seventy miles from Rheims, was apparently a royal bishopric. One royal abbey, possibly St. Rieul, reconstructed by Robert II, was located there. Queen Adelaide founded St. Frambourg at Senlis. Lot, *Hugues Capet*, Index, s.v. Senlis. Newman, *Domaine royal*, pp. 97, 205, 212, 216, 221. Apparently King Hugh maintained a royal residence at Senlis. Richer iv.xlii.

·181. SENLIS. June 1, 990
Compliments Archbishop Egbert on his perspicacity with regard to Archbishop Arnulf; begs for a lenient attitude towards himself

To Egbert, Archbishop of Trier

Although I have tested Your Prudence in many ways, recently I learned to know it better when, in a subtle answer you censured the complaint [1] that, in the name of Archbishop Arnulf, I had embellished. Since my conscience has been tormenting me about this, I have thus feared lest I be displeasing in your eyes, because I had already begun to dissatisfy myself. I was regarded not [simply] as the companion of the wicked, but as the leader [2] of enormous crimes, I, who under the regime of my Father Adalbero of blessed memory, served in the school of all the virtues.

Now, however, I am living at the royal court, and offering the words of life with the priests of God. Not for the love of Charles nor of Arnulf [3] will I suffer longer to be made an instrument of the devil by proclaiming falsehoods contrary to truth. So, I beg to be found worthy of your kindness as of yore, for I am laying bare my soul to be judged by you in order that through me you may know what you should learn about the betrayal of Rheims. [4]

This is Letter 172 in Havet.

1. Letter 177. Egbert's answer is not preserved.

2. Letter 175. Charles, by leaving Gerbert in charge of Rheims, produced the impression that Gerbert, not Arnulf, was his chief assistant. Introduction, p. 12; Lattin, *Peasant Boy*, pp. 134-35.

3. Possibly Egbert had used these words ironically in his reply.

4. See Letters 185-88; 201, p. 238; *Acta concilii S. Basoli,* Chaps. VI, XI, XIV, LV,; *Concilium Mosomense,* Olleris, pp. 180-82, 185, 235, 247.

182. SENLIS. June 1, 990

Reminds the bishop of Verdun, Adalbero, of their close friendship; requests the return of his friend Lelius

To ADALBERO, BISHOP OF VERDUN [1]

I shall not be wordy with you, the partner and confidant of all my plans. For, you know why I remained so long at Rheims after the departure of my blessed Father Adalbero to God, and whither, both before and after the betrayal of the city, I was striving to go. Often, also, you have taken to heart that Terencism: "If you cannot do what you wish to do, then wish to do what you can." [2]

Now, indeed, I am not unmindful of your favors and affection towards me, and I still maintain toward you and yours that love which I have declared, judging myself made more blessed on this account. For, why should I not love those who cherish me? Indeed, I feel that you are delighted that I have fled the gatherings of wicked men [3] and that I have been restored to ecclesiastical fellowship.

Hence, with your accustomed wont, transact the business of a friend, to wit: have Lelius return from the Alsatians or Swabians, and let a worthy substitute for [our] beloved Aquila [4] be sought out so that the end of our works [James 2 : 22] may result in perfect charity [Col. 3 : 14].

This is Letter 173 in Havet.

1. At the beginning of· 989 Bishop Adalbero sought medical aid for his failing health in Salerno, Italy. The results were disappointing so he traveled to northern Italy where he remained for some time. Then he returned to Verdun in the early spring of 990 and resumed his episcopal duties. Letter 182 proves this and the fact that he was in close and frequent communication with Gerbert. Later Adalbero returned to Italy where he died April 18, 991. *Gesta episcopum Virdunensium,* MGSS IV, 47; Bubnov, II, 475, n. 65.

2. Terence *Andria* ii.i.5-6. See Letter 61.

3. Duke Charles and Archbishop Arnulf. Gerbert seems to have been thinking of Psalms 94 : 20, and 1 Corinthians 10 : 20-21. Some writers interpret Gerbert's words here to mean that he had been excommunicated because of association with Charles, but the inclusive excommunication (which did not include Gerbert) was not promulgated until July, 990. Letters 185 and 189.

4. Lelius and Aquila may have been pupils of Gerbert. The unusual names

may have been nicknames, Lelius being derived from Cicero's *De amicitia,* and Aquila from the book of Acts. Cicero dedicated his essay *De amicitia* to Scipio Africanus, whose close friend was Laelius. Hence, Gerbert may have applied the name to a very close friend who was also known to Bishop Adalbero. Letter 189 proves that Aquila was the name of someone close to Gerbert, possibly a converted Jew, since the Biblical Aquila (Acts 18 : 1-3; 1 Cor. 16 : 19; Romans 16 : 3) was a converted Jew who was St. Paul's principal assistant. However, Alcuin called the Bavarian Arn, bishop of Salzburg from 785, "Aquila," [i.e., "The Eagle"], because of his keenness of insight and spiritual strength, since in Old German *arn* = eagle. Duckett, *Alcuin,* p. 140.

183. SENLIS. June 1, 990
King Hugh (?) seeks closer friendship with Duke Henry (?) and requests aid

[To Duke Henry (?), in the Name of King Hugh (?)]

While we are embracing your precious and matchless friendship more eagerly we endure the ill will of many men, especially those who are upsetting your seigneur's[1] plans [so they will be] against us. Evil increases from day to day. Multiplied are our enemies who arrogate to themselves greater boldness in the hope of dividing the kingdoms. If, therefore, you are as excellent a person as we hope and believe, make us aware of the fact that you are not against us, for we have preferred your love to the love of King Otto. Let our enemies feel that peace between the kingdoms is due to you, [peace] which they are denying can be made without their advice.

Furthermore, because a route through enemies is difficult for trustworthy legates, I beg you to fulfill the office of our legates. Whatever you judge honest, promise in our behalf. Thus, venture for us absent as if we were present.[2] And if you find anything to reply to us, please do so as quickly as possible by letters or messengers so that while our rivals[3] remain in ignorance our mutual friendship may be strengthened through the most trustworthy messengers. We are saying this for the following reasons: because we are unwilling, without a definite reason, to send legates of greater authority with great danger to themselves,[4] and because a meeting of kings is a thing of labor and at this time useless in every respect because of the ill will on both sides. Even if you have felt that the plans of wicked men are equally valuable, and that friendship could not be made useful and honorable for you, still, because it is of the utmost importance, we implore counsel and aid from you at one and the same time. Do not permit a useless hope to delude us whom hitherto you have considered worthy because of a kind of friendship and relationship.[5]

This is Letter 174 in Havet. This letter is most intelligible if King Hugh was the addressor and Duke Henry of Bavaria the addressee. Empress Theophanu was expected soon in Germany, and Hugh wished to have a powerful partisan to plead with her for aid. Lot, *Hugues Capet*, p. 22, argues for Queen Mathilda of Burgundy as the addressee.

1. Otto III.

2. Many German nobles met with Theophanu at Frankfort, June 16th, (DO III 62) but the roads from Senlis towards Frankfort were probably controlled by Heribert of Troyes, a partisan of Duke Charles. So, Hugh hoped Henry would represent him. See Letter 129 relative to Theophanu's earlier unsuccessful effort to secure cessation of hostilities.

3. Duke Charles.

4. Such legates would have carried various marks and insignia to convince Henry and especially Otto III of their credibility, and therefore they would have been easily recognized in enemy territory.

5. *Affinitatis* (nom., *affinitas*), relationship by marriage, or in a remote degree, or even by a community of interests. Actually, King Hugh was a first cousin of Duke Henry and of Queen Mathilda (see introductory note, above). Mathilda, however, was a sister of Duke Charles, and as a Carolingian might understandably have supported Charles's efforts to defeat Hugh.

184. SENLIS. June 30, 990
King Hugh (?) assures the recipient (Duke Henry?) of his services and seeks friendship

[To Duke Henry (?) in the Name of King Hugh (?)]

Your happiness gratifies and comforts us. For where there is one flesh and one blood, there there is one love. That day has passed when your grief produced an unavoidable sadness in us, nor let it ever return.[1] Now, indeed, in peace, just as then in distress, we are devoting ourselves and our possessions to your service so that if either by force or ingenuity you try to undertake anything great and worthy of yourself, you may use our resources, to wit, industriousness, advice, natural capacity, and soldiers. But if you desire quietude and silence both now and in eternity, may we enjoy peace and quiet with you.

Do not let the rivals of your name boast that they are more capable of injuring us than you are of aiding. If possible, let there be an honest appearance of friendship between your seigneur [2] and ourselves. Prescribe what is to be done and what avoided. Do not allow us to be surrounded with treachery and deceit because we have determined not to follow any man against you, even though he be our friend.

This is Letter 175 in Havet. The recipient was a blood relative of the sender, who certainly was King Hugh, using Gerbert's pen. Thus, Duchess Beatrice, Queen Mathilda of Burgundy, Mathilda's daughter, Countess Bertha, and Duke Henry of Bavaria all qualify. However, this letter seems to reply to a letter from Duke Henry, written in response to Letter 183. See M. Uhlirz, *Untersuchungen über Inhalt und Datierung der Briefe Gerberts*, pp. 148f.

1. Uhlirz, *Untersuchungen* (see introductory note, above), suggests that these words refer to Duke Henry's incarceration, 978-84.
2. Otto III.

185. **SENLIS. July 1, 990**
Gerbert, for the bishops of the Rheims archdiocese, denouncing the priest Adalger and his accomplices, and publishing the anathema against them

THE DENUNCIATION AGREED ON AT SENLIS BY THE BISHOPS OF THE [ARCH]DIOCESE OF RHEIMS IN LIEU OF A DECREE

How far will your unrestrained license extend itself, O satellites of that other betrayer, Judas? What limit of crimes will your leader's newly manifested audacity reach? We are speaking of the priest Adalger [1] as your leader, whose very name pollutes the name of the priestly office.

You, disgraceful priest, do we therefore address. Why, after those bloody weapons with which you occupied yourself at Laon, did it seem to you that you, once more become a worthless apostate, should betray Arnulf, archbishop of Rheims, when previously, like a most trustworthy guardian, you slept with him, you were his attentive table companion, you offered him advice, you administered the sacraments? Do you suppose that you can escape the inflexible ecclesiastical severity or the judgment of Omnipotent God? You opened the gates of the city, you let in the enemy; the venerable temple of the Mother of God, which should be revered by barbarians themselves, you besieged as if it were the camp of an enemy.

And also [we address] you, almost all of the plunderers, whom enormous benefits had obligated to the church, and who are saying: "As heirs let us possess the sanctuary of God" [Gal. 4 : 7], you who, clothed in mail and helmet, with shields and lances, bore the military standards before the altar of the Blessed Mother of God, you whose polluted hands seized pastor, clergy, and people within the Holy of Holies, whose custody you divided up, whom you delivered over to prison and whom you still hold; will you, I ask, escape divine justice?

You, by whose deception and fraud, advice, and aid so great a crime was committed, certainly are conspirators, with those who were the ringleaders [2] of such great villany, so you impious brigands, having at the same time sinfully conspired and having divided up the property of the citizens of Rheims as if it were the booty of war, must equally suffer the punishment of a sinner. Nor should you who have perpetrated no less unreliable tricks against Adalbero, bishop of Laon, be omitted. In order to cut off the budding heresy that asserts Charles's rights over everything, even in sacred places, we are taking away the right of the sacred offices from both the church of Rheims and that of Laon, each polluted by sacrilege, however dissimilar, until each shall be legally reconciled.

And, lest anyone may think that we favor such monsters of men or will give our assent to such behavior, and even more to inform them that we have been exposed to all sorts of dangers for the faith by which we live, we thus confirm, establish and corroborate our sentence:

ANATHEMA AGAINST THE CRIMINALS

By the authority of Omnipotent God the Father, the Son and the Holy Spirit, by the intervention and aid of the Blessed, Perpetual Virgin, together with all the saints, by the authority and power also handed down by the apostles and bestowed on us, we excommunicate, anathematize, damn, and separate from the limits of the Holy Mother Church the priest Adalger, member of the devil, betrayer of the archbishop, clergy, and all of the people of Rheims; and also those who were the originators of this betrayal, the authors, the perpetrators, the accomplices, the promotors, the plunderers of the citizens, and the transferers of their movable property under the pretense of sale.[3] To these villains we add the attackers of the bishop of Laon and his wickedly oppressive torturers.

Let it be done as the Scripture says: "Who said, Let us take to ourselves the houses of God in possession. O my God, make them like a wheel; as the stubble before the wind. As the fire burneth a wood, and as the flame setteth the mountains on fire; so persecute them with thy tempest, and make them afraid with Thy storm. Fill their faces with shame; that they may seek Thy name, O Lord. Let them be confounded and troubled forever; yea, let them be put to shame, and perish: That men may know that Thou whose name is Lord, art alone the Most High over all the earth" [Psalm 82].[4]

Furthermore, because they have not pitied the widow and the orphan, nor respected the temple of God, but have usurped the control of the churches for themselves, may their sons become orphans, and their wives, widows; may the usurer search out all their substance, and foreigners ravage their labors. Let their faithless sons be taken away, and be ejected from their homes, and let them beg. May their days be few, and let another receive their posts of honor. By double destruction, destroy them, O Lord our God, unless they repent and make satisfaction to the Catholic Church by effective penance.

Translation based on the text in *Acta concilii S. Basoli*, Olleris, pp. 185-86. Drawn up by Gerbert who had the fullest knowledge of the matters contained therein, it was read to the bishops at Senlis. Instead of passing a formal decree they accepted the document as read. Later Bishop Gui of Soissons offered it in evidence at the Council of St. Basle to prove that the assembled bishops at Senlis went as far as they had thought expedient with regard to Archbishop Arnulf by including him in the anathema by implication only, without naming him.

1. The bishops at the Council of St. Basle deprived him of his priestly office in order not to subject him as a priest to perpetual anathema. Olleris, pp. 235-36.

2. Duke Charles, and, by implication, Arnulf.

3. *Sub hasta* [under the spear]. A spear was stuck into the ground to indicate the place of sale of booty gained in battle.

4. This is from the Authorized Version of the Bible as that is closer to Gerbert's Latin than the Douay-Confraternity translation.

186. SENLIS. July 2, 990

The Rheims bishops are sending herewith a copy of the revised anathema against the plunderers of the church of Rheims to Rothard, bishop of Cambrai

[To Bishop Rothard in the Name of the Bishops of the Rheims Province]

The bishops[1] of the diocese of Rheims greet Reverend Father Rothard.[2]

Because our brother and fellow bishop Arnulf was captured within his own church and now is unable to carry out satisfactorily what is his right, owing, it is said, to the strength of the enemy, we, who are not unmindful of our duty, have therefore repeated herein what we previously said [3] with his advice against the notorious plunderers. The following [exception] has been added, namely, that with respect to food and drink, we have not abused mercy [by an act] contrary to divine and human justice, as he himself said.[4] But our anathema, in addition, condemns the dukes, counts, and accomplices of the whole faction, and we have suspended this church from divine office, judging that other [churches] can suffice for the Christian faithful. Accordingly, we are sending to you a copy of the decree of anathema,[5] and we exhort, advise, and pray you to applaud our decision, and to take similar action.

This is Letter 176 in Havet.
1. See Letter 195.
2. Died September 20, 995. Rothard was the only suffragan bishop of the Rheims archdiocese outside the French kingdom.
3. Letter 173.
4. See Letter 173, and the speech of Bishop Walter of Autun at the Council of St. Basle (Olleris, p. 184).
5. Letter 185.

187. SENLIS. July 10, 990

The bishops of the Rheims diocese apologize to Pope John XV for not consulting him earlier about Archbishop Arnulf and request papal condemnation of him

[To Pope John in the Name of the Bishops of the Rheims Province]

To the Most Reverend Lord Pope John,[1] the bishops of the diocese of Rheims.

For a long time we have realized, most blessed Father, that we should seek the opinions of the Holy Roman Church regarding the ruin and downfall of the sacerdotal order. But, oppressed by a multitude of tyrants, and removed [from you] by the length of the lands, we have thus far been unable to fulfill our desires. Now, finally, we are bringing before you the new and unprecedented [2] crime of Arnulf, archbishop of Rheims, who, now become a notorious apostate, holds in the church the place once held by the betrayer Judas: he, though once a son of the church of Laon, after seizing its bishop [Ascelin] through fraud and treachery, invaded his church, and, as a crowning point of his damnation, captured Rheims, which had been entrusted to him, and its clergy and people.

Our summons,[3] or rather, our salvation-bringing exhortation does not move him, nor the many times repeated admonition of his brother archbishops of the provinces, nor his profession [4] made according to the canons before God and the angels, nor the text of the chirograph read within sight of the Church,[5] nor the numerous oaths that he swore, nor the words from the wonderful councils. Many, many churches stand widowed of their pastors through his crime; innumerable persons are perishing without priestly benediction and confirmation; he himself, despising divine and human laws, practices tyranny with a tyrannical faction. He plans ruin for our kings from whom he has so freely received such great honor.

Finally aroused to the monstrous acts of this most wicked man, therefore, we turned to the Word of the Lord Who says: "If thy brother sin against thee, go and show him his fault, between thee and him alone. If he listen to thee, thou hast won thy brother. But if he do not listen to thee, take with thee one or two more so that on the word of two or three witnesses every word may be confirmed. And if he refuse to hear them, appeal to the Church, but if he refuse to hear even the Church, let him be to thee as the heathen and the publican." [Mat. 18 : 15-17].

Come to the aid of a sinking church, O Father, and render against the criminal an opinion that is made known by the sacred canons or rather by Truth itself. Let us feel that you are another Peter, the defender and corroborator of the Christian faith; let the Holy Roman Church render a verdict of damnation against a criminal whom the whole Church condemns. Let your authority support us both in the deposition of this apostate and in the consecration of a new archbishop who can be placed over the home of God, and also [uphold] our brother bishops who have been called upon to make the necessary promotion so that we may learn and know why we ought to put your apostolate above the others.[6]

Translation made from the text in *Acta concilii S. Basoli,* Olleris, pp. 202-3. There is no absolute proof that Gerbert wrote this letter, but its language, style, and content seem to indicate his authorship. Lot, *Hugues Capet,* p. 25, also believes that Gerbert wrote Letters 187 and 188. T(etbald?), archdeacon of

Rheims cathedral carried Letters 187 and 188 to Pope John XV in Rome. See Letter 193.

1. Pope John XV (985-96). See Letter 188.

2. He had allowed his city to be captured and his church to be desecrated.

3. The council of bishops at Senlis summoned Archbishop Arnulf three times between the time of his release by Charles in March, 990, and the promulgation of the anathema which, by implication, included him (Letter 185). Arnulf completely ignored the first two, but finally agreed to meet Bishop Gui of Soissons at Chavignon where Gui brought the third citation. Arnulf still refused to appear at Senlis, and admitted his swearing of an oath to his uncle, Duke Charles. *Acta concilii S. Basoli*, Olleris, p. 216; Lot, *Hugues Capet*, pp. 262-63.

4. This profession of faith had probably been sent to Pope John XV at the same time as Arnulf's request for the pallium. Letter 168.

5. In Letter 201, pp. 237-38, Gerbert wrote that the oath of fealty was sworn inside the church. The importance of the place lay in the religious sanction supporting an action taken even within sight of a church, because of the Sacrament. See Letter 188, especially, n. 2.

6. This was not a remark insulting to the pope, as some writers have interpreted it, but a call to him to take the Rheims affair in hand with a firm attitude. The Rheims bishops could not have appealed to Rome earlier, because they were at first not aware of Arnulf's complicity, and as they gradually learned of it they preferred to believe that he was an unwilling captive of his uncle.

188. SENLIS. July 10, 990
*King Hugh Capet explains Archbishop Arnulf's treachery to
Pope John XV; requests the pope's decision*

Hugh by the Grace of God King of the French to the Most Blessed Pope John

Aroused by new and unusual events, we have ordered that your advice must be most eagerly and carefully sought, since we know that you devote all of your time to divine and human studies. Take under consideration what has been done, and write back in reply what ought to be done in order that respect for sacred laws may be revived and the royal power not be nullified.

Arnulf, the son[1] of King Lothair, so they say, whom we took to our bosom like a father, even after his alarming hostility and the crimes that he practiced against us and our kingdom, was freely given the archbishopric of Rheims and swore an oath of allegiance[2] such that it would invalidate past and future oaths. He wrote a chirographic document[3] of fealty which he read aloud, corroborated, and had others corroborate. He compelled his knights and all the citizens to swear an oath that they would persist in fidelity to us if at any time he should fall into the power of enemies.[4]

Contrary to all these assurances, as the most reliable witnesses [5] can verify, he himself threw open the gates [6] to enemies; and the clergy and people entrusted to his fidelity he allowed to be distributed as captives and booty.

Granted that he was delivered over to the power of another, as he wishes it to appear.[7] Why [then] does he force citizens and knights to perjure themselves? Why does he prepare arms against us? Why does he fortify the city and camps against us? If he has been captured, why is he not set at liberty? If he is overwhelmed by the enemy's force, why does he not wish to be aided? And, if he has been freed, why does he [not] return to us? The palace summons him, but he refuses to come. The archbishops and his fellow bishops invite him, but he responds that he owes them nothing.[8]

Therefore, you who are the apostles' successor, decide what ought to be done with this second Judas lest we blaspheme the name of God, and lest, by chance, aroused by a justifiable sorrow and your silence, we attempt the downfall of the city and the burning of the whole diocese. If you are unwilling to render a formal judgment to us who seek one because of our lack of knowledge, do not offer the excuse that the judgment is God's.[9]

Translation made from the text in *Acta concilii S. Basoli*, Olleris, p. 202. As with Letter 187, the language, style, content, and occasion for writing all suggest Gerbert's authorship. See the introductory note to Letter 187. At the Council of St. Basle it was stated that the legates bearing Letters 187 and 188 were at first well received by the pope. Then legates from Charles's partisan, Count Heribert of Troyes, arrived with gifts, including a beautifully shaped white horse, so that (the Council said) Pope John turned against the king's legates. He kept them waiting outside his palace doors for three days, and they finally returned to France in disgust without a further hearing. Olleris, pp. 203-204. They reached Senlis September 15th.

1. Letter 163, n. 1.

2. Arnulf swore his fealty on the Eucharist during the celebration of the Mass. Some shocked bishops considered this a sacrilege. Richer iv.xxx-xxxi.

3. See Letters 187 and 201, pp. 237-38; and Richer iv.xxix, lx.

4. Cf. Letter 190 in which Gerbert protests against having an oath which was sworn to one person bind the swearer to a third person.

5. Gerbert and Bishop Bruno of Langres were eyewitnesses.

6. Actually the priest Adalger opened the gates of Rheims to Duke Charles. Introduction, p. 12; Olleris, p. 182.

7. See Letter 177, n. 3. The same word *addictus* (delivered up) is used in Letter 188 here to indicate Arnulf's excuse for his submission to Charles.

8. See Letter 187, n. 3.

9. Tertullian (*De pudicitia* iii.xxi) believed some sins are so grave as to be irremissible, and therefore they must be reserved to the judgment of God. J. T.

McNeill, and H. M. Gamer, *Mediaeval handbooks of penance* (Records of civilization, No. 29; New York, 1938) p. 15. The real issue was Arnulf's treason (infidelity) against King Hugh. Compare the deposition of Bishop Sisebert of Toledo for treason against the Visigothic King Egica in 693; and of Hildemann of Beauvais, and Ebo of Reims for the same reason. F. R. Murphy, "Julian of Toledo and the Fall of the Visigothic Kingdom in Spain," *Speculum,* XXVII (1952), 23, n. 51; *Acta Concilii S. Basoli,* Olleris, pp. 200-201.

189. NEAR RHEIMS. August 25, 990

Gerbert promises Abbot Joubert of St. Thierry to secure permission from Kings Hugh and Robert for him to hide his grain in the city

To Abbot Joubert [1]

Because you bear our burdens [Gal. 6 : 2] and rejoice in our fortunate situation we thank you, as we should. We are not so far removed, nor do we take such advantage of this good, now that the Divinity smiles upon us, that we are unable to make our old friendship serviceable. Therefore, I will attend to your requests and, as far as I am able by persuasion to utilize the favor of the kings, I will remove the army from the neighborhood of Rheims until you have hidden in the city whatever [grain] you have left in the fields.

May you, then, look after my son Aquila [2] until you can return him to me by very trusty friends.

In addition, lest you be ignorant of what the synod of the bishops of our diocese decreed, I am hereby sending you and your associates a copy of the decisions [3] so that henceforth you may know what you ought to follow, what to avoid.

This is Letter 177 in Havet. In early August, 990, Duke Charles was seizing and storing all possible grain near Laon, Soissons, and Rheims. Kings Hugh and Robert then renewed their campaign against him, making a speciality of burning the fields. Richer iv.xxxvii. Hugh's army undoubtedly assembled at Senlis, drove northeastward towards Soissons, then turned southeastward towards Rheims. Hugh, Robert, and Gerbert accompanied the army. For this scorched earth policy Hugh could not have waited until the return of his ambassadors to Pope John XV, since they had left Senlis about July 10th. Letter 188; Lot, *Hugues Capet,* pp. 27, n. 1, 260.

1. Abbot of St. Thierry (situated about four miles from the city of Rheims). His brother Gerard was a pupil of Gerbert and later bishop of Cambrai (1012-48). *Gesta episcoporum Cameracensium,* MGSS VII, 465; Havet, p. 157, n. 1.

2. Apparently, Aquila (Letter 182, n. 4) had sought refuge in St. Thierry after his return, since he learned that Gerbert had escaped from Rheims.

3. Letter 185.

190. **NEAR RHEIMS.** September 1, 990

Gerbert officially announces his severing of relations with Archbishop Arnulf and Duke Charles

MEMORANDUM OF GERBERT'S REPUDIATION OF ARCHBISHOP ARNULF

For a very long time as I kept turning over and over in my mind the unhappy state of our city and did not find any way to exterminate the evildoers without the slaughter of the good people, at length the following solution seemed satisfactory as one which would remedy the present misfortunes and safeguard our friends in the future.

So, we are changing one only for one—a lordship for a lordship—and, thus freed, we abandon your benefits [to us] to your ill will and to that of our rivals [toward us] lest, because of these [benefits] an argument of violating promised fidelity [1] be raised against us, that could be extended to bind us by any sort of friendship to your uncle [Charles]. For nothing is owed to one person, according to the agreement by which we live, when fidelity has been pledged to someone different.[2] For, if we wish you to be safe, how are we benefiting your uncle? Likewise, if we help your uncle, in what way can we wish you to be safe?

This controversy we are settling by departing for other persons so that we may owe neither to you nor to that one anything except gratuitous benevolence. If you accept it, please save for me and mine the homes, that with our own labor and at great expense we built, together with their furnishings. Also, the churches that we obtained by solemn and legitimate gifts [3] according to the custom of the province we pray you not to seize by prejudicial decisions. As for the rest we do not ask for much.

After this has been done you may honestly summon to your service one who at one time did not have to bow his neck.[4] Nor is there any doubt that, if you exceed these limitations, everything that we possess, just as we received it from many persons, you will have bestowed with an oath on our rivals at the very time when, corresponding to your affection, we were recommending the most sagacious plans in your behalf. We shall [then] be unable to forget bygone evil deeds since we shall be reminded by the present disclosures.

This is Letter 178 in Havet. Gerbert wrote out this repudiation apparently when King Hugh's troops had some chance of recapturing Rheims. Letter 189 and Richer IV.xxxvii-xxxix. Hugh, fearing that Arnulf might make a claim upon Gerbert's loyalty because of his oath to Arnulf (n. 1 below), probably compelled Gerbert to write this document.

1. See Gerbert's speech at the Council of Mouzon on June 2, 995. "Nor did I consign to prison the man [Arnulf] to whom, in the presence of faithful witnesses, I had recently taken an oath of fidelity." Olleris, p. 247.

2. See Letter 188, n. 4.

3. At the Council of Mouzon Gerbert mentions "the possessions which the especially outstanding largess of the great dukes had bestowed upon me through your generosity." Olleris, p. 247.

4. Cf. Letter 8.

191. RHEIMS. June 21, 991
The notification of Gerbert's election as archbishop of Rheims, drawn up by himself

ELECTION OF GERBERT ARCHBISHOP OF RHEIMS

Always, indeed, dearest brothers, the judgments of God are just but ofttimes hidden. For, behold, after the death [1] of Father Adalbero of blessed memory, urged on as we were by the shout of the crowd, since the Scripture says: The voice of the people is the voice of the Lord [Isa. 66:6], and by the regulations of the sacred canons, requiring us to learn the wish and vote of the clergy and people in the election of a bishop, we placed over ourselves and the church of Rheims a certain royal offspring.[2]

By incautiously following the requirements to the letter, as well as by investigating too little the true revelation of divine scripture, the keenness of our minds was dulled. That cry, indeed, that voice of the people shouting: "Crucify, crucify" [Luke 23:21; John 19:6], was not the voice of the Lord. Therefore, not always is the voice of the people the voice of the Lord. Nor should the votes and desires of all of the clergy and people be sought in the election of a bishop, but only those of the sincere and uncorrupted, if we hope to gain the one least open to bribery. In the opinions of the Fathers the rule says: "The crowd is not allowed to elect those who are called to the priesthood, but let the decision be that of the bishops since they are to make proof of him who is to be ordained as to whether he has been trained in speaking, in faith, and in episcopal life." [3]

Therefore, following these constitutions of the Fathers, with the favor and agreement of both of our princes, august Lord Hugh and most excellent King Robert, and also with the assent of those among the clergy and the people who are God's, we, the diocesan bishops of Rheims, are choosing as our archbishop Abbot[4] Gerbert, mature in age, prudent by nature, tractable, affable, and merciful.[5] Nor do we esteem that unstable young man, vaunting his ambition and administering everything with rashness, more than this one. Nor, indeed, do we endure being forced to listen patiently to such persons as those by whose knowledge and advice we know ecclesiastical and civil rights cannot be administered.

Since this quality must be especially looked for in a bishop, particularly in one who as metropolitan is placed above others, we are electing therefore this Gerbert who has been [our teacher (?)].[6] We have known his life and habits from young manhood. We have experienced his zeal in divine and human affairs. We seek to be informed through his advice and instruction. Therefore, we confirm his election by subscribing our names, and we establish and corroborate it by the common consent of all good persons.

This is Letter 179 in Havet. During the nine months elapsing between Letters 190 and 191 the following events occurred: King Hugh and Duke Charles, each with troops, met but failed to join battle, and withdrew. Count Eudes seized Dreux but failed to render the aid promised to Hugh. A fictitious reconciliation between Charles and Bishop Ascelin and between Arnulf and Hugh was brought about by Ascelin. Through the deception of Ascelin, Charles and Arnulf were captured at Laon on March 29th or 30th. Hugh then entered Laon and imprisoned Arnulf and Charles with his family. A council of bishops and abbots met at St. Basle-de-Verzy of Rheims, June 17-18, 991, and compelled Arnulf to abdicate his office of archbishop of Rheims. Gerbert was elected archbishop on the following Sunday (June 21st). *Acta Concilii S. Basoli*, Chap. LIV; Richer IV.xl-xliv; Havet, p. 159, n. 3; Lot, *Hugues Capet*, pp. 27-30, 76-78.

1. January 23, 989.
2. Arnulf.
3. Dionysius Exiguus, *Codex canonum ecclesiasticorum* cxvi, PL LXVII, 166.
4. Gerbert was still legally abbot of Bobbio.
5. These words conform to the general formulae of election of bishops and abbots such as can be found in Villanueva. Vol. XIV, 309, in 949, election of Aimeri as abbot of the monastery of Santa Maria de Amer: "Aimeri ... adorned with good habits, humble, chaste, modest, sober, gentle, compassionate, and well instructed in the Old and New Testament"; Vol. XV, 279, in 976, election of Abbot Dodo of Camprotund, drawn up in the more extravagant language used by Bishop Miró (Letter 33) of Gerona: "Dodo ... for a long time most judiciously trained under monastic discipline, whom we know to be adorned with good habits, tastefully educated in wisdom, shining in charitableness, outstanding in humility, astute in prudence, noted for compassion and piety, and fully instructed according to the Benedictine Rule"; Vol. X, 290, in 1017, election of Borrell as bishop of Rodez: "He is prudent, tractable, temperate in habits,

chaste of life, sober, humble, compassionate, hospitable, learned in the law of the Lord, and skilled in simple words."

6. Blank in MS L of about 15 letters. I suggest *scolasticus noster*.

192. RHEIMS. June 21 or 28, 991

PROFESSION OF FAITH OF GERBERT, ARCHBISHOP OF RHEIMS

I, Gerbert, by the surpassing pleasure of God soon to be archbishop of Rheims, in simple words affirm all the previous articles of faith. I assert that there is one God, the Father, the Son, and the Holy Spirit, the whole Deity of one essence and consubstantial in the Trinity, and I pronounce the three Persons coeternal and co-omnipotent. I confess each of the single Persons in the Trinity to be the True God, and all three Persons to be One God. I believe that the Divine Incarnation was not only in the Father, not only in the Holy Spirit, but as much in the Son, just as He who was the Son of God the Father on his divine side, became the Son of the Mother of man on his human side.

And I confess that He assumed flesh in the womb of His Mother, having a human, thinking mind, possessing at the same time both natures, God and man, one Person, one Son, one Christ, one Lord of all creatures, of whom He is the Creator, Lord, and Leader, together with the Father and the Holy Spirit. I assert that He suffered by the real Passion of the flesh, that He died by real bodily death, and that He was resurrected by the real resurrection of the flesh and of the spirit, by which He shall come to judge the quick and the dead. I believe the author of the New and the Old Testaments to be one and the same, the Lord God. [I believe] that the devil became evil not from his nature but through his free will.

I believe that the resurrection comes with this flesh which we wear, and not some other. I believe in the future judgment when each will receive punishments or rewards in proportion to what he has done.

I do not prohibit marriage, nor condemn second marriages. I do not forbid the eating of flesh. I confess that reconciled penitents ought to be allowed communion. I believe that in baptism all sins are forgiven, as much that one which was committed originally as those which are voluntarily committed, and I profess that outside of the Catholic Church none is saved. I affirm the Holy Synods to be the six [1] which the Universal Mother Church established.

This is Letter 180 in Havet. Gerbert was consecrated archbishop probably on June 28, 991, the Sunday following his election. This *Promissio fidei* is identical, with a few slight variations and one addition, to the one prescribed in the pretended fourth council of Carthage, which is found in Pseudo-Isidore *Collectio canonum*, PL LXXXIV, 199B-200B. This, in turn, is similar to the *Promissio fidei episcopi* which is No. lxxiii of the *Liber diurnus*.

1. Councils of Nicaea, 325; Constantinople, 381; Ephesus, 431; Chalcedon, 451; Constantinople, 553, and 680. This last sentence is an addition taken from the *Liber diurnus*, for Pseudo-Isidore *Collectio canonum* (introductory note above) does not mention councils. Cf. Letter 201, n. 33, which does not mention the two councils of Constantinople. A *Pontifical* for the use of Rheims cathedral gives a procedure which was undoubtedly followed at Gerbert's consecration. CG XXXVIII: Reims, I, 413, MS 341 (C. 163), s. XI.

193. RHEIMS. December, 992
King Hugh requests Pope John XV to receive his ambassador T., and suggests a meeting at Grenoble or elsewhere in France

HUGH, KING OF THE FRENCH, TO POPE JOHN

I and my bishops, through T.,[1] archdeacon of the church of Rheims, have sent letters[2] to Your Holiness, in which we explained to you our case against Arnulf. But, above all, we add this now: I beseech that you decide justly regarding me and my followers, and that you do not believe doubtful statements as the truth. We know that we have done nothing in opposition to your apostolate.

And if, because we are far away, you do not believe us entirely, learn the truth as we will offer it to you when present in person. The city of Grenoble whither the Roman pontiffs were accustomed [to go] to meet with the kings of the French,[3] is situated on the boundary of Italy and France. This is a possible meeting place, if pleasing to you. But, if you are disposed to visit us and our realm, we shall receive you with the highest honors as you cross over the Alps, and with the deference due you shall accompany you during your visit and as you return. We say this with all affection in order that you may perceive and know that we and our followers do not wish to avoid your decisions. Accordingly, we petition that you receive kindly the embassy of Archdeacon T. so that while he will have been securing what he seeks, he will make us happy at his return and render us zealous in obedience to you.

This is Letter 188 in Havet. Between Letters 191 and 192, or 192 and 193, there should be a letter which Gerbert mentions as having written to Abbot

Raymond of Aurillac after Gerbert's election. See Letter 196.

Abbot Leo of SS. Boniface and Alexius in Rome and Bishop Dominic of Sabina (Letter 198, n. 7), papal legates sent to deal with the conflict over the Rheims archbishopric, convoked a synod at Aachen, where the German court was celebrating Easter on March 27, 992 (DO III 89, 91). The French bishops ignored the summons to Aachen, and Kings Hugh and Robert refused to hold any conversations with Leo. Pope John XV cited Hugh and Robert to Rome. This is Hugh's answer. Lot, *Hugues Capet*, pp. 83-87; Boye, "Quellenkatalog der synoden Deutschlands," NA, XLVIII (1924), 63; M. Uhlirz, *Jahrbücher des deutschen Reiches unter Otto II. und Otto III*, Vol. II: *Otto III*, pp. 153-54, 166, 466, 478-79, 481.

1. Perhaps Tetbald, who appears in the Acts of the council of Mont-Notre-Dame en Tardenois in 972. Bubnov, II, 813, n. 74.

2. Letters 187 and 188.

3. Roman pontiffs had occasionally journeyed to France, even though we have no record of any who met French kings at Grenoble. In 753-54 Pope Stephen II went to Ponthion to meet Pippin (JL I, 272-73); in 804-5 Leo III went to Rheims (JL I, 311ff.); in 816 Stephen IV went to Rheims (JL I, 317); in 833 Gregory IV went to France (JL I, 324); and in 878 John VIII went to France (JL I, 398ff.). Holland, *Traffic Ways*, p. 52. Thus, Hugh's invitation to Pope John XV is not as unusual as Havet (p. 174, n. 6) claims.

194. RHEIMS. After May 16, 993
Gerbert suggests to Bishop Arnulf of Orléans a pact of un-animity in support of their similar attitude towards the monks of St. Denis

GERBERT TO ARNULF, BISHOP OF ORLÉANS [1]

Much has the Divinity vouchsafed to mortals, O guardian of my soul, on whom It bestowed faith and did not gainsay intelligence. Hence, Peter denied Christ, the Son of God, yet faithfully confessed Him whom he had denied [Mat. 16 : 16]. Hence it is that the just man liveth by faith [Rom. 1 : 17; Gal. 3 : 11]. So, to this faith [2] we join intelligence, because the foolish are said not to have faith. That significant decision of a generous mind shows that you have this faith. The continuity of your words shows how you wish it to be perpetuated between us.

I am therefore grateful, and to the giver of such gifts I return thanks, both because he has preserved a friend for me who disagrees with me in nothing, and because he did not believe our rivals, speaking half-truths, but no actual truths. It is Thy office, good Jesus, to make of one mind those that dwell in one house [1 Peter 3 : 7]. Before Thee, I, Your priest, confess this, that I esteem, cherish, and love Arnulf, Your venerable bishop, and that in my heart and on my lips

I place him above all the members of my rank whom I now know. Therefore, let all fraud and treachery be absent, let peace and brotherhood be present so that whoever injures one will have injured the other.

With Christ's protecting power, neither tyrannical force nor the harsh threats of the kings uttered against us at Eastertime will deter me from what I have begun. Indeed, we are accused of having unjustly condemned the monks of St. Denis.[3] We are urged to celebrate the divine services before these condemned persons and not to act contrary to the privileges granted by the Roman Church to the monastery of St. Denis. To these orders we answer that we will assent to privileges promulgated under the authority of the canons, and we will not accept as law whatever be decreed contrary to ecclesiastical laws.[4]

However, since the weight of the affair recoils especially against me, I thought that it was not my jurisdiction, nor did I consider that I was rushing in to the injury of my lords, as I have been accused of doing, but that rather it appears to concern those [5] through whose fault arises the evil of which they complain. When the decision of the secular clergy had prevailed over the party of the monks. . . .[6] That these things are so, Fulk, son of Your Blessedness, is a witness, who hearkened to the bitterness of my soul till his eyes overflowed with tears. For I was indeed suffering and do suffer greatly. . . .[7]

I do not know what informer accused you of being an ambusher, as it were, of the royal honor, and who. . . .[8] No vehemence of mine, thus, has raged against you, as someone reported to you, nor have I by harsh speech disparaged an absent friend.[9] In fact, in daring to make excuses for you, I have subjected myself, as almost accused, to the dogs of the palace.

Therefore, let it be betwixt us, as you wish, "Yea," but not "Yea" and "Nay" [2 Cor. 1 : 19]. Let there be mutual aid and consultation which I believe even in sacred matters ought to be confirmed by pledges, if this pleases Your Sublimity, in order that with all fear of suspicion removed we may be of one heart and one soul [Acts 4 : 32].

This is Letter 190 in Havet. King Hugh had caused a synod of bishops to meet at the monastery of St. Denis near Paris at Eastertime, probably in 993 (Easter was on April 16th), to decide upon the payment of tithes claimed by both the secular clergy and the monks of St. Denis. Abbo, abbot of Fleury, a promotor of political monasticism, actively supported the contention of the monks, who, in turn, so aroused the inhabitants of the town of St. Denis that they riotously dispersed the synod. Rumor spread rapidly especially at the royal court that Bishop Arnulf of Orléans had had a hand in this riot. Arnulf (not to be confused with Archbishop Arnulf of Rheims) began an immediate investigation, and wrote to Gerbert whom he accuses of denouncing him before Hugh. Letter 194 replies to Arnulf's letter, and its date is determined by the fact that a period of at least a month after the synod would have been occupied by the rumors and the investigation of Arnulf. Havet, p. 176, n. 8; Lot, *Hugues Capet*, p. 88, n. 1.

1. 972–December, 1003. Arnulf was noted for his noble birth, wealth, generosity, and integrity, and his staunch defense of the rights of the secular clergy. He was an archenemy of the monastic leader Abbo, whose monastery of St. Benoît sur Loire (Fleury) was in his diocese, near Orléans. King Hugh entrusted to Arnulf the most important prisoners captured at Laon in 991— Duke Charles and his family, and Archbishop Arnulf. Gerbert's acquaintance with Bishop Arnulf dated from at least Easter 981, when Arnulf came to Rome with Hugh Capet. Richer III.lxxxiv. He took an active part in the Council of St. Basle. Olleris, pp. 176, 180-81; Letter 219; E. certain, "Arnoul, éveque d'Orléans," BEC, 3e sér., IV (1853), 421ff.; A. Prévost, "Arnoul, éveque d'Orléans," DHGE, IV, 616-17.

2. Throughout this letter Gerbert plays upon the double meaning of the word *fides* [faith and fidelity].

3. See introductory note above. Hugh's censure of Gerbert must have occurred at Easter, 993. (Gerbert had participated in the council, which had condemned the monks of St. Denis near Paris, at Hugh's invitation.) Easter, 992, can scarcely be meant, because Hugh would not have so criticised his new archbishop only nine months after his consecration (Letters 191 and 192). Moreover, in 994 Hugh asked Abbot Mayeul of Cluny to reform St. Denis, but he required some persuasion to undertake the task. The negotiations with Mayeul were probably begun prior to Easter, which fell on April 1st in 994, since these negotiations extended over a considerable period and Mayeul died on May 11th on his way to St. Denis, after accepting the commission. In 994, then, Hugh would scarcely have been threatening Gerbert for not undertaking the settlement of the St. Denis controversy when he was attempting to secure Mayeul for the very same purpose.

4. JE 2499, May 27, 798, PL CXXIX, 967A-968A. The authenticity of this papal privilege is questionable. Havet, p. 177, n. 1.

5. The monks of St. Denis, supported by Abbot Abbo of Fleury.

6. Space of 20 letters in MS L, and in the margin some undecipherable, debased Tironian notes.

7. Space of 20 letters in MS L, and in the margin some undecipherable, debased Tironian notes.

8. Space of 18 letters in MS L, and in the margin some undecipherable, debased Tironian notes.

9. The basis for Arnulf's unwarranted accusation against Gerbert is not known. As a result of Arnulf's investigation Abbo was suspected of having instigated the riot at St. Denis, and tried to counteract this by writing a *Vindicatio* (PL CXXXIX, 456-72), a weak bit of writing, lacking in ingenuity. Convinced now of Abbo's guilt, Arnulf blasted him with a sharply worded work entitled *De cartilagine* (About Gristle, published by P. Lauer, *Mélanges de l'École française d'Athènes et de Rome*, XVIII [1898], 493ff.).

195. RHEIMS. February - April 15, 995

*Gerbert and the bishops of the Rheims province demand the
restoration of church property and threaten excommunication*

GERBERT AND ALL[1] THE BISHOPS OF THE RHEIMS DIOCESE TO THE EN-
CROACHERS UPON THE SAME

From Gerbert, by the grace of God àrchbishop of Rheims, Gui of
Soissons,[2] Adalbero of Laon, Ratbod ot Noyon,[3] Rothard of Cambrai,
Eudes of Senlis,[4] Fulk of Amiens, Baldwin of Thérouanne, Hervé of
Beauvais,[5] bishops through the grace of the Holy Spirit, to N. and
to G[ausbert?][6] and to those encroachers, scoundrels, and tyrants
whose names are written below.

For a long time because of its moderation the priesthood has with-
stood your angry rage, and hitherto has patiently endured it. But how
long will your insanity set itself against our sane minds? How long
will the feigning of the wicked disturb the quiet of the guileless? You
murder the clergy and do not cease your thefts from clergy, monks,
and paupers.

Therefore we, all the bishops of the diocese of Rheims, summon
Your Consciences, and invite you to make satisfaction. We are allowing
time for penitence until the first of next month. Then we shall either
recognize you as the fruitful branches of the church or with the
sword of the Holy Spirit cut you off from the field of God as useless
wood.

This is Letter 199 in Havet. Fulk, one of the bishops sending this letter,
probably became bishop of Amiens only at the beginning of 995 (Letter 200,
n. 1); another bishop, Rothard died August 18, 995 (*Gesta episcoporum Camera-
censium*, MGSS VII, 448 and n. 71, 449; Bubnov, II, 774, n. 1); in June and July
Gerbert was occupied with the councils of Mouzon and of St.-Rémy of Rheims.
Therefore, the meeting of the bishops who sent this letter undoubtedly occurred
before June 2, 995 (date of the council of Mouzon). Since the matter was to be
dealt with further on the first of the following month, the date of this letter
must have been not later than April 1st, because Gerbert was in Mouzon on
June 1st.

Letter 195 apparently deals with violence against the monastery of St. Riquier
(dept. Somme) in the diocese of Amiens, and supplements two documents issued
by Pope John XV relative to the same crimes (PL CXXXVII, 850C-852A). This
was a royal abbey, whose abbot (at this time Engelard) was chosen by the
Capetians. Probably Hugh requested Gerbert to convene a bishops' meeting to
take strong action against the thieving nobles. Lot, *Derniers Carolingiens*, pp.
116-18, 381-82; *Hugues Capet*, pp. 189, 230; Newman, *Domaine royal*, pp. 84, 93,
97, 204, 212-13.

2. The bishops of Châlons-sur-Marne, Arras, and Tournai were absent.

Probably the bishops of Cambrai and of Noyon represented the latter two bishoprics, since they had been united to Cambrai and Noyon respectively since the sixth and seventh centuries. Lot, *Hugues Capet*, pp. 218-19, 427-29; Newman, *Domaine royal*, pp. 221, 223.

2. See Letter 112, n. 6.

3. Or Rabeuf, February 12, 989-June 21, 997. See Letter 157, n. 2; Gams, *Series episcoporum*, p. 589.

4. See Letter 141, n. 2.

5. Letter 106, n. 1.

6. The name Gausbert appears in JL 3861 as that of a viscount who had stolen property from the monastery of St. Riquier (Centula). PL CXXXVII, 850C-D. The papal document is addressed also to Counts Arnulf [of Valenciennes?] and Baldwin of Flanders as despoilers of St. Riquier so that possibly the "N." of Letter 195 should be "A." (Arnulf).

196. RHEIMS. July 15, 995
Gerbert informs Abbot Raymond and the monks of St. Gerald of Aurillac of his election as archbishop of Rheims and of the difficulties he has encountered, and requests prayers

GERBERT TO THE ABBOT AND BROTHERS OF ST. GERALD

Distracted to the utmost by the preoccupations of important business in behalf of my see and my official position, I have been able to indicate to you neither by messengers nor by letters what has thus far happened to me. Now because Brother...[1] just as I wrote [2] through an earlier carrier of letters, while I was fleeing the city of Rheims for God's sake, by God's grace I was placed at its head.

This fact aroused races and peoples to hate me, and, because they are unable to rely on their own powers, they seek to wound by laws. More tolerable is the clash of arms than the debates of laws. Although by oratorical ability and a wordy explanation of the laws [3] I have satisfied my rivals as far as it concerns me, thus far they have not yet abandoned their hatred.

Be with your son, therefore, reverend fathers, and render him aid by prayers poured out to God. The pupil's victory is the master's glory. To all of you together I render thanks for my installation,[4] but more especially to Father Raymond [5] whom, after God, I thank above all mortals for whatever knowledge I possess. Now....[6]

Farewell, your holy congregation....[7] Farewell to those once known to me and linked by ties of brotherhood, if any of you remain whose faces I know well though whose names I often forget. Not through arrogance have I forgotten them but, hardened by the gross-ness of barbarians, or, as I might say, completely changed, what I learned as a boy I lost as a youth, and what I desired as a youth, I have despised as an old man [1 Cor. 13 : 11]. Such are the fruits you offer me, O desire; such are the joys that the honors of the world give birth to. Therefore, believe me who have tasted them. For, as much as princes attain external glory, by so much do they suffer internal crucifixion.

This is Letter 194 in Havet.
1. Space of 15 letters in MS L.
2. This letter is lost. See introductory note to Letter 193.
3. Undoubtedly the publication of the *Acta concilii S. Basoli* and Gerbert's speeches at the councils of Mouzon and of St.-Rémy.
4. See Letter 192, introductory note.
5. Abbot of St. Gerald of Aurillac. See Letters 23, n. 7, and 102.
6. Space of 12 letters in MS L.
7. Space of 20 letters in MS L.

197. RHEIMS. July 30, 995
Gerbert advises an unknown ecclesiastic about penance for an adulterer

ARCHBISHOP GERBERT TO [AN UNKNOWN]

You ask advice as to whether he who has polluted his wife's sister by adultery ought to return to the prior union after he performs penance, or to go to the other. The first, indeed, is allowed, the second is completely prohibited. In title 48 of the African Councils: "In accordance with evangelical and apostolic discipline, it is enjoined that neither a man deserted by his wife nor a wife deserted by her husband should marry another, but that, with a view to reconciliation in each case, they should remain in the same status. But, if they should disobey this injunction, let them be brought to penance.[1] But, if a woman shall have married another, let her not receive communion before the death of him whom she deserted,[2] unless by chance the necessity of some infirmity compels giving it."[3]

Let this adulterer perform penance, therefore, according to the law pertaining to those who have polluted themselves by incest, but let it be a ten-year penance. Also, in the case of the woman [adulteress], notwithstanding her blood relationship, and it can be brought about that she confesses her loss of chastity, claiming that she is driven on by the fire of youth, then one must fear that she will be tempted by Satan; for such a case we know of nothing better than Pope Leo's words in similar cases: "A young woman" he says "who cannot be continent, can be restrained by the remedy of becoming a wife." [4] To this can be added only that if this adulteress cannot control herself, let her marry, thus saith the Apostle, only in the Lord [1 Cor. 7 : 39].

This is Letter 195 in Havet.

1. *Concilium Milevitanum* ii.xvii, and *Concilia Africana* lxix, in Mansi, *Sacrorum conciliorum Collectio*, new and enlarged ed., IV, 331, 502; Regino *De ecclesiasticis disciplinis* ii.civ, PL CXXXII, 304B.

2. *Is quem reliquit* in MS Berlin Phillipps 1718 and in the Duchesne edition, against MS L, *his quem reliquid*.

3. *Concilium Eliberitanum* ix, in Mansi, *Sacrorum conciliorum Collectio*, new and enlarged ed., II, 7; Regino *De ecclesiasticis disciplinis* ii.ciii, PL CXXXII, 304B.

4. PL LXVII, 290, No. 25.

198. RHEIMS. September 1, 995

Gerbert, apologizing sarcastically to the papal legate, Abbot Leo of SS. Boniface and Alexius, for his "unsatisfactory" conduct of his office, suggests that Leo dictate his future actions

GERBERT TO "POPE" LEO [1]

Since I realize your great goodwill towards me,[2] I judge myself fortunate in the friendship of such a great man. The fact that our servitude has not complied exactly with your wishes as, to be sure, it should have, ought not to be ascribed to ill will, but to necessity.[3]

Midst the multifarious struggles constantly harassing us, indeed, we can find scarcely one person to whom we may safely reveal the secrets of our heart, to such an extent have deceit and treachery, pretense, and dissumulation in turn seized the citadel of virtue for themselves.

After you left me,[4] we, therefore, could make use of no mutual exchange of letters except that one which we directed to you under the sign of the triple cross.[5] Thus, we have placed our affairs under your disposition so that whoever, by chance, shall injure us will be seen to have inflicted injury upon Lord "Pope" Leo. Henceforth it will not be our right to decide in what, how much, whom, and when [6] we ought to please, because the diligent service of our ministry will be for Lord Leo.

I greet Lord Amizo,[7] a bishop to be revered in everything, for I am presuming much on his wisdom and eloquence, and on his outstanding reliability of character, as by this I make myself submissive [8] to his service.

This is Letter 196 in Havet. The only time Abbot Leo departed from Gerbert was after the council of St.-Rémy of Rheims, July 1, 995 (Richer iv.cviii; Olleris, pp. 251-56). Furthermore, Gerbert wrote him one letter (now lost) after this departure. The bitter, sarcastic tone of Letter 198 suggests that it must have been written after he had learned the contents of Leo's denunciatory letter to Kings Hugh and Robert written during his return journey to Rome in July, 995 (MGSS III, 686; Olleris, pp. 237-43). The time consumed by these events was: two weeks for half of Leo's journey to the place where he wrote the letter, two weeks for the letter to reach Hugh and Robert, another week for Gerbert to have received news of its contents. One paragraph of Leo's letter is directed specifically to the author (whom he does not name) of the *Acta concilii S. Basoli* (Olleris, p. 238, last paragraph). Cf. Letter 199.

1. *Ger. Leoni Pontifici. Pontifex* means "bishop" or "pope," and Gerbert uses it to mean "pope" in Letters 93, 172, and 193. Abbot Leo in his letter (introductory note above) uses *pontifex* to mean "pope." Since Leo was neither bishop nor pope, Gerbert must be applying the word *pontifex* to him sarcastically.

2. Cf. the similar phrase in Letter 165, which Gerbert later (in letter 181) admitted was hypocritical. In Letters 129 and 174 Gerbert uses the same phrase with sincerity.

3. Cf. the council of Mouzon, "If by chance this [election of Gerbert] deviated at all from the sacred laws, urgent necessity, not ill will, caused it." Olleris, pp. 248-49.

4. See introductory note above.

5. *Sub triplicatae crucis signo.* This letter is not in Gerbert's Collection and is lost. The significance of these words is not clear since the word *triplicata* is unusual. It is used in Macrobius *Commentarii in somnium Scipionis* i.xx.16, with which Gerbert was familiar. Number symbolism may explain the meaning here. The number three, representing the Three-in-One, possessed great significance, and could mean that Gerbert was relying upon the judgment of God rather than that of man (more specifically of Pope John XV). In addition, the cross was thought of as representing the number 5 (the fifth point being the intersection of the arms), and the 5 points might generate the number 25, a circle or circular number. Tripling the cross, then, would produce the number 75. Gerbert's name in the vernacular was Girbert and this adds up to 76. Therefore, the 3 crosses plus himself as would equal the 76 of his name. See V. Hopper, *Medieval Number Symbolism* (New York, 1938), pp. 11, 42, 73, 99, 121, 151-52, 158, 164-65, 171, 184-85.

6. *Quid, quantum, quibus, et quando.* These were five of the seven questions put by the rhetoricians to cause the writer or orator to justify his discussion. Victorinus *In Rhetoricam Ciceronis* i.xx.21. Gerbert's use of the words is two-edged—to vaunt his learning, which Leo had criticised, and to accuse Leo of being a dictator, or, as Gerbert would say, a tyrant, for thus depriving men of their free will to the detriment of the Church.

7. A nickname for Dominic, probably bishop of Sabina, who had assisted Leo at the council of Aachen in 992. Bubnov, II, 741, n. 113; 844, n. 30; Lot, *Hugues Capet*, p. 84, n. 2. Bubnov dates Letter 198 incorrectly at the end of 995 or beginning of 996, and believes Dominic was the bishop of Ferentino. Lot dates it incorrectly as just prior to the council of Aachen in 992. *Annales Weissemburgenses continuatio*, a. 993 [992], MGSS III, 70, "A synod was held at Aachen by Dominic, bishop of the Roman Church."

8. *Obnoxium*. Since this word can also mean "obnoxious", Gerbert may be just as sarcastic here as in the rest of the letter. However, at the council of Aachen Dominic may have appeared favorable to Gerbert.

199. RHEIMS. September 1, 995
Gerbert protests to Pope John XV about his treatment by the latter because of Arnulf

GERBERT TO POPE JOHN

The deepest grief overwhelms me as I learn that I have been removed from the fellowship of your very sacred apostolate,[1] and that I am considered guilty of the crime of intrusion. So, from the depths of my soul I groan. For up to now I have so conducted myself in the church of God that I have been in charge of many persons, but I have injured no one. I did not publish the sins of Arnulf, but instead I publicly disassociated myself[2] from the sinner. God and those who know me are my witnesses that it was not with the hope of usurping his office, as my rivals say, but lest I should partake of another's sins.

This is Letter 197 in Havet.

1. Leo had written to Kings Hugh and Robert (Olleris, pp. 238, 239): "Wherefore it is clearly apparent that you have separated the Roman Church, your Mother, from yourselves since you have not feared to write such scurrilities about her... Truly, Father Arnulf [of Orléans] and I do not know what apostate son of his [Gerbert], weighed these things little when they dared to write against the Roman Church such things as not even the Arian heretics wrote." Leo's reference is to Chap. XXVI of the *Acta concilii S. Basoli* (Olleris, pp. 204ff.).

2. Letter 190.

200. RHEIMS. October 1, 995
Gerbert upbraids one of his suffragan bishops (Fulk, bishop of Amiens?) for lax administration of his office

[ARCHBISHOP GERBERT TO BISHOP FULK (?) [1]]

We do not bear it with equanimity that we have not occasionally made use of conferences with you, for, by means of these, mutual charitableness becomes lasting, disconnected matters coalesce, bitterness is softened, similar problems are aired, and those present settle many matters agreeably. However, since the events of these times will not permit this, epistolary brevity will explain the difficulties between us.

We bespeak your good will towards Brother...[2] so that our intercession for him may have some weight with you; and let our letter obtain more for him than possible gifts offered by anyone. Prevented by the difficult times, we have been unable thus far to convene [in synods] regularly and to inquire into the conduct of God's business. Now because a commiserating God offers a breathing space we think...[3] and we advise and pray that abandoning every excuse you interest yourself in this matter.

All priests equally may propose the form of discipline and the form of knowing and observing the sacred canons founded in the spirit of God and consecrated by the reverence of the whole world; but it is most especially imposed upon us bishops to instill acceptably into the flock under our care such precepts by the example of the habits and lives we pastors follow. Why, therefore, do we place money ahead of justice? Why do we trample upon the rights of sacred laws by illicit cupidity? We mention [4] these matters in order that you may think about, mull over, and judge the complaints that we constantly endure—not as a tyrant with the prejudice of tyrants, but as a priest with the judgment of priests.

Curb these disturbances, settle these quarrels. Overcome your tenderness of years by sobriety of manners. Let continuous reading and constant questioning stimulate your mind. Why was the judgment...[5] concealed from us? Why, if he is appealing to a larger audience, has he been deprived of his possessions? And even if he is not appealing, but has been despoiled while keeping silent, why has this decision rendered against him not been reported to us? If you have done these things knowingly, the law has been defied. If unknowingly, then in order that you may exercise forbearance, this must be the agreement: that whatever has illegally been taken from this priest be restored legally, and afterwards, if it seems proper, that a judicial process be reinstituted in accordance with the laws.

Do not consider that my son R.[6] lacks confidence in his own cause because he has not gone to meet you as agreed. Since many affairs have absorbed our attention we have been unable to send him to be examined by you until the fifteenth day before the kalends.[7] On the basis of your very friendly disposition towards us we beseech that by all means these delays be not prejudicial to him. And, if you shall have carried out these details calmly, and pass judgment on him at his trial without the testimony of persons, you will make us greatly indebted to you for your service.

This is Letter 198 in Havet.

1. This is an administrative letter, and Fulk is the only young suffragan bishop of the Rheims province known. According to Havet (p. 188, n. 1), 995 is the first sure date of Fulk's episcopate, although Gams, *Series episcoporum* gives 993.

2. Space of 12 letters in MS L.

3. Space of 15 letters in MS L.

4. *Dicimus*, suggested by Havet, p. 188, n.*d*, and accepted by Bubnov, II, 847, n. 39, because MS L and the Duchesne edition have *dominus*, which does not make sense.

5. Space of 15 letters in MS L.

6. The identification of this "R." with the one in Letter 222, as made by Havet, p. 189, n. 3, and Bubnov II, 848, n. 41, seems doubtful since the "R." of the latter letter is called the common son of Gerbert and of Haimo of Verdun.

7. October 18th, if the October dating of this letter is correct.

201. RHEIMS. December 31, 995

Gerbert sends to Wilderode, bishop of Strasbourg, the account he requested of the facts of Arnulf's trial as well as the authorities justifying his prosecution

[GERBERT TO BISHOP WILDERODE]

Gerbert sends greetings to Wilderode, bishop[1] of the city of Strasbourg.

INTRODUCTION

The ignorant often marvel at, but the learned know how many good things result from both a sacred association, well begun and better continued, and a holy friendship, because good is the cause of good things, and what gives birth to good must of necessity be good. Whence would arise families, whence cities and kingdoms, unless stabilized by association and friendship?[2] For what else has drawn mortals to the cultivation of the wilderness except association with

God? The universe [3] itself, sometimes at variance, sometimes friendly, reconciles its own contrary powers.[4] The same union binds the physical man to the spiritual. The whole body of good derives from the greatest good, which is God, and through the great good of association and friendship preserves order according to the eternal law of its founder.

Therefore, in judging me one must seek this good of friendships, so noted and felicitous, for itself [and] not, as some claim, for another reason. Just as Seneca says in his *Moralia:* [5] "A wise man, even if he despises himself, still desires to have a friend, if for no other reason than to exercise friendship, not that such great virtue may lie in it, and not, as Epicurus says, that he may have someone who is devoted to him while [he is] unfortunate [and] willing to aid him [when he is] destitute and in chains, but that he may have someone to whom he is devoted when such a person is unfortunate and whom he might free from hostile custody."

These ideas your generous and prudent mind seem to have grasped intelligently, for you have revived me through the sweet speech of your faithful intermediary, though I am far distant and scarcely known to you even by name. Because you made an effort to have explained to yourself both my fortunate and unfortunate circumstances, in your present good office you prove how great a prelate Alsace obeys. Let me, therefore, pour into the ears of so great a judge the stream of evils of these recent times in order that, every angle of the cause being considered, you may render an accurate judgment to the party that justice requires.

NARRATION

Arnulf, the son, 'tis said, of King Lothair, was condemned in a council [6] of the bishops of all of France, after he had captured his bishop [7] and his bishop's city by surrounding him with deceit and fraud. After brigandage and incendiarism and the spilling of much human blood, and then after the demise of Adalbero [8] of blessed memory, in the hope of securing peace he was given the archbishopric of Rheims, although reconciled [9] solely through the efforts of Bishop Ascelin of Laon. He swore the fear-inspiring oaths and acknowledged in a document the fealty to be maintained to his kings, which he both

recited aloud in a meeting in the church and corroborated by signing
with his own hand.[10]

Six months had not yet elapsed after his consecration, when behold
like a tempest an enemy invaded the city that he betrayed,[11] polluted
the sanctuary of God, seized the spoils, and captured both clergy and
people.[12] Though true that after these events Arnulf placed his
thieves under an anathema [13] and ordered the bishops of France and
Lower Lorraine to do likewise, still he took away the estates of the
church that he had bestowed on his knights with a oath and conferred
them on enemies.[14] The band of conspirators against his king and his
king's army he led forth into battle under the standards of Charles.

Meanwhile, messengers and conciliar letters [15] implored the Roman
pontiff to aid the distracted church. But he offered no counsel,
neither by messengers nor by advisory letters. Therefore, a council,
acting upon the agreement of the solicitous bishops, through messengers and conciliar letters, bearing a kindly warning, for eighteen
successive months [16] [asked] Arnulf to desist from the furor he had
created and to purge himself according to law from the crime of
betrayal and rebellion that drove him on. Arnulf refused.

But, when he perceived the worst evil doers withdrawing from him
to further their own wickedness, terrified, he approached the king,
and by new pledges and with new conditions imposed, once more
became a partaker of the royal table.[17] Since the king's wrath was
thus abated, he believed that he had nullified all his criminality, but
soon, backsliding, he broke his sacred pledge by not fulfilling its
terms. But, the faction to which he belonged, disregarding how often
they are cheated, how often deprived of their property, seize the
citadel of Laon. Arnulf is found among the enemies of the king.[18]

He is brought before a council [19] that demands that he account for
so many and such disgraceful acts. For a long time he deliberated
with himself and his friends, then burst forth with the confession of
his sins, produced other witnesses [20] before his confessors,[21] recorded
his crimes in a document that he signed after reading it aloud before
the Church. His priest's insignia he laid down, and abdicated his
office while his confessors and attesting and responding witnesses
chanted: "In accordance with your confession and signature cease
from your office." [22]

BODY [23]

So much is agreed upon regarding Arnulf's disgraceful acts and crimes. But his defenders [24] are divided by two points of view. Some, indeed, claim that the king had granted forgiveness to the priest Arnulf for all his sins, saying that after a pardon the latter had done nothing requiring a pardon. Others claimed the injury to be to the Roman pontiff as if he [Arnulf] ought not to be deposed without the former's authority, and unless the latter has resumed his office.

But to discuss these matters, reverend father, because a subject classified under the judicial genus of causes [25] is considered now through judgment, now through authority [writings] (that is, by points of dispute conjectural, definitive, translative, qualitative,[26] as well as by legal issues [27]) first, it seems to me, one should deliberate on judgment and truth, on custom and law, even on differences in the laws and in what order things are to be considered, specifically ecclesiastical causes. Once these have been ascertained, the issues will easily be evident.

"Plainly," says Augustine,[28] "it is true that reason and truth must be preferred to custom. However, when truth supports custom, nothing ought to be more firmly held to." Also, in his book *De baptismo*, among other things: [29] [That this must be done] "in order that the more potent truth and universal medicine, resulting from salvation-promoting unity, would heal whatever had begun to invade some minds through disputes of this sort, even if the ancient custom of the Church did not hold this, and afterwards the Catholic excluded it by the most powerful sanction—the consent of the world."

We learn that law is established partly by nature, partly by authority. The law of nature, indeed, is apparent. So far as law consists in authority it is partly human, partly divine. In both divine and human affairs it prescribes what must be done or not done. Therefore, after the law of nature, there was established the law now of letters, now of kindness, each of which when supported by Divine Authority is more serviceable inasmuch as Divinity surpasses humanity. And because the law of kindness transcends the law of letters, this same subtle and multiple [law], emanating as if from the Divine Font, [was] accepted by the Apostle, and explained first, by the decretals of the pontiffs of the Prime See, then, through the councils of innumerable prelates, and as if through certain pure rivulets has been lead almost into infinity.

Above all, in this law, as we mentioned, authority must be considered. For it matters greatly whether God speaks or man; and if man, whether an apostle or simply a bishop. Furthermore, among bishops there is likewise a great difference, depending on their authority. For the number, knowledge, or even place, as it seems to some, confers this authority. Number refers to their number in councils where many Catholics agree. Likewise, knowledge in particular and in divine matters is preeminent. As for the place it is a question as to whether it is one of the large cities.

Again, number, knowledge, and place now differ from each other and even vary in themselves. Number is overtopped by number, or by plurality, or by the weight of reasoning and truth; by plurality when among persons equally good and learned, one part disagrees with another; and by the weight of reasoning and truth, as in the case of the famous council of Rimini when the decision was quashed by number, i.e., the small number of bishops present.[30] Likewise, the individuals in the plurality should be taken into consideration as well as the meeting places with reference to other [cities] and with reference to themselves.

Therefore, let laws embody the highest ideal and above all that which Christ, the apostles, and the prophets set forth. Then, let the ideas consonant with theirs and corroborated by the consent of all Catholics obtain a second strength [by embodiment] in laws. In the third place, may those opinions have weight that individual men, skilled in knowledge and eloquence, have offered to the light of knowledge.

Lest, perchance, I seem to be speaking in a court and to vitiate the decrees of the pontiffs of the Roman Church, let me cite as the witness for my contention Gelasius, pontiff of the Roman See. Here, indeed, in the catalogue of the divine books, the following excerpt adds the Councils of Nicaea, Constantinople, Ephesus, Chalcedon to the preceding authentic writings:[31] "We have decreed that any council established by the holy fathers, according to the authority of these four [councils] must be preserved and received." Thence he passed from the universal to the particular and added: "Likewise, the works and tracts of all of the orthodox fathers who have deviated in nothing from the consortium of the Roman Church, nor have separated from its faith and preaching, but have been partakers of its communion to the last days of their lives, we decree shall be read." As to how the decrees of this see should be received, he intimates as follows: "Likewise the decretal letters which at various times the blessed popes dispatched from the city of Rome for the comfort of different fathers ought to be received with veneration." And thus designating by name certain special ones to be read, and as to what should be thought about both letters and writings he expressed himself most intelligently and carefully: "But when this shall have come into the hand of a Catholic," he said, "let the saying of the blessed apostle take precedence: 'test all things; hold fast that which is good.'" [1 Thess: 5 : 21].

Hence, Hincmar, venerable bishop of Rheims, writing about this ambiguity to his nephew, likewise interpreted the passage on distinctions: [32] "From these words of Gelasius one should accordingly note the distinction between synodal councils, and the letters of apostolic men before the era of councils, written at various times for the comfort of various fathers, and which, he says, should be accepted with veneration. Also, he decreed that any councils instituted by the holy fathers, according to the authority of the four,[33] must be accepted and observed. In his decretals also he spoke to the same effect: [34] 'Wherever and whenever heresy sprang into being,' he says, 'our Catholic fathers and learned pontiffs together with the assemblage sanctioned anything for the benefit of faith, truth, and the Catholic and Apostolic Communion, that accords with the manner of the Scriptures and the preaching of our predecessors. And one after another they wished it to remain fixed and unchanged, and in the same cause, in spite of [possible] new suppositions, they did not allow a reexamination of what had been already decided.'

"No one versed in ecclesiastical dogmas is unacquainted with how much difference exists between those councils that he decreed should be accepted and received and that the succeeding Catholic fathers wished to remain fixed and unchanged, and those letters, written at different times for the comfort of various persons, that he says should be received with veneration. Thus, if we shall have begun to desire to hold and keep certain opinions contained in certain of those letters against those that we formerly wished to preserve, by so doing, you see, we shall be deviating from the sacred councils that we should have accepted, held, guarded, and followed in perpetuity. And by departing ruinously from the custom held by the Catholic Church since our fathers convened in the sacred Nicene Council, who, as Leo says,[35] still live with us in their constitutions, and, holding nothing as certain, we shall come upon the sect of the *Genethliaci*,[36] that is, the Astrologers, who consider everything as uncertain.

"And the Blessed Gelasius, now, shows that these letters in certain points contravene not only the sacred canons, but that even diverse letters contradict themselves, written as they were, he says, at diverse times for the comfort of diverse persons. Hence, perchance, against me you will say: 'Therefore you falsely attack the Apostolic See in its sacred pontiffs, because [as you say] they thought wrongly and decreed what was untenable.' To you I shall answer what the apostle said to those contradicting themselves about keeping the non-Jewish law as they queried, 'Is the law then contrary to the promises of God?' 'By no means.' [Gal. 3 : 21]. 'The law indeed is holy, and the commandment holy, and just, and good' [Romans 7 : 12], but proper to persons and times, which 'was enacted on account of transgressions, being delivered by angels through a mediator, until the offspring should come to whom the promise was made' [Gal. 3 : 19].

"Together with that apostolic man blessed Gelasius I say that we must accept with veneration those letters of holy and apostolic men that were issued by the Apostolic See at various times for the comfort of diverse persons (just as Gelasius says) and were arranged in orderly collections by those same priests of the Lord, whom Scripture calls angels [messengers]. We must accept those, I repeat, that were suitable to their times up to the period when our fathers established laws valid forever by meeting as one body in their sacred councils, each father being under the guiding influence of the Holy Spirit, just as the pontiffs of this same Apostolic See are insisting, because otherwise we need not rely on them.

"And just as the apostle speaks of the law: 'For if there were a law which could give life, justice would truly be the law' [Gal. 3 : 21].

"So, I say, saving reverence to the Apostolic See, that if the contents of these same letters were suitable for their own times, and all the ideas contained therein at the same time both merited preservation and were suitable for subsequent ages to preserve and uphold, our Catholic fathers and learned pontiffs in sacred councils would not have established laws binding forever. With blessed Gelasius, therefore, I maintain that those letters should be received with veneration, and when they are read, just as Gelasius himself advises, that apostolic sentence should precede that says: 'Test all things; hold fast that which is good' [1 Thess. 5 : 21]. And I am not speaking thus to say thereby that certain things are not good, but that they are not consonant in everything with the sacred canons of the fathers and with the councils. Just as the apostle says: 'The law is good and holy, and the commandment holy, and just and good' [Romans 7 : 12], but for its times."

Likewise, when the same Hincmar speaks of the difference in sacred laws, among other things he says as follows:[37] "Certain ideas, at length, handed down by the apostolic men, just as they are read in these same letters, or as they are found taken over from Roman laws, thus are preserved by the authority of ecumenical councils, and certain of these things have been changed in councils. But some of those that have been legislated on in regional councils, are adhered to unchanged by the authority of the ecumenical councils and henceforth must be kept inviolate, just as the Catholic doctors and the teachers of the Church point out, as I have shown above, partly through their own words. And, besides the words of Blessed Augustine which I have cited in this work, in his book *De baptismo* he says, first showing there is a difference between a collection of letters, where such aforementioned letters of the apostolic men are preserved, and a regional or a general council: 'I see,' he says, 'what I myself can still examine, namely, that I may answer to those half truths, resulting from no general council nor even a regional one, but from a collection of letters that earlier influenced both Agrippina and Cyprian himself as well as those persons in Africa agreeing with them, and perchance some persons in widely separated lands across the sea, to think that something should be done which both the ancient custom of the Church did not uphold, and which afterwards the Catholic [Church] excluded through its most powerful sanction—the consent of the whole world—in order that the more potent truth and universal medicine resulting from salvation-promoting unity might heal whatever had begun to seize some minds through disputes of this sort.' [38]

"Likewise, he shows the difference between regional and ecumenical councils as follows, saying: 'It is safe for us not to be wordy through any temerity of opinion on that subject, that whatever was begun by no Catholic regional council was terminated by no plenary one. Moreover, we are unassailable in asserting by word of mouth what has been confirmed by the assent of the Universal Church under the governance of our Lord God and Savior Jesus Christ.' In addition, he shows the difference between authentic writings and regional and ecumenical councils, and also between earlier and later councils. 'Who,' he asks, 'does not know that the Holy Catholic Scripture is contained within its definite limits—true as much of the Old as of the New Testament? And that it takes precedence over all later letters of bishops so that there can be no doubt or argument about it as to its truth or rightness? And that bishops' letters, past or future, written after the Canon was established, may be discussed by the possibly wiser words of anyone more learned in the subject, by other bishops of weightier authority, by discerning scholars, and by councils, as to whether anything in them deviates from the truth? And [that] these councils, convoked in separate regions or provinces yield without ambiguity to the authority of the ecumenical councils, created by the whole Christian world? And that these earlier plenary councils are often amended by later ones, since this will open to some experiment what had been closed, and what was being concealed will be recognized, without any grain of sacrilegious haughtiness, without any swelled neck of arrogance, without any quarrel from livid envy but with holy humility, with the Catholic peace, with Christian love?' [39]

"And again: 'Wherefore let them consider the one thing that is apparent to all, that Cyprian's authority, if followed, should be followed rather in preserving unity than in changing the custom of the Church; that if, also, we take his council into consideration, it must be superseded later by a council of the Universal Church, a member of which he rejoiced to be; and he often warned that others should imitate him in maintaining the binding together of the whole body. For to posterity later councils will supersede earlier ones, and the whole most rightfully always takes precedence over its parts.' [40] For Cyprian did not represent the universality of the Holy Catholic

Church, though he remained in its universality and never lost touch with its roots; [41] yet the Celestial Farmer exculpated him when he was flourishing upon those roots in order that he might become more fruitful. Blessed Augustine spoke similar words about other councils.

"As for the sacred and mystic Nicene Synod, just as I have pointed out from the words of Leo and of others, nothing has ever been changed by any pontiff of the Apostolic See, or by an ecumenical or regional council, a change which could be nothing except void. Gelasius in his decrees says the same: [42] 'It is not concealed from us,' I say, 'that in the storm of the Arian persecutions, many bishops, restored from exile after the return of peace, had united the disturbed churches in certain provinces by banding together brother bishops with themselves, not however, to change anything that the Nicene Synod had defined relative to faith and Catholic communion, nor to smite anyone with a new damnation for his lapse, but, according to the tenor of that decree, to judge a person condemned unless he had repented, and the consequence would follow that he would, without doubt, be subject to damnation unless he corrected it.' "

Once more the same Hincmar to the same person: [43] "Let me repeat to you what Blessed Augustine says about the sacred councils: [44] 'All such matters, accordingly, that are not contained in the authorities of the Holy Scriptures, nor are decisions reached in the councils of bishops, nor are confirmed by the custom of the Universal Church, but are infinitely varied by the differing events of diverse places so that one can scarcely ever find any cases that men followed in their deliberations, where the opportunity presents itself I think they should be extirpated without any hesitation.' How pleasing Blessed Augustine's words are to you, you shall see. In my difficulty it seems safer and more beneficial to my insignificant self to follow the sacred councils with him and to inculcate in all who shall wish to listen to me not to follow those matters that he thinks should be cut out, leaving aside the sacred councils, rather than those ideas that have been cut out and dissected, that you propose should be pursued, because different cases reveal in themselves that they cannot be maintained and followed altogether.

" 'Therefore, in this,' said Innocent to Bishop Decentius of Gubbio,[45] 'the priests of the Lord must follow what the Roman Church holds, whence, beyond a doubt they originated, lest, while they strive after foreign doctrines they seem to overlook the head of their institutions.'

"What the Roman Church preserves and the priests of the Lord should follow, Gelasius also demonstrates, saying: [46] 'We are confident that now no Christian may truthfully be ignorant of the decision of any synod that by its assent the Universal Church has approved, and that it is necessary to follow no see ahead of others except the first, that by its own authority both confirms and protects every synod with continued guidance and in behalf of its primacy, which St. Peter, the apostle, received from the voice of the Lord, and which the subsequent Church nevertheless always held and retained.'

"Behold, according to the law and to the gospel you have a plenitude of witnesses, testifying as to the councils that one must follow, and as to not pursuing foreign ideas, since the apostle also admonishes: 'Do not be led away by various and strange doctrines' [Hebrews 13 : 9]. Therefore, I mention these foreign doctrines along with Innocent because after this time they began to convene in sacred councils in the Catholic Church. Those doctrines that were of little force in their own time, as far as the sacred councils saw that they must adopt them, flowed from [general] ecclesiastical usage, up to those [usages] that recently you began to revive, as far as they were due to your efforts, in order that those things to which you desirously aspire you could freely transform into the desire of your heart, and not be legally coerced or judged by anyone. However, they do not hold the same opinion as you, nor do the doctors and teachers of the Church agree with you."

These words, indeed, Hincmar said. Again one should reiterate the position that the Nicene Synod obtains in divine laws, and through what witnesses it has become illustrious. "Pope Leo [47] said to Anatolius: [48] 'That establishment of the Nicene canons was truly ordained through the Holy Spirit, and no part of them is ever dissolvable. Let no synodal councils flatter themselves because of the size of the assembly, nor let any larger number of priests dare to be compared or preferred to those 318 bishops, since the Nicene Council was consecrated by so plenary a privilege of the Divinity that, though ecclesiastical decisions may be reached through fewer or more, whatever differs from their resolutions is absolutely invalid.'

"Regarding this privilege St. Ambrose says: [49] 'Not by human effort nor by any arrangement did the 318 bishops convene at the council. But, as in their number, through the sign of His Passion and His Name, Lord Jesus proves that he was present at their council, for the cross is in the 300, the name of Jesus is in the 10, and the 8 in the priests.' [50] 'And to me,' said Hilary,[51] 'that very number itself is sacred in which Abraham, the victor over wicked kings, is blessed by him who is the model of the eternal priesthood.'

"And, likewise, Blessed Pope Leo says: [52] 'Those holy and venerable fathers who in the city of Nicaea, after the condemnation of the Arian sacrilege with its impiety, established the laws of ecclesiastical canons to last to the end of the world, and in its [the Council's] constitutions they still live throughout the whole world, and whatever is ever presumed other than what they determined let it be quashed without delay.' Thus, St. Leo says, to the Augusta Pulcheria: [53] 'No one may dare grant anything to anyone contrary to the statutes of the canons of the fathers which were established long years ago in the city of Nicaea by spiritual decrees so that, if anyone might wish to decree something different, let him rather cease trying than break those decrees. If pontiffs throughout all the churches keep these inviolate, as they must be kept, tranquil peace and unwavering harmony will exist. There will be no dissensions over the apportionment of honors, no litigation over ordinations, no ambiguities about privileges, no struggles against alien usurpation, but by the equitable law of charity, the rational order of customs and offices will be followed, and verily he will be great to whom all ambition is foreign.' "

So much for the difference between divine laws. As to what distinctions have a bearing on the preceding matters, a few words will suffice. They must detail in what ways Arnulf is dead forever as a priest, but first we must offer a few considerations as to the kinds of sins, of judgments, and of judicial procedure.

Accordingly, there are crimes against God and against man. Moreover, of these crimes some are hidden, some are overt. Whence it is manifest that the judgments and the degree of the sentences are meted out in accordance with the quality of the crimes. Hence it is written: "Who sins secretly let him repent in secret; who sins publicly, in public."

"Here [54] arises a two-fold judicial procedure: One [example] concerning which the apostle speaks [to wit]: 'If any man be called immoral' [1 Cor. 5 : 11] and he is willing for this epithet to be known, as Augustine says in his book *De poenitentia*, whatever decision is given against anyone is rendered according to proper judicial procedure and with integrity. For he was unwilling that man be judged by man from arbitrary suspicion, or even that an extralegal judgment should be arrogated, but rather by the law of God according to ecclesiastical procedure, whether he confessed of his own accord, or was accused and convicted. For, if name-calling alone sufficed, many an innocent person must perforce be condemned, because often a crime is falsely imputed to someone.

"How this legal procedure should be followed St. Gregory indicated in his letter of instruction to the Defender John as he departed for the Spains,[55] to wit, that some may be accusers, others witnesses. The type of case, therefore, [should be taken into consideration] in order that the testimony alleged in the writings may be recited under oath in the presence of the accused, and that the accused may have an opportunity of responding and defending himself, and that the examination of persons accusing and persons testifying shall be carried out legally. The Lord Himself acknowledged this judicial procedure when he revived the girl lying dead at home, and—though in revelation causes are not known to everyone—he offered as witnesses [only] some of his disciples, but both the father and the mother of the girl [Luke 8 : 51]

"There is, indeed, another method of judicial procedure in order that credence may be given to the [testimony] about events in cases where [sufficient] witnesses are lacking—not that they are few because of being shut up in a cubicle, but because many admittedly knew the events, as when there was a huge accompanying crowd outside the city gate [Luke 7 : 12] in the case of a person raised up [from the dead].

"Of this judicial procedure the apostle says: 'I, indeed, absent in body, but present in spirit, have already, as though present, passed judgment in the name of our Lord Jesus Christ on the one who has so acted—you and my spirit gathered together with the power of our Lord Jesus Christ—to deliver such a one over to Satan for the destruction of the flesh' [1 Cor. 5 : 3-5]. And just above this: 'So that he who has done this deed might be put away from your midst.' Whence Ambrose says: 'A sinner whose misdeed is known ought to be expelled from association with you.' Everybody, you see, knew his crime, and in such a case the misdeed could not be erased by witnesses nor the crime by any subterfuge.

"With respect to the perpetrator of obvious crimes, even if he cannot be brought to judgment, Pope Boniface, writing to the seven provinces, says of Maximus, who avoided meetings by his unwillingness to attend: [56] 'No one doubts,' he says, 'that an innocent person seeks to be absolved, because he thereby escapes a harmful sentence. But the artful scoffing of those who believe craftiness of action to be wisdom will never receive the name of innocence. For, admittedly, they think to escape judgment by delays. But, it matters not whether in the present examination all allegations are proved, since just as often absence itself will also be an admission of guilt equal to a confession that has been secured. And, if he shall have neglected to be present, absence will gain no postponement of sentence.' So judged Celestine in the case of Daniel, *quondam* bishop of the Gauls.[57]

"Because no one should be judged hastily, nor out of turn, nor a person not warned, nor one not summoned, the law of obvious crimes says concerning the indictment of this sort of offender: 'Whoever shall have been summoned by three decrees of the judge or shall have been cited before the judge by three edicts, or by a single peremptory one in place of all, namely, that which precludes debate, and if he be unwilling to appear before that judge to whom he has been denounced, he can be judged guilty as if of contumacy. By no means can the case be withdrawn through an appeal as long as the contumacy charge stands.' [58]

"Celestine's letter to Nestorius, the decision of the council of Ephesus on the same subject,[59] and St. Gregory's letter to John all prove the truth of the statement about the three decrees, summoning a person, as if it were gospel truth. Regarding the written peremptory summons, the African Council explains in the case of Cresconius that if the person summoned shall have refused to repent, thus being guilty of contumacy by his contempt, he can be immediately removed by judicial authority.' " [60]

And the same council held, regarding priests who conspire, jealously watching over their parishioners, and refuse to come to a council, fearing perchance lest their sins will be made public, that not only may the parishes not retain them, "but they must also be forced from their own churches that evilly favored them, and that also public authority reject them, and the cathedral heads remove them so that, as rebels, they lack public authority over their own." [61]

CONFIRMATION AND EXAMINATION ARRANGED IN ALTERNATE ORDER

O prudent priest, you have observed that Arnulf's sins are numbered not among the secret, but among the public ones; also, that the bishops of the Gauls did not establish new laws against Arnulf, but were the diligent executors of already established laws.

And, since he refused to obey the laws, by a peremptory law, namely, the summons by letters dispatched by the bishops of all Gaul, declaring, by virtue of their judicial authority, that he is guilty of contempt and contumacy, his year-long contempt and contumacy resulted in his being excluded from his church and in the silencing of his voice.

Surely, he could not object either [on the grounds] that he had been summoned outside of his province, as if to foreign councils where it would have been difficult for him to produce witnesses, because hostages and oaths had been proffered for him in great abundance; or [on the grounds] that he was judged outside of his province by those who were ignorant of his case. But, although admonished by letters and legates for eighteen months, he was unwilling to answer that the wrong had been carried to the Roman primate. Now, neither his hiding behind silence, nor any new regulation can be prejudicial to already established laws.

O, the crafty scoffing of wicked men! God says that a sinning brother should be chided and warned even to the ears of the Church, and if he heeds not the admonitions he shall be considered a heathen and a publican. The African council says he must be coerced by the power of the prince and must be expelled from the Church. [62]

Yet, you say that Arnulf, who engages in arson, sedition, betrayals, disgraceful acts, captures, and thefts from his own men, while he plots his kings' destruction, and betrays his land to the enemy, despising divine and human rights, ought not to be deprived of communion, nor be deprived of his see except by order of the Roman bishop, although the apostle says that the prince "not without cause carries the sword" [Romans 13 : 4] but "for vengeance on evildoers, and for the praise of the good" [1 Peter 2 : 14].

Your favor [I crave], all you who have promised fidelity to your kings and wish to observe it as promised, and who have not betrayed nor arranged to betray the clergy and people entrusted to you. Be favorable [to me], I repeat, you who shudder at the deeds of such great crimes. O favor those who obey God's command that a sinner who does not obey the Church must be held as a heathen and publican [Mat. 18 : 17], and who says further: "Woe to you, scribes and pharisees" [Mat. 23 : 13-29] who "transgress the commandment of God to keep your tradition" [Mat. 15 : 3].

Once more I beg and implore, favor those who comply with the prince of the apostles when he says: "We must obey God rather than men" [Acts 5 : 29] and with the apostle declaring, "If any man preach a gospel to you besides that which you have received, even an angel from heaven, let him be anathema" [Gal. 1 : 8-9]. And the Prophet agrees: "Woe to you that call evil good, and good evil" [Isa. 5 : 20]. And lest anyone adduce envy against us, as if we were derogatory of the privileges of the Roman Church, let him listen to Jerome as he speaks: "Whenever authority is in question, that of the world is greater than that of the city." But if a person greater than a priest is sought as authority, add as witness that great ecclesiastic, Pope Leo: [63] "The privilege of Peter does not hold," he says, "where a judgment is rendered not from his sense of justice." Be it so. In any matter not so far judged, let the new judgment depend on Peter's sense of justice, and hence let it be carried to the Apostolic See, as to a divine oracle.

But why have judgments been rendered by those who are uninformed as to what ought to be judged? Or how did the 318 fathers establish laws to last forever if their statutes are completely altered or limited at the wish of anyone? The priest Apiarius was condemned by the Africans but was restored to communion by the Romans. The African bishops wrote to Pope Celestine that this was apparently carried out contrary to the Nicene Council.[64]

Those who slander us say that Arnulf, as the highest ecclesiastic, ought to be judged only by the highest ecclesiastic, the Roman. St. Augustine says [65] that if the accusers of Caecilian, primate of all Africa, might convict him of crime after his death because they could not do so during his life, by saying that he was ordained by those who surrendered Sacred Books, or that he himself was such a traitor, so even after his death they pronounced an anathema against him without hesitation.

Therefore, the bishops of the Gauls should be permitted to pronounce anathema against the living Arnulf, heathen and publican that he is, who has confessed and has been convicted. They should be permitted, I repeat, to follow the evangels, the apostles, the prophets, the sacred councils, the decrees of apostolic men not inconsistent with those of the four [councils] that always have been, and should be, valid.

"If thy eye is an occasion of sin to thee," says Christ, "pluck it out, and cast it from thee" [Mat. 18 : 9]. And the apostle: "With the heart a man believes unto justice, but profession of faith is made unto salvation" [Romans 10 : 10], likewise: "If we judged ourselves, we should not thus be judged" [1 Cor. 11 : 31].

And the Nicene council said: [66] "If any, priests or bishops, have been advanced without examination and, when they are investigated, have confessed the sins that they have committed, and if [then] they be overcome by other sins, and excited men, contrary to the canon of the law, have laid hands upon them as they are confessing, such [men] the canon does not sustain, but abandons. For the Catholic Church defends this [act of confession] as meriting no blame."

Now Arnulf, of his own accord, has confessed that he had repudiated his oath to his kings, [the oath] that he had recited and subscribed to. He confessed to those crimes that his confessors know but made this confession only after his life, members [of his body], and punishments had been remitted to him, and after the bishops had placed him under an anathema lest he offer any lies about himself. He has passed judgment upon himself, like Judas, like Achar, like Achitofel, and he even listed his crimes in a document like Potamius, archbishop of Braga,[67] doing this according to the tradition of the Apostolic See, and according to the nature of his deed.

Pope Zosimus, writing to Aurelius and the seven provinces, says among other things: [68] "Lazarus not long ago was condemned as a false accuser by the decision of the solemn bishops in the council of Turin, when he impugned the life of the innocent Bishop Briccius by false accusations, after the former had unjustly attained the priesthood through the same Proculus who with others in the council had assented to his condemnation, and by whose letters he was made conscious of his [evil] life so that of his own accord he abdicated."

And Pope John wrote to all the bishops established throughout the Gauls about the quondam Bishop Contumeliosus, saying: [69] "We agree to grant you the prosecution of the case against the aforesaid Bishop Contumeliosus, to allow him permission for penance, [and] when clearly admitting his error, let him confess as of a certain day and year." Also St. Gregory writes to Archbishop John of Prima Justiniana [Skoplje]: [70] "Nemesion, the beloved bearer of these presents, coming to us, indicated, just as was contained in the copies of the proceedings which he brought hither, that Paul, bishop of the city of Diadine," and a little after, "also presented the memorandum in which he confessed the truth of those acts of which he had been accused, and that after he had been deposed in accordance with the bishops' sentence he therefore had [again] been ordained bishop with the consent of Your Fraternity."

As to moderation and restraint in this sort of memorandum, Leo, writing to all the bishops in Campania, Samnium, Picene, and other provinces, says: [71] "Great wrath moves me and deep grief saddens me because I have discovered that some of you are unmindful of the apostolic tradition and are undismayed at being entangled with error," and farther on as to what punishment is exacted of the faithful: "Do not publicize separate sins in a confession written in a memorandum, for the conscience of the sinners will suffice to induce avowal to priests only by secret confession. For, as laudable as seems fullness of faith which men are not afraid to blush at because of the fear of God, yet not everyone's sins are of this sort. Let this objectionable custom be abandoned in order that those who demand penance shall not fear to have them made public, and lest many be held back from the remedial benefits of penance, while they either blush or fear that their deeds may be revealed to their enemies who might smite them with the force of the law."

And [it is] St. Gregory's [opinion], just as is very often found in his letters, that a bishop, after having given a memorandum respecting his infirmity of body, may remove himself from office if he wishes and another person may prove that he was called in the former's place. To cite one of the many instances, that of Archbishop John: [72] "If," he said to Deacon Anatolius, "this same very reverend John petitioned to be allowed to vacate his episcopal office possibly because of its burdensomeness, it should be granted in accordance with the writing setting forth the petition."

But if from Gregory's decision a bishop languishing in health can receive a successor after a memorandum has been given, what sort of envy is it to receive a successor by a council's decision after a memorandum had been given, if Arnulf [in fact] be dead in God's mind and in that of the Church? But perhaps you answer: "He claims that falsehoods were spoken of him." The African Council decided in the case of that bishop who lied about his communication with the Donatists that he should lose his episcopacy, and the decision was made according to the credence placed in his profession and signature.[73]

According to the decision of the synod [74] over which St. Caesarius, bishop of Arles, vicar of the Apostolic See, presided, just as is found in the letters of the see itself, the rule of the Council of Antioch prevailing, "A council is complete where a metropolitan ecclesiastic is present." [75] According to the canons of Nicaea and of other councils, and confirmed by the authority of the Roman See and preserved in continuing regularity, one should be held twice a year by the assembling together of all of the bishops of a province. Separate cases that possibly shall have come to light are to be received in these [councils] for correction, so that, as Gregory says, past offenses may be corrected and a rule established for the future. Said the aforementioned synod of many metropolitans with their suffragans, presided over by Caesarius, "We do not deem it alien to the utility of the Church, fellow bishops, that you know that whichever ordained person, either of the deaconate, the priesthood, or the episcopate shall have said that he was defiled by mortal sin, must be removed from the said ordinations, [because revealed] as criminals by their true confessions, or by the falsity of their lies."

Now, one cannot be absolved who shall have pronounced the cause of death in himself, words that against another will be punished, since everyone who causes his own death is greater than a murderer, as the Lord says in the Gospel: By thy words thou wilt be justified, and by thy words thou wilt be condemned [Mat. 12 : 37]; and likewise: Out of thy own mouth I judge thee [Luke 19 : 22]; and the prophet David answered him who lyingly claimed that Saul had killed the Lord's Christ: Thy blood be upon thy own head: for thy own mouth hath spoken against thee [2 Sam. 1 : 16]. And St. Gregory said to Maximus, bishop of Solitanus, regarding Andrew that "judgment ought not to be demanded in a cause that he himself has judged." [76]

If now, as the bishops then claimed, Arnulf confessed the truth about himself, this rendered him alien to the pontifical office and ministry, owing to his crimes, and he is then a criminal. If his confession be false, it must be rejected, just as that of a witness testifying falsely against himself since, as the Lord says in the Decalogue, which is strengthened by the Evangel: "You shall not bear false witness against your neighbor" [Ex. 20 : 16; Mat. 19 : 18; Mark 10 : 19; Luke 18 : 20], no one may bear false witness against his neighbor, how much less may he bear it against himself. Both the sacred canons and also the public laws will not permit criminals to accuse a highborn person nor to testify against him, and by so much less will they permit one such to attain an ecclesiastical grade or to remain in an ecclesiastical grade, just as Zosimus wrote about Lazarus who was condemned as a false accuser by the decision of the most solemn bishops in the Council of Turin. As Leo said to Rusticus.[77] "A private withdrawal to God's mercy, which must be deserved, must be sought for lapses of this sort where, if worthy satisfaction is made for them, the results may be fruitful."

The Toledan councils of long ago, establishing their own laws to strengthen the position of kings, order Arnulf [already] confessed and convicted, to be deprived of his office without delay, and to be concealed in everlasting prisonment without communion to the day of his death. Moreover, Pope Celestine [78] demonstrates that very often a person justly condemned was in vain led to [further] examination, knowing, as Prosper says against Cassian, that a condemned person's responsibility is not to examine the judgment but only to carry out the remedy [prescribed] in the decision, and ordered Caelestius to be driven out of the territory of all Italy, as if he were not demanding an audience for discussing the affair, and he decreed that the statutes of his predecessors and the conciliar decrees be kept inviolate to the same degree so that whatever once merited being expunged he would in no way allow to be reexamined.

It has been shown, as I think, that the Roman pontiff could not, in all justice, be seen to have suffered any injury, also that Arnulf was condemned not without the authority of the Roman pontiffs, and that he ought not to receive their support through laws. All of this we more fully exposed in the [Acts of the] council of Rheims.[79]

The first part of the plea of the defenders of Arnulf's case is invalid in its very self, to wit, that the kings had granted, to Arnulf forgiveness for his transgressions, and that afterward he committed nothing not pardonable.[80] The jurisdiction of souls has been entrusted to ecclesiastics certainly, not to kings. But, the power of binding and loosing at will was not bestowed on these pontiffs. Whichever person, dead in sin, Christ has restored to life, a priest will absolve, and whomever the criminal himself may implicate, the priest will bind. Christ showed this in the revival of Lazarus. Peter showed it in the damnation of Simon Magus.

Now truly to those who try otherwise, the prophet shouts: They were killing souls which should not die, and saving souls alive that should not live [Ezek. 13 : 19]. In explaining this passage Gregory says: [81] "Often in binding and loosing the pastor is moved to substitute his own wishes, and therefore does not follow the merits of the cases. Hence it happens that he may be deprived of this power of binding and loosing if he exercises it according to his own desires, not according to the customs of the subjects." Whence rightly the prophet says as above, "They were killing the souls." For, is he who condemns a just man not killing someone who is not dying? And is he who tries to absolve a criminal by prayer, not attempting to revive a dead person? For, often it happens that either he condemns those undeserving of it, or he himself, though bound, frees others."

"And [82] the law of the Catholic Emperor Justinian, which the Catholic Church esteems and keeps, in chapter 441,[83] decreed that no bishop nor priest should excommunicate anyone before his case be tried, and on this account the ecclesiastical canons ordered this to be complied with. If, however, anyone shall have excommunicated a person contrary to these [canons], the excommunicated may return to the grace of Holy Communion by the authority of an older priest. Moreover, let him who illegally pronounced the excommunication abstain from Holy Communion to the extent that it seems to the elder priest that what he did unjustly he is making amends for justly."

"Hence, St. Gregory wrote to Bishop John who was guilty of illegal excommunication, saying among other things: [84] 'Since the decrees of your aforesaid sentence have previously been quashed and rendered invalid, we decree that after you have been deprived of Holy Communion for the space of thirty days, by heavy penance and tears you beg from Omnipotent God remission for such a great aberration. And if we shall learn that you have carried out our sentence too negligently, you will learn that it is not only injustice but also the contumacy of Your Fraternity that, with God's aid, must be punished more severely.' And again in another place: [85] 'If at any time or in any place you attempt by description to act contrary to what we have determined, we decree that, after having been deprived of Holy Communion, you may not receive it except at the point of death, except by an order conceded by the Roman pontiff. We are ordaining these things in a definition consonant with the holy fathers in order that whoever does not understand obedience to the holy canons is unworthy of receiving Communion or of administering it at the holy altars.' "

Foolishly, therefore, Arnulf believes that he has received absolution for his sins from the kings, although to his great danger the power seems to have been bestowed on the bishops. What seems more worthy of derision than admiration is the argument of his supporters in that they say that afterwards he committed nothing not pardonable. For, since it is written, "the words of a priest are either true or sacrilege," how ought one to be purified, who afterwards polluted his mouth by perjury, and profaned the sacrosanct by sacrilege? Doubtless by that [same right hand] which, though addicted to so many perjuries and implicated in so many crimes, he has never withdrawn from the sacred mysteries, and which he has not blushed to offer with the Holy Eucharist to be kissed by the wicked and those damned by himself and by the bishops of the whole of Gaul?

EPILOGUE BY ENUMERATION, AND APPEAL

I think that the learned bishop must be satisfied that Arnulf appears condemned by right, by the laws of the Evangels, of the prophets, of the sacred councils, and also of the decrees of the prelates of the Roman Church, by scholars and by eloquent men who declared and attested opinions consonant with the preceding. But now I, insignificant in station and a priest (not through my own merits), I address myself to thee and mention the particulars about myself to thee, great priest of God. I am that one who, though tossed on land and on high,[86] while I aimed at the findings of the philosophers, while I shunned the undisciplined peoples, still did not escape; and now I, I repeat, who at the notorious betrayal of the city of Rheims, was no small part of the betrayed great city of Rheims and of its captured and despoiled population, flee to thee as to the safest haven. Therefore, stretch forth thy salvation-bringing hand to me as I am tossing about hither and thither, comfort me who am weary, and I will repay thee in kind, if chance permits. For the revivified servant of an Amalekite became the leader of David [1 Sam. 30 : 11-16]. It is not gold we ask, not estates we seek, only once more that kindness, which has been intercepted.

Consuming envy and blind cupidity have disseminated through the mouths of the wicked that I had invaded the see of another, that the pastor was captured, accused, and thrown out at my instigation. That such is not so, Your priestly Honor, France is witness, and also her kings and nobles. Nor can anyone, in truth, prove that I begged to have him degraded from this office. Those who elaborated greatly on this while I was unaware of it know this. It is known by my brother priests and fellow bishops, who, after the degradation of Arnulf, I swear, forced me to undertake this office. If, by chance, you ask of us again why this was done, I confess I do not know, I repeat, I do not know, why I, destitute and an exile, aided neither by birth nor wealth, was preferred to many persons who were wealthy or conspicuous for the nobility of their parents, unless by Thy gift, good Jesus, who lifts up the poor out of the dunghill to sit with princes [Ps. 112 : 7-8] and to hold a throne of glory. Thou Dispenser and Apportioner of all these gifts, Thou Author of peace and love, Thou knowest that I have always honored Germany and Lorraine as my lady, have cherished them as a mother, have languished over their adversities, have been joyful over their good fortune, now I ask again from Thee the sweet affections which I have lost, and I pray that Thy bishop, Wilderode, be made a restorer of the favor unjustifiably lost and the interpreter of my innocence before the prelates [87] and before his king [Otto III], for the favoring of whom since the time of King Lothair I have been delivered over to the swords of the enemy.

And now, indeed, evil is being returned to us for good by those whom we considered the lovers of peace, protectors of the innocent, combatters of the impious. The whole church of France lies ground by [the heel of] tyranny. Salvation was hoped for not from the French, however, but from these! But Thou art man's one salvation. Rome herself, hitherto considered the mother of all the churches, is said to abuse good, to bless evil persons, to make common cause with those to whom "welcome" should not be said [2 John 1 : 10], and to condemn those zealous for Thy law, abusing the power of loosing and binding received from Thee, even though with Thee it is not the judgment of priests but the lives of sinners which are sought, nor can it be man's right to justify the impious and condemn the just.

These, dearest brother, are the facts that I have embellished with rhetorical material for the sake of begetting the fellowship of friendships and of retaining good will. Moreover, I shall devote myself and my following to you and yours, just as I eagerly await your opinion, and not only with respect to the above account but also with respect to the account of the council of Rheims of which I am the interpreter, successful or not. If, in this account, the content and the manner of discourse shall have pleased his learned ears, [88] my most secure reward will be to have pleased so great a man.

This is Letter 217 in Havet. It is really a rhetorical brief, condensing the material in the *Acta concilii S. Basoli* (Olleris, pp. 173-236). See n. 26 below. Gerbert made two copies of it and sent the other one to Bishop Notker of Liége, together with Letter 202. A council was to be held on February 5, 996, at Ingelheim in preparation for Otto III's departure for Rome. The German bishops were to discuss the Rheims dispute at Ingelheim, and Bishop Wilderode requested Gerbert to brief him about the controversy. In writing his account Gerbert welcomes Bishop Wilderode as "the interpreter of my innocence before the prelates and before his king" (p. 259), and this proves that the material of

Letter 201 was to be presented to a council where Otto III was to be present, i.e., the council of Ingelheim. Then the German bishops would present the case to a council in Rome to be held in the presence of the pope. See n. 88 below; Richer IV.cviii; M. Uhlirz, *Untersuchungen über Inhalt und Datierung der Briefe Gerberts*, pp. 173-75.

1. December, 991-July, 999. See Letter 240.
2. Cicero *De inventione* I-II.iii.
3. *Mundus*. In the language of Gerbert and Richer, *mundus* means "universe," not simply "world."
4. The "Contrary powers," a Platonic concept found in the *Timaeus* (Letter 161, n. 2), refer, among other things, to the varying motions by which the planets follow their courses, sometimes opposite to the apparent general motion of the universe, sometimes in harmony with it, all ruled by eternal law.
5. Seneca *Epistulae morales ad Lucilium* I.ix.8.
6. Council of Compiègne, June 4, 988. Letters 131, n. 6; 163.
7. Ascelin. Thus, Arnulf had been a cleric of the church of Laon.
8. Archbishop of Rheims. He died January 23, 989.
9. Bishop Ascelin twice reconciled Arnulf with King Hugh. The first time, which Gerbert mentions here, preceded Arnulf's election as archbishop of Rheims, when Ascelin strenuously supported Arnulf's candidacy. The second time, described by Richer IV.xli-xlv, followed Arnulf's return to Rheims from his pretended imprisonment by Duke Charles after Arnulf had betrayed Rheims and had allowed himself to be captured.
10. Letter 188; *Acta concilii S. Basoli*, Olleris, p. 180.
11. Rheims. The enemy was Duke Charles, Arnulf's uncle. Olleris, p. 236.
12. Letter 187.
13. Letter 173.
14. Letter 190.
15. Letters 186 and 187.
16. December, 989 (the first session of the council of Senlis) to June 18, 991 (the council of St. Basle).
17. Richer IV.xlv.
18. Richer IV.xlvii. As a result of Ascelin's and King Hugh's pretended reconciliation with Arnulf, Ascelin brought about Arnulf's capture at Laon (n. 9 above).
19. St. Basle. See n. 16 above.
20. Thirty abbots and clerics. *Acta concilii S. Basoli*, Olleris, p. 227.
21. Archbishop Siguin of Sens, Bishops Arnulf of Orléans, Bruno of Langres, Gotesman of Amiens. *Acta concilii S. Basoli*, pp. 218, 226.
22. *Acta concilii S. Basoli*, Olleris, pp. 234-35; *Richer* IV.lxxi-lxxii.
23. Cicero *De inventione* I.xxii; Quintilian *De institutione oratoria* I.li.13.
24. See Letter 204, n. 4.
25. See R. McKeon, "Rhetoric in the Middle Ages," *Speculum*, XVII (1942), 14. This seems to be a rhetorical distinction from Victorinus.
26. Compare Richer's description (IV.lxxiii) of the *Acta concilii S. Basoli* as to their usefulness in learning the questions of rhetoric: [This book] "replete with objections and answers, with harangues and orations, with invectives, conjectures, and definitions, sets forth the account, discusses it, and rounds it off." See also Cicero *De inventione* I.viii.10.
27. *Status*, a word used for "issue" or "question" by Martianus Capella v.443 ff.
28. *De baptismo contra Donatistas* IV.5, PL XLIII, 157, cited by Hincmar *Opusculum adversus Hincmarum Laudunensem*, xxv, PL CXXVI, 387-88. Gerbert uses

Hincmar's work extensively throughout the remainder of this justification to Wilderode.

29. Augustine *De baptismo contra Donatistas* III.2, PL XLIII, 139.

30. A spurious council. Havet, p. 208, n. 1.

31. The three following quotations are from Hincmar *Opusculum adversus Hincmarum Laudunensem*, PL CXXVI, 384B. The Letter of Gelasius is JK 700.

32. The following quotation is from Hincmar *Opusculum adversus Hincmarum Laudunensem*, PL CXXVI, 384C-386A.

33. The Councils of Nicaea in 325, of Constantinople in 381, of Ephesus in 431, of Chalcedon in 451. Cf. Letter 192, n. 1.

34. JK 664.

35. St. Leo the Great, Letter CVI.iv, PL LIV, 1005B.

36. Casters of horoscopes. No conclusion as to Gerbert's attitude on the subject may be drawn from the use of this word here, since he is quoting from Hincmar. See Augustine *De doctrina christiana* II.xxi.32, and xxix.46, PL XXXIV, 51, 57.

37. The following long quotation is from Hincmar *Opusculum adversus Hincmarum Laudunensem*, PL CXXVI, 388A-389C.

38. Augustine *De baptismo* III.2, PL XLIII, 139.

39. *Ibid.* II.3, PL XLIII, 128-29.

40. *Ibid.* II.9, PL XLIII, 135.

41. Augustine *Epistolae*, XCIII.x.40, PL XXXIII, 341.

42. JK 664.

43. The following is from Hincmar *Opusculum adversus Hincmarum Laudunensem*, PL CXXVI, 390B-391A.

44. Augustine *Epistolae* LV.xix.35, PL XXXIII, 221.

45. JK 311, March 19, 416.

46. JK 664, February 1, 495.

47. From Hincmar *Opusculum adversus Hincmarum Laudunensem*, PL CXXVI, 392D-393C.

48. *Epistolae* CVI.ii, PL LIV, 103B-C.

49. St. Ambrose *De fide* I.xviii.121, PL XVI, 556.

50. Written in Greek, $\tau\iota\eta$, because in the Greek number system τ equals 300, ι equals 10, and η equals 8. The Greek tau (τ) suggested the ancient cross; the iota (ι) was the first letter of Jesus' name—Iesu; the eta (η) was considered a full number and hence symbolized the priests assembled in the first full, or ecumenical council—the council of Nicaea in A.D. 325. See Macrobius *In somnium Scipionis* I.v.15-18; V. Hopper, *Medieval Number Symbolism* (New York, 1938), pp. 75-76.

51. St. Hilary *De synodis*, 86, PL X, 538-39. Cf. Genesis 14:14, 18, 19. The number is 318, which, of course, was considered a prefiguring of the 318 priests at the council of Nicaea.

52. *Epistolae* CVI.iv, PL LIV, 1005B.

53. *Epistolae* CV.ii, PL LIV, 999A.

54. The quotation beginning here is from Hincmar *Opusculum adversus Hincmarum Laudunensem*, PL CXXVI, 400D-402B.

55. PL LXXVII, 1295.

56. Dionysius Exiguus *Codex canonum ecclesiasticorum*, PL LXVII, 266C-267C.

57. *Ibid.*, PL LXVII, 277B.

58. The three summonses were simple summonses without punishment threat. However, in lieu of these, one formal peremptory summons might be issued for cause, containing a punishment clause. A judgment of contumacy could be entered if the individual failed to appear, and, if not absolved within a year, he

could be judged on the basis of heresy. W. Fanning, "Citation," in *Catholic Encyclopedia*, III (New York, 1908), 791-92.

59. PL L, 475B, 515A.

60. Dionysius Exiguus *Codex canonum ecclesiasticorum*, PL LXVII, 196A.

61. *Ibid.*, PL LXVII, 197D-198A.

62. *Ibid.*

63. *Sermones* iv.iii, PL LIV, 151. St. Jerome was only a priest.

64. Dionysius Exiguus *Codex canonum ecclesiasticorum*, PL LXVII, 227D-230B.

65. *Epistolae* clxxxv, PL XXXIII, 794A.

66. Dionysius Exiguus *Codex canonum ecclesiasticorum*, PL LXVII, 149.

67. *Concilium Toletanum* x, a.656, in J. Mansi, *Sacrorum conciliorum nova, et amplissima collectio* XI (reproduction in facsimile, Paris and Leipzig, 1901, of Florence, 1765 edition), 40-41.

68. PL XX, 662B-663A, cited by Hincmar *Opusculum adversus Hincmarum Laudunensem*, PL CXXVI, 316C.

69. JK 886, April 7, 534.

70. PL LXXVII, 1241; mentioned by Hincmar *Opusculum adversus Hincmarum Laudunensem*, PL CXXVI, 307D. However, Gerbert's quotation seems to have been made from the *Registrum* of St. Gregory, a copy of which was at Rheims according to Hincmar and to the editors of the Congregation of St. Maur. P. Ewald, "Studien zur Ausgabe Registers Gregorii," NA, III (1878), 464, 470.

71. JK 545, March 6, 459.

72. PL LXXVII, 1167B.

73. Dionysius Exiguus *Codex canonum ecclesiasticorum*, PL LXVII, 221B, cited by Hincmar, *Opusculum adversus Hincmarum Laudunensem*, PL CXXVI, 620B.

74. See Hincmar *Opusculum advresus Hincmarum Laudunensem*, PL CXXVI, 620C.

75. PL LXVII, 162.

76. PL LXXVIII, 1059.

77. PL LXVII, 288, No. 16.

78. This is not listed among the Acts of Pope Celestine (422-432) in JK.

79. *Acta concilii S. Basoli* (Olleris, pp. 172ff.). This indicates that Letter 201 was written after the *Acta* were.

80. Gerbert insists that Arnulf's was an ecclesiastical crime, not merely a secular one.

81. St. Gregory *Homilia in Evangelia* ii.xxvi.5, PL LXXVI, 1200, cited by Hincmar *Opusculum adversus Hincmarum Laudunensem*, PL CXXVI, 410C-D.

82. The following quotation is from Hincmar *Opusculum adversus Hincmarum Laudunensem*, PL CXXVI, 411C-412B.

83. Justinian *Novellae* cxxiii.xi.

84. PL LXXVII, 608.

85. PL LXXVII, 611.

86. Virgil *Aeneid* i.3.

87. At a future council.

88. This indicates that Gerbert thought of the present letter as a brief to be spoken or read.

202. RHEIMS. January 2, 996
*Gerbert requests Bishop Notker of Liége to reconsider his
adverse opinion of himself, occasioned by the dispute over the
archbishopric of Rheims*

To Notker, Bishop of Liége [1]

We are not unaware of the source that has influenced your soul
to anger against us, and, because of our office, we ought to offer
without serious dispute as much as is to your advantage in order that
this source may dry up and your wrath be calmed down. Therefore,
at the request of the venerable Wilderode, bishop of Strasbourg,
the day before yesterday I wrote down an account of the evils of our
time,[2] and the matters of agreement and disagreement between the
parties which I revealed there, I have sent to you as an impartial judge,
so to speak.

And now I am working with all possible means to have a general
council summoned, though not of the whole world—an impossibility
as my enemies remind me—but at least of the whole jurisdiction of
our princes. In this way a free opportunity of assembling and of
discussing may be given not only to the inquisitive but also to our
enemies. As much, indeed, as evil is absent from us, that much do we
rely upon our innocence so that we not only do not avoid a regular
judgment but even strive after it as if it were fleeing to the world's
end. Now that they have been summoned a third time, if they are
unwilling to show themselves, both the appeal and the refusal to take
issue are deprived of sense by the peremptory character of the law.

In this matter you should notice whom the wrath of God threatens
when he says: "Woe to that one through whom scandal does come"
[Mat. 18:7].[3] Since the Apostle Paul says: "We, indeed, preach
Jesus Christ—to the Jews indeed a stumbling block, and to the Greeks
foolishness" [1 Cor. 1:23-24], the woe is not to Paul but to those who,
as the Prophet says, call good evil and evil good [Isa. 5:20]. "The
Lord knows who are His" [2 Tim. 2:19]. He knows who are moved
through zeal for Him [Num. 25:13; 4 Kings 10:16; Rom. 10:2].
But "if God is for us, who is against us?" [Rom. 8:31].

I pray and beg you, therefore, through whatever piety you have, not
to believe more of me from my enemies than from yourself. You
are testing whether I am the one who was devoted to you, honoring

you in everything, indeed, faithful to friends in common with you, a lover of justice and truth, without treachery and haughtiness. For, I enjoyed your friendship and that of your followers, which, since lost through no fault of mine, I ask from Your Virtue; and, if this be denied, greatly will I mourn, but, if I receive it, equally much will I rejoice.

This is Letter 193 in Havet. See the introductory note to Letter 201.
1. See Letter 38, n. 1.
2. Letter 201.
3. Apparently this was such a well known quotation at the end of the tenth century that MS L has here only the initials of the words: *quidem s. g. a. s.* (i.e., *quidem scandalum Grecis autem stulticiam*).

203. RHEIMS. January 15, 996
Gerbert is sending to Hervé, bishop of Beauvais, his beloved cleric D., educated and skilled in craftsmanship

To HERVÉ, BISHOP OF BEAUVAIS [1]

May you consider it both honest and useful to you that we have kept our beloved D.[2] for so long. [We have done so] not because of ill will towards you but for the sake of his great usefulness to you. Now, indeed, as you request, we are sending to Your Kindness this man who, through love for us, is leaving behind his native region, his relatives, and even all sorts of friends, an inestimable treasure whom we are transferring from our bosom to your jurisdiction.

Therefore, receive this man learned in the liberal disciplines, and accurately instructed in the craft of artisans,[3] whom many persons sought after with much money, but whom we retained. We desire that you look after him and treat him so well that your kindness will banish from him the grief of parting from us. Be generous to him with a munificent liberality becoming to Gerbert, archbishop of Rheims, the giver, and to Hervé, bishop of Beauvais, the recipient.

This is Letter 200 in Havet.
1. See Letters 106, n. 1; and 195.
2. Possibly Drogo, teacher of Anselm the Peripatetic, who taught at Parma. The name Drogo was common in the region of Paris, Toul, Troyes, and Mâcon. His teaching at Parma duplicates Gerbert's in rhetoric and dialectic. However, nothing is known of Drogo's skill in crafts. If "D." and Drogo are identical, he might have accompanied Gerbert to Italy in 997, for "D." seems to have gone to Gerbert at Sasbach (Letter 223). On Drogo see Manitius II, 708-14.
3. *Opificum* (nom. *opifex*). Workers in gold and silver, and those skilled in the use of precious stones, were highly valued by churches and monasteries

which constantly desired ecclesiastical objects made of these materials. At Auxerre, in the eleventh century, the cathedral chapter established prebends as remuneration for the positions of goldworker, of painter, and of glassworker in order to provide the cathedral with more or less permanent artisans in these crafts. *Gesta episcoporum Autissiodorum*, PL CXXXVIII, 282; Lesne, III, 104, n. 7; 182; 184.

204. RHEIMS. February 15, 996
Gerbert protests to Abbot Constantine of Micy about the political mission of Abbot Abbo of Fleury to Rome

GERBERT TO CONSTANTINE, ABBOT OF MICY [1]

I am greatly amazed at the mission of venerable A[bbo]. [2] Indeed, he pretended. . . . [3] However, all of these things are not troubles but are the beginnings of troubles. Greater is his complaint and what he seeks than am I who am humble and of little account. True is the proverb: "Your affair is in peril, when the nearest wall burns," [4] and also the Divine Word: "Begin ye at my sanctuary" [Ezek. 9 : 6], that is, at the foundation of the kingdom, and at the citadel. Furthermore, we know what persons are associated with this treacherous act. Since this is so, the priestly dignity, or rather importance, is obscured, the position of the kingdom is in jeopardy.

But if this be done without consulting the bishops, the power, importance, and dignity of the bishops is nullified. And such persons neither ought to, nor can, deprive a bishop, even a wicked one, of priesthood. But if they [the bishops] be consulted, the witnesses of his condemnation prove to be these very persons who decided that they should not judge him and who have dared to disregard his confession and his signature in Arnulf's document of abdication which they themselves drew up. [5]

Call to mind his capture and extended incarceration, [6] and the ordination of another [7] to his seat. The consecrators, the ordained, and the persons ordained by this latter will be accused of false pretenses. Even the kings themselves will appear as sinners in each of the sins.

Let no one be pleased by the shattering of something while he himself remains unharmed, and let no one be deceived by the false assurance of a promise, since cases depend not on the indulgence of judges but on the strength of the causes.

This is Letter 191 in Havet.

1. Whether Constantine was abbot of St. Mesmin of Micy at the time of this letter is disputed. Weigle, "Studien zur Überlieferung der Briefsammlung Gerberts," DA, XIV (1958), 158-64, argues that Constantine did not become abbot of St. Mesmin until after November, 1004. He concludes this from the fact that Abbot Abbo of Fleury in a letter (PL CXXXIX, 436-38) mentions Robert as abbot of Micy, Fulk as bishop of Orléans, and Constantine as dean of Micy. Fulk became bishop only in December, 1003. On the other hand, Andreas of Fleury, *Vita Gauzlini*, Chap. 2, in P. Ewald, "Reise nach Italien im Winter von 1876 auf 1877," NA III (1878), 352, states that Bishop Arnulf of Orléans (972-December, 1003) consecrated Constantine as abbot of Micy. However, there may be no conflict here. The monks of Micy rebelled against Abbot Robert, according to another of Abbo's letters (PL CXXXIX, 438A), and probably Constantine became abbot in his place. Later Robert was reinstated and Constantine was demoted to dean to become abbot again later. Gerbert's letter, then, coincides with the period when Robert had been chased from office (temporarily).

2. Letter 151, n. 3. In Abbo's letter to Abbot Leo of SS. Boniface and Alexius he mentions his journey to Rome where he found the "Roman Church widowed of a worthy pastor," i.e., by the death of John XV (about April 1, 996), and he returned to Fleury before the selection of the new pope, Gregory V. PL CXXXIX, 460. Hence, Abbo left Fleury for Rome in early February, 996. Gerbert feared that Abbo would destroy any favorable impression that the German bishops and Otto III might make on Pope John XV in his favor as the result of his Letter to Wilderode (201). Cf. n. 5 below.

3. Space of 25 letters in MS L.

4. Horace *Epistulae* i.xviii.84.

5. Arnulf's principal defenders at the council of St. Basle (991) were Abbots Abbo and Romnulf of Sens, and John, teacher at St. Germain of Auxerre. Olleris, pp. 188-89, 215-16; Richer iv.lxvi. Whether they actually participated in the preparation of Arnulf's document of abddication is unclear in Richer iv.li. See also Letter 201, at p. 238; and Olleris, pp. 234-35.

6. He was captured March 29, or 30, 991, and was still in prison. Richer iv.xlvii-xlix; Lot, *Derniers Carolingiens*, pp. 274-76; Lot, *Hugues Capet*, p. 29.

7. Gerbert. Letter 191.

205. RHEIMS. February 15, 996
Gerbert demands restoration of church property under penalty of excommunication

[Archbishop Gerbert to an Unknown]

It is necessary that you, an unmarried daughter, respect and cor-roborate the agreements and decisions of your admirable [1] father. Because you have annulled these stipulations, moreover, and persist in denying what you have recently done, we summon you to recognize your sin. You, also, R., we order to cease from plundering the property . . . [2] and to restore what you have wickedly stolen. And, do not think I shall overlook you . . . [3] you, I repeat, with the tonsure of a cleric but a tyrant in life and habits, along with your accomplice N. All of you, I insist, show yourselves deserving of the fruits of penance of the Catholic Church. By the sword of the Holy Spirit we shall drive you like heathens and publicans [Mat. 18 : 17] from the Catholic Church.

This is Letter 201 in Havet.
1. MS L, *virginem spectabilem patris* [admirable daughter of a father], but Vatican Barberini has *virginem spectabilis patris*, which is the reading adopted.
2. Space of 25 letters in MS L.
3. Space of 25 letters in MS L.

206. RHEIMS. February 15, 996
Gerbert informs a pastor (Fulk?) about warning letters sent to his scoffers and advises posting of a notice of excommunication if they continue

[ARCHBISHOP GERBERT TO BISHOP FULK (?)]

After receiving your complaint, reverend father,[1] we wrote to our brother abbots [2] and fellow bishops relative to that very matter, and we also dispatched reproving letters [3] to those who scorn you. Therefore, because you are the guardian of peace and love, Your Prudence should receive them kindly as erring sons if they shall have repented.

But, if they persevere in evil, which God forbid, then we order that the document of our summons be placed for reading in the well-known place of the church; and then, that a sentence of excommunication, written out accurately and pronounced solemnly, be affixed in the well-known place; and [finally] that a copy of it be directed to us in order that the same may be carried out in our churches.

Because you begged that an educated cleric be sent to you who could be of aid in these and other matters, when my D.[4] shall have returned, we shall take pains to see that he zealously serves your commands.

This is Letter 202 in Havet.
1. These words and the tone of this letter suggest that the recipient was a bishop, probably Fulk, bishop of Amiens. Letter 207.
2. All the manuscripts and the Duchesne edition have: *scripsimus cum fratribus et coepiscopis nostris* [we with our brothers and fellow bishops wrote] and this would refer to Letter 195, which dealt with a different problem (probably St. Riquier). Havet, p. 192, and Bubnov, II, 849, n. 44, suggest the correction *confratribus* [to confreres] in place of *cum fratribus* [with our brothers].
3. Letter 205. This was probably sent to each person named therein.

4. Letter 203, n. 2. Since D. was with the bishop of Beauvais, the addressee of Letter 206 was not the latter.

207. RHEIMS. May 1, 996
Gerbert complains to Fulk, bishop of Amiens, of his un-restrained actions, especially in seizing church property

GERBERT TO BISHOP FULK OF AMIENS [1]

Among all sorts of preoccupations with important events no trouble pesters us more than the frequent reports of your excesses. Even though the care of the whole of the city of Rheims has been enjoined upon us, yet are we burdened most of all by you who, through im-maturity of age and unstable habits have not yet learned to bear the weight of the priestly office.

Thus, why have you, before the time of the council,[2] invaded the very parishes [under dispute], contrary to the agreement determined between us? Nor is your action less serious if what you have seized belonged to the church, since such action is not permitted except by law. The assumption of arms, and violation of churches, as if all acts were permitted the priest in the church, approach illegality. But the Apostle saith: "All things are lawful for me, but not all things are expedient" [1 Cor. 6 : 12; 10 : 22]. They are lawful through free will, which you have employed badly, but are not expedient through laws which you have defied.

Thus, we urge Your Fraternity to correct the errors of your ways, and, if it pleases you, to make amends to us whom you have offended, so that once these excesses are acknowledged, you may correct your many errors.

This is Letter 206 in Havet.
1. See Letter 206.
2. Undoubtedly a provincial council, held by Gerbert, otherwise unknown.

208. PAVIA? August 1-5, 996
Gerbert writes to Pope Gregory V in the name of Otto III commending Abbot Peter to him

[EMPEROR OTTO TO POPE GREGORY]

From August Emperor Otto by the grace of God, to the Most Reverend Pope Gregory.[1]

Because a propitious Divinity links us not only by blood but also by a distinctive kind of preeminence among all mortals, we ought not to be disparate in the quality of our zeal for the cult of the Lord. Therefore, measuring your genius according to the deep feelings of our soul, let us commend to Your Apostolate this Abbot Peter, in order that you may eagerly work out whatever honest and useful acts, as you will have ascertained them both from him and from our legate, ought to be executed for his monastery, so that while we honor the memories of martyrs in common,[2] we likewise may experience their benefits in common.

Farewell.

This is Letter 213 in Havet. Otto III was in Italy in 996 from April to August (DO III 191ff.), during which time he designated his cousin Bruno as the new pope (Gregory V) and had himself crowned emperor (May 21, 996). Otto III stayed in Pavia from August 1st through August 5th (DO III 221-25).

1. May 3, 996-February 18, 999. Bruno (see introductory note) was the son of Duke Otto of Swabia and Carinthia, and the first cousin once removed of Otto III.

2. In 1001, a Peter was abbot of San Lorenzo in Campo in Perugia. Since the Abbot Peter mentioned in this letter was abbot over a monastery dedicated to a martyr, he may be the same person. Or, possibly Otto III planned the establishment of a monastery honoring a martyr, for which Peter had already been chosen abbot. See Schramm, *Kaiser, Rom, und Renovatio*, I, 135-37, for a discussion of Otto III's devout feelings.

209. PAVIA? August 1-5, 996
Gerbert, in the name of Emperor Otto III, informs Rainald, count of Marses, of changes in abbots near Benevento, and requests that he aid Abbot Rotfrid

[To COUNT RAINALD, IN THE NAME OF EMPEROR OTTO]

From August Emperor Otto, by the grace of God, to Count Rainald,[1] greetings.

The variety of the matters of business of our kingdom sometimes compel us to indite varying orders. Thus, it happens that, owing to certain exigencies, we have recently bestowed upon the monk John the abbey of St. Vincent located at Capua,[2] although Abbot Rotfrid[3] has been neither adjudged guilty of a crime nor deposed. Hence, out of compassionate respect, we are granting to the same Abbot Rotfrid the cell of St. Mary, with all things belonging to it, located in the county of Marses [4] in the place called Apinianici [5] plus the remaining possessions of St. Vincent located in the same county; also, the cell of St. Mary in the district of Benevento named Lugosano [6] with all of St. Vincent's possessions situate in Beneventan territory. Therefore, we admonish you and the prince of Benevento,[7] because of fealty owed to us, since these possessions are nearby you, that you assist Abbot Rotfrid in holding the aforementioned property without any contravention.

.

This is Letter 214 in Havet. See Letter 208, introductory note.

1. Count Rainald of Marses, son of Count Berard, a Frank (i.e., from south-west Germany), and father of Count Oderisius. He is frequently mentioned in Leo *Chronica monasterii cassinensis*, Chaps. VII, X, XIII, XXVI, XXXII, the last reference being in June, 1012. MGSS VII, 634ff. See n. 4 below.

2. St. Vincent of Volturno (province of Campobasso, Italy), founded in 703, now destroyed. The monk John became Abbot John IV, first mentioned as such in July, 997. He died April 28, 1007. Havet, p. 201, n. 5, citing Muratori, *Scriptores rerum italicarum*, I, 473, 493; V. Federici, "Ricerche per l'edizione del *Chronicon Vulturnense* del monaco Giovani," BISI, LVII (1941), 87.

3. Or Roffrid, abbot of St. Vincent of Volturno, August 11, 984-August 11, 998. He appears in documents only up to June, 996. Havet, p. 201, n. 5.

4. "The county of Marses occupied the region near Lake Fucina and its principal place was the city *civitas Marsicana* [Marsica], a village which today is ruined, near Pescina (province of Aquila, Italy). Pescina is the seat of a bishopric, the title of whose bishop is the bishop of Marses, *episcopus Marsorum*." Havet, p. 201, n. 6.

5. Empress Theophanu, while in Rome on January 2, 990, had confirmed the possession of this now ruined village near Pescina to St. Vincent of Volturno. MG *Diplomata* II, 876. Havet's date, January 2, 989, is incorrect, since Theophanu reached Rome only late in the year 989 (Letter 168, n. 2). Previously, in 981, Otto II had twice confirmed to the monastery of Farfa this same monastery of St. Mary of Apinianici (DO II 244, 249), but on July 7, 981, he confirmed possession of it to St. Vincent of Volturno (DO II 251).

At first, Count Rainald heeded Otto III's letter (209) but in May, 998, he was ordered to return Apinianici to St. Vincent of Volturno with the statement that he had been in illegal possession for two years. Havet, p. 201, n. 7; Bubnov, II, 868, n. 4.

6. Province of Avellino, Italy.

7. Pandulf (or Paldolf) II, 981-1014, son of Landulf III of Benevento. G. Ladner, "The 'Portraits' of Emperors in Southern Italian *Exultet* Rolls and the Liturgical Commemoration of the Emperor," *Speculum*, XVII (1942), 188, n. 2. M. Uhlirz, *Jahrbücher des Deutschen Reiches unter Otto II. und Otto III*, Vol. II: *Otto III*, p. 215, n. 85, suggests that Otto III must have sent a letter of similar content also to Prince Pandulf. Such a letter is not extant.

210. **PAVIA?** August 1-5, 996

Emperor Otto III, by means of Gerbert's pen, thanks his grand-mother, Empress Adelaide, for her maternal care and hopes his coronation as emperor pleases her

[To the August Empress Adelaide, in the Name of Emperor Otto]

From August Emperor Otto, by the grace of God, to the ever August Empress Lady Adelaide.

Because the Divinity, in accordance with your wishes and desires, auspiciously conferred upon us the rights of empire,[1] we do, indeed, adore Divine Providence and render true thanks to you. For we have known and experienced your maternal affection and zealous piety, because of which we cannot fail in honoring you. Therefore, since your renown is exalted when we are advanced, we greatly hope and pray that the commonwealth is being enlarged through us,[2] and that, after being expanded, it is being ruled successfuly in its [new] condition.

Farewell.

This is Letter 215 in Havet.
1. See Letter 208, introductory note.
2. MS V, *per vos* [through you], but this contradicts the beginning of the sentence. MS V sometimes confused *vos* [you] and *nos* [we, or us], and *vester* [your] and *noster* [our], indicated in the Havet edition in his Letters 6, n. *c*; 140, n.*b*; 150, n. *c*; 186, notes *i, k, l*; and 187, n.*e*.

211. **PAVIA.** August 5, 996

Emperor Otto III, through the pen of Gerbert, announces to Pope Gregory V his departure from Italy and his arrangements for the eight counties under dispute

[To Pope Gregory, in the Name of Emperor Otto]

From August Emperor Otto by the grace of God to the Very Reverend Pope Gregory.

I am overcome by vehement grief because the unseasonable weather has prevented me from satisfying your desires. For I am urged on by an affectionate piety towards you, but the necessity of nature, which restricts everything by its own laws, puts into opposition the quality of the Italian climate and the frailty of my body. Changed only bodily are we on this account; mentally we remain with you, and we are leaving the foremost men of Italy as aid and comfort to you—Hugh of Tuscany,[1] faithful to us in everything, and Cono, count of Spoleto and prefect of Camerino,[2] to whom, because of our love for you, we have entrusted the eight counties which are under dispute.[3] For the present, furthermore, we have placed our representative [4] in charge of them in order that the people may have a ruler and render to you the works and services due.

This is Letter 216 in Havet. Since Otto III was about to leave Italy, as he did in August, 996, this letter must have been written at Pavia. See Letter 208, introductory note.

1. See Letter 90, n. 1.

2. See Letter 91, n. 1.

3. Pesaro, Fano, Senogallia, Ancona, Fossombrone, Cagli, Jesi, and Osimo, which Otto III later bestowed upon Sylvester II (DO III 389), over which, as here, he was to exercise only a partial control. They were counties whose possession in friendly hands was very important to Otto III to assure him safe access from Ravenna down the Adriatic coast on the way to Rome. In 962 Otto I had bestowed these counties upon the papacy (DO I 235), and Gregory V wished to make good these claims. Otto III claimed the counties as imperial property and entrusted their military defense to Margraves Hugh and Cono and their financial and judicial administration to a legate or *missus*. Schramm, *Kaiser, Rom und Renovatio*, I, 161ff.; M. Uhlirz, "Italienische Kirchenpolitik der Ottonen," MIOG, XLVIII (1934), 307ff.

4. *Legatus*, the emperor's representative in judicial and financial administration, who was to hold court and collect the public imposts, especially those for provisioning the ruler's soldiers and animals (*fodrum*). However, he must permit Pope Gregory V to enjoy the usufruct of these counties. Schramm, *Kaiser, Rom und Renovatio*, I, 149, 162.

212. RHEIMS. February 25, 997

Gerbert expresses to Adelaide, dowager queen of France, his consternation over bad news but illness prevents him from seeing her; offers advice on punishing a soldier

GERBERT TO QUEEN ADELAIDE [1]

The too wicked and almost incredible report [2] has affected me with such grief that I have almost lost the light of my eyes in weeping, but when you order me to come to you to offer consolation—an excellent idea, indeed—you command the impossible. For my days have passed away [Job 17 : 11], O sweet and glorious lady. Old age [3] threatens me with my last day. Pleurisy fills my sides; my ears ring; my eyes fill with water; continual pains jab my whole body. This whole year has seen me lying ill in bed, and now, although scarce out of bed, I have suffered a relapse, and am seized by chills and fevers on alternate days.[4] If any respite from pains comes, however, I shall not be unmindful of your favors.

The definition of the Council of Nicaea relative to the deprivation of communion appears sufficient, namely that persons refused [communion] by some should not be received (by others), still we shall obey your command both in these and in any sort of honest and proper matter. But because the salvation of souls must be handled with great moderation and no one should be precipitately removed from the body and blood of the Son of God through whose mystery the true life is lived, since a man is dead when excommunicated justly, even though he be alive. Therefore, we deem a military man worthy of being first warned by us, to discover whether he will repent and render satisfaction to Your Reverence.

Just recently, indeed, we removed him along with certain other persons from the threshold of the Church because of these and other excesses. Afterwards they will be separated from the body of the Lord, and then from communion with all of the faithful so that by the increasing degrees [of punishment] he may be warned of his soul's salvation, and also so that the contagion of one person may not infect the people of God, because they are living together as a military group —an evil necessity of this time—and so that he alone may bear the fruits of his evil, ignominy, and ruin.

This is Letter 208 in Havet. The date is based upon the assumption that this letter is addressed to Queen Adelaide, not Empress Adelaide (n. 1 below), and that the news (n. 2 below) refers to the decrees of the council of Pavia, January, 997 (Letters 214, introductory note and n. 5; 216, introductory note).

1. All the manuscripts and the Duchesne edition have here "Adelaidi Imperatrici Ger." However, the letter does not offer sense if to Empress Adelaide of Germany. Moreover, Gerbert is here answering a letter from Adelaide, but in Letter 217, written a month or so later, he does not know where Empress Adelaide is! It is to be remembered that the headings indicating addressor and addressee were not necessarily put there by Gerbert. See Letter 13 to Empress Adelaide, which carries the heading G. *Adalaidi Reginae*, which is just the reverse of the present confusion in titles.

2. This was certainly the news of the decrees of the council of Pavia, perhaps brought directly to Queen Adelaide by the layman who had presented the cases of the Rheims archbishopric and of King Robert's marriage to the council (Olleris, p. 545).

3. If Gerbert was born in 945 (Introduction, p. 3) he would now be fifty-two years old.

4. Gerbert's description indicates that he had been suffering from tertian fever, a form of malaria, contracted probably during his journey to Italy, July-September, 996 (Letters 207ff.) so the "year" of his illness was actually about six months. Practically nothing is known of Gerbert's activities from September, 996 to February 15, 997 so that he may, indeed, have been very ill. Note the

effect of the Roman climate upon Otto III and Bishops Wilderode of Strasbourg and Franco of Worms. Letters 211; 240, n. 3; and 241, introductory note. Many instances of the morbid effect upon foreigners of the malaria-infested Rome are listed by Anna Celli-Fraentzel, "Contemporary Reports on the Mediaeval Roman Climate," *Speculum*, VII (1932), 96-106. She does not, however, mention Gerbert. See also her work cited in Letter 48, n. 7.

213. RHEIMS. March 15, 997

Gerbert assures Archambaud, archbishop of Tours, of his assistance in the latter's dispute with the monks of St. Martin of Tours

GERBERT TO ARCHBISHOP ARCHAMBAUD OF TOURS [1]

Not without fraternal compassion have we taken up your quarrel.[2] Therefore, we do not postpone such counsel and aid as we are able [to give]. As for the fact that a cleric of St. Martin [3] has rejected your benediction, as you report, act according to the Scripture: "He took no delight in blessing, and may it be far from him" [Ps. 108 : 17]. The Lord teaches that wheresoever you shall have been rejected, you shall shake off the dust of your feet, for a testimony against them [Mat. 10 : 14; Mark 6 : 11; Luke 9 : 5].

This is Letter 207 in Havet.

1. 980-1000. Archambaud had married King Robert and his near-cousin, Countess Bertha, at the end of December, 996, in spite of the fact that Gerbert had refused to do so. Richer iv.cviii; Lot, *Hugues Capet*, pp. 104, n. 2; 109; 110, n. 1. The council of Pavia, January, 997, then cited both Archambaud and Robert to appear before a papal synod or be suspended from communion. Olleris, p. 545; Richer iv.cviii.

2. With the monks of St. Martin of Tours (n. 3 below). Gerbert did not harbor resentment over the fact that Archambaud's action in marrying Robert and Bertha was an affront to himself (n. 1 above).

3. St. Martin of Tours, located outside the old Roman town of Tours, claimed exemption from the jurisdiction of the bishop, who was also archbishop of the province. King Robert controlled the abbey and the new village outside the walls, while the old village belonged to Count Eudes I of Blois. The monks were organized as canons (Letter 215). Lot, *Hugues Capet*, pp. 182, n. 1; 188, n. 3; 226; 231; 433; Newman, *Domaine royal*, pp. 202, 204.

214. RHEIMS. March 15, 997

Gerbert urges Siguin, archbishop of Sens, not to submit to the judgment of the council of Pavia, because this would admit guilt

GERBERT TO ARCHBISHOP SIGUIN OF SENS [1]

Your Prudence found it necessary, indeed, to avoid the craftiness of shrewd men, and to hear the voice of the Lord saying: "If any shall say to you, behold, here is Christ, or lo! there, do not follow after" [Mat. 24 : 23]. Rome is said to be the one who will justify these things that you condemn and who will condemn what you think just.

And we say that to condemn those things which seem just and to justify what is considered evil are God's province, not man's. "It is God who justifies, who shall condemn?" asks the Apostle [Rom. 8 : 33-34]. Consequently, if God condemns, He will not be the one who justifies.

God says: "If thy brother sin against thee, show him his fault between thee and him alone," and the rest of the words through "let him be to thee as the heathen and publican" [Mat. 18 : 15-17]. How, therefore, can our rivals say that in the deposition of Arnulf the decision of the Roman bishop should have been awaited? Have they been able to show the Roman bishop's judgment to be greater than God's?

But the first bishop of the Romans, nay, rather the prince of the apostles themselves, exclaimed: "We must obey God rather than men" [Acts 5 : 29]. Declared also that master of the world, Paul: "If any shall preach unto you anything other than that ye have received, even an angel from heaven, let him be anathema" [Gal. 1 : 8-9].

Because Pope Marcellus burned incense to Jove,[2] did all bishops, therefore, become incense burners? I firmly maintain that if the Roman bishop himself shall have sinned against his brother and, though often advised, shall not have listened to the Church, that Roman bishop, I say, is, according to the Word of God, to be considered a heathen and publican. For the loftier the position, the greater the ruin. Even though he leads us unworthy mortals through his power over communion, he cannot, therefore, separate us from communion with Christ, because none of us agrees with him when his opinion is contrary to the Evangel, nor should a priest be removed from office, moreover, unless he has confessed to, or been convicted of a crime, especially since the Apostle says: "Who shall separate us from the love of Christ?" [Romans 8 : 35] and also: "For I am sure that neither death nor life [will]" [Romans 8 : 38].

But what greater separation is there than to remove anyone of His followers from the body and blood of the Son of God, who daily is sacrificed for our salvation? But, if he who buys temporal life either for himself or for another is a murderer, by what name shall he be called who buys eternal life?

Nor can the words of Gregory, referring to the people, be truly said of bishops. "Whether," he said, "a pastor compels [them] justly or unjustly, the flock must respect the opinion of the pastor." [3] For the bishops are not the flock, but the people [are]. By as much as the life of the pastor is separated from the flock should the life of the priest be distant from his people.

Therefore, you ought not to be suspended from Holy Communion [4] like a confessed and convicted criminal. Thus far, indeed, no legal sentence of condemnation could have been pronounced against you, as if you were a rebel and fugitive, especially since your acts and conscience are unstained, you who have never avoided the sacred councils; nor can it be, according to law. No legal sentence has been pronounced, because Gregory [I] says: "A sentence pronounced without writing does not merit being considered a sentence." [5] Nor can it be pronounced according to law, because Pope Leo the Great says: "The privilege of Peter does not hold wherever a judgment does not arise from the justice of the case." [6]

Do not, therefore, give our rivals such an opportunity that the priesthood, which everywhere is one, just as the Catholic Church is one, seem to be so subjected to one person that when he has been corrupted by money, friendship, fear, or ignorance, no one can become a priest except one whom these "virtues" commend. Let the common law of the Catholic Church be the Evangels, the Apostles, the Prophets, the canons established by the spirit of God and consecrated by the reverence of the whole world, and the decrees of the Apostolic See not discordant with them. And let him who through contempt shall deviate from these laws be judged according to these and be degraded according to these. Therefore, let there be continuous peace forever and ever for the one keeping these [laws] and carrying them out according to his abilities.

We hope that you are faring well. . . .[7]

Again farewell, and do not willingly be suspended from the sacred mysteries. For he who, when accused, stands silent before the judge, confesses his guilt; or he who while the judge is deciding, resigns himself to punishment, likewise confesses. Now, a confession is made either for the sake of salvation or of perdition: for salvation, when one admits truths about himself; for perdition, when he fabricates or allows to be fabricated false statements against himself. To keep silent [before] a judge is, therefore, to confess.

Furthermore, to confess false and mortal crimes is the act of a murderer, because everyone who causes his own death [8] is a greater murderer. And the Lord says: "Out of thy own mouth I judge thee" [Luke 19 : 22]. The false accusation must, accordingly, be repulsed, and the illegal judgment despised lest, while we desire to appear innocent, we are proved criminal before the Church.

This is Letter 192 in Havet. It deals with the application of the decrees of the council of Pavia (n. 5 below) by Archbishop Siguin of Sens. If the council was held the last week in January, 997, the news would have reached Sens in 3 or 4 weeks; within two weeks Siguin's obedience to the decrees would be apparent; and in another week Gerbert would have received news of Siguin's action.

1. See Letter 114, n. 1.

2. "According to a tradition rejected today, St. Marcellus, bishop of Rome from 296 to 304, had sacrificed to idols during the persecution and was adjudged guilty by a council of three hundred bishops (PL VI, 11-20; St. Augustine *De baptismo unico* xci, 27, PL XLIII, 610; JK, p. 25)." Havet, p. 180, n. 5.

3. *Homilia in Evangelia* II.xxvi.6, PL LXXVI, 1201.

4. He had been suspended from office by the council of Pavia. See n. 5 below.

5. No official record of the council of Pavia exists, and it is known only by the summary sent to Willigis, archbishop of Mainz, in his capacity of papal vicar in Germany (JL I, 492), printed in MGSS III, 694 and Olleris, pp. 544-46. "It has pleased this holy council that all the bishops of the west who participated in the deposition of Archbishop Arnulf, and who, after having been summoned by definite citations, scorned the council at Pavia, and through a lay person sent irrelevant causes to confuse the council, be suspended from episcopal office... [and] those deposed without apostolic authority remain innocent." Apparently Abbot Leo brought the decisions of this council to France by word of mouth. Lot, *Hugues Capet*, pp. 115, 284, n. 2. Gregory I's words are found in his *Registrum* XIII.xlv, PL LXXVII, 1300.

6. *Sermones* IV, 3, PL LIV, 151.

7. Space of 15 letters in MS L, with debased Tironian notes in the margin.

8. Spiritual death, which results from sin.

215. **VILLAGE OF ST. DENIS. March 28, 997**
A bishops's council orders the canons of St. Martin of Tours to heed their archbishop, Archambaud, or appear at a council on May 9th

To the Canons of St. Martin [1] in the Name of the Bishops

From all the bishops who attended the council in the church of St.

Paul [2] to all the canons of the monastery of St. Martin.

After hearing the report of your rebellion against our brother, bishop of the city of Tours,[3] we are sending you these letters. They carry our unanimous decision that you either make peace with your bishop or attend the court [4] to be held at Chelles [5] on May 9th to adduce reasons for your long-continued quarrel. If this be not carried out, know that you will be visited with the censure of canonical punishment.

This is Letter 209 in Havet. Easter, March, 28, 997, seems a likely time for the council, since councils were usually held on Sunday, and since this date would allow sufficient time for the canons of St. Martin to obey the orders before the future date of May 9th mentioned in the letter. It was certainly not held later than March 28th because Gerbert left Rheims within the next week (Letters 219, introductory note; 220). Havet, p. 197, n. 6; 198, n. 1; Lot, *Hugues Capet*, p. 278.

1. The monks of St. Martin of Tours were organized as canons of a cathedral. For a brief account and bibliography see E. Duckett, *Alcuin* (New York, 1951), pp. 285, 307.

2. The council of bishops may have met at the collegiate church of St. Paul in St. Denis near Paris for two reasons: the memory of the riot at St. Denis, in the monastery (Letter 194, introductory note), was still fresh in their minds; and King Robert was fond of coming to St. Paul's to pray. Probably, then, Robert was at this meeting (cf. n. 4 below). Havet, p. 197, n. 6.

3. Archambaud. See Letter 213.

4. *Placitum*, the word used usually for the judicial session presided over by the king or count or their representatives. N. Estey, "The meaning of *Placitum* and *Mallum* in the Capitularies," *Speculum*, XXII (1947), 439. The use of this word, with its nonecclesiastical meaning, strengthens the idea that King Robert was present at the meeting in St. Paul's. Estey (pp. 436 and 438) calls attention to the fact that Charlemagne forbade holding courts on Sunday, though May 9, 997 was a Sunday.

5. Dept. Seine-et-Marne, canton Lagny.

216. RHEIMS. April 1, 997

Gerbert begs Siguin (?), archbishop of Sens, not to apply the decisions of the council of Pavia with such severity; hints that he may flee from Rheims

[GERBERT TO ARCHBISHOP SIGUIN (?)]

With how much moderation the salvation of souls must be dealt with, Your Fraternity, knows, and one should ponder deeply over the matter in order to do nothing in excess.[1] While you are executing the severe judgment [2] against the church of S[ens?], you have, indeed, overstepped the limits established by the Fathers. For what councils or decrees have forbidden the baptizing of infants, or the burying of the faithful in hallowed ground? But if this place be kept closed legally by your interdict, or, in ecclesiastical language, ban, the innocent parishioners ought to be permitted to move elsewhere and legally to participate in their sacred rites.

Accordingly, I advise Your Paternity to soften the execution of the judgment and to deal with the whole affair in such a way that you will be pleasing in the eyes of the Divine Majesty, and not displeasing in the judgment of your fellow bishops.

After [3] suffering the manifold tumults of these evil times for so long now, I am fleeing to you for solace as to the safest harbor. As for the rest, either your assistance will comfort us, or we must seek foreign [4] aid.

This is Letter 203 in Havet. It is Gerbert's second letter protesting the application of the decrees of the council of Pavia, January, 997. See Letter 214, especially introductory note, and n. 5. Since the church of "S." is mentioned below it must mean Sens, and therefore the letter was written to Archbishop Siguin as Letter 214 was. Either Siguin had answered immediately, affirming his interdict, or Gerbert had received complaints from persons in his diocese.

1. Terence *Andria* 1.i.33, 34.
2. Decree of the council of Pavia.
3. In MS L there is a space between the preceding part and the first word of this sentence (*Varios*). What follows does not seem really to belong to this letter.
4. Otto III, or Empress Adelaide. Letter 217.

217. RHEIMS. April 1, 997

Gerbert commends himself to the remembrance of Empress Adelaide and relates the dangers surrounding himself

GERBERT TO EMPRESS ADELAIDE [1]

Very often, O Majesty, whom many-sided virtue has always inhabited and possessed, Your Piety alone has come to my mind as I was meditating on where fidelity, truth, piety, and justice make their home. To you, therefore, as to a special temple of compassion,[2] I flee as a suppliant; and once more I ask your ever beneficial counsel and aid. For, because...[3] they turn their fury against me alone, passionately demanding my life;[4] and added to this mass of evils....[5] Even Rome, which should be a solace, rages. I beg and beseech you, therefore, that by your command your kingdoms assume a gentler attitude. Since all of me is yours, wherever I am, I await your considerate attention and relief. Of this alone I am certain—that we wish to carry out what manifestly pleases you.

This is Letter 204 in Havet.
1. See Letter 216, n. 4.
2. *Misericordia.* There was a Roman goddess of that name, of whom Gerbert could have learned in Quintilian (*De institutione oratoria* v.xi.38). From his own journeys to Rome Gerbert must have known of temples erected to such a goddess.
3. Space of 25 letters in MS L.
4. Virgil *Aeneid* xii.398; ii.72.
5. Space of 18 letters in MS L.

218. RHEIMS. April 2, 997?

Congratulates an unknown bishop or abbot upon his restoration to his official position; he is returning a youth in whom both of them are interested and hesitates to undertake his education

[Archbishop Gerbert to an Unknown Bishop or Abbot]

Since the Divinity has always shown that human affairs are ruled by His eternal wisdom, so in our time He has wished you especially to be the channel of His wisdom. For, He has exalted you and cast you down, and then, modifying and reducing this humiliation by His goodness, He has restored you to your see [1] with the attendant highest approbation of many persons. So, He has ordered you, like so much gold purified in a furnace,[2] to shine more brightly in His house. I praise and glorify His pity and compassion, accordingly, not only on your account but also on my own, for I, as a pilgrim, was, as you might say, fleeing the whole world when He ordered me to cease wandering and to remain in a certain land.[3]

I am directing to you my greatly beloved whose godfather [4] you wished me to be, but whether you ought to send him to be educated by us is not ours to decide. For, if we refuse, we may perchance appear ungrateful, and, if we agree, any evil befalling the boy because of the difficult times will be attributed to our fault.

This is Letter 205 in Havet. Gerbert was returning the protégé mentioned in the letter because he was planning to leave Rheims. This protégé, if ready for education by Gerbert, must have been at least thirteen years of age (n. 4 below) so Gerbert had known the addressee a long time. He could have been an abbot, for Gerbert uses *sedes* [see] in Letter 171 to mean "abbey." However, Ascelin of Laon is almost the only person known who might fit Gerbert's description.

He had been imprisoned by Duke Charles in 988, but he had been restored to his episcopal see by 991. Then he was imprisoned by King Hugh in 993, but was restored again by April, 995. Letter 253, n. 1.

1. Bishopric or abbey. See introductory note above.

2. Ps. 12 : 6, though here silver, not gold is mentioned. See Seneca *Epistolae morales* v.9, where fire rather a furnace is mentioned.

3. Virgil *Aeneid* 1.629. This sounds as if Germany were meant. In such case, this letter was written after Gerbert left Rheims in April, 997.

4. *A sacro fonte.*

219. AACHEN. April 12, 997

Gerbert expresses his affection for, and gratitude to, Bishop Arnulf of Orléans and requests him to take charge of his property in France

GERBERT TO ARNULF, BISHOP OF ORLÉANS [1]

Speech is inadequate to explain the affection of my soul towards you who, to be sure, taught, warned, and prescribed what course I should follow and what avoid when I was endangered by the slightest movement of my head.[2] And now, indeed, according to my knowledge and ability, with heart and soul I repay such thanks to you as I am able, and I entrust myself and all I own to your protection and disposition, as I hold forth the almost certain hope that the notable beginnings will have happy [endings], and because a synod. . . .[3] Thus, I earnestly beseech that the overwhelming troubles which at present vent themselves wholly on me shall not envelope our church. When, then, after a little, a propitious Divinity will allow me to breathe again, in your very presence [4] we shall await your judgment in these and in other matters.

This is Letter 210 in Havet. Gerbert probably joined Otto III's court before the latter left Aachen. Otto III was in Aachen April 9, 997 and in Dortmund on April 18th. DO III 240 and 242.

1. See Letter 194, n. 1.

2. Possibly a reference to advice given Gerbert not to perform the marriage of King Robert and Countess Bertha, for such a refusal was dangerous to Gerbert who needed Robert's support to maintain his position as archbishop of Reims.

3. Space of 18 letters in MS L. The synod referred to was probably a papal synod planned for Christmas in Rome (or, at least, in Italy).

4. Thus, Gerbert planned to return to France, if the papacy rendered a decision favorable to him. Letter 221 at end of letter.

220. **AACHEN.** April 12, 997
Gerbert thanks Adalbero, bishop of Metz, for receiving him so kindly

GERBERT TO THE BISHOP OF METZ [1]

As if set upon a candlestick [Mat. 5 : 15f.; Mark 4 : 21f.; Luke 8 : 16f., 11 : 33] let [the light of] your excellence shine forth, manifested in many directions before, and now so abundantly radiating its affection by words and deeds. Thus, because the Apostle says: "Rejoice with them that rejoice, weep with them that weep" [Romans 12 : 15], you received me joyfully as I was freed by God's grace from the undeserved persecution of my brothers, and you grieved at not having undergone dangers with me. I therefore render thanks to you though absent, and when present I will compensate by service, if acceptable. For the rest . . .[2] as for the other matters worth mentioning we know nothing certain as yet.

This is Letter 211 in Havet.
1. Adalbero. See Letter 65, n. 1.
2. Space of 25 letters in MS L.

221. **MAGDEBURG.** June 5, 997
Gerbert refuses to return to Rheims until his claim to the arch-bishopric has been decided definitively by a papal synod

To QUEEN ADELAIDE [1]

To the glorious ever august Queen Lady Adelaide, from Gerbert, archbishop of Rheims by the grace of God, and to all of his colleagues and fellow bishops of the diocese of Rheims, farewell in Christ.

The letter in your name carried joyful beginnings and contained agreeable information, but was terminated in a disheartening manner. To be sure, it showed the sweet affection of your heart toward me, and advised me to hasten to return to my own see.

But what kind of an answer could your harsh conclusion expect? For thus it reads: "Know, if only you will weigh the implications of this small matter, that we shall utilize both the property and advice of our vassals without giving consideration to claims on your part."

With me in charge of the city of Rheims, when was it, is it, or will it be not permitted to you[2] to use [my] counsel and the property entrusted to me? Or, was this permitted more readily when Arnulf held it? But that man took it away from you by deceit and fraud. I kept it for you by watching constantly and laboring incessantly against the deceits and treacheries of many persons.

Astonishing! Unbelievable! that you do not perceive the plots of your enemies. For they, seeking to restore Arnulf to his see, to the disturbance of your kingdom, think that this restoration will not be safe for them unless they earlier lose me through any pretext whatsoever. We recognize this to be certainly true for the double reasons that when I was recently living at Rheims you decreed that he be set free, and that, as has been indicated to me through letters from friends at Rheims, the Roman Abbot Leo [3] had secured his freedom as a condition precedent to obtaining confirmation of the new marriage [4] of my lord, King Robert.

My belief that the situation is dangerous is strengthened by present events, since Chaumuzy [5] was invaded by Gibuin,[6] nephew of Gibuin. I believe the number of villages was very great, and the inhabitants of Rheims cannot suffice to hold them unless the inhabitants of Châlons are invited to secure estates. What then? If Arnulf is freed, or if Gibuin, or any other is enthroned in my seat, it is inconceivable that my return would be without danger to my head. Even if you will not take notice of it, I ought not to doubt that this is so.

Your kindnesses I realize, indeed, should be extolled before all mortals. I am aware of the very sweet devotion of your heart towards me, which I will repay by my prayers even if unable to repay by my merits.

Hence, in order not to burden you with my troubles I shall keep silent altogether about myself whom the Divine Grace has freed from immeasurable dangers, and whom as far as I alone am concerned It is arranging for and caring for with all felicity. So, in the terrible name of Omnipotent God, I pray and beseech you to aid the desolate and wasted church of Rheims, if in any way you are able. Because it is the head of the kingdom of the French, if it perishes, necessarily the members will follow. And how will it not perish, placed as it is under the names of two men, as if between the hammer and the anvil, while it approves of neither as a leader, as it tosses about midst the waves of the sea without an oarsman?

What, then, do you think can be accomplished if, without the decision of the Church, a third[7] be added to the number? Truly, I am not saying these words as if [I were] a soothsayer or a prophet. Remember, furthermore, that not only my knights, but also the clerics conspired so that no one would eat with me, no one assist in the sacraments.[8] I keep silent about the vilification and contemptuousness. I say nothing of the violent injuries often inflicted on me by many persons. To these conditions you call upon me to return, and to make me suffer worse things your letter adds threats.[9]

To what purpose, O Divine Majesty? Do they think me so very foolish or so separated from you that I do not see the dangling swords, or that I would wrack your church by schism? Indeed, I am acutely aware of the cunning of these wicked men, but if so decreed I will defend the unity of the church against all schisms by my death.

Therefore, I ask, my ever august lady and my brother bishops, who because of their judgment against the traitor Arnulf, have been subjected to an anathema[10] whether justly or unjustly, that they bear with me as I am patiently awaiting the judgment of the Church. For, the church which I was charged with governing by the decision of the council of bishops I am unwilling to relinquish except by such judgment, nor do I plan to hold it again, as if by force, contrary to the decisions of the bishops whose judgment prevails.

While I await these decisions, I endure, not without sorrow, an exile that many persons think pleasant. My mind dwells on the illustrious features of my lord, King Robert, on his happy face and our accustomed conversations,[11] and likewise upon your words full of wisdom and importance, as well as upon the pleasing friendliness of princes and bishops, the deprivation of which makes this life burdensome.

My only consolation is the affection, kindness, and generosity[12] of the illustrious Otto, the Caesar, who loves you and yours so much that day and night he besieges me with the question as to where and when he can see you more intimately and can embrace and speak with King Robert, my seigneur, about the same age and resembling him in intellectual enthusiasms. Therefore, if the journey to Rome that greatly occupies my attention because of the [anticipated] council should be postponed now, about the first of November you may expect me who am your very faithful interpreter of these matters and obedient to you in everything.

This is Letter 181 in Havet. Otto III left Gerbert at Magdeburg while he proceeded northeast into Slavic territory to campaign against the Slavs (DO III 244-47). Thietmar (iv.lxi), who actually saw Gerbert at Magdeburg, records his presence there. See also H. Voigt, *Der Verfasser der römischen Vita des heiligen Adalbert* (Prague, 1904), p. 3; Lowis, *History of the Church in France*, p. 117; Schramm, *Kaiser, Rom und Renovatio*, I, 96.

M. Uhlirz, *Untersuchungen über Inhalt und Datierung der Briefe Gerberts*, pp. 153-59, argues that after Gerbert's return from Italy (Letters 208-11) (about August 1, 996, according to her), he exercised his office as archbishop less than a month and then fled first to Lorraine, then to Mainz where Otto III had arrived in early October. Thus, she dates Letter 221 in the period October 15th-24th (n. 1 below). As a result of her assumption that Gerbert fled from Rheims at the end of August, 996, her dating and interpretations of Letters 221-31 vary considerably from those given here. See also M. Uhlirz, *Jahrbücher des Deutschen Reiches unter Otto II. und Otto III*, Vol. II: *Otto III*, pp. 217, 220-27, 487-93.

1. Letter 129, n. 1. King Hugh died October 24, 996, but Queen Adelaide still exercised considerable authority. Richer iv.cviii; Lot, *Hugues Capet*, pp. 185, 298-303.

2. I follow MS V, *vobis* [to you], against MS L, *vestris* [to your followers].

3. Abbot of SS. Boniface and Alexius in Rome, and papal legate. See also Letters 226 and 227.

4. Letters 213, notes 1 and 2.

5. This seigneury belonged to the archbishop of Rheims until modern times. Havet, p. 164, n. 5.

6. Gibuin II, nephew and successor of Gibuin I. See Letter 65, n. 6.

7. Gerbert.

8. At the council of Mouzon, June 2, 995, Gerbert promised to refrain from celebrating mass for a limited period. Olleris, p. 250.

9. MS V stops at this point, and in the margin is the notation: "The old manuscript did not contain more," and "The remainder is transcribed from Vignier's *Historica gallica* [*La Bibliothèque historiale* (Paris, 1587), II, 633]."

10. Letter 214, n. 5.

11. Compare the similar description of Otto II in Letter 42.

12. Letters 223, introductory note; and 229, notes 1 and 2.

222. **MAGDEBURG?** July 5-8, 997

Gerbert worries over lack of news from Emperor Otto III, who should concern himself with Italian affairs; he forwards a letter dealing with same

GERBERT TO THE EVER AUGUST EMPEROR OTTO

Gerbert to the ever august Caesar, glorious Lord Otto.

Each passing day completes a whole year for me. Full of cares and anxieties I can scarcely endure the days and nights while my messengers do not return and I lack news from Your Majesty. The Scythian [Slavic] [1] land augments my cares; Italy multiplies them. If we abandon the Scythians, I am apprehensive. If we do not go to the Italians, I am terrified. Why the Italians? [2] Because, as their legates come announcing their own misfortunes, they dramatize yours. Why is it, I beg by your [3] leave, that the imperial majesty is so contumaciously despised? And by whom?

I shall be astonished if such men, regarding excellence as cowardice as we all know and it is unnecessary to mention, have abused your patience [4] with impunity. As further proof of these events I am dispatching to you the letter sent to me. [5] Although it describes injuries to me, they concern you even more, and in so far as I consider them wrongs to you I do not regard them as wrongs to me alone.... [6]

This is Letter 219 in Havet. See Letter 221, introductory note. Letter 222 was written at the time when the news of the capture and burning of Arneburg (north of Magdeburg) had reached Magdeburg just as Bishop Sigfred of Piacenza had arrived there. The disaster at Arneburg occurred on July 2d, while Otto was in Gandersheim, somewhat to the west (DO III 248), and the news would have reached Magdeburg on the 5th or late on the 4th. Apparently, Bishop Sigfred had sought Otto III first at Magdeburg but found only Gerbert there. Gerbert sent Letter 222 and the letter received from Italy along to Otto, whom Sigfred finally met at Eschwege, July 17th (DO III 250).

1. *Scythicus axis*, an archaic expression, used by the Romans to designate peoples living to the north and northeast in Europe. M. Uhlirz ("Die Scythae in den Briefen Gerberts von Aurillac," MIOG, LIX [1951], 411-415), by dating Letters 222 and 225 in early November, 997, interprets "Scythians" to mean Hungarians. She dates the letters too late, hence her conclusions are inacceptable.

2. Vignier, *Bibliothèque historiale*, II, 637, has *Quia Italis*, [Because to the Italians], while MS V has *Quia Itali* [Because the Italians]. The passage makes more sense if the "s" was actually a question mark and the words therefore in the original of Vignier and MS V had been *Quia Itali?* The translation is based upon this. Bubnov, II, 878, n. 22, suggests: *Quia Itali st*, i.e. *Quia Itali sunt* [Because they are Italians].

3. Havet, p. 232, following Vignier (*Bibliothèque historiale*, II, 637) gives *nostram* [our], but MS V has *vestram*, which I follow here.

4. Cicero *In Catilinam* i.i.

5. From Italy, probably from Bobbio, which still looked to Gerbert as abbot, and with whom the monks continued to exchange infrequent letters or news. Another disturbing event which had occurred in northwest Italy only a short time previous to this letter (i.e., on March 17th) was the murder of Bishop Peter of Vercelli by Margrave Arduin's followers. In 1002, Bobbio favored Arduin as king so perhaps he had already been active in the region of Bobbio in 997.

6. MS V copied *etc.* here which Vignier (*Bibliothèque historiale*, II, 637) had

printed after *puto* [I consider] as his own words, not those of the letter. They indicate that the letter was longer in the manuscript used by Vignier, which is now lost.

223. SASBACH. Last week of July 28, 997
Compliments Bishop Haimo of Verdun on finally understanding certain unstable Lorrainers; recommends D. to him

GERBERT TO THE BISHOP OF VERDUN [1]

Our common sons, R.[2] and D.[3] have rejoiced us by their information of a sweet change of affairs.[4] For, as the Apostle says: "Evil communications corrupt good manners" [1 Cor. 15 : 33]. So, not being of simple mind, you have suddenly sensed the unstable and perplexing attitudes of certain Lorrainers who are honey-tongued, but bitter of heart; and you have turned against their many stupid remarks, as they deserve. But, because they could not longer make sport of Your innate Prudence, we rejoice that you have fully grasped their pretense and deceit. Therefore, [trust] our son D. as a faithful interpreter of all that you and I should know in common, for we shall have been able to instruct him fully in the knowledge of things.

Farewell.

This is Letter 212 in Havet. Gerbert left Magdeburg almost immediately after writing Letter 222 to take possession of the estate of Sasbach (either in Baden, between Achern and Bühl, or north of Breisach), bestowed on him by Otto III. Introduction, p. 15; Letter 227. Soon R. and D. visited him at Sasbach, bringing news of Bishop Haimo.

1. Haimo (Haymo, Heimo), May, 991-April 21, 1024. He succeeded Adalbero II (Letter 182, n. 1). Johnson, *German Episcopate*, p. 254, incorrectly dates Haimo's election 988.
2. See Letter 227, n. 5. "R." was possibly the same as "Ri." in Letter 154, and "R." in Letter 200.
3. Probably the same as "D." in Letter 203.
4. Gerbert refers to Bishop Haimo's changed opinion about certain Lorrainers.

224. SASBACH. August 15, 997
Complains to Emperor Otto III of the lack of direct news from him and reports a case of starvation at Gorze

GERBERT TO OTTO CAESAR

Bishop Gerbert sends the homage of service that he owes to the ever august Caesar, glorious Lord Otto, Emperor of the Romans

With difficulty do we who are separated from you by the land's length endure your absence and the fact that an exceedingly round-about report of your maneuvers, so brilliantly executed as always, has brought us not one shred of news [directly] from you.

Just as it is not my purpose to write you at this time about the life and habits of Count Harmand,[1] so I am especially concerned to inform you of the wails and groans of brother W. That noble man bewails the fact that his brother is being destroyed by hunger near Gorze,[2] regardless of his rank and that of his family, and this leads to everlasting disgrace.

If this is true, why do they desire such harsh torments for him? What more painful death than hunger? Hunger alone, disdaining death itself and yet contrary to the law of nature itself causing death, overshadows all kinds of punishments. Eradicate such monstrous wickedness I beseech and to a begging brother restore a brother who, according to report, still breathes. Let captors and captives be particularly mindful of the treatment of the latter lest, after regaining liberty, the captives either themselves or through their followers may injure the captors or their friends because of the imprisonment.

This is Letter 182 in Havet. Otto III made his second campaign against the Slavs in Havelland during the year 997 between July 17th and August 20th (DO III 251 and 252). Letter 224 was written perhaps before the conclusion of the second campaign. See Letter 221, introductory note, about Otto III's first Slavic campaign in 997.

1. Possibly the same as Count Herimann, son of Count Godfrey of Verdun. In such case, his captor might have been Duke Thierry of Upper Lorraine. Lot, *Hugues Capet*, pp. 292-94. However, a brother "W." of Count Herimann is unknown. Bubnov (II, 781) believes that Count Harmand was the captor. "W." might refer to Bishop Wilderode of Strasbourg (Letter 201). As an archbishop Gerbert could call another bishop "brother."

2. Nine miles southwest of Metz in the Moselle department.

225. **LEITZKAU** or **MAGDEBURG?** August 15-23, 997
Emperor Otto III (?) or one of his court (?) regrets Gerbert's absence; the Slavs are surrendering, and John Philagathos will soon

[To GERBERT]

We ascribe to impossibility the fact that up to now you have not come to us, and we are hereby thanking you for your good will towards me. We are unable to prescribe when, in truth, you will be able to do this. Because the many races of Scythians [Slavs] are eager to submit themselves to the rule of our Caesar, and John the Greek [1] promises that he is about to do likewise—a fact which greatly pleases us—we are as yet doubtful whither we ought to turn the army that is at hand.

This is Letter 220 in Havet. The news of John Philagathos' (n. 1 below) capitulation reached Otto III in eastern Germany during or at the conclusion of the latter's second Slavic campaign of 997 (July-August). Either Otto or one of his followers wrote to Gerbert who was, by then, at Sasbach (Letter 224). Otto was at Leitzkau, a short distance southeast of Magdeburg, August 20th (DO III 252), and soon thereafter at Magdeburg. Schramm, "Die Briefe Kaiser Ottos III. und Gerbert von Reims," *Archiv für Urkundenforschung*, IX (1924), 105. Letter 225 seems to answer Letter 222, and to indicate that Otto's presence was more necessary in Germany than in Rome. Letter 224 was written by Gerbert at the same time, apparently, as Letter 225, and they must have crossed each other in transit.

Vignier (*Bibliothèque historiale*, II, 638) states that this is "the letter of an unknown, found among Gerbert's letters." The writer addresses the recipient with the familiar form of "you" (*te*), and this indicates that he was on familiar terms with Gerbert, or that he was Gerbert's superior. M. Uhlirz, *Untersuchungen über Inhalt und Datierung der Briefe Gerberts*, pp. 184ff., suggests that Archbishop Willigis of Mainz wrote the letter, and this seems very possible. However, her date—November, 997—based upon her assumption that the *Scythae* were Hungarians, not Slavs, produces a different interpretation of a portion of the letter. See also Uhlirz, "Die 'Scythae' in den Briefen Gerberts von Aurillac," MIOG, LIX (1951), 411-15.

1. John Philagathos, a Greek from Calabria, said to have been of servile origin, who became abbot of Nonantola (DO II 283) in 982, and then bishop of Piacenza in 988. As a favorite of Empress Theophanu he even became the godfather of Otto III and exerted considerable influence over him after Theophanu's death in 991. In 994, Philagathos was sent to Byzantium to seek the hand of a Greek princess as Otto III's bride. Returning to Italy at the end of 996, he was created [anti-]pope as John XVI about the end of January, 997, by the powerful Roman noble, Crescentius, with the encouragement of the Byzantine Ambassador Leo who had returned with him. Schwartz, *Die Besetzung der Bistümer Reichsitaliens*, p. 189; Schramm, "Die Briefe Kaiser Ottos III. und Gerbert von Reims," *Archiv für Urkundenforschung*, IX (1924), 92, 94, 106-7; Schramm, "Kaiser, Basileus, und Papst in der Zeit der Ottonen," *Historische Zeitschrift*, CXXIX (1924), 443-46; Schramm, "Neun Briefe des byzantinischen Gesandten Leo," *Byzantinische Zeitschrift*, XXV (1925), 97-100.

226. AACHEN. September 7, 997

Emperor Otto III queries whether Gerbert is pleased with events in France and suggests an imperial messenger to Pope Gregory V in Gerbert's behalf

[HIS PUPIL OTTO TO MASTER ARCHBISHOP GERBERT]

Otto, most faithful of his pupils in steadfast preseverance, to

Gerbert, master beloved above all others and most loving of arch-bishops.

If the outcome of events[1] accords with your desires there is no person who rejoices more than we. If, however, this result is anta-gonistic to what your noteworthy merits deserve—a thing we hope not—we are affected by the same sorrow as yourself.

To continue, we are aware that your industrious, careful foresight takes no small care of the condition of our affairs. Hence, we desire to indicate to you the sort of state your affairs are in. We are, there-fore, compelled to continue to speak realistically by reporting that your adversary Arnulf,[2] son of deception, even now directs his journey to the pope [Gregory V]. This we learned through the report of Abbot Leo.[3] Because this has happened, here is the tenor of our advice: that with this very Leo we dispatch our messengers to the pope to act as intercessor for you to vouch for your faith.

May you live and flourish, and forever continue happy.

This is Letter 218 in Havet. It is answered by Letter 227. September 2, 997, Otto III was at Thorr, near Cologne (DO III 253), and from September 29th to the end of October he was surely in Aachen (DO III 254-62).

1. Arnulf was reported (falsely) to have been released from prison. Note 2 below.

2. Arnulf was actually released from prison only in January or February, 998. Abbot Abbo of Fleury traveled to Pope Gregory V in Arnulf's behalf about the end of September, 997. *Epistolae Abbonis*, PL CXXXIX, 419; *Vita Abbonis*, PL CXXXIX, 401, 403; Lot, *Hugues Capet*, pp. 124-25, 267ff.

3. Letter 221, n. 3.

227. SASBACH. September 12, 997
Congratulates Otto III upon his Slavic victories; accepts his aid against Arnulf; and complains that Sasbach has been taken from him

GERBERT TO OTTO

The least of his bishops[1] always and everywhere offers the homage of the service that he owes to the ever august Caesar, his most worthy Lord Otto.

Since, among human affairs, we consider nothing sweeter than your supreme power, you could make known to us, solicitous in your behalf, nothing sweeter than the great renown of your empire and your great and dignified perseverance. For, what, indeed, is more splendid in a prince, what firmness more praiseworthy in the leader, than for him to force his legions to invade hostile territory, to withstand the attack of the enemy by his presence, and to expose himself to the greatest dangers for his fatherland, for religion, and for the safety of his followers and of the commonwealth?

Because these affairs have terminated successfully, we are less upset by Abbot Leo's [2] embassy, directed to you regarding that Arnulf. This embassy, moreover, does not worry us. He relied on as true either what is entirely false,[3] but which Abbot Leo demanded as having been promised by my French compatriots; or what, if it is true, I know that your innate good will toward me both can and will cause you to prevent such audacious schemes.

Because when our Leo [4] was hastening to you swift as a bird on September 8th, as he himself wrote, there first arrived a letter, delayed, I believe, by bad winds, confirming that nothing had been done about Arnulf. But just as he carries with him other ideas, thought up with great cleverness, so they must be carried out through wise plans.

Your Gerbert says an everlasting farewell to you, and because you so generously bestowed [on me] magnificent Sasbach in order that I may live in splendor, your Gerbert dedicates himself forever to your everlasting command. And because R. greets you,[5] your Gerbert transfers himself to your everlasting service. These gifts which you so liberally had bestowed, but which have been taken away by some-one—I do not know why—your Gerbert begs to be restored [6] to him. May the last number of the abacus [7] be the length of your life.

This is Letter 183 in Havet. It answers Letter 226.

1. Here Gerbert refers to himself as bishop. Both Gerbert and Leo of Vercelli (see also n. 4) served in Otto III's chapel, as evidenced by DO III 270 (January 19, 998, at Cremona): *Gribertus musicus seu Leo qui Uuannus, capellani ipsius domni imperatoris* [Gerbert the musician and Leo called Warin, chaplains of the lord emperor]. Since Leo was called a "bishop of the palace" (*episcopus palacii*) in 996, although he did not become a bishop (of Vercelli, 998-1026) until 998, Gerbert must also have been called a bishop. Ter Braak, *Otto III,* p. 108; M. Uhlirz, "Italienische Kirchenpolitik," MIOG, XLVIII (1934), 279, n. 4.

2. Letters 221, n. 3; and 226.

3. Letter 226, notes 1 and 2.

4. Leo Warin (*Uuanus,* n. 1 above), a former cleric of the cathedral of Hildesheim, where he had been taught by Bernward (later bishop), one of Otto III's tutors. Skilled as a poet, politician, and administrator, Leo was a man of lively genius, well educated, and better acquainted with Roman law than any man of his time. H. Bloch, "Beiträge zur Geschichte des Bischofs Leo von Vercelli," NA, XXII (1897), 78ff.; Manitius, II, 511-17; Schramm, *Kaiser, Rom*

und Renovatio, I, 100, 115, 119-20. Leo, on his way from Italy, was coming down the Rhine by boat to Aachen.

5. MS L has *Et quia R. s.[alutem] v[obis] d[icit].* Probably "R." is the same person as "R." in Letter 223, who may have been Richard of Rheims, later abbot of St. Vannes of Verdun (Letter 154, n. 1).

6. See Letter 229, n. 2.

7. 999,999,999,999,999,999,999,999,999. See Letters 7 and 232 (near the end). Gerbert's abacus consisted of 27 columns. Richer iii.liv.

228. SASBACH. September 21, 997
Gerbert espresses to Archbishop Willigis (?) his satisfaction in their friendship and his pleasure at being relieved from the burden of cares at Rheims

[GERBERT TO ARCHBISHOP WILLIGIS (?)]

To the Very Reverend Father Lord Willigis (?) [1] from his son Gerbert.

In a noteworthy speech you declared holy friendships and close fraternal association to be as sweet as they are useful, and you have deemed me worthy, both now and for the future, to be an associate and companion in the Divinity's great reward. For what else is true friendship except the especial gift of the Divinity?

Leaning on your friendship, then, both by presuming good results from it and by hoping for better in the future, I do not fear the return of Arnulf to the city of Rheims. But, if it shall have happened as related by Hungerius,[2] who favored it, then I am confident that I am being freed from Ur of the Chaldees,[3] and that I shall not be lacking in obedience to your service. This event will accomplish what I have always wished, have always hoped for, by making me his inseparable companion [4] so that we can guide the exalted empire for him. What, therefore, could be sweeter? What more outstanding?

Thus, you should not have sighed over the affair of a friend, nor should you in the future, since all things will be entirely successful if the Divinity is favorable [Rom. 8 : 28], when they have occurred through a wish and deliberation in common, that is, by your advice, by the aid of friends, and by compelling ourself to seek out and obtain every favorable advantage.

Farewell, and rejoice that the affairs of our Caesar have been conducted well, and that mine are progressing auspiciously.

Again and many times farewell.

This is Letter 184 in Havet. Gerbert wrote this letter, but to whom is uncertain (n. 1 below). The words "our Caesar" at the end of the letter indicates that the recipient was a German and the formal salutation shows that he was an important ecclesiastic. M. Uhlirz, *Untersuchungen über Inhalt und Datierung der Briefe Gerberts,* pp. 163-65, 201, argues convincingly that the recipient was Archbishop Willigis, or, less likely, the vice-chancellor Heribert.

1. *Domino et reverentissimo patri ill. G. filius* in MS L. In Gerbert's Register of his letters, *ill.* was undoubtedly written *Guil.* or was a Tironian note.

2. Hungerius may be identical with Otto III's representative, mentioned in DO III 154 and in a document dated May 3, 998. Böhmer, *Regesta imperii,*Vol. II, Pt. 3: *Regesten unter Otto III,* No. 2: *998-1002* (new ed. M. Uhlirz), No. 1278a.

3. See Letter 88.

4. *Comitem individuum.* This refers to Otto III. See Letter 232 for the same expression.

229. NEAR SASBACH. October 12, 997

Gerbert complains to Otto III of being ousted from his new estate of Sasbach by one of Otto's men and reminds his emperor of his long service to the Ottos

GERBERT TO THE AUGUST CAESAR OTTO, ALSO ROMAN EMPEROR

From Gerbert to the ever august Caesar, glorious Lord Otto.

I know that I have and do offend the Divinity in much. But I do not know by what contradiction I am said to have offended you and your followers so that my service is so suddenly displeasing. Would that either I might never have been permitted to receive such gifts,[1] offered with glory by your generosity, or, once received, I had not lost them in such confusion. What should I think of this?

What you most certainly gave, you were either able to give, or you were not. If you were not able to, why did you pretend to be able to? If you were able to, what unknown, what emperor without name, commands[2] our emperor, so noted and famous throughout the world? In what shadows is that scoundrel lurking? Let him come forth into the light and be crucified so that our Caesar may freely rule.

Many persons believed that I stood in great favor with Your Piety. Now one must exert one's self to secure patrons, the same persons I once undertook to support; and greater trust is to be placed in my enemies than in friends. My friends have told me that all things are advantageous for me and everything favorable. My enemies have foretold, in either a prophetic or a rabid spirit, that there will be no gifts, no benefices for me, that the pleasant beginnings will have harsh endings. Such things I have experienced more than I wish, and they are not befitting the imperial person.

For three generations I might say, to you, to your father, to your grandfather,[3] midst enemy and weapons, I have exhibited the most incorruptible fidelity; for your safety have I exposed my person, however small, to raging kings and frenzied people. Through wilderness and solitude, beaten by the assaults and attacks of thieves, tortured by hunger and thirst, by cold and heat [2 Cor. 11 : 25-27], in all disturbances I stood firm so that I chose death rather than not to see the son of Caesar, then a captive, on the throne.[4] I have seen him rule, and I have rejoiced. Would that I might rejoice to the end and finish my days with you in peace.

This is Letter 185 in Havet.
1. The domain of Sasbach. Letter 223, introductory note.
2. Otto III had bestowed the estate of Sasbach upon Gerbert as if the domain belonged to the imperial fisc. Some powerful official close to Otto, disputing this ownership, ousted Gerbert, claiming he was acting by the wish of Otto. Moreover, Gerbert's mild protest in Letter 227 at being dispossessed of Sasbach had apparently elicited a letter from Otto confirming the action of the dispossessor.
3. Otto III, Otto II, and Otto I.
4. See Letters 24 and 34f. M. Uhlirz, *Untersuchungen über Inhalt und Datierung der Briefe Gerberts*, p. 166, suggests that possibly these words mean that Gerbert actually saw Duke Henry of Bavaria surrender Otto III to his mother Empress Theophanu at Rohr, June, 29, 984.

230. AACHEN. October 21, 997

Emperor Otto III writes a letter for himself inviting Gerbert to become his teacher and enclosing an original verse

EMPEROR OTTO TO GERBERT, HIS TEACHER

Otto himself writes Gerbert, most skilled of masters and crowned in the three branches of philosophy.[1]

We wish to attach to our person the excellence of your very loving self, so revered by all, and we seek to affiliate with ourself the perennial steadfastness of such a patron because the extent of your philosophical knowledge has always been for Our Simplicity an authority not to be scorned. Not to be ambiguous but to enjoy plain speaking with you, we have firmly resolved and arranged that this letter shall make clear to you our desire as to the extent of our choice and the singleness of our request in order that your expert knowledge may be zealous in correcting us, though not more than usual, unlearned and badly educated as we are, both in writing and speaking, and that with respect to the commonwealth you may offer advice of the highest trustworthiness.

We desire you to show your aversion to Saxon ignorance by not refusing this suggestion of our wishes, but even more we desire you to stimulate Our Greek Subtlety to zeal for study, because if there is anyone who will arouse it, he will find some shred of the diligence of the Greeks in it. Thanks to this, we humbly ask that the flame of your knowledge may sufficiently fan our spirit until, with God's aid, you cause the lively genius of the Greeks to shine forth.

Pray explain to us the book on arithmetic [2] so that when fully taught by its lessons we may learn something of the attainments of the ancients.

Whether it pleases you to act upon this invitation, or displeases you, may Your Paternity not postpone making a reply to us by letter. Farewell.

> Verses have I never made
> Nor in such study ever stayed.
> When to its practice myself I apply
> And can write successfully,
> As many men as has Lorraine,
> To you, then, songs I'll send the same. [3]

This is Letter 186 in Havet. It answers Letter 229. Otto III was in Aachen until October 27, 997 (DO III 262).

1. Natural (physics), moral (ethics), and rational (logic). This was the Platonic division of philosophy known through Isidore's *Etymologiae* ii.xxiv.3-8. Gerbert, however, followed the Aristotelian division known through Boethius, Cassiodorus, and a later section (pars. 9-16) of the same chapter of *Etymologiae*. See his dispute with Otric in Richer iii.lix-lxi; and Letter 122, n. 1.

2. Probably a manuscript of Boethius *De arithmetica*, sent as a gift by Gerbert to Otto, and believed to be MS Bamberg Class. 5 (HJ. IV. 12), written on purple parchment in gold and silver letters, a truly royal book. The manuscript, a product of the school of Tours, had been written for Charles the Bald soon after 832 but before his coronation as emperor. The dedication verses to Charles found on fols. 1v-2r, 62v-63r, 139r-139v seemed to apply equally well to Otto III and were long believed to have been written by Gerbert. See Bubnov, I, 326ff.; and *Gerberti opera mathematica*, pp. 148-50. Even Otto III may have believed in Gerbert's authorship, since he answers with a poem (Letter 230, at end) when mentioning the Arithmetic. K. Pivec, "Briefsammlung Gerberts," MIOG, XLIX (1935), 45, suggests that Gerbert may have composed the verses and added them to the already constituted manuscript.

How Gerbert could have acquired the manuscript is unknown. When Charles the Bald died he divided his books among St. Denis (near Paris), St. Mary in Compiègne, and his son Louis the Stammerer. J. W. Thompson, *The Medieval Library* (Chicago, 1939), p. 59, n. 24. Another Bamberg manuscript of Boethius *De arithmetica*, Class. 8 (HJ. IV. 13), a.900-50, came from Rheims. Carey, "Scriptorium of Reims," *Studies in Honor of Rand* (New York, 1938), p. 58. G. Friedlein, *Boetii De institutis arithmeticae libri duo* (Leipzig, 1867), p. 1, mentions many marginal notes in a second hand. See also Letter 232 about Otto III's intellectual studies.

3. *Quot habet viros Gallia, Tot vobis mittam carmina.* The *quot-tot* was a favorite form of love-greeting in the middle ages, derived from Ovid, Virgil, and others.

231. NEAR SASBACH. October 25, 997
Gerbert accepts Otto III's invitation to join his court as a teacher

Gerbert to Otto Caesar

Gerbert, archbishop of Rheims,[1] by the grace of God, [sends] whatever is worthy so great an emperor to the ever august glorious Lord Otto.

Not because of our merits, though perchance because of solemn vows, are we able to make answer to your surpassing kindness that deems us worthy of perpetual obedience to you. If we are aglow with the slightest spark of knowledge, it redounds to your glory through the excellence of your father who nourished it and the magnificence of your grandfather who matched it.

What shall I say? We are not bringing our own treasures to yours,[2] but rather are giving back what we once received, some of which you have enjoyed already,[3] some of which you are very soon to enjoy as is evidenced by the honest and useful invitation, so worthy of Your Majesty. For, unless you were not firmly convinced that the power of numbers contained both the origins of all things in itself and explained all from itself,[4] you would not be hastening to a full and perfect knowledge of them with such zeal. Furthermore, unless you were embracing the seriousness of moral philosophy, humility, the guardian of all virtues, would not thus be impressed upon your words.

Not silent, moreover, is the subtlety of a mind conscious of itself since, as I might say, oratorically you have shown its oratorical capabilities as flowing from itself and its Greek fountain. I do not know what more evidence of the divine there can be than that a man, Greek by birth, Roman by empire, as if by hereditary right seeks to re-capture for himself the treasures of Greek and Roman wisdom.

Therefore, Caesar, we obey the imperial edicts not only in this, but also in all things whatsoever Your Divine Majesty has decreed. For we who consider nothing sweeter among human affairs than your command cannot fail in obedience to you.

This is Letter 187 in Havet. It was undoubtedly written immediately after the receipt of Letter 230, which it answers. The latest date when Otto III is known to have been at Aachen was October 27, 997 (DO III 262). See also Letter 232.

1. Gerbert here reminds Otto III to address him not merely as teacher (*magister*) but by a title corresponding to the dignity of archbishop of Rheims.

2. MS V, *vestris*, instead of MS L, *nostris* [ours].

3. A reference to their learned discussions earlier in 997. Introduction, p. 15; Lattin, *Peasant Boy*, pp. 136-39.

4. The verses on the Boethius manuscript sent to Otto III by Gerbert (Letter 230, n. 2) contain the same idea. St. Augustine in various *Sermons* (lii, cclii, cclxiv; cclxx, PL XXXVIII, 352, 353, 1177-78, 1216, 1240) discusses the power of number, likewise Martianus Capella VII.731ff., Boethius *De arithmetica* I.ii, and Macrobius *Commentarii in somnium Scipionis*, who writes (I.vi.8), "This number one, the beginning and end of all things, though it itself knows no beginning or end, pertains to the highest god and separates our knowledge of him from knowledge of the things and powers following."

232. REICHENAU? December 26, 997

Gerbert sends to Otto III the philosophical tract De rationali et ratione uti; prefaces it with this letter, and concludes it by adding another personal note

[GERBERT TO THE EVER AUGUST EMPEROR OTTO]

Bishop Gerbert sends the homage of service that he owes to the ever august Caesar, glorious Lord Otto, emperor of the Romans.

While we lingered in Germany during the hotter part of the year,[1] obligated as heretofore and henceforth by allegiance to the emperor, some hidden spark of your divine mind secretly struck fire in us and refined the flux of our thoughts into words. It revealed to everyone qualities discussed in very difficult phrases by Aristotle and the greatest men. One such was the wonderful ability of any mortal to have such depths of thoughts midst the strifes of war being prepared against the Sarmatians [Slavs],[2] since from them flowed such note-worthy penetrating ideas like streams from the purest source.

For you remember, and we continually recall to mind many noble and learned scholars who used to be with us, among whom were some bishops,[3] notable in wisdom and distinguished for their eloquence. However, we saw none of them who explained any of these questions properly, because certain problems too removed from use produced beforehand no hesitancy in them, and certain problems frequently aired could not be solved. Therefore, you in your divine prudence, regarding ignorance unworthy of the sacred palace, commanded me to discuss what others had argued in various ways in a [tract] *De rationali et ratione uti.*

At that time, indeed, both a lassitude of body [4] and more serious matters [5] postponed this. Now that good health has been restored, and I am now midst public and private cares on this very Italian journey, and in all allegiance about to be your inseparable companion, I shall set forth briefly my conclusions on this question lest Greece shall boast of herself alone both in imperial philosophy and in Roman power.

Ours, ours is the Roman Empire. Italy, fertile in fruits, Lorraine and Germany, fertile in men, offer their resources, and even the strong kingdoms of the Slavs are not lacking to us.[6] Our august emperor of the Romans art thou, Caesar, who, sprung from the noblest blood of the Greeks, surpass the Greeks in empire and govern the Romans by hereditary right, but both you surpass in genius and eloquence.

Therefore, in the presence of so keen a judge let us first state certain preliminaries, or rather sophistical statements of scholars, then investigate the findings of philosophers on these points, and thence the many-sided and thorny dialectic will offer the conclusion of the proposed question.

[The text of the tract *De rationali et ratione uti* [7] appears here.]

I have set forth, O Caesar, that which, though remote from the seriousness of a priest, still is not foreign to an emperor's zeal for learning, for I prefer to displease others than not to please you, not only in this respect but in all things worthy of your command. May you, therefore, read this in the midst of your mathematical exercises.[8] Whether I may have offered anything worthy of the sacred palace, the [intellectual] efforts of the nobles [9] will give the answer, and logic, when consulted, will not be silent, nor, indeed, let me fear any censure if I have worked to accomplish what could please the sacred ears.

This is Appendix II in Havet. By December 31, 997, Otto III had reached Pavia (DO III 264), where Gerbert joined him by January 19, 998 (DO III 270; Letter 227, n. 1). See n. 6 below as to the probability that Letter 232 was written at Reichenau.

1. In August, 997 Gerbert was at Sasbach. Letters 223 and 224. Lot, *Hugues Capet*, pp. 287-88, 290-91, 297.

2. The region east of the Vistula, in the central section of the Dnieper river, was called Sarmatia by the Romans. Gerbert's words indicate that Otto III and he began philosophical discussions before Otto's first Slavic campaign of 997, i.e., between May 18th (DO III 244 at Merseburg) and June 5th (DO III 245 at Arneburg, north of Magdeburg) at Magdeburg.

3. Among them were probably Leo Warin (Uuanus), Willigis of Mainz, Giselhar of Magdeburg, Henry of Würzburg. DO III 245-49.

4. This was undoubtedly a return of the tertian fever suffered in 996-97 (Letter 212, n. 4), but not the identical illness, as believed by Havet, p. 237, n. 2.

5. Part of this serious business was the fact that Gerbert had been dispossessed of Sasbach. Letters 227, 229.

6. Not only the Slavic tribes recently conquered by Otto III, but also the assistance of the Polish Duke Boleslaw Chobry. Thietmar iv.xxviii. Gerbert's words seem to have a close association with the miniature of Otto III in a Josephus manuscript of Bamberg (MS Bamberg Class. 79 [olim E. III. 16]) in which four female figures labeled *Sclavania, Gallia, Germania, Italia* [Slav-land, Lorraine, Germany, and Italy], offer their gifts to Otto III. It was executed at the monastery of Reichenau, probably during this Italian journey of Otto's and was apparently known to Gerbert. P. Schramm, *Die deutschen Kaiser und Könige in Bildern ihrer Zeit*, I (Leipzig, 1928), 194-95.

7. Olleris, pp. 299-310.

8. See Letter 230.

9. Gerbert hoped to stimulate the court nobility (including the bishops) to logical discussions and thinking along with Otto III. Compare the intellectual atmosphere of Charlemagne's court, described in Duckett, *Alcuin*, pp. 85-117.

233. RAVENNA? February 25 - March 25, 999?

Gerbert apologizes to Adalbold for not sending him more geometrical figures, but explains the difference between arithmetical and geometrical procedures for finding the area of a triangle

[GERBERT, ARCHBISHOP OF RAVENNA (?) TO ADALBOLD] [1]

Gerbert greets his still beloved and ever to be cherished Adalbold with honest fidelity and unchanging sincerity.

You have requested that if I have any geometrical figures of which you have not yet heard,[2] I should send them to you, and I would, indeed, but I am so oppressed by scarcity of time and by the immediateness of secular affairs that I am scarcely able to write anything to you. However, lest I continue mentally disobedient, let me write to you what error respecting the mother of all figures[3] has possessed me until now.

In these geometrical figures which you have [already] received from us,[4] there was a certain equilateral triangle, whose side was 30 feet, height 26, and according to the product of the side and the height the area is 390. If, according to the arithmetical rule,[5] you measure this same triangle without consideration of the height, namely, so that one side is multiplied by the other and the number of one side is added to this multiplication, and from this sum one-half is taken, the area will be 465. But I have carefully discussed[6] that geometrical [rule] which, using the theory of the height, measures the area as 390 feet, and I allow to the height only $25^5/_7$[7] of a foot, and the area $385^5/_7$. So, let this be the universal rule of finding the height of every equilateral triangle: always give a seventh [more] to the side, and allow the remaining six parts for the height.

In order that you may comprehend better what I have said, let me exemplify it in smaller numbers. I give you a triangle having a length on the side of 7 feet. I measure this thus according to the geometrical rule. I take a seventh from the side and the six which is left I give to the perpendicular. I multiply the side by this, and I say: 6 times 7, which gives 42. Of this, the half, 21, is the area of the said triangle.

If you measure this same triangle through the arithmetical rule, then you say: 7 times 7, and it makes 49, and you add the side so that it will be 56, and you divide to obtain the area, you will find it to be 28. Thus, in a triangle of one size only, there are different areas, a thing which is impossible.

However, lest you are puzzled longer, I shall reveal to you the cause of this diversity. I believe that you know what are said to be linear feet, what square, what cubic feet,[8] and that for measuring areas we are accustomed to use only square feet. The triangle touches only a part, no matter how small, while the arithmetical rule computes them as a whole. Let me draw a figure[9] in order to make clearer what has been said.

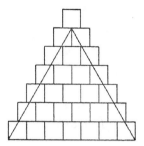

Thus, in this little diagram you have 28 feet, though not whole. Whence the arithmetical rule, taking a part for the whole, takes the half with the whole. The skill of the geometrical discipline, rejecting the small parts extending beyond the sides, and counting the halves about to be cut off and the [squares] remaining within the sides, computes what is shut in by the lines thus. For in this diagram, which measures 7 on a side, if you seek the perpendicular, it is 6. Multiplying this by 7 you fill it as if it were a squared figure [rectangle] whose breadth will be 6 feet, side 7, and you thus determine its area to be 42. If you halve this, you leave a triangle of 21 feet.

To comprehend this more clearly, lend your eyes to it, and always remember me.

Translation based on Bubnov, *Gerberti opera mathematica*, pp. 487, 44-45. The first paragraph of the body of the letter exists in MS Vatican Barberini VIII. 92, s. XII, fol. 487, and does not appear in the PL and Olleris editions of this letter. Gerbert's words in the first paragraph seem to indicate the period when he was preparing to leave Ravenna to become pope in Rome. Pope Gregory V died February 18th, and the news would have reached Ravenna by February 25th at the latest. Gerbert had become archbishop of Ravenna April 25, 998. See JL 3883.

1. Adalbold (Adelbold, Albald, Albold), was a cleric of Liége under Bishop Notker, and studied with Heriger, teacher and then abbot (990-1007) of Lobbes (Laubach). Adalbold became teacher at Lobbes after the date of this letter. He wrote to Gerbert, after the latter had become pope, about finding the volume of a sphere (published in Olleris, pp. 471-75, Bubnov, pp. 302-9, and elsewhere). In 1010, Adalbold became bishop of Utrecht, and died in 1026. Manitius II, 743-48; U. Berlière, DHGE, I, 524-25.

2. Gerbert had already sent to Adalbold a copy of a manuscript of the collected surveying literature, as handed down from the Roman surveyors (*agrimensores*) but put together in the seventh century, of the class of manuscripts designated by Bubnov as TBbba, which contained at least parts of: Pseudo-Boethius *Geometria*, Isidore on geometry from his *Etymologiae*, Cassiodorus on geometry from his "Institutes of secular studies" (Book II of his *Institutiones*), work on the *podismus* (linear measure by feet), the surveyors Epaphroditus and Vitruvius Rufus (anonymus here), summary formulae for

polygons, excerpts from Balbus, excerpts from Pseudo-Hyginus, an anonymous work on measuring fields, names of boundaries and fields, fragment of Julius Frontinus on the quality of fields, fragment of the spurious Commentary of Aggenius on Frontinus, Siculus Flaccus, fragment of Euclid I, a portion of Book IV of the *Geometria* of an anonymus author (originally printed with Gerbert as author). This was either the very same manuscript of the *Agrimensores* which Gerbert had found while at Bobbio in 983 (Letter 15, n. 5), or a copy of it. Bubnov, *Gerberti opera mathematica*, pp. 472-76, 556 (correcting p. 43, n. 4).

3. Cf. Boethius *De arithmetica* II.viii, who calls the triangle "the mother of all numbers" because it represents the number "one," i.e., unity, from which all numbers are derived. Boethius's discussion centers around Greek triangular numbers.

4. The figures accompanied the manuscript described in n. 2 above.

5. Boethius *De arithmetica* II.vii-ix; Bubnov, *Gerberti opera mathematica*, p. 44, n. 5.

6. This discussion is lost.

7. The use of a fraction of this type was unusual, because Egyptian fractions which used the number one as the only numerator (1/2, 1/3, 1/7, etc.) were still used and continued to be long afterward. Where possible, Roman duodecimal fractions (*deunx*, 11/12, *dodrans*, 3/4, etc.), based on the twelfth parts of the *as* (1), were used. In his *Geometria* iii.24, Gerbert refers to *minutias usitatas* [common fractions], i.e., Roman fractions, and to other fractions which he calls *intellectuales* [conceived of in the mind], i.e., our fractions, like the 5/7 he uses here. Bubnov, *Gerberti opera mathematica*, p. 64, notes 9 and 10.

8. Gerbert here uses *pedes longi, quadrati, crassi* for linear, square and cubic feet. In his *Geometria* ii.6, he uses *linearis, constratus*, and *solidus*. Bubnov, *Gerberti opera mathematica*, p. 56.

9. The figure that belongs with this letter has been printed with the title "L'abaque de Gerbert" (The abacus of Gerbert) by J. Leflon, *Gerbert*, p. 79. It has nothing to do with the abacus.

PAPAL PRIVILEGES

PAPAL PRIVILEGES

234. ROME. April 15-18, 999?

Sylvester II notifies all the faithful about establishing the monastery of Helmarshausen; and to the monks grants the right of electing the abbot and of choosing an advocate upon the death of Count Ekkehard.

SYLVESTER, BISHOP, SERVANT OF THE SERVANTS OF GOD.

To all the orthodox of the righteous faith. If [1] by our pontifical power we try to strengthen and exalt places and monasteries constructed by religious persons and by those dedicated to God, we trust that, without doubt, this will be useful both for securing favorable conditions in our present life and the reward of eternal blessedness.

Therefore, be it known to all our faithful in Christ, present and also future, how Count Ekkehard and his wife Mathilda for the sake of their souls and those of their parents, by a conspicuous act of benevolence constructed a monastery in a place called Helmarshausen [2] and installed a congregation of monks in honor of the Holy Savior of the world...[3] with all things belonging to it, and whatever shall be given from this time forth.

Therefore, be it be established by apostolic authority that the said monastery administer its gift just as the abbey of Corvey [4] is known to administer its; also, that it freely possess the property of its own right, to wit, all of the urban and rustic places and diverse lands, cultivated and uncultivated, with all of their appendages, that have been or will be granted by Christians. Further, permission is granted to the monks serving God there to elect an abbot for themselves according to the monastic Rule of St. Benedict. Besides, it also pleases our authority [to grant] that the aforementioned constructor of the monastery shall exercise the office of advocate while he lives, but that after his demise the abbot with the brothers may according to their ability choose as advocate anyone they deem more useful.

If anyone, by rash boldness, however, shall attempt to contravene this document of our apostolic confirmation, though this seems impossible, let him be advised that he will have been held fast by the chain of the anathema of Our Lord [and] [5] of Peter, prince of the apostles, to be consumed in the everlasting fire with the devil and his most vicious retinue, and also with Judas, betrayer of Our Lord and Savior Jesus Christ, sent down into the Tartarean depths to perish with the wicked. May he who is, indeed, the guardian and respecter of this our privilege receive the grace of benediction and eternal life from the Lord.

Written by the hand of Peter, notary and secretary of the Holy Roman Church, in the third [first] year of the pontificate of Lord Sylvester, in the month of April, in the twelfth year of the indiction.[6]

JL 3924. This is translated from Bubnov, I, 334-35; and P. Kehr, "Die älteren Urkunden für Helmarshausen," NA, XLIX (1930), 110-11.

Sylvester II's earliest document (the text of which is lost) seems to have been a privilege granted to the nuns of the Holy Savior and St. Vitus of Elten, issued presumably between April 9th and 15th. W. Erben, "Excurse zu den Diplomen Otto III," MIOG, XIII (1892), 572-74.

1. This formula differs from any in the *Liber diurnus,* and apparently was not used prior to the time of Sylvester II, being related to DO III 235. See also two other closely related diplomas of Otto III: 256 and 356.

2. In Hesse.

3. A portion of the sentence is apparently missing. P. Kehr, "Die älteren Urkunden für Helmarshausen," NA, XLIX (1930), 94, n. 2.

4. Do III 256 (partially false) also contains the reference to the abbey of Corvey.

5. Added from *Liber diurnus* 101.

6. Apparently the lower portion of the original papyrus document was so destroyed at the time it was copied into the Helmarshausen copybook that only portions of the two closing formulae (the *scriptum* of the notary, and the *data* of the librarian) were legible. The copyist, by combining the remains of the two formulae, produced two different dates.

The indiction years were periods of fifteen years computed from the 1st of September, used by the later Romans for tax purposes. Christians computed the indiction years from A.D. 313, based upon the conversion of Constantine the Great and the Roman empire to Christianity. They are read "the twelfth year of the indiction," not the "twelfth indiction," because each fifteen years a new indiction period began. Thus, the four years of Sylvester II's pontificate covered the twelfth, thirteenth, fourteenth, fifteenth years of one indiction period and the first year of the next. The twelfth year of the indiction was 999, which was the first of Sylvester II's papal reign and the third of Otto III's imperial reign.

235. ROME. April 18, 999

Sylvester II notifies the diligent faithful about establishing the rights of the monastery of St. Lambert of Seeon under the Holy See, and also defines the rights therein of its founder, Count Aribo.

SYLVESTER, BISHOP, SERVANT OF THE SERVANTS OF GOD.

If, by our pontifical authority, we try to strengthen and uplift places and monasteries constructed by religious persons and by those dedicated to God, we believe that, without doubt, we shall thereby secure the reward of double blessedness.

Therefore, let all the diligent faithful of God's Holy Church, both present and future, know how Count Aribo [1] for the care of his soul and those of his parents, by a notable act of beneficence, constructed a monastery in honor of the blessed martyr Lambert in a certain spot of his property once called Burgilis, but now called by the inhabitants Sewa [2] of St. Lambert Martyr. Acting thus to increase the chances of future reward, he requested that its freedom of dominion be validated in conformance with the authority of St. Peter, prince of the apostles. [3] On that account, therefore, since our apostolic authority has been persuaded by the pious intercession of the most glorious august Emperor Otto III, [4] we allow the aforesaid monastery of St. Lambert Martyr, through the terms of this privilege to have free dominion, to wit, that the monks serving God there may elect an abbot for themselves, according to the Rule of Abbot St. Benedict. [5]

In addition, it has also pleased our authority to grant that the monastery's aforementioned protector [Aribo] shall exercise the office of advocate [6] while he lives; but after his demise the abbot with the brothers may, according to their ability, choose as advocate anyone they deem more useful; [7] and that without any sort of objection by anyone he [the abbot] may both enjoy quiet possession with complete security, and control all urban and rural places, and various cultivated and uncultivated manors, with all of their appurtenances, that any

Christians have granted or will grant, and after him [the same for] all of his successor abbots in perpetuity.

Therefore, by the sanction of the Holy Roman Church we confirm to this oft-mentioned monastery through the gift of our privilege that neither we nor any of our successor pontiffs, nor any emperor nor king may have the power of selling or of bestowing it as a benefice, or of giving it away; and that no duke, archbishop, bishop, count, nor any person may dare to disturb or injure or to appropriate any of its property without the assent of the abbot.[8] And as consideration and evidence of the freedom granted, twelve *denarii*, in honor of the twelve apostles, shall be brought every year to the shrines of the apostles Peter and Paul.[9] But if it is impossible to offer this every year let it be paid within a twelve year space. And each day from this time forth let one collect be said at Mass for the living Roman pontiff. The same for the deceased ones.

If [10] anyone, by rash presumptuousness, however, shall attempt to try to do anything against the terms of this apostolic confirmation of ours, though such behavior is unbelievable, let him know that he has been bound by the chain of the anathema of our Lord [and of] Peter, prince of the apostles, to be consumed in the everlasting fire with the devil and his most vicious retinue, and with Judas, betrayer of the Lord and Savior, Jesus Christ; and at the same time, having been sent down into the Tartarean depths, let him perish with the wicked.

(Let it be fully known to all Christ's faithful that if this command of mine cannot remain stable permanently, though God forbid, soon, without the objection of any rulers let this abbey under the control of the aforesaid freeborn man freely return to the property of the next heir of the family of the aforesaid Count Aribo. Let him not use this grant for his own advantage but let him faithfully uphold [it] until it [the abbey] may again be held peacefully, just as other free abbeys ought to be provided with royal protection.)[11] Whoever, indeed, shall be the guardian and respecter of this our privilege, may he receive the grace of benediction and eternal life from the Lord.[12]

Written by the hand of Peter, notary and secretary of the Holy Roman Church.[13]

Given [14] on April 18th in the year of the Lord's incarnation 999, in the twelfth year of the indiction.

JL 3900. A. Brackmann, I, 73, No. 1. This is translated from Olleris, pp. 155-56. Letter 235 is mentioned in a privilege issued by Innocent II, April 11, 1139 (JL 7971).

1. *Arbo* in DO III 318. Count Aribo (whose wife was Adala) belonged to an important South German family, related to Duke Henry IV of Bavaria (later Emperor Henry II). He was the founder also of the monastery of Göss in Steiermark. J. Egger, "Das Aribonenhaus," *Archiv für österreichische Geschichte,* LXXXIII (1897), 406-7; K. Dumrath, "Das Benediktinerinnenkloster Göss, seine Stellung zu Kaiser und Papst," in *Festgabe Hans Hirsch,* MIOG, Ergänzungsband XIV (1939), 83-87.

2. A church had existed here since 924. The monastery of St. Lambert of Seeon was given to the church of Salzburg in 1201 and was suppressed in 1803. Brackmann, I, 72-73.

3. For an analysis of papal protection and its relationship to imperial or royal protection see A. Brackmann, *Studien und Vorarbeiten zur Germania Pontificia,* I (Berlin, 1912), 8; and H. Hirsch, "Untersuchungen zur Geschichte des päpstlichen Schutzes," MIOG, LIV (1942), 364-433.

4. On April 15, 999, Otto III had taken St. Lambert of Seeon under his protection (DO III 318), thus making it a royal abbey, possessing the juridical rights deriving from the emperor's protection, particularly the right of exemption from local (county) authority. The intercessor, frequently mentioned in royal diplomas, appears but infrequently in Sylvester's documents. In fact, the reference here to an intercessor indicates that this privilege was based on DO III 318 (in which Duke Henry of Bavaria was intercessor).

5. By the end of the tenth century the right of the monks to elect their abbot became a usual privilege bestowed by the papacy. See the expanded formula in Letter 261; and H. Hirsch, "Untersuchungen zur Geschichte des päpstlichen Schutzes," MIOG, LIV (1942), pp. 414-15. The "free dominion" (*arbitrium*) granted here thus consisted of the monastery's rights: (1) to elect an abbot, (2) to choose an advocate in the future, and (3) to have its property free from impairment by outsiders.

6. A lay person, usually of the nobility, in this case the founder of the monastery, chosen to protect a monastery's rights in secular matters, particularly in lay courts.

7. More frequently the office of advocate in the case of "free" abbeys (those belonging to a lord or bishop) became hereditary. P. Dollinger, *L'évolution des classes rurales en Bavière* (Paris, 1949), pp. 39-40.

8. The altar of the abbey church, dedicated to St. Lambert, was the center of the property-complex. Ordinarily, the land could be sold or mortgaged by the lord, but it could not be diminished nor could its use be changed. However, the present document forbids not only the lord, but also those other persons who had acquired rights in the abbey—the emperor and the pope—to make any change in the status of its property without the abbot's consent. See U. Stutz, "The Proprietary Church as an Element of Mediaeval Germanic Ecclesiastical Law," in G. Barraclough, *Mediaeval Germany* (Studies in Mediaeval History; Oxford, 1938), II, 42-43.

9. The usual place of payment was at St. Peter's tomb in Rome, but under Sylvester II payments could be made elsewhere, as here. The shrine of SS. Peter and Paul was located in the oratory of St. Lawrence in the church of St. John Lateran, where were the relics of the heads of the two apostles. "Latran," DACL, VIII, Pt. 2 (1929), cols. 1624-25, 1628-30. "The payment here was only the evidence for the assurance of protection, which was actually provided by the kingship." Brackmann, *Studien und Vorarbeiten zur Germania Pontificia* I (Berlin, 1912), 8.

10. The punishment formula (*poena spiritualis*) of the sanction (*sanctio*) taken from *Liber diurnus* 101 (ed. Sickel), was used ordinarily in documents confirming possessions. Portions of this formula were taken over from the sanctions in imperial documents. This one is found in the *Variae* of Cassiodorus (IV.42; VIII.28, in MGAA XII). The anathema, first used at the synod of Rome of 484, is equivalent to excommunication. Various Biblical, mythological and historical persons and places appear in the modifications of the original formulae. J. Studtmann, "Die Pönformel der mittelalterlichen Urkunden," *Archiv für Urkundenforschung*, XII (1932), 251-374, esp. 251, 258-59, 264-65, 269-71.

11. The section I have put in parentheses seems to be an interpolation taken from an imperial diploma. The notification formula (*notum sit omnibus Christi fidelibus*) is unusual in papal privileges but very frequent in royal diplomas. The acknowledgment that Seeon is now a royal abbey strengthens the belief in an interpolation. C. Daux, "La protection apostolique au moyen age," *Revue des questions historiques*, LXXII (n. s. XXXVIII) (1902), 32; A. Brackmann, *Studien und Vorarbeiten zur Germania Pontificia*, I (Berlin, 1912), 8.

12. The benediction or *Benedictio* formula.

13. This formula (the *Scriptum* formula) is incomplete, probably due to the copyist, because it should contain the month and indiction year.

14. *Data*, signifies the actual delivery of the privilege, and the time at which the librarian authenticated Sylvester II's signature.

236. ROME. April 19, 999

Sylvester II to Luizo, abbot of the monastery of San Salvatore and San Benito of Leno, Brescia (Lombardy), granting rights over the manor of Pancianum.

SYLVESTER, BISHOP, SERVANT OF THE SERVANTS OF GOD, to his very dear son in the Lord, Luizo, abbot of the monastery of our Lord and Savior and of Father Saint Benedict, built by pious King Desiderius [1] of divine memory in a place called Leno [2] in the county of Brescia, to you and your successors forever.

Because requests reasonably and suitably made by the faithful ought to be granted, we, as a result of our pious founder's devotion must nowise restrict our liberality in bestowing privileges.

Therefore, because you have petitioned us that a certain manor called Pancianum, belonging to the monastery of Leno in the county of Brescia, built by the aforenamed Desiderius of good memory, magnificent king of the Lombards, be decorated by a privilege of the Apostolic See, and also that the aforesaid manor, where he had established a cell itself as a permanent dwelling for monks, be never subjected to the control of any other authority, power, or rule, accordingly, through our authority, manifested by this privilege, we freely grant to your pious desires what you have asked.

And therefore we prohibit any priests or men, except the currently ordained abbot in the aforesaid monastery of Leno, from exercising any jurisdiction, power, authority, or regulation over the said cell constructed in the county of Brescia (Montinensi [sic]) and consecrated to the honor of Father Saint Benedict and the apostles St. Philip and St. James, or over the hamlets,[3] huts, churches, and vineyards belonging to it. By this apostolic authority of ours we decree further that no person, great or small, shall presume to inflict any injury on this same cell or on the parish church of St. Mary belonging to it, or on the serfs of God living there, or on the servants of both sexes, or also on the freemen living all over the lands[4] of the same cell, or on any property, movable or immovable, belonging to it.

And we equally confirm and corroborate to the same manor or cell the legal jurisdiction over the serfs and the freemen, and the tenths[5] and first-fruits of all their work in every place rightfully and legally belonging to the aforesaid parish church of St. Mary, or to the cell itself, just as it is possessed by virtue of the document granted to this very place and corroborated by its actual founder and [those] kings and emperors, his successors, as well as by our predecessor pontiffs of the Holy Roman Church.

We freely grant what ought to be granted without limit, requested by any prelates you please, namely, the altar, also the consecration of churches, the chrism,[6] and whatever pertains to the sacred ministry of the monks and canons, both free and dependent, enjoining under apostolic censure, we order that no mortal shall presume to have any legal jurisdiction in any parts of this manor or cell, or to judge, or to hold any law court without the permission of the abbot, or shall dare in any way to alienate the possessions of this place, ecclesiastical or secular, or to inflict any injury there, or to demand or require either provisioning of horses or soldiers or the expenses of entertaining officials[7] or any public functions. Moreover, all of these things enumerated above, by our apostolic authority we confirm, grant, and corroborate to you, Luizo, our son in the Lord, and to your successors from the present twelfth year of the indiction through this page of our privilege, according to the aforesaid manner.

If anyone, rashly daring, however, attempts to contravene this privilege of ours—an unanticipated act—just as it has been granted and corroborated by our apostolic authority, and if he shall not abandon his persevering in this, let him be aware that he is bound by the chain of an anathema by the Father, Son, and Holy Spirit and by the authority of Saint Peter, prince of the apostles, in whose place undeservedly we function, and that he will be cremated in the torture of the everlasting fire with the devil and with Judas, betrayer of our Lord Jesus Christ.

But whoever, out of pious consideration, shall continue to respect all of these regulations by upholding the provisions of this privilege of ours pertaining to the cult of God, shall receive the grace of benediction from the most merciful Lord God and shall merit being a partaker of the eternal life forever and ever. Amen.

℞ FAREWELL.

Written by the hand of Anthony, regional notary and secretary of the Holy Roman Church in the twelfth year of the indiction.

Given on April 19th by the hand of John, bishop of the church of San Albano,[8] in the above [written] month and in the above written twelfth year of the indiction, in the first year of the pontificate of Lord Pope Sylvester the Younger.

JL 3901. Kehr, *Italia pontificia*, VI, Pt. 1, pp. 343-44, No. 1. This is translated from Olleris, pp. 157-58. This privilege was used in a false privilege of Alexander II to the nuns of Santa Iulia of Brescia (JL 4542; Kehr, *Italia pontificia*, VI, Pt. 1, p. 344).

1. Lombard king, 756-74.

2. Leno was an imperial abbey (cf. Letter 235, n. 4) to which many kings and emperors granted privileges, among them Otto I (DO I 240, a. 962), Otto II (DO II 243, a. 981), and later Otto III (DO III 405, a. 1001).

3. That the *villae* here were only hamlets, consisting of a manor house, dwellings of the tenant cultivators, and scattered land parcels, seems clear from both the prior and later history of the region. The Lombards did not live together in compact groups. *Cambridge Economic History*, I, 172, 231. No important villages or towns developed from the *villae* of Pancianum.

4. Since the sub-Alpine Leno has a border location these freemen were undoubtedly *arimanni* whose ancestors earlier settled mainly on public land in frontier regions or near strategic spots or roads. They assumed both agricultural and military obligations to cultivate land to sustain themselves and to protect the roads and provide military defense, at the same time paying a small rent. Derived from Byzantium, the system was similar to the establishment of border troops (*agri limitanei*) by the Romans. F. Schneider, "Die Entstehung von Burg und Langemeinde in Italien; Studien zur historischen Geographie Verfassungs- und Sozialgeschichte," AMNG, LXVIII (1924), 102ff., esp. 109-16, 133, 168; *Cambridge Economic History*, I, 33-34, 49, 52, 172, 196-97.

5. C. E. Boyd, "The Beginnings of the Ecclesiastical Tithe in Italy," *Speculum*,

XXI (1946), 158-72; C. E. Boyd, *Tithes and Parishes in Medieval Italy* (Ithaca, N.Y., 1952).

6. See the interesting article on church dedications by Lee Bowen, "The Tropology of Mediaeval Dedication Rites," *Speculum*, XVI (1941), 469-79. "The chrism was composed of oil and balsam which preserves from corruption and so signifies charity." *Ibid.*, p. 478, n. 12. It was used in the sacraments and rites of baptism, confirmation, dedication, etc.

7. *Paratas*, an exaction required to pay the expenses of visiting public officials, such as the emperor or king, the *missi* (direct representatives of the emperor) and legates, or bishops and archdeacons in their tours of inspection of the parishes. Du Cange, V, 86f. This was one of the most burdensome of the exactions.

8. Librarian of the Holy See.

237. ROME. April 26? 999

Sylvester II to Adelaide, abbess of the monastery of St. Peter and St. Servatus Confessor of Quedlinburg, reaffirming the privileges granted by previous popes and exempting the monastery from the control of any bishop except the Roman pontiff

✠ SYLVESTER, BISHOP, SERVANT OF THE SERVANTS OF GOD, to Adelaide,[1] venerable abbess of the monastery of Quedlinburg,[2] and to her successors to the headship of the aforesaid place, and to all there who, in accordance with canonical regulation, serve God, St. Peter, prince of the apostles, and St. Servatus Confessor in whose honor the aforesaid monastery was constructed and by whose merit it flourishes excellently, forever.

...[3] Therefore, because the rights and the unavoidable obligations of divine laws require that whatever may legitimately and reasonably be requested from our apostolic benevolence, be denied to no one, we deem it proper that if we have discovered in the privileges of our predecessors or in other sacred ecclesiastical documents, statements and facts worth preserving, we should reaffirm these if requested, by reiterating the evidence of their permanence.

On this account, therefore, and persuaded by the pious intercession of the most glorious august emperor of the Romans, Otto III, and by the sacred petitions of his illustrious sister, Lady Adelaide, the above mentioned venerable abbess, for we have the power to take the initiative with all such liberality as this within the bosom of the Mother Church lest we should offer any objection to one making requests by the force of apostolic authority, we have partially renewed the privilege in its own words according to the copies of our predecessors and have [partially] added to it, ratifying this in order that this same place of Quedlinburg [located, it appears, on a mountain] [4] may manage its own affairs to include the abbess, the handmaidens of Christ and servants of the holy order, and those serving God and the holy apostles, Peter and Paul, and St. Servatus there, as well as all its possessions, such as churches and villages, which legally are regarded as much divine as secular; and that subject only to the Highest See, that of Rome, and to its apostolic occupant, namely, the universal [5] pope, and immune from the yoke of obedience to anyone else, and flourishing under perpetual freedom, it may grow by God's favor.

Thus, in the event of the death of the abbess of this place, to fill such lack they shall fittingly elect for themselves, without consideration of rank, a prelate whom probity of life and habits shall betoken as most useful for such an office, [and it shall be] according to their decision alone, without any contradiction by emperors, kings, or princes.

Furthermore, we firmly establish this through the weight of the apostolic adjuration that no bishop at all shall presume to enter the said premises except only the Roman pontiff; [and] that without the voluntary consent and esteemed invitation of the abbess herself the former may not assume there any small or important case of law, nor may he dare to celebrate the mysteries of the Mass there unless obligingly invited for the sake of kindness. The free apostolic dominion [having been granted?] to the abbess of the aforementioned place...[6] we bestow grace by granting that a bishop, whom they have invited or one whom they prefer, perform the providently unifying services of their Roman Order, which is their dear head, services of a threefold sort, beginning first with consecration and the sacrament of baptism, through the middle up to the common fate of a funeral and the last honors of the funeral services to the reward for sacred ministry; [and] they may have power to exercise the cult of the Roman religion without any objection now and in the future.

If, however, any scorner of this page or any obstinate violator of this decree exists, we bind him by the everlasting, indissoluble damnation of anathema in order that he submit and be turned over to the punishments of God and of Peter, prince of the apostles and also of all the saints. By the unchangeable authority of our apostolate we place under the control of the aforesaid place and the abbesses presiding there the two monasteries within Quedlinburg, that of the nuns of St. Mary on the mountain, and of the canons of St. Wibert in the village, with Walbeck situated in the pagus of Sueuon and Vuinatha-husum located in the pagus of Hartugo. And if anyone, by chance, shall attempt to change this, though God forbid, let him, by the prescribed anathema, be a companion of Judas in eternity.

Written by the hand of Peter, notary and secretary of the Holy Roman Church, in the month of April, in the twelfth year of the indiction.

✠ [Gerbert] who is also Sylvester, bishop.[7]

[BULLA] [8]

JL 3902. This is translated from Bubnov, I, 330-31.

Otto III issued two diplomas at Rome for Abbess Adelaide of Quedlinburg, April 26, 999 (DO III 321 and 322). In view of the close papal and imperial co-operation evidenced by the proximity of the dates of the imperial and papal privileges for Seeon (Letter 235), undoubtedly Sylvester issued a privilege to Quedlinburg on the same date as, or very close to, the date of Otto III's privileges for the same.

1. Oldest daughter of Otto II and Empress Theophanu. She was not formally consecrated abbess until September 29, 999, although her Aunt Mathilda, abbess of Quedlinburg, had died February 7, 999. *Annales Quedlinburgenses,* a. 999, MGSS III, 75; Thietmar iv.xxvii.

2. Founded in 930 in the diocese of Halberstadt. Chevalier, *Repertoire: Topo-bibliographie,* II, 2490.

3. A comparison with the beginning of the *arenga* (see Introduction, p. 26) in Letters 235 and 236 indicates that about four lines are missing here, un-doubtedly due to the damaged condition of the papyrus original when the twelfth-century copy was made. Ewald, "Zur Diplomatik Silvesters II," NA, IX (1884), 351.

4. Ewald, "Zur Diplomatik Silvesters II," NA, IX (1884), 350, n. 2 suggests this because two diplomas granted by Otto I to Quedlinburg (DO I 89 and 313) use this descriptive phrase.

5. Modern writers often use this word to describe Sylvester II as if he were the first to use it. However, *Liber diurnus* 73 (ed. Sickel, pp. 69-70), a much earlier formula for a bishop's profession of faith, contains it, *vobis ... summo pontifici seu universali pape* [to you ... the most exalted bishop and universal pope]. "Universal" is likewise applied to Pope Gregory V, who preceded Sylvester II, in a document in PL CXXXIX, 269A.

6. Here a portion of the papyrus original was destroyed.

7. Sylvester II's signature on the original privilege was in Tironian notes (see Introduction, pp. 21, 25), parts of which were copied onto the Quedlinburg parchment copy. Bubnov, I, 269 reproduces these notes in Table IV.B.3, tran-scribing them (p. 271) as *be-ne va-le-te* [farewell]. However, I consider that they resemble a mutilated form of *qui et Sil-ves-ter e-pis,* a signature lending an air of authenticity to the document whose genuineness has been questioned.

8. Sylvester II's original lead bulla had been removed from the disintegrating papyrus original and attached to the twelfth-century parchment copy in Magdeburg cathedral. Bubnov, I, 331, does not mention this lead seal (bulla), which apparently was not well made. Ewald, "Zur Diplomatik Silvesters II," NA, IX (1884), 350, n. 2.

238. ROME. May, 999?

Sylvester II to an abbot, advising him on his suspension from office for two years for simony, based upon the rule for bishops in such cases

SYLVESTER, BISHOP, SERVANT OF THE SERVANTS OF GOD, sends greetings and apostolic benediction to Abbot....[1]

Concerning the matter on which you sought our advice, we have postponed answering you for the reason that we do not have the authority in books here in Rome.[2] We remember having left in France those very books in which we read the particular opinion. However, we recall some of the ideas which we believe can satisfy your request.

In these same books relative to the advancement of bishops by purchase [simony] one reads that, if any such shall be found, he shall be deprived of his episcopal office for two years, two days a week he shall abstain from wine and cooked food, and he shall eat only after completing [the reading] of the Psalter.

We note that this accords with the traditions of the earlier fathers who sanctioned the deposition of bishops in this manner. The suspension from office shall be [the equivalent of] a deposition for any such [bishop], but whoever is removed from office may not be deprived of communion. However, the two-year suspension shall carry as much penance as deposition alone. Indeed, whoever shall return to his office after his two-year suspension and the performance of penance shall be reconciled with compassion as if after a deposition.

Therefore, begin the aforesaid biennium after the octave of Pentecost [June 15], and you may be restored to your office by virtue of this decree. If you can entrust the guardianship over the brothers and the burden of caring for the whole monastery to any one of the brothers, do so. If not, however, even though you be heavy-laden, you must endure the whole patiently. Increased heat causes a purer metal to pour forth from the furnace.

JL 3930. This is translated from Olleris, pp. 153-54. Sylvester's remarks about his books left in France suggest a time soon after his consecration (April 9, 999).
1. Blank in Vatican copy.
2. This hints at the smallness of the papal library in the period. See Lattin, *Peasant Boy*, p. 151.

239. ROME. May 7, 999?
Sylvester II confirms to the church of Vercelli the control of the county of Santhià

In the name of the Holy Trinity, indivisible and eternal, SYLVESTER, POPE,[1] SERVANT OF THE SERVANTS OF GOD.

Let it be clear to all the living and to posterity that, owing to the meritorious intercession and worthy petition of our son Lord Otto [III], most pious emperor, through this privilege of our authority we affirm that the county of Saint Agatha[2] with all its public appurtenances, and all castles, hamlets, fishing and hunting rights,[3] markets, customs dues, and every exaction,[4] shall henceforth remain as a unit and continue unchanged under the control of the holy church of Vercelli.[5] The outstanding generosity of the same[6] Lord Otto, emperor of pious memory, granted this unconditionally for the love of God and of the Confessor St. Eusebius who rests there by that decree [which stated] that no one living, emperor or king, margrave or count, neither an Italian nor a German nor any person soever, shall dare cleverly or rashly to offer any opposition or damage at any time to the aforesaid church.

But, if by chance, anyone shall attempt to impair the imperial grant, and a disorderly transgressor of this confirmation of ours shall strive to disturb the Holy Church of God, let Omnipotent God Himself say anathema and maranatha[7] against him [who is] abandoned and driven afar by the whole society of the faithful, and cursed by the Virgin of Virgins and by Michael, highest of the archangels, and by St. Peter, the key-bearer and prince of the apostles, and let all the curses be heaped upon him read in both Testaments of the Bible; and let every church, whitersoever scattered about the globe, that looks to the faith of the Holy Apostolic See, strike him; let it copy this and believe absolutely that he eats and drinks midst sinners, that he sleeps, plays, sits, stands,[8] and always turns towards them, and that his life will be death without end, devoid of remedy until these possessions shall be wholly restored to the oft-mentioned Holy Church and its guardian.

In order that this confirmation of our authority may remain irrevocably valid through fleeting time, in our day and in those of our successors, according to our custom we have ordered that it be subscribed and sealed with our bulla.[9]

[BULLA]

JL 3903. This is translated from Olleris, pp. 158-59. Kehr, *Italia pontificia*, VI. Pt. 2, p. 12, No. *19*. (Bibliography on Vercelli on pp. 5-7). Since this privilege was prepared outside the papal chancery, its authenticity has been questioned. But convincing proof has not yet been offered that it was not issued by Sylvester II. C. Manresi, "Alle origini del potere dei vescovi sul territorio esterno della città," BISI, LVII (1941), 293, 298, insists that Bishop Leo of Vercelli (Letter 227, n. 4) falsified numerous documents, among them this privilege. See however, M. Uhlirz, *Jahrbücher des Deutschen Reiches unter Otto II. und Otto III*, Vol. II: *Otto III*, 296, who relates it to two diplomas of Otto III (DO III 323, 324), issued on May 7, 999, and thus believes it be authentic. The introductory formula in Letter 239 is characteristic of imperial diplomas, not of papal documents.

1. Although the appellation *papa* [pope] was used as early as Siricus (384-98), the word *episcopus* [bishop] was a much more common designation for the bishop of Rome. "Pape," DACL, XIII (1937), col. 1343, and n. 3.

2. Santhià, the old Roman *Vicus viae longae*, 14½ miles northwest of Vercelli, almost halfway to Ivrea, and important for control of the roads to the western Alpine passes. Queen Theodolinda of the Lombards had changed its name to Saint Agatha. *Enciclopedia italiana*, XXX, 181.

3. The hunting rights must have been more important in Santhià than the fishing rights, because there was much forest and woodland here in addition to the arable land.

4. Such as bridge, road and gate tolls, payments for use of the forest, of the common or pasture, or the rivers or other water.

5. In Lombardy, on the Sesia river, halfway between Milan and Turin, a place very important to Otto III for the control of this northwestern section of Italy and important to the tenth-century margraves.

6. Otto III must have petitioned for this grant for Vercelli, but before it was issued in final form he died. The word the "same" (*ejusdem*) and the words "of pious memory" (*piae memoriae*) could not refer to Otto III in 999. Apparently, there was an interpolation here, the purpose of which is not clear.

7. 1 Cor. 16:22: "If any one does not love Lord Jesus Christ let him be anathema. Maranatha." The last word is Aramaic and means "Our Lord has come," or "Lord, come Thou." In the formula of the text "maranatha" is mistakenly used as a terrible curse.

8. Similar to an expression in Gregory I *Registrum epistolae* VII.xxvi.

9. These formulae were appropriate to the imperial chancery, but not to papal usage. However, DuCange (VI, 240c) gives an example of the use of sealing (*sigillare*) a document with a lead bulla. This means in the case of the pope that a bulla is to be hung onto the open document as a further authentication.

240. ROME. May, 999

Sylvester II to Wilderode, bishop of Strasbourg, granting control over the nunnery of Andlau, a possession of the Roman Church, to the church of Strasbourg, and confirming the possessions of the church of Strasbourg

SYLVESTER, BISHOP, SERVANT OF THE SERVANTS OF GOD, to all the orthodox of the holy faith.

The divine precepts of both the sacred canons and the venerable fathers, so very salutary for us, etc.[1]

Therefore, it is manifest that the abbey of Eleonis, commonly called Andlau,[2] known to belong of right to the Holy Roman Church, has been completely lacking not only in religious life known to have existed there once, but also in chattels, owing to the thefts of lay persons. When this information reached the ears of our predecessor Gregory [V] of blessed memory, he pondered how to aid the aforesaid abbey. Therefore he granted it to Wilderode,[3] venerable bishop of the church of Strasbourg, to protect and defend, and at the same time to restore the religious observance after completely ousting the lay power.

˙ Moreover, by apostolic authority, ratifying the privileges of our predecessor, we grant that, in accordance with his regulation, the aforesaid abbey shall be subject in perpetuity to the protection and defense of the Strasbourg church; and by the authority of our privilege we confirm all its possessions, either already acquired or capable of being acquired, and completely alienate them from the power of all lay persons. And whatever lay person shall presume to exercise any control over it, let him realize that he has been excommunicated by our authority.

We are granting this decree not to remove it from the jurisdiction of St. Peter, but, because it is far away from us, we are entrusting its protection to the aforesaid church as a lesser to a greater, imposing the condition that as acknowledgment of our rights three albs [4] yearly be brought to us. But, if neglected in the first year, it will be doubled the second year; if the same in the second, it will be tripled in the third, and if neglected in the third, similarly it will be quadrupled. If now the aforesaid are not paid in the fourth year, the church of Strasbourg will forever lose the abbey; this will be so if such neglect of obligation occurs while the bishop is living. In addition, whatever property the church of Strasbourg has previously acquired or shall possibly acquire, whatever it has justly and legally received from any person either in the city or outside, both chattels and realty, we affirm by apostolic authority not only privately but also publicly [5] to belong rightfully to it, and we shall kindle the dread curse of anathema especially against all who might plot against this decree.

Written by the hand of Peter, notary and secretary of the Roman Church, in the month of May, in the twelfth year of the indiction.

Given by the hand of John, bishop of the church of San Albano, and librarian of the Holy Roman Church, in the year of the Lord's Incarnation 999, in the first year of the pontificate of Lord Pope Sylvester, with Otto III ruling, in the sixteenth year of his reign.

JL 3904. This is translated from Olleris, pp. 159-60.

1. Certain formulas used by the papal secretaries were so well known that only the beginnings appear in the privileges, with *etcetera*, so that the recipient would know that the remainder of the formula (here from *Liber diurnus* 92) was intended. Cf. JL 3888. Santifaller, "Verwendung des *Liber diurnus*," MIOG, XLIX (1935), 259, 269, 271, 322.

2. Benedictine nunnery in Basse Alsace, canton of Molsheim, founded about 880. Chevalier, *Repertoire: Topo-bibliographie*, I, 112; DHGE, II, 1575.

3. JL 3891, known only from Sylvester II's privilege. See Letter 201 as to Bishop Wilderode. He died at Benevento, undoubtedly from malaria, presumably a few days before July 8, 999, as that is the recorded date of his burial. Rupert *Vita S. Heriberti archiepiscopi Coloniensis*, PL CLXX, 397B.

4. *Camisiales*, a long linen garment worn by practically all ecclesiastics, the alb being a special form. These were undoubtedly manufactured in the nunnery. Lesne, III, 242, and n. 2.

5. This was not merely a private document of confirmation of property, but a public decree that should be read from the church, and perhaps be copied and circulated.

241. ROME. August 1-14, 999

Decree of Sylvester II in favor of the monastery of Lorsch, exempting it from all control except that of the king and of the pope

SYLVESTER, BISHOP, SERVANT OF THE SERVANTS OF GOD, to all the sons of the Holy Church of God.

We wish it to be known to all persons present and future, that the abbey called Lorsch [1] was of old subject to the dominion of kings and popes only; afterwards, however, owing as much to changing conditions as to increasing sins, it had degenerated from its former condition.

Now, however, admonished by our beloved son Otto, august Caesar, through the recommendation of Willigis, archbishop of Mainz, and of Franco,[2] bishop of Worms, and of their followers and of all of the bishops of this same province, and likewise of Bernehar, bishop of Verden,[3] we order, by our authority, that the aforesaid abbey return to its former status, to enjoy the freedom which clearly it once possessed, to wit, to be subject only to the jurisdiction of kings and popes and to banish, indeed, any other control.

As long as the abbot and the monks of this place shall live religiously and blessedly they may remain in peace and quiet and without the objection of any person. If, however, they shall abandon religion and devote themselves to unpermitted and secular business, we decree that the Roman pope must warn and correct them. If they do not mend their ways after being warned by him, we turn them over to the royal power. Therefore, we wish this privilege, embodying our decree, to remain valid and inviolable for all time. But if anyone shall presume to make it void, first let him incur the wrath of God and let him be anathema maranatha.

Written by the hand of Peter, notary and secretary of the Holy Roman Church, in the month of October [August?] in the twelfth year of the indiction.

FAREWELL.

JL 3905. This is translated from Olleris, p. 161. The date given in the printed text at the end is erroneous. Bishop Franco of Worms died August 28, 999. *Annales necrologici Fuldenses*, MGSS XIV, 208. About two weeks earlier Otto III had bestowed Lorsch on the church of Worms, a grant that appears to conflict with Sylvester's privilege to Lorsch. Either or both may be false. *Vita Burchardi episcopi*, MGSS IV, 833. Presumably Sylvester II's privilege was of approximately the same date as Otto III's diploma. Had Bishop Franco been deceased at the time of Sylvester's privilege he would have been called "of blessed memory" (*beatae memoriae*). Its absence indicates that Franco was still alive. Possibly the privilege was granted in August, but was not registered until October.

1. In the diocese of Worms, in Hesse-Darmstadt. Werinher the Pious was abbot, March, 999-1001. MGSS XXI, 400.

2. August 4, 998-August 28, 999. Franco was the brother of the canonist Burchard of Worms who, in the year 1000, was Franco's third successor. *Vita Burchardi Wormaciensis episcopi*, MGSS IV, 833; Thietmar, MGSS IV, 785; Ter Braak, *Otto III*, pp. 226f.; DHGE, X, 1245-47.

3. On the Aller river, at this time in the archbishopric of Mainz, but later in

that of Bremen. The especial mention of Bernehar of Verden suggests a controversy as to which archbishopric included Verden.

242. ROME. November 23, 999

*Sylvester II to Théotard, bishop of Le Puy, recognizing him
as the legally elected bishop of Le Puy-en-Velay*

SYLVESTER, BISHOP, SERVANT OF THE SERVANTS OF GOD, to Théotard,[1]
venerable bishop of the holy church of Puy,[2] his dearly beloved son
in the Lord.

As often as questions of the Church arise from evil it is necessary
that the adjudication of the complaint rest upon synodal advice and
that what shall have been decided shall be abided by according to
the synodal definition.

Wherefore, because it is clear that in the general council held in
Rome, Stephen,[3] invader of your church, was rightly condemned by
Lord Gregory [V], our predecessor,[4] and was deprived of every
priestly office because he had been chosen by the living bishop, Gui,[5]
his uncle and predecessor, without the willingness of the clergy and
people, and had been ordained bishop after the latter's death by only
two bishops.[6] And because it is clear that, since the privilege of
choosing another bishop had previously been granted to the clerics
serving the Lord in the church of Le Puy, it was decreed in the same
synod that their choice should be ordained by the Roman pontiff,[7]
we declare to their priesthood that you have been elected bishop by
them and that we are eager for you to be ordained bishop since with
our apostolic authority we favor their choice.

Furthermore, because a compassionate heavenly clemency and in-
describable piety therefore deemed me worthy of being elevated to
the apostolic heights in order that we may faithfully discharge the
duty assumed toward the care of the lambs of the Lord, with pastoral
solicitude, we urge you, dearest brother, to guard with intelligent care
the flock entrusted to you, and so to regulate yourself by good habits
and to put on the ornament of the mind that by your example you
may lead imitators to the joys of eternal blessedness. The grade of
bishop, indeed, we grant by our authority through the decision of
this privilege, so that you may hold all things belonging [8] to your bishopric, just as your predecessor held them, in quiet possession and

without the opposing claim of anyone, and that you may possess them securely and may trustworthily make such disposition as pleases Your Reverence.

Furthermore, by our apostolic authority we command you that if any bishops or royal highnesses shall have the rash temerity to presume to excommunicate [9] you or your place or shall attempt to bind you in the chains of anathema—an unthinkable act—you, by relying upon our support shall view this excommunication as null and with good intentions shall perform the office committed to you. If, however, anyone, by presumptuous audacity, shall attempt to thwart the terms of this apostolic gift of ours that we have promulgated let him be advised that he will be enmeshed by the chain of the anathema of our Lord [and] of Peter, the prince [of the apostles], and of Paul, and that he will be punished by the penalty of eternal damnation unless he shall have made satisfaction before he exits this life.

Written [by the hand] [10] of Peter, notary and secretary of the Holy Roman Church, in the month of November, in the thirteenth year of the indiction.

✞ FAREWELL. Sylvester, who is also Gerbert, bishop.[11]

Given on November 23d through the hand of John, bishop of the holy church of Albano, and librarian of the Holy Apostolic See, in the first year of the pontificate of Lord Pope Sylvester II, Lord Otto III, great and pacific emperor, crowned by God, ruling in his fourth year, in the month and indiction written above.

JL 3906. This is translated from L. Delisle, "Rapport au Ministre de l'instruction publique, des cultes et des beaux-arts, sur l'administration de la Bibliothèque nationale pendant l'année 1875," BEC, XXXVII (1876), 109-11.

This is one of the few extant original privileges issued by Sylvester II (Introduction, p. 25). In addition to the larger fragment in the Bibliothèque Nationale in Paris, used by Delisle, there are two small fragments at the Musée Crozatier in Le Puy. Ewald, "Zur Diplomatik Silvesters II," NA, IX (1884), 323, 329; M. Prou, "Deux Fragments des bulles sur papyrus au musée du Puy," BEC, LXIV (1903), 577; H. Omont, "Bulles pontificales sur papyrus," BEC, LXV (1904), 575ff.; P. Kehr, "Ältesten Urkunden Spaniens," ABB, 1926, No. 2, pp. 21-22.

1. A religious from Aurillac, bishop of Le Puy, 998-1016. Gams, *Series episcoporum*, 2d ed., p. 603.

2. Puy-en-Velay (dept. Haute-Loire).

3. The third son of Stephen, count of Gévaudan, and of Adelaide, sister of Gui of Anjou. De Vic et Vaissete, *Histoire général de Languedoc*, IV, 401.

4. Gregory V presided over a general synod in the church of St. Peter in the presence of Otto III, which issued the decrees indicated in the text, probably at the end of 998 or beginning of 999. Otto III was in Rome, November 30, 998-

January 10, 999 (DO III 305-308). Lot, *Hugues Capet*, pp. 121, n. 6, and 127, n. 2, places the synod in the first half of 998, when Otto III was likewise in Rome (DO III 276-300).

5. Gui II, 975-97, younger son of Fulk the Good, count of Anjou, and of Gerberga. De Vic and Vaissete, *Histoire général de Languedoc*, IV, 401.

6. Dagobert, archbishop of Bourges, and Rodene, bishop of Nevers. The Roman synod of 998 had excommunicated them (n. 4 above).

7. The bishops of Le Puy long adhered to the privilege of being directly under the papacy and thus of being exempt from the jurisdiction of the archbishops of Bourges. U. Chevalier, *Cartulaire de l'abbaye de St.-Chaffre du Saint Benoît suivi de la Chronique de Saint Pierre du Puy* (Paris, 1884), p. 160.

8. *Venientia*. However, the context indicates that this should have been *pertinentia* [belonging to].

9. The power of excommunication rests with ecclesiastical, not with secular, authorities.

10. Delisle here incorrectly read *signum* [seal or sign], which is meaningless in papal chancery practice, for *scriptum* [written], which is the usual word. He also omits the next two words, which should be *per manus* [by the hand].

11. Signature in Sylvester II's hand in Tironian notes, reproduced in Bubnov, I, 269, with transcription on p. 271. Delisle transcribed the notes as *Sil-ves-ter qui et Ger-ber-tus pa-pa*, but the last word is incorrect, since the Tironian note stands for [*e*]*pis*[*copus*] as in the other signatures.

243. ROME. December 31, 999

Sylvester II to Erkanbald, abbot of Fulda, confirming him as abbot and exempting the monastery from all control except that of the Holy See

SYLVESTER, BISHOP, SERVANT OF THE SERVANTS OF GOD, to his very beloved son Erkanbald,[1] venerable abbot of the sacred monastery of our Savior, Jesus Christ, and to all of your abbot successors of this same monastery in perpetuity.

Pontifical duty compels us to favor the utility of all of the holy churches of God and to render suitable decisions to them according to which each may remain in its proper condition.

Wherefore, dearly beloved son, we confirm to you and to your successors in perpetuity everything which your predecessors legally and reasonably requested from our predecessors. Therefore, through the authority of our privilege we grant and confirm to you the monastery of Fulda,[2] that Boniface, most holy martyr of Christ, first constructed and [then] enriched magnificently by the votive offerings of kings and princes and by his own means, with all cells, churches, manors, and all their appurtenances, so that henceforth no future abbot shall presume ever to receive consecration except from this apostolic see. Of all the monasteries of Germany we assign to you and to your successors the first rank of sitting and of judging and of holding a council. No bishops, archbishops, nor, by chance, patri-archs,[3] may celebrate the solemnities of the Mass on an altar under your protection. Let the person of no prince presume to subject to any mortal either a whole or a part of the possessions of the monastery, nor to give such under the name of a benefice, but let the church of Fulda, always free and secure, zealously serve the Roman see alone. If, though God forbid, any abbot of your monastery shall become notorious through any crime, we decree and command that he not incur the judgment of an accusation until he shall be heard and examined by our apostolic see.

It is granted to you, dearest son, and to your successor abbots to call upon the apostolic see to defend you and your church, according to the custom of bishops, and to defend yourself by the shield of the Roman majesty against all your rivals. As we weigh this matter, we direct that at convenient times you may satisfy our solicitude as to whether the monastic life is being carried on in regular fashion and whether harmony among the brothers is being maintained with eccle-siastical zeal, lest perchance, under the pretext of this privilege, though God forbid, both your disposition to uprightness and its direction may be twisted from the norm of justice. In accordance with the decree of Zachary,[4] our predecessor, we forbid any woman to enter this same monastery.

But above all we direct and warn that no one shall carry off or give to anyone any of the revenues and incomes or tithes and other do-nations offered to God by St. Boniface Martyr and many other princes, except the legitimate benefices of the *ministeriales*,[5] but that just as your sainted patron established, all revenues shall be apportioned and regulated, as much those apparently belonging to the dwelling for the poor and the gate for guests as those [belonging] to the brothers' necessities.

Over all of these items we decree through the document of this privilege, which we confirm by the authority of the prince of the apostles, that if anyone shall dare violate this charter of our privilege, let him be accursed and, incurring the wrath of Omnipotent God, be excommunicated from the company of the saints, and let the dignity of the said monastery as indited by us remain in every case forever inviolate.

Written by the hand of Anthony, notary and secretary of the Holy Roman Church.

FAREWELL.

Given on the 31st of December through the hand of John, bishop of the holy church of Albano and librarian of the holy apostolic see, in the first year, with God's favor, of the pontificate of Lord Sylvester the Younger, pope, with the pacific Otto III ruling, in the third [fourth] year of his reign, the thirteenth year of the indiction.

JL 3907. This is translated from Olleris, pp. 161-62.

1. 997-1011. Erkanbald later became archbishop of Mainz, April 1, 1011-September 15, 1020.

2. Benedictine abbey in the diocese of Mainz, region of Cassel (Hesse-Nassau). Fulda was the first German monastery exempted from the jurisdiction of the bishop, through the privilege granted in 751 by Pope Zachary (JE 2293). W. Levison, *England and the Continent* (Oxford, 1946), pp. 26-27.

3. The Pseudo-Isidorian Decretals employ the terms "primate" and "patriarch" as identical in meaning. In Germany the archbishop of Mainz was called the primate.

4. JE 2293, November 4, 751.

5. *Ministeriales* were serfs owing chiefly non-agricultural services to the overlord. They acted as stewards or managers of manors or estates, as messengers, as bodyguards for the lord during his travels, or as castleguards at home, or even furnished military service ahorse or afoot. As long as the stipend that they received for their services came from servile tenures, they were considered servile even though sometimes called noble, but if, after being freed, they came into possession of free tenures they might achieve free social status. By the twelfth century they had developed into the petty nobility in Germany, most of whom, in spite of wealth and the responsibilities of their offices, remained servile in status and did not become members of the aristocracy. Thompson, *Feudal Germany*, pp. 323-30; Otto Freiherr v. Dungern, "Constitutional Reorganisation and Reform under the Hohenstaufen," in G. Barraclough, *Mediaeval Germany* (Studies in Mediaeval History; Oxford, 1938), II, 205-13; P. Dollinger, *L'Evolution des classes rurales en Bavière* (Paris, 1949), p. 235.

244. ROME. December, 999?

Sylvester II to Arnulf, archbishop of Rheims, restoring him to complete authority over the archbishopric of Rheims, and decreeing that his previous abdication shall not be cited against him

SYLVESTER, BISHOP, SERVANT OF THE SERVANTS OF GOD, to his beloved son in Christ, Arnulf,[1] archbishop of the holy church of Rheims.

To the apostolic pinnacle belongs the duty not only of advising sinners, but also of actually lifting up those who have lapsed and by means of the insignia of their restored office [2] of transforming those deprived of their own official grades in order both that Peter's power of loosing be unshackled and that everywhere dignity of office shine to the glory of Rome.

Therefore, we have thought it fitting to assist you, Arnulf, arch-bishop of Rheims, who were deprived of your pontifical honor because of certain excesses, in order that you may believe that this damage can be redressed through the gift of Roman compassion because your abdication lacked the assent of Rome.[3] For this highest attribute belongs to Peter, which no mortal capacity may equal.

Therefore, through the decrees of this privilege of ours we grant, that after the ring and the crosier have been returned to you, you may administer the archiepiscopal office, and in the customary way enjoy all of the perquisites belonging to the holy metropolis of the church of Rheims. You may use the pallium for stated solemnities, you may possess the right of consecration of the kings of France [4] and of the bishops suffragan to you, and by our apostolic authority you may exercise all public authority that your predecessors appear to have had. In addition, we direct, that no person, neither in a synod nor in any place soever, shall in any way presume to allege the crime of your abdication against you or to break out into words of reproach against you, but that everywhere our authority shall protect you even when a feeling of guilt shall seize your own conscience.

Over and above all we grant and confirm to you the archbishopric of Rheims as a whole, with all the bishops suffragan to you,[5] with all of the monasteries, parish churches, altars,[6] and chapels, as well as manors, castles, villages, farms, and with everything belonging to the church of Rheims, saving the inviolable testament of St. Remi,[7] apostle of the Franks.

Under the adjuration of Divine Judgment and the interdict of a curse we enjoin by apostolic censure succeeding popes or any great or small persons from infringing this privilege of ours. But if anyone, indeed, though God forbid, shall attempt to violate this decree, ana-thema to him.

JL 3908. This is Appendix IV in Havet.

1. The signature at the end of DO III 339, December 2, 999, "Arnolf, bishop of the ... church, was present and signed," suggests the possibility that Arnulf of Rheims was present in Rome at this time.

2. See Introduction, p. 12, and Letter 191, introductory note, relative to the removal of Arnulf from the archbishopric of Rheims.

3. See Letter 221.

4. Robert II may have been crowned at Rheims in 987. After the time of Hincmar the archbishops of Rheims more and more took upon themselves the function of consecrating the kings of the West Franks, to the detriment of the rights of the archbishop of Sens. However, Rheims first became the official coronation city of the French kings only in 1179. E. Eichmann, "Die sogenannten Römische Königskrönungsformel," *Historisches Jahrbuch*, XLV (1925), 523, n. 16; Leflon, *Gerbert*, pp. 126ff., 190.

5. Letter 195.

6. *Titulis*. These were the church altars to which priests and deacons were consecrated and which they were not supposed to leave. DuCange, VI, 596b.

7. P. Varin, *Archives administratives de la ville de Reims* (Collection de documents inédits sur l'histoire de France, 1ᵉ sér., Paris, 1839), I, 2-23, No. ii. Two versions exist—that of Hincmar in his *Vita s. Remigii*, and that of Flodoard in his *Historia ecclesiae Remensis* (History of the Church of Rheims), the first of which is shorter and more generally accepted.

245. ROME. May, 1000

Sylvester II to a monastery of Arezzo, confirming its possessions and granting exemption from all authority save that of the pope, even in the consecration of the abbot

...[1] on account of the state of the kingdom, by the command of Lord Otto the third, the unconquered ... for the soul of the august emperor and its redemption we decree through the [notification?] of this authority of ours, that all places urban and rustic, namely, manors, cottages, churches, vineyards ... cultivated and uncultivated estates, with the male and female farmers [2] and serfs that some faithful Christians have bestowed on this same monastery [3] apparently coming into the possession of this same pious place through some earlier gifts, you ought to possess quietly in great security and all of your successor abbots forever in such a way that your holy church shall be under the jurisdiction of no other church excepting only the Holy Roman Church, and that no duke, margrave, count, viscount, or any sort of great or small person ... may dare to invade, injure, or disturb all the aforesaid possessions that appear to belong; and we, strengthening [our decision] by a proclamation of Divine Judgment, by confirmation, and by the interdict of anathema, decree that no bishop or any priest whatsoever shall presume to consecrate the abbot in that same monastery of yours. For the abbots who are to be consecrated shall be chosen from this congregation upon the advice of the brothers together and shall be brought to us and our successors for benediction and consecration, and this which we establish by our privilege shall remain firm and inviolable now and in the future.

If anyone, however, unbelievable as it seems to us, shall rashly and boldly attempt to contravene this privilege of our apostolic confirmation, let him know that he has been bound by the chain of the anathema of the Lord and of Peter, prince of the apostles, to be consumed in the everlasting fire with the devil and his most vicious retinue and with Judas, betrayer of our Lord and Savior Jesus Christ, and at the same time, having been plunged into the Tartarean depths, let him perish with the wicked. Whoever, indeed, shall be the guardian and respecter of this our privilege, may he receive the grace of benediction and eternal life from the Lord.

[Written] by the hand of Peter, notary and secretary of the Holy Roman Church in the month of May in the thirteenth year of the indiction.

FAREWELL.

[BULLA]

JL 3910. This is translated from Bubnov, I, 333-34. Kehr, *Italia pontificia*, III, 164, No. *1*. The privilege, on papyrus with lead bulla attached, existed in the seventeenth century in the Archivio di SS. Fiora e Lucilla, a part of the Archivio Capitolare of Arezzo, but it had disappeared by the year 1731 when only the empty tube which had contained it was found in the Archivio. P. Kehr, "Mizellen. Aus Sant'antimo und Coltibuono," *Quellen und Forschungen aus italienischen Archiven*, X (1907), 217.

1. This and the subsequent lacunae are due to a defective copy in the Arezzo Archive.

2. *Cum colonis vel colonabus.* From Roman times the *colonus* and the *colona* were semi-free cultivators of the soil, who were attached to the seigneur of the land. Their condition was hereditary, and they were transferred from one owner to another with or without transfer of the land. To the owner they rendered certain services. Socially, they were considered freeborn and so they differed from slaves who themselves were pieces of property, i.e., the land of the *colonus* was servile, but he was not, whereas the person of the slave was servile, but his land might (and usually was) or might not be servile, depending upon its history. In the early tenth century *ingenuus* [freeborn] was used as a synonym of *colonus* and indicated the same class of society—tenants paying rent and furnishing services, whom we indiscriminately call serfs. Leclerq, "Colonat," DACL, III, Pt. 2, cols. 2242-63.

3. The monastery in question was possibly San Gennaro in Campoleone, in

the bishopric of Arezzo in Tuscany, a bishopric directly dependent on the Holy See.

246. ROME. June 12, 1000

Sylvester II to Emperor Otto III, complaining of lack of direct news from Otto, informs him of the riot in the church at Orte during Mass and requests restoration of papal possessions in the Sabina region.

SYLVESTER, BISHOP, SERVANT OF THE SERVANTS OF GOD, [greets] his beloved Otto, ever august Caesar, glory of the whole empire, and, in addition, [sends] the apostolic benediction.

Many facts that you heard [garbled] through lying rumor, I have entrusted to Gregory of Tusculum [1] out of precaution for you. But I protest that what happened to us at Orte [2] during the sacred solemnities of the Mass should not be accepted lightly. For the persons who were contributing nothing for our service incited a tumult and a riot in the church against those who were offering little Roman gifts to us, shouting that they should be offered by others. Their anger burned hotter because a certain poor woman had dared to complain to us about their judge, as if that complaint had been made from a grudge against the count. And so, within the holy of holies swords were drawn, and we withdrew from the city amidst the swords of frenzied enemies. The first lodgings, [3] that should have been ours, disappeared at our approach, although they had been standing the day before. The second suffered the same fate. But more of these details anon.

Now I pray this one request, if not on our account at least on yours and your followers', that our rightful possessions in the Sabina region, controlled by others, shall be restored to our authority through the representative of both of us in order that the present abundance of crops shall relieve scarcity.

Given on June 12th.

JL 3913. This is translated from Olleris, pp. 150-51. The year 1000 was the only year in which Otto was far separated from Sylvester II in the month of June, when the former was returning to Italy from Aachen: June 11, Hohentwiel (DO III 370-72); June 20, Chur (DO III 273-74); July 6 (or earlier), Pavia (DO III 375); August 15, probably Rome (Schramm, *Kaiser, Rom und Renovatio*, I, 148-52).

1. The papal naval prefect, first mentioned as such in DO III 339, December 2, 999.

2. Anciently Horta (in text, *Orta*), 43½ miles northeast of Rome, on the road to Perugia, in the Sabina region, then controlled by the Crescentius family who undoubtedly caused this outbreak against Sylvester II. Schramm *Kaiser, Rom und Renovatio*, I, 149; W. Kölmel, "Rom und Kirchenstaat," AMNG, LXXVIII (1935), 29. It is directly dependent upon the Holy See.

3. *Hospicia*. This indicates that temporary lodgings were set up when the pope traveled. The rebellion against the papal-imperial authority apparently extended along the whole road from Orte to Rome.

247. ROME. November, 1000

Sylvester II to Emenon, abbot of the monastery of Déols, confirming possessions, granting exemption from all except papal authority, and even exemption from a general excommunication in the whole diocese of Bourges

SYLVESTER, BISHOP, SERVANT OF THE SERVANTS OF GOD. To his beloved son in the Lord, Emenon, venerable abbot of the monastery of Déols,[1] and to all your successor abbots after you forever.

The desire which is manifested towards [maintaining] the stability of religious purposes and of holy places ought to be fulfilled under the Lord's authorship without any delay, and as often as our assent and the customary apostolic authority is requested to further its utility, it is appropriate for us to come to your assistance beyond the consideration of kindness and properly to strengthen you in complete security, as is reasonable, in order that on this account the most important reward may be inscribed for us in the starry heights by the Lord, the Founder of all things.

And, therefore, because you have requested us to strengthen the aforesaid monastery of Déols by a pronouncement of apostolic authority confirming that all its possessions in that very place ought to remain inviolate by perpetual right, and establishing and corroborating by a page of privilege from us that [it remain] free from every burden or from the control of any person, accordingly, moved by your prayers and by love for our Chancellor Peter,[2] and influenced especially by the example of our venerable predecessors, John [XI], Leo [VII], Stephan [VIII], John [XIII], Leo [VIII], Zachary,[3] and many others, we declare it established through the privilege of this authority of ours that all places and monasteries, to wit, Vodolion in honor of SS. Donatian and Rogatian Martyrs, Pontigny in honor of St. Tyrsus Martyr, and St. Austregesill in the fortified village of Turre, and a great many other monasteries and churches, and urban and country places, towers, manses, manor houses, castles, cottages, vineyards, lands, woods,[4] and various cultivated and uncultivated estates with their male and female farmers and serfs and whatever very faithful Christians have bestowed on this same place or will in the future, and whatever seems to belong to this religious spot through gift, you ought to possess quietly with great security and all your successor abbots after you forever, in such a way that no person, neither archbishops, bishops, counts, nor anyone of any rank or order, may commence any quarrel against this same religious place over its possessions or instigate any intrigue nor exercise any power there.

But if anyone be so presumptuous—and God forbid—let him be advised that he has been excommunicated by apostolic penalty and authority, unless he shall have made amends with suitable reparation.

Also, in such case, should it happen that the whole bishopric of Bourges, in whose diocese the aforementioned monastery with its adjacent cell named Vodolion appears to be situated, be excommunicated by the bishop of the same for some cogent reason, all the monasteries and all the churches subject to this place and all the monks with all persons under their control, that is, with all male and female serfs and daily workers[5] of the same place shall always remain immune from this excommunication.

It is permitted to the monks serving the Lord there to perform the divine office and to bury their own, with the understanding that they may not receive within the borders of the monastery other men from other places who have been excommunicated by the bishop of Bourges, whether they are living or dead, but these monks shall fulfill their vows to the Lord behind closed gates.

We assent to the above, moreover, and we adjuge it confirmed by apostolic authority in order that the aforesaid abbey shall by perpetual right always be subject to the Holy Roman Church, according to ancient usage, and that as an acknowledgement in nowise to be violated, and out of respect for [the rights of] the Roman pontiff, twelve *denarii* shall be paid each year by the abbots of this place.

If anyone, by rash boldness, however, shall attempt to infringe the terms of this apostolic confirmation of ours—an incredible act—let him know that he is bound by the chain of the anathema of our Lord and of Peter, prince of the apostles, to be consumed in the everlasting fire with the devil and his most vicious retinue, and with Judas, betrayer of our Lord and Savior Jesus Christ, and, as soon as he has been toppled into the Tartarean depths, let him perish with the wicked. Whoever, indeed, may have been the guardian and respecter of this privilege of ours, he shall merit receiving the grace of benediction and eternal life from the Lord.

Written by the hand of Peter, notary and secretary of the Holy Roman Church, in the month of November in the fourteenth year of the indiction.

This is translated from W. Wiederhold, "Papsturkunden in Frankreich. V: Berry, Bourbonnais, Nivernais und Auxerrois," NAG, Beiheft 25, No. 1 (1910), pp. 25-26.

1. Or Bourgdieu (dept. Indre, canton of Chateauroux), founded in 917 by Ebbe the Noble, lord of Déols. *Liber censuum* I, 200, n. 1.

2. Letter 248 contains the only other reference to a chancellor for Sylvester II. Chancellor Peter does not seem to be the same as the notary Peter who wrote this letter.

3. Referring to six documents, as follows: (1) JL 3585 (March, 931), receiving Déols under the protection of the papacy; (2) JL 3603 (January 5, 938); (3) not in JL; (4) JL 3725 (January 2, 968); (5) not in JL; (6) a falsification, mentioned also in JL 4211A of Leo IX for Déols (April 13, 1050).

4. The text has *salinas*, but JL 4211A (n. 3 above) gives the more correct word *syluas*, i.e., woods. See C. Parain and M. Bloch in *Cambridge Economic History*, I, 161-62, 269-70, as to the importance of woods and forests in medieval economy.

5. Unfree persons who rendered services to their seigneurs every day without leisure, the heaviest burdens, exactions, and disabilities being placed upon them of all the unfree. Their whole subsistence depended upon their seigneur. Dollinger, *L'Evolution des classes rurales*, pp. 265ff.

248. ROME. November - December, 1000

Sylvester II to Peter, bishop of Asti, upbraiding him for refusing to appear at synods and citing him to appear on the Sunday after Epiphany

✠ SYLVESTER, BISHOP, SERVANT OF THE SERVANTS OF GOD, to Peter, bishop of Asti.[1]

Already our letters summoning you to a synod are burdening the chancellor by their number, all to no avail. The whole world cannot endure the stench of your obscene infamy. The Immaculate Virgin, the Universal Church, does not stop me from crying out about the dishonor to it. Though summoned to a synod you refuse [to attend] and avoid hearing the citations of the canons. You prefer to putrefy midst your dung with the beasts of burden rather than to shine among the pillars of the Church. We, however, who are Peter's representative, are trying to restore the brightness of the Church. Therefore, by apostolic authority we cite you to a synod on the Sunday [2] after Epiphany . . .[3]

JL 3911. Kehr, *Italia pontificia*, VI, Pt. 2, p. 173, No. 5. This is translated from P. Kehr, "Papsturkunden in Rom. I: Eigentliche Vaticana," NAG, 1903, pp. 31-32. The present letter refers to several letters previously dispatched to the same recipient, Bishop Peter of Asti, and whose texts are not extant. This summons to Bishop Peter to attend a synod in Rome must have been dispatched some time before the Sunday after Epiphany (January 6th). Otto III was present at the synod (DO III 387-90), which must have been held in the year 1001, since Otto III was not in Rome in January, 1000 (DO III 343-46), nor in January, 1002 (DO III 422-24). In the year 1001, Epiphany (January 6th) fell on Sunday so the date of the synod was January 13th, the Sunday following Epiphany. Synods were usually held on Sunday. Schramm, *Kaiser, Rom und Renovatio*, I, 152, n. 4.

1. 992-1005? F. Bonnard, "Asti," DHGE, IV, 1173. Asti, 28 miles southeast of Turin, in the province of Alessandria, was a suffragan bishopric of Turin. In this northwest section of the Italian peninsula Margrave Arduin (Letter 222, n. 5), an enemy of the German overlordship, possessed a strong following, and among them Bishop Peter appeared as an important supporter. Arduin was already under a sentence of perpetual penance, decreed by Sylvester II's first synod (May, 999) for his participation in the murder of Bishop Peter of Vercelli (March 17, 997). MG *Constitutiones* I, 53.

2. January 13, 1001 (See introductory note above). Present at the synod were twenty Italian bishops, four German bishops, and among the laity the second most powerful rulers in Italy and Germany—Margrave Hugh of Tuscany and Duke Henry of Bavaria. *Vita Bernwardi*, MGSS IV, 768f.

3. The lower portion of the page of MS Vatican latin 1343, s. XI, from which this document was published (introductory note above) was cut off, but in Kehr's opinion only a few words are missing. Kehr, "Papsturkunden in Rom, I: Eigentliche Vaticana," NAG, 1903, p. 31.

249. ROME. December 26, 1000

Sylvester II to Count Daiferio, his sons and grandsons, granting the territory of Terracina as a benefice for three generations in return for military service, and on condition of payment to the papal treasurer of three gold solidi

℞ SYLVESTER, BISHOP, [SERVANT] OF THE SERVANTS OF GOD, to his beloved son in the Lord, Count Daiferio [1] and your sons and grandsons.

As often[2] as the favors that it is hoped we will bestow conform to justice and law, it is fitting for us to grant with pleasure and to render a favorable reply to the requests of petitioners.

Accordingly, because you have asked us that in return for your faithful service which you have been accustomed to render obediently to us and to our predecessor pontiffs of the Holy Roman Church, and especially because of the military service that you promised to perform with devoted reverence to us and our successors, by our generous gift we give and bestow on you and your sons and grandsons, under the legal title of benefice, the upper and lower city named Terracina[3] with all of its towers and walls and with all of its legal jurisdiction, and the whole county of Terracina with lands and woods, fields and marshes, banks, waters and their fishing rights, and with every public toll, and any of the said city or county belonging to our treasury[4] which is in the neighborhood; beginning at the headland at the water's edge, it extends through Agapito's field, thence goes to Droga and thence to the river near San Donato, and along this river to Sassa and even to Sonnino and to Portella, and even to the lake, and along the lake it goes near the river of Santa Anastasia, and then it extends to the sea twelve miles away. Inclined by your prayers we grant to you by the issuance of this document of ours all of these possessions legally belonging to the Holy Roman Church, which we serve through God the Creator, to be held and enjoyed.

Because it is well known that these and other possessions had been indifferently bestowed on others when they [the popes] turned their attention to [immediate] profit and [thus] lost the greatest possessions of the Church with [only] the smallest sort of rent [in return], this sort of gift we are changing completely for the better so that what we bestow under the name of benefice through this document of our grant shall be for military service.[5] This sort of return[6] we deem proper, that knights shall offer allegiance in peace and arms in war for the honor and safety of the Holy Roman Church.

But lest ecclesiastical property should pass into the possession or ownership of anyone we, disregarding any [present] difficulty, have decreed that from this present fourteenth year of the indiction three gold *solidi* shall be paid under the title of rent to the treasurer of the Holy Roman Church, to wit, in the month of January. But if it cannot be paid in the first year, the rent of the first and second years ought to be paid in the second year. Inclined by your prayers, through the terms of this decree with the county of Terracina and with everything pertaining to it, as recorded above....[7]

Enjoining by apostolic censure under the witness of divine judgment and the prohibition by anathema, that no men or kings, neither margrave, prince, bishop, lay person, or men established in any rank or office shall dare to be annoyingly active in the affairs of this same county or in any way presume to carry off or to alienate the things or possessions belonging to it; but rather they [the counts] shall continue in its rightful [possession] and ownership forever.

If, however, anyone, beyond our anticipation, shall presume by abominable boldness to transgress the matters that we have decreed for stabilizing the affairs of the said county, let him know that he has been bound by the chain of anathema and destined for the most horrible torture of everlasting fire with the devil and all the wicked ones.

But, on the other hand, whoever out of [pious] [8] consideration shall be a guardian and observer [of this], let him merit receiving from our most merciful Lord God all manner of grace of benediction, and the absolution and indulgence of all of his sins and the blessedness of celestial life with the saints and the elect of God.

Written by the hand of John, secretary of the Holy Roman Church, in the month of January in the fourteenth year of the indiction.

⚜ FAREWELL. Sylvester, Gerbert, Roman bishop

I HAVE SIGNED

✠ Given on the 26th of December through the hands of John, bishop and librarian of the Holy Apostolic See. In the second year of the pontificate of the Lord Sylvester, most holy pope. In the fifth year of the rule of Lord Otto, great and peaceful emperor, crowned by God, in the month and year written above.

JL 3912. Kehr, *Italia pontificia*, II, 121, No. *1*. This is translated from I. Giorgi, "Documenti Terracinesi," BISI, XVI (1895), 63-65, who publishes the text from a copy made in 1466, which existed in the Archivio of Terracina. This privilege was later utilized as the basis of a forged document for the citizens of Terracina. Kehr, *Italia pontificia*, II, 118, No. 3.

1. Daiferio (Darferio) seems to be the Daoferio, count of Traetto, son of Count Gregory of Castro Argento and nephew of John III (966-78?), duke of Gaeta, and a member of the Hypati family. I. Giorgi, "Documenti Terracinesi,"

BISI, XVI (1895), p.71. In 1001 he subscribed a document as "most worthy consul, duke and count of Terracina." Kehr, *Italia pontificia*, II, 120. Sylvester II bowed to the persisting Roman legal tradition in Italian thought by making his grant of Terracina for three generations.

2. *Liber diurnus* 115. Santifaller, "Verwendung des *Liber diurnus*," MIOG, XLIX, 269, 270, 272, 322.

3. Terracina, a maritime city, was in the southern part of the province of Rome, bordering the Patrimony of St. Peter on the south. Its location was of strategic importance to the papacy in its struggles against the south Italian princes, the Byzantines, and the Saracens. From 970 it had belonged to Crescentius II, son of Crescentius de Theodora, who possessed it until the downfall of his family in Rome in 998. K. Jordan, "Eindringen des Lehnswesen," *Archiv für Urkundenforschung*, XII (1932), 39; W. Kölmel, "Rom und der Kirchenstaat," AMNG, LXXVIII (1935), 32, 40.

4. *Palatium.* For the use of *palatium* [papal treasury] see Letter 259; Ewald, "Zur Diplomatik Silvesters II," NA, IX (1884), 346-48 (this adds to the examples in Lunt); and W. E. Lunt, *Papal Revenues* (New York, 1934), I, 6.

5. This was the type of feudal landholding with which Gerbert, as a Frenchman, was familiar, and represents a step in the feudalization of the papacy.

6. *Pensio*, which Sylvester II contrasts with the *census* (rent in money or kind or services) heretofore received by the papacy for these lands. In Italy, the *pensio* was the legal recognition of ownership. Schramm, *Kaiser, Rom und Renovatio*, I, 276; Jordan, "Eindringen des Lehnswesen," *Archiv für Urkundenforschung*, XII (1932), 39-40.

7. Lacuna in the fifteenth century copy from which the document was published by Ignazio Giorgi (see introductory note).

8. Supplied from the similar formula in Letters 236, 261, and 264.

250. ROME. 1000?

Sylvester II notifies all who foster the Christian faith of the taking of the monastery of SS. Gervaise and Prothaise of Langogne under the protection of the Holy See and of granting it immunity from secular control

✠ SYLVESTER, BISHOP, to all who foster the Christian faith.

We wish it known that the spouses Viscount Stephen and Angelmoda through a deed of gift have bestowed upon our Holy Roman Church the church [monastery] of SS. Gervaise and Prothaise, constructed at their own expense, situated in the county of Gévaudan, and that they made this gift for the salvation of their souls upon the sacrosanct tomb of St. Peter, to the effect that the aforesaid spouses and their heirs in perpetuity will pay to St. Peter fifteen *solidi* each third year out of regard for the right of the Holy Roman Church.[1]

Wherefore, it has pleased us to receive the aforesaid church, with all of its estates, villages, huts, and demesnes, both cultivated and uncultivated, and with all property and possessions belonging to this same church, to be sustained under our protection, and to fortify it with the shield of our watchful care.

Therefore, by apostolic authority we decree and order by an unavoidable amendment that no king, marquis, duke, count, viscount, or any person of either high or low estate shall dare to disturb or molest that church in any way, nor shall presume to carry off or to appropriate anything belonging to it or to seize it as booty. Moreover, anyone who shall attempt to do this, unless he repents, will be pierced by the javelin of divine curses, bound by the unbreakable chain of Peter, prince of the apostles, and wounded by the sword of our anathema, so let him at the final catechism perish irrecoverably with the devil.[2]

JL 3931. This is translated from W. Wiederhold, "Papsturkunden in Frankreich. VII: Gascogne Guienne und Languedoc," NAG, 1913, Beiheft, pp. 34-35.

The account of the founding of the monastery of SS. Gervaise and Prothaise of Langogne (dept. Lozère) in the Cartulary of St. Chaffre (U. Chevalier, *Cartulaire de l'abbaye de St.-Chaffre* [Paris, 1884], No. ccclxxvi, p. 132) states that Pope Gregory V acknowledged and confirmed the placing of SS. Gervaise and Prothaise under the protection of the Holy See. The account of the founding in the cartulary of Langogne mentions a confirmation by Sylvester II and includes a portion of it (De Vic and Vaissete, *Histoire général de Languedoc*, V, 332, xxx). The donors of Langogne (Viscount Stephen of Gévaudan and his wife Angelmoda) made two trips to Rome, the first one apparently in September-October, 998, when Gregory V confirmed their gift of property for the monastery which was to be built. The second Roman journey resulted in Sylvester's privilege, accepting the completed monastery under the protection of the Roman Church. The spouses could scarcely have returned home late in 998, had the monastery built, and returned to Rome before the beginning of the year 1000.

1. Actually, Langogne was made a priory of St. Chaffre (dept. Haute Loire), which was held responsible for the payments to the Roman Church. *Liber censuum*, I, 203-4.

2. In the account in the Cartulary of Langogne (introductory note above), this privilege ends: *Dato privilegio ecclesiae Cosmae et Damiani* [The privilege was given in the church of Cosme and Damian]. However, this does not seem to be an integral part of the privilege but a statement of fact.

251. RAVENNA. May 1-7, 1001

Sylvester II to Salla, bishop of Urgel, confirming possessions of the bishopric and exempting it from secular control

✠ SYLVESTER, BISHOP, SERVANT OF THE SERVANTS OF GOD to Salla,[1] the very reverend bishop of the holy church of Urgel and to your successors forever.

A desire, evidencing itself as persisting through the ordination of religious heads and the stability of holy places must be encouraged under God's authorship without any delay, and as often as our assent and customary apostolic authority is requested for furthering its utility, it is appropriate for us to come to your assistance beyond the consideration of kindness and to strengthen you legally in your security of possession, as is reasonable, in order that on this account the greatest reward may be inscribed for us also in the starry heights by God, the Founder of all things.

And, therefore, because you have requested us to protect the aforesaid bishopric of the holy church of Urgel by a document of apostolic authority and to confirm that all its property that it appears to have and to hold justly and legally ought to continue by perpetual right undisturbed as such; therefore, we, having been moved by your prayers and expressing our decision through this privilege of our authority, we decree that all places urban and rural, to wit, manors, manses, manor houses, castles, cottages, vineyards, lands and various estates, cultivated and uncultivated with their tenths and first fruits, male and female serfs [farmers] and slaves,[2] and *aldiones*,[3] which [possessions] have been given by some very faithful Christians to the same episcopacy in the county of Cerdaña,[4] in the districts of Llivia, Berga,[5] Pallars,[6] Ribagorza,[7] Jestobiensis, Cardós,[8] Anabiensis, Tirbiensis [Turbiensis?], and the place of St. Deodata with its land, also the fortified village of Sanaugia with its land, Calbiciniano, Feners at the foot of the mountain, Letone and Clopedera with their woods and lands; in the district of Vich,[9] Castelleto and Turrizella with their borders, in Marfano that alod which belonged to Bishop Guisad;[10] in Gerona the village of Adeiz with all its alodial land[11] and its parish; also in Urgel the village called Bescharam (or Bascharam) with its borders, and that parish of Alasse and that village of Boxedera, Nocolone, Sardinia, Salellas with the fief and alod belonging to the count,[12] in the village of St. Stephen the count's fief and alod, in the village of Andorra[13] all the count's alods and that village of Montanicello and of Cubilare with their boundaries, the fortified village of Carcobite with its boundaries, and the village of Sallente[14] with its boundaries and the fief of Arcavelle,[15] also the monastery of San Pedro de Escalas[16] with all its appurtenances and the tower which belonged to Marcuz, and another tower in the region of Celsona which had belonged to Bellone; and the third part of the customs with the imposts from the market,[17] and everything that through any gifts was seen to belong to this religious place previously acquired by you or by your successors in the future, you ought to have, hold, and possess in perpetuity peacefully and quietly in complete security; in such a way that no king, no prince, no count, no marquis, no judge, nor any person great or small may presume ever to use any force or to trespass upon this same episcopacy or its appurtenances.

If anyone, by rash presumptuousness, however, shall attempt to try to do anything against the decision of this apostolic confirmation of ours—which seems unbelievable—let him know that he has been bound by the chain of the anathema of our Lord and of Peter, prince of the apostles, to be consumed in the everlasting fire with the devil and his most vicious retinue, and with Judas, betrayer of the Lord and Savior, Jesus Christ, and at the same time, having been submerged in the Tartarean depths, let him perish with the wicked. Whoever, indeed, shall be the guardian and respecter of this our privilege, may he receive the grace of benediction and eternal life from the Lord.

Written by the hand of Peter, notary and secretary of the Holy Roman Church, in the month of May in the fourteenth year of the indiction.

✠ FAREWELL. Sylvester, Gerbert, Roman bishop

I HAVE SIGNED

JL 3918. This is translated from A. Brutails, "Bulle originale de Silvestre II pour La Seo de Urgel (Mai 1001)," BEC, XLVIII (1887), 521-26. Plate VIII in Kehr, "Ältesten Papsturkunden Spaniens," ABB, 1926, reproduces a portion of the papyrus original of this privilege. This original in the Archivo Capitulare of the Seo de Urgel is in poor condition because of insects. The privilege does not carry the day of the month, but it must have been at least three weeks before the council that Bishop Salla summoned at the end of May as the result of the privilege. Villanueva, XII, 214, n. 3; Kehr, "Das Papsttum und der katalanische Prinzipat," ABB, 1926, pp. 16f. Salla's request for this confirmation of rights originated in a conflict between the inhabitants of Cerdaña and Berga, aided and abetted by Countess Ermengarda, widow of Olive Cabreta, who not only refused to make payments to the Seo de Urgel, but even seized some of its property. The conflict continued until the death of Count Ramon Borell III in 1018, and involved not only the aforementioned regions but also Narbonne, Carcassonne, Roda, and Barcelona. Villanueva X, 288ff., 291ff.; Rovira, III, 342, 578.

1. 981-1010. He was the son of Viscount Isarn and Ranlo, and brother of Bernard, viscount of Conflent who was the father of St. Armengol, successor to Salla (or Sanla) in Urgel.

2. The words used here, *cum... colonis vel colonabus, servis et ancillis et aldionibus* do not properly describe the condition of the unfree population of Catalonia but are suitable for Italy (especially Lombardy) and Bavaria. (Their use probably is due to the fact that Letter 251 is modeled after JL 3871 for St. Peter of Pavia. Santifaller, "Verwendung des *Liber diurnus*," MIOG XLIX [1935], 322.) Serfdom in Catalonia was based upon a contract between the serf and the seigneur so that the serf had some few more rights than elsewhere. Usually, through the *precarium*, or contract based upon petition, he became attached or ascribed to the domain in return for the protection afforded by the seigneur, lay or ecclesiastical. However, if the contract provided that he might regain his freedom, this was possible and frequent in Gerona and Vich. Certain of the semi-free, though attached to the land, possessed the rights of testamentary disposal of their property, and of marriage without permission of the seigneur. The slaves (*servis et ancillis*) were mainly Saracens, a large number of whom appear in the early part of the next century. Rovira, IV, 240-41, 243, 248-49; Smith in *Cambridge Economic History*, I, 346ff.

3. The *aldiones* were semi-free persons, owing recognized obligations to a master who, however, did not possess as much control over them as in the case of serfs. DuCange, I, 175, mentions them particularly in Lombard law, but no examples are offered from Spain. The use of this word may be due to the model from which the privilege is derived (n. 2 above), and it may therefore not be the proper word here to describe a class of the semi-free in Catalonia.

4. Originally a Catalan county in the eastern Pyrenees, now divided between France and Spain, bordered on the north by the county of Foix, on the east by the county of Roussillon, on the south by the county of Berga, on the west by the county of Urgel (now in the province of Lérida) and the valley of Andorra. *Enciclopedia universal ilustrada*, XII, 1212f.; map in Rovira IV, 385.

5. One of the Catalan counties, at the foot of Mt. Queralt, on the right bank of the Llobregat, now *partido judicial* of the *provincia* and *audiencia* of Barcelona, and diocese of Solsona. *Enciclopedia universal ilustrada*, VIII, 228ff.

6. *Paliarensis*, one of the Catalan counties, between the Pyrenees and Montsech, now in the province of Lérida.

7. The most northwesterly of the Catalan counties, bordered on the east by the county of Pallars.

8. *Cardosensis* [Vall de Cardós], a valley in the county of Pallars. *Enciclopedia universal ilustrada*, XL, 535.

9. See Introduction, p. 1.

10. Probably Guisad II, bishop of Urgel 942-78. Villanueva, X, 100, 256.

11. In the Spanish March one finds at this time a considerable amount of alodial land, i.e., freeholds, land not subject to the payment of rents or services. Much of such land was acquired during the Reconquest by the ruling families as successors to the French monarchs, as a kind of payment for settling in this region, or by the right of *apprisio*, i.e., "squatting" on the land, with the obligation of making improvements either by cultivation or by building or repairing buildings for defense.

12. Armengol I (Ermengol), second son of Count Borrell II and Countess Ledgard.

13. It borders the county of Urgel on the north and Cerdaña on the northwest. Even today it is under the joint control of the bishop of Urgel and France. In 952 Borrell II had bestowed upon the church of SS. Felix and Martin the tithes which he owned in Andorra. P. Pujol i Tubau, "De la cultura catalana medieval: Una bibliotheca dels temps romànics," *Estudis universitaris catalans*, VII (1913), 3.

14. Probably in the *provincia* of Lérida, municipio of Pinell. *Enciclopedia universal ilustrada*, LIII, 485f.

15. Arcabell, now a *municipio* in the diocese of the Seo de Urgel, *provincia* of Lérida, in the valley between the Segre and Balira rivers. *Enciclopedia universal ilustrada*, V, 1274-75, map between pp. 432-33.

16. A church for canons, built in 913, in the district of Llordá, changed into a Benedictine monastery in 960. Villanueva, XII, 30-31; 227ff.

17. The location of Urgel at the confluence of the Segre and Valira rivers, where Cerdaña and the valley of Andorra open, made it an important gateway to France, and hence important for trade. P. Kehr, "Papsturkunden in Spanien. I. Katalanien," ABG, XVIII (1926), 165ff.

252. ROME. June - August 31, 1001

Sylvester II to Robert, abbot of St. Mary Magdalen of Vézelay, forbidding alienation of its property or the granting of any benefice except payment to the Holy See; permitting election of the abbot; anathematizing violators of the monastery property; condemning simony; exempting the monastery from the power of the bishop

SYLVESTER, BISHOP, SERVANT OF THE SERVANTS OF GOD, sends greetings to his beloved son Robert, religious abbot of the holy monastery of Vézelay,[1] and to all the congregation of this same monastery, forever.

As often as the favors that it is hoped we will bestow instantly conform to what is reasonable, it is fitting for us to grant with pleasure and to render a favorable reply to the requests of petitioners.

Accordingly, therefore, because you have asked us to issue a privilege of the Apostolic See, just as had already been done by our predecessors of pious memory, Pope Nicholas [I] [2] and John [VIII or XV],[3] to the monastery of Vézelay over which you are known to preside, and which, as is known, was long ago constructed in the kingdom of Burgundy, the diocese of Autun,[4] in the district of Auxois, by Gerard, most noble and Christian man, and his wife Bertha in honor of our Lord and Savior Jesus Christ and in veneration of Blessed Mary, Mother of Our Lord; and which was offered by the aforesaid founders devoutly and by an instrument of deed to St. Peter, prince of the apostles; we, influenced by your prayers, have gladly decreed that this be done.

Through the privilege of the apostolic authority we affirm and order that no emperors, no kings ever, no prelates, no one at all of any rank, shall be permitted under the pretext of any cause or occasion to diminish or carry off or put to their own use any of the real or personal property bestowed upon and granted to the same monastery by the said founders or by any other persons, or property given legally in the future; but all property which has been offered there or shall in the future be offered we wish and direct shall be held unimpaired without disturbance from the present time, the fourteenth year of the indiction, for the sustenance of the said monastery and the uses of the abbots and monks serving God there under the Rule of Father Benedict on this condition: that none of our successor pontiffs in this See, in which we serve God the Author, shall at any time or any place allow that any of this property shall be granted as a benefice to anyone, or exchanged, or be granted in the future for any payment whatsoever, excepting only the payment in the founders' deed of gift making this Holy Roman See the heir of this said monastery, that they assigned, so that our successors are to receive one pound of silver yearly,[5] and to you and your successors and the monks living there now under the Rule of the aforementioned Father Benedict [we grant] the election of a pious father over this same monastery, and let them be zealously active in the exercise of their pastoral office against all disturbances.

Therefore, we decree that, when the abbot of the said monastery dies, no one else shall be ordained there by crafty deceit, but rather only him whom the monks by common agreement shall have elected through fear of God and according to the regulation of the Rule of Blessed Benedict, and whose ordination the pontiff of this Apostolic See shall approve.[6]

Wherefore, we have decreed, and by apostolic authority we give assent to, and through this apostolic privilege of ours we affirm that no king nor pontiff, abbot or count, nor any great or small person who is corrupted by avaricious desire or deceived by a diabolical suggestion, shall dare or presume in any manner to lift a hand against your office, O venerable Abbot Robert, or to molest you either with respect to your property or to your office, or to trespass, steal, or commit acts of violence against any of the possessions of the monastery that we and our predecessors had granted and confirmed to you and your predecessors by a document of privilege. If he does so, let him be advised that on the authority of God and of St. Peter through our apostolic excommunication he has been separated from the body and blood of our Lord Jesus Christ and from access to the Church.

To remove this place from avaricious eyes we are subjoining to this present section that it is permitted to no kings, bishops, priests, or any of the faithful, either through themselves or through a substitute, to dare to accept anything in any form whatsoever in the guise of a gift for the ordination of the abbot, or clerics, or priests, or for the dispensing of baptism, or consecration of the church, or for any of the matters pertaining to this same monastery; nor is it permitted for the same abbot to give anything to secure his ordination.

The bishop of the [episcopal] city of this diocese may not perform public Masses there, unless invited [7] by the abbot of the same monastery, nor say the Stations [of the Cross] in the same monastery lest the quietude of the servants of God be in any way disturbed by a gathering of the people nor may he presume to demand lodgings there. We do not deny that you should receive faithful and religious men and exhibit the kindness that the Apostle orders shown to all, according to the means and ability of the place, and we actually urge it.

If, indeed, any kings, bishops, priests, abbots, judges, counts, or [any] secular person shall attempt to controvert [the terms of] this document [embodying] our decree, let him know that after being struck with the apostolic anathema whereby he will be deprived of the authority of his office and rank, he will appear a criminal before the Divine Judge; and unless he shall deplore his evil acts, let him be a stranger to the most sacred blood of Our Lord Jesus Christ and be subjected to the everlasting condemnation of severe punishment.

May the peace of Our Lord Jesus Christ be with all of those who uphold justice for this same place so that they may receive here the fruit of good deeds, and may find the rewards of eternal peace with the Eternal Judge.[8]

JL 3920. This is translated from Olleris, pp. 165-67. This privilege is based on JE 2831 (n. 2 below). Santifaller, "Verwendung des *Liber diurnus*," MIOG, XLIX (1935), 256.

1. Dept. Yonne, arondissement of Avallon. Vézelay was really in the duchy of Burgundy because the kingdom of Burgundy had not included this region for over two hundred years. Duke Henry I (965-1002), brother of King Hugh

Capet, was duke of Burgundy and protector of Vézelay. Lot, *Hugues Capet*, pp. 228, 434.

2. JE 2831, May, 858-67. Hirsch, "Päpstlichen Schutz," MIOG, LIV (1942), 367, 380. Hirsch (p. 367) shows that the prohibition of Masses by outsiders, mentioned farther down in Letter 252, was derived from a letter of Pope Gregory I (*Registrum* v.49).

3. John VIII (872-82) issued JE 3189, September 29, 878. In 986 John XV issued a privilege to Vézelay that is not in JL. Wiederhold, "Papsturkunden in Frankreich," NAG, Beiheft, 1910, p. 23, No. 4, to Abbot Eldrad. Sylvester II mentions the privilege of only one John. Was this an oversight?

4. Walter was bishop of Autun, 993-1023. Lot, *Hugues Capet*, p. 229, n. 3.

5. *Liber censuum*, p. 189a: "In the bishopric of Autun. The monastery of St. Mary Magdalen of Vézelay one pound of pure silver." This payment was evidence that Vézelay could claim papal (apostolic) protection.

6. Cf. Letter 237 which does not mention that the newly elected abbess must be approved by the pope.

7. This section relating to the bishop is taken from JE 2831. Cf. Letter 237.

8. Gregory I, *Registrum* xiii.xii.

253. TODI. December 27, 1001 - January 11, 1002?
Sylvester II to Bishop Ascelin (Adalbero) of Laon, reprimanding him for his crimes and citing him to appear before a general council in Rome during Passion Week

Sylvester, bishop, servant of the servants of God, to Ascelin of Laon.

You should not wonder at [the omission of] the greeting and apostolic blessing since you have ceased to be a man of upright character, although you bear a bishop's title. If faith links mortal man with God, no less does faithlessness make rational man equal to irrational animals. Inasmuch as the sum total of reasoning power is to know one's self, we are completely dumfounded that you have abandoned your natural condition by barbarously perpetrating new [1] and unheard-of crimes.

A letter from King Robert [2] and his bishops, accusing you before the people and the universal clergy of these public crimes, has reached the apostolic and the imperial hands. When the archbishops of Rheims and of Tours [3] invited you with other brothers to a council held at Compiègne, after receiving assurances by their oaths for the security of your life, of your person, and of freedom from capture, you finally promised that you would attend. You came to beg compassion, according to this same letter, since, deservedly conscience-stricken, you shuddered at the council's severity.

You manifested your inability to make answer to the laws cited against you. You did not deny that you had committed offenses against your lord, the king. Demanding only indulgence of the general council, you obtained the favor of the king by renewed perjuries. After giving hostages, to wit, your archdeacon and a knight, you promised that you would return the towers of Laon. Then, as you guided your master,[4] the archbishop of Rheims, going to receive the return of the towers, like a Judas you wished to lay hands on him. Indeed, your imprisonment of others unmasked the fraudulent deception you had conceived against him.

O thou Judas, repeating the betrayal of a master in our time and defiling the name of bishop, you who wish to betray your master the archbishop, you would not spare your lord the king if you could. You hold in prison knights surrendered to you and fear not that you have tricked your king. How often we have warned you by exhortatory letters and how we have sweated to pluck you from these dangers.

However, since we are unable to restrain you from the crowd of sinners rushing headlong to their ruin, we command you to come to Rome in the approaching Passion Week,[5] and we warn you to present yourself before the general council to be held there. Therefore, no excuse will suffice to permit you to scoff at our summons, because you will be subject to conciliar censure in this same council, and absence will be of no avail. Do not resort to the excuse of the difficulties of the roads, because in the Lorraine kingdom [6] no ambuscades will threaten you, and Italy certainly offers no terrors. No excuse will have any effect except illness of body, but in that case witnesses must be sent who can confirm your sickness, reply to your accusers, and justify you before the law.

JL 3914. This is Appendix V in Havet.

King Robert captured Laon in 999. *Annales Elnonenses minores* a.999, MGSS V, 19. Then Sylvester II wrote several letters to Bishop Ascelin (see the text). King Robert's letter arrived when Otto III and Sylvester II were together. An Easter synod was planned to be held in Rome. The period December, 1001-January, 1002, best conforms to the time necessary for all of these events. Pope and emperor were together at Todi on December 20, 1001 (DO III 421) and for some days thereafter, and an Easter synod was planned for 1002 (Letter 256, introductory note). Schramm, *Kaiser, Rom und Renovatio*, I, 182, n. 1 gives literature about the date.

1. Ascelin (Adalbero) had earlier been arrested as a traitor (about 993) for having plotted to aid Otto III against Kings Hugh and Robert with the aim of securing the archbishopric of Rheims for himself. Richer iv.xcvi-xcviii. He had again assumed his episcopal functions by April, 995 (Letter 195). It is perhaps Ascelin's incarceration to which Gerbert refers in Letter 218.

2. Sylvester II may have·written to King Robert of the French at the same time as to Ascelin. Cf. Papire Masson's words in his *Vita Silvestri Secundi,* added to J. Masson's edition *Epistolae Gerberti* (Paris, 1611), p.79, "I read a manuscript of his [Sylvester II's] letters to Robert, king of the French."

3. Arnulf and Archambaud.

4. *Magister.* This has been interpreted to mean "teacher," thereby referring to Gerbert, but such does not appear to be the meaning here, since the events referred to occurred after Gerbert left France. Hence, Arnulf is meant here.

5. March 28-April 5, 1002? See introductory note above.

6. Havet (p. 242, n. 5) supposes that the suggested route would have been: Verdun, Metz, Strasbourg, and along the Rhine. Ascelin would then have gone to Chur and Pavia. This was not the usual route from Rheims. Holland, *Traffic ways,* Appendix I, Table iii, route J.

254. TODI. December 27, 1001?

Sylvester II to Ravenger, abbot of the monasteries of Stavelot and Malmédy, taking them under papal protection and urging them to choose an abbot from Stavelot, if possible, otherwise from Malmédy

SYLVESTER, SUPREME AND UNIVERSAL POPE AND VICAR OF ST. PETER, SERVANT OF THE SERVANTS OF GOD, [sends] true devotion in Lord Jesus and mutual accord of brotherly love to the venerable Abbot Ravenger of Stavelot and Malmédy,[1] and to all desiring to live piously in Christ.

Since it is a fact that after the lying of our first parents the human race has been addicted to this mode of conduct almost to the exclusion of free will so that, according to the voice of the Psalmist, man is placed over others to curb the illicit appetites of human desire, and we are circumscribed not only by civil law but also by ecclesiastical rules and regulations. The establishment of their authority has progressed so much that the holy places of the saints which, founded by the devoted faithful and thus transferred to the Divine Cult, which have obtained many unusual benefactions from diverse persons, [now] request decrees, not only royal but also imperial, to confirm their immunity; and they also seek privileges from our authority for their stability.

Therefore, at the request of the venerable Notker, bishop of Liége, the abbey of Stavelot and Malmédy, nobly constructed by the munificence of ancient kings and emperors, and always protected as much by the authority of our predecessors as by royal immunity, we have taken under the same protection of our immunity.

Let them always have an abbot, and, furthermore, let the prevailing rule be, by the leave of Malmédy, that because St. Remacle, builder of each monastery and previously bishop and pastor of Tongres, preferred to choose for himself a place of burial in the other of them (that is, in Stavelot), let them have the first opportunity at the election, if there shall be found among them a person of superior merits and learning. However, if there be no such one there, then let a preeminent man be found at Malmédy, and let him assume the headship of both places rather than to introduce there someone taken from outside.[2]

JL 3928. This is translated from Olleris, pp. 170-71.

Notker, bishop of Liége, petitioner for this privilege, was in Todi for the synod of December 27, 1001, and probably secured this privilege at that time, or within the next two weeks, since there were several postponements of the synod. Thangmar, *Vita Bernwardi* MGSS IV, 768; Tschan, *Saint Bernward of Hildesheim*, I, 190-91. However, the whole privilege both in words and in formulas is so different from the others issued by Sylvester II that its authenticity is seriously doubted.

1. In Belgium. The communities as well as the monasteries have been associated together throughout their history. Ravenger II was abbot June 4, 980-November 9, 1007.

2. This unusual arrangement for choosing an abbot was taken almost word for word from JL 3867 (Gregory V, June 2, 996) which itself copied the words from DO I 220. Lerche, "Privilegierung der deutschen Kirche," *Archiv für Urkundenforschung*, III (1911), 173-74.

255. TODI. January, 1002

Sylvester II to Geribert, viscount of Barcelona, reprimanding him for not appearing before the Christmas synod and citing him to appear before the Easter synod for a decision on his claim to the castle of Ribas

SYLVESTER, BISHOP, SERVANT OF THE SERVANTS OF GOD. To Geribert,[1] greetings and apostolic benediction.

We can no longer endure the complaint of the bishop of Barcelona [2] against you. Last March he made such complaint, and therefore I advised you to come with him before our presence at Christmas [3] when I purposed to resolve the cause of this complaint, but you failed to make an appearance, thus preventing my decision.

For the sake of God and of St. Peter, again I advise you to come and by apostolic authority I command you to be present in Rome at our synod in the approaching Easter[4] lest the church of Barcelona, agitating me beyond endurance with its outcries, shall exasperate me to the point of punishing you, though I be reluctant. Come, therefore, and present yourself with the bishop of Barcelona[5] for a decision about the castle of Ribas.[6] If the church ought to lose it according to the laws, we are unwilling that it shall ever hold it, and if legally it belongs to you we are unwilling that you should lose it.

However, if, after being warned by these two letters of ours you are contemptuous of coming and postpone appearing before our presence at the time indicated, you will be deprived of entrance into any church, because you have oppressed the Church, and then you will be made a stranger to the association with Christians, and you will remain bound under our apostolic anathema until you repent and make suitable amends to the aforesaid bishop.

This is translated from F. Fita, "Bula inédita de Silvestre II," BAH, XVIII (1891), 248-49.

1. Since the office of viscount had become hereditary in Catalonia, Geribert, as the son of Viscount Guitart of Barcelona, became viscount after his elder brother, Viscount Udalart, was captured by the Saracens at the siege of Barcelona, July 6, 985.

2. Aëtius, 995-1010. A. Andrès, "Aetius," DHGE, I, 669-70, with bibliography; Rovira III, 464ff.

3. Synod of Todi, December 27, 1001 (Letter 254, introductory note).

4. Synod of Rome, April 5, 1002.

5. Possibly a letter was sent also to Bishop Aëtius, as this would have been the proper procedure.

6. *Partido judicial* of Villanueva y Geltrú, *provincia* of Barcelona, southwest of Barcelona. *Enciclopedia universal ilustrada*, LXVIII, 1458ff. This castle, also called Bell-Lloch and Sant Pere de Ribes, probably consisting of several wooden towers in the district of Olerdola (Olerdula), near Sitges, with walls and considerable land, was only one of a number built near the Saracen border in the plain of the Panadés (or Penadés) and in the mountains southwest of Barcelona.

A knight named Peter had reconquered the castle of Ribas after the Saracen invasion of 985, and in 990 Bishop Vivas had granted him possession of it as a free alod, granting a charter of freedom from exactions likewise to the community, since previous to 985 the see of Barcelona controlled it. Peter's only obligation was the repair and maintenance of the castle "as was the custom with the citizens of Barcelona, and at the *castrum* of Olerdola." Màs, IX, 45, No. 106.

How Geribert had gained control of it after Peter is unknown. Ribas remained in the family for in 1030 Geribert's wife, Ermengard, bequeathed parts of the land there to her relatives. In 1039, however, their son, Folch Geribert, returned it to the See, admitting that his father had "detained" possession of it. Geribert's claim may have rested on the fact that he had kept the castle in repair. Fita, "Bula inédita de Silvestre II," BAH, XVIII (1891), 247, 249; F. Carreras y Candi, "Lo Montjuich de Barcelona," MABL, VIII (1903), 238, 241f., 323f., 325, Appendix iv, 367f., 382, Appendix ix; Màs IX, iv, No. 367; Rovira III, 325-26; IV, 233-34.

256. ROME. January, 1002?

Sylvester II to Peter Orseolo II, doge of Venice, urging him to undertake the reform of the Venetian clergy by calling a synod to deal with this, under his patriarch's headship

SYLVESTER, BISHOP, SERVANT OF THE SERVANTS OF GOD, [sends] to Peter, doge of the Venetians and of the Dalmatians, greetings and the apostolic blessing to his beloved son.

Midst the diverse heartaches caused by disorder we are unable to attain the inward harbor of joyfulness, because we see clergymen of all grades neglecting the precepts of the Catholic religion. This knowledge has, in fact, deprived us of sleep, while tears flow in rivers down our cheeks and we gasp for breath.

Of what moment is it to speak of the ends of the earth when your principality, our very neighbor, does not blush to sell openly the sanctuaries of God through its bishops, when your bishops and priests all openly secure wives, and, like money-changers and money-lenders, pursue worldly wealth, making use of lay business for the divine office? Assuredly, the coals of this wickedness are being heaped upon your head,[1] for you must exterminate this iniquity. You on whom God bestowed power ought not to be thus forgetful of that same God.

By our apostolic authority, therefore, we advise that you, together with your patriarch, hold a general synod dealing with all matters entrusted to you, and that you unshrinkingly excise all evils that should be cut away from the bosom of the Church, and that you accomplish results to prevent your aforementioned disease from creeping through your neighbors and beyond, to your complete perdition. Do this soon enough, moreover, so that if any very serious problem arises among you it can be brought to our general synod at Easter. Whatever may not completed [at your synod] owing to the difficulty of its solution, will not lack solution once brought to our presence.

Write back to us more definitely and openly about our ambassadors sent into Dalmatia.

Kehr, *Italia pontificia*, VII, Pt. 2, p. 18, No. 26, and p. 50, No. 68.

This is translated from H. Omont, "Quatre Bulles inédites des papes Silvestre II et Pascal II," BEC, L (1889), 567-58. Doge Peter Orseolo II (991-March, 1009) assumed the title of "Doge of Dalmatia" after his conquests in the Adriatic, upon which he embarked May 29, 1000, the first great conquest by the Venetian fleet. Hence, Sylvester II wrote Letter 256 after Doge Peter's Adriatic conquest, and at a time when a general synod was planned for the approaching Easter. In the year 1001 Sylvester II was either in Ravenna (DO III 396) on Easter (April 13th) or had just left for Rome. However, Letters 253 and 255 mention a general synod planned for Easter (April 5th), 1002. Schlumberger, *L'Epopée byzantine*, II, 316-20; Kehr, "Rom und Venedig bis ins XII. Jahrhundert," *Quellen und Forschungen aus italischen Archiven und Bibliotheken*, XIX (1927), 82; E. Kantorowicz, *Laudes regiae; a Study in Liturgical Acclamations and Mediaeval Ruler Worship*. (University of California Publications in History, XXXIII; Berkeley, Calif., 1946), 147-48.

1. Romans 12 : 20. Sylvester II's reversal of the meaning is intended to be subtle flattery.

257. **ROME. January, 1002?**
Sylvester II to Vitale IV, patriarch of Grado, upbraiding him for the conduct of the clergy in his diocese and urging him to cooperate with Doge Peter Orseolo II in summoning a provincial synod

SYLVESTER, BISHOP, SERVANT OF THE SERVANTS OF GOD, to Vitale,[1] patriarch of Grado, greeting and apostolic benediction.

Secular judgments are being rendered everywhere, all people are being improved by laws, contagions both trivial and deep-seated are being exterminated, and most apparent is the uplifting of worldly glory. Ecclesiastical dignity alone is neglected because those who belong to the clergy do not know the restraints of reproof, and completely postpone the acquisition of such knowledge, denying as they do that God's laws for the people are suitable for them and at the same time disregarding any observance of the institutes of the canons.

In addition, it is a fact that those who are placed over men for the guidance of souls are following the irrationality of dumb animals: they carry on public business among other priests in your established diocese; they ruin the churches; they are unashamedly associated with women. The Bride of Christ, once beautiful through her most precious ornaments, alas, nowadays is disfigured by this deformity.

Weigh this crime with an earnest and careful mind, brother. Take counsel with yourself over this matter, and by our apostolic authority make arrangements with our beloved son, the doge of the Venetians, for a synod in the immediate future. Then, issue a general order to all the clergy under his dominion, summoning them to this same synod. Let the rules of the canons guide you. Exercise your impartiality strictly and the power of a Catholic prince piously with regard to the acceptance of [proper] persons there, and [let there be] no simoniacal giving of gifts but only the tradition handed down by the holy fathers.

Whatever points you can resolve, do so, but whatever you are unable to conclude bring to the general synod that we shall hold this approaching Easter,[2] for no controversial matter that then requires a decision in our presence will transcend our ability, aided as we are by God's mercy.

Kehr, *Italia pontificia*, VII, Pt. 2, p. 50, No. 67. This is translated from H. Omont, "Quatre Bulles inédites des papes Silvestre II et Pascal II," BEC, L (1889), 568-69. Kehr dates this privilege 999-1003. See Letter 256, introductory note as to the date.

1. Son of Doge Peter IV Candiano and Giovanna. This doge was murdered in 976, and the Orseolo family seized the helm. Vitale was patriarch from 961-62. Kehr, "Rom und Venedig bis ins XII. Jahrhundert," *Quellen und Forschungen aus italischen Archiven und Bibliotheken*, XIX (1927), 79. Sylvester II issued a privilege to Vitale, probably at the synod of April 5, 1002, or later, confirming his patriarchal title and his metropolitan jurisdiction over Venice and Istria. Dandolo *Chronica*, in Muratori, *Rerum italicarum Scriptores*, new ed., XII, Pt. 1 (Bologna, 1931), 201. (See Appendix C: "Sylvester II's Privileges... Whose Texts Are Not Extant," No. 50.)

2. April 5, 1002. See Letter 256, introductory note.

258. ROME. June 1, 1002?

Sylvester II issues a proclamation demanding the restoration of the decorations stolen from the gates of the chapel of St. Michael in Hadrian's tomb

...honor through all things

...and since the decorations on the gates of St. Michael Archangel[1] on Hadrian's tomb were recently taken down and carried off [nefariously?][2] at night, by this apostolic command we order them restored to their places. Furthermore, unless this shall have been carried out before the natal feast day of the apostles,[3] those who either committed this sacrilege, or agreed to it, or are a party to it by concealing them [4] will be placed under the heaviest sort of anathema until they repent, making satisfaction through suitable amends.

Given on June 1st.

JL 3922. This is translated from MS Bamberg E.III.3, fol. 56v, and Olleris, p. 152. Kehr, *Italia pontificia*, I, p. 154. Only the month and the day are given at the end of the letter. The year 999 seems excluded because Otto III was in Rome in May-June (DO III 324-25) and could have dealt with the theft. In June, 1001, Sylvester II was with Otto III outside Rome. Letter 246, with a date of June 12th, seems to have been added first to MS Bamberg E.III.3, fol. 56v, hence Letter 258 with a June 1st date added below Letter 246 refers to June 1, 1002. However, M. Uhlirz, *Jahrbücher des Deutschen Reiches unter Otto II. und Otto III*, Vol. II: *Otto III*, 562, argues that because Letters 246 and 258 were copied onto the same manuscript they belong together in time, and therefore dates Letter 258 in the year 1000.

This proclamation is on the verso of the next to last folio of the autograph manuscript of Richer and is added in a different contemporary hand below Letter 246. Between them an ink line has been drawn. Below the line is written in lighter ink *p[er] omnia honor*, but whether this belongs with Letter 258 is not clear. On the next line the letter begins *et quum nuper*. Something preceded the *et*, as it does not begin with a capital letter. (Olleris's text fails to show this.)

1. Peacocks of bronze were attached to the grilled doors of the chapel. "Hadrien," DACL, VI, Pt. 2, col. 1981. Pope Boniface IV (d. 615) is believed to have built this chapel to St. Michael atop the huge square-based cylindrical mausoleum of the Emperor Hadrian (completed by Antonius Pius in A.D. 139) in memory of Pope Gregory I's vision of the saint during a procession to pray for relief from the pest. The mausoleum had been used as fortress as early as A.D. 537, and the garrison stationed there needed a chapel. Its beauty and its height were a marvel to all and many early medieval writers mention it, "this church of the Holy Angel, reaching even to heaven," "situated among the clouds." In length the chapel was about 32½ feet. Later a statue of St. Michael replaced the chapel. O. Richter, *Topographie der Stadt Rom.* (2d ed., Handbuch der Altertumswissenschaft, III, 3. Abteilung, 2. Hälfte; Munich, 1901), 278-80; H. Quentin, *Martyrologes historiques* (Paris 1908), p. 561.

2. *Tempore nocturno* in Olleris, p. 152, but I read the manuscript *re pre nocturno*, which might stand for *reprehensibiliter* [nefariously].

3. June 29th.

4. The decorations? Or the thieves?

259. ROME. November, 1002

Sylvester II to Winizo, abbot of the monastery of the Holy Savior of Amiato, confirming possession of the church of St. Cassian with its dependencies and two woods and exempting it from civil control

SYLVESTER, BISHOP, SERVANT OF THE SERVANTS OF GOD sends greetings to Winizo, a son very dear to us in the Lord Jesus Christ, venerable abbot in the most sacred monastery of the Savior, our Lord Jesus Christ, which is seen to be constructed on the mountain called Amiato[1] in the county of Chiusi, and to the members of the holy congregation of the same monastery dwelling there, and to your successors forever.

Being mindful of the divine compassion, we assumed the burden of rule in order to favor the wishes of those whose requests are legitimate and, by balancing the equities, to assist all who need it, especially those who, [having adopted] religious garb for the name of our Lord Redeemer, have at any time of life betaken themselves to monastery walls to exhibit unremitting services and to sing the praises of His power. For we are adorned with pontifical merits as long as we, for cogent reasons, shall by our command have restored the rights belonging to each one, and we shall deliberate with pastoral compassion as to whether this completes whatever is needed.

Because, indeed, it [depredations] happened many times in the aforenamed monastery, though your hands attempted restraint... therefore we grant and confirm to you and to your successors forever, to wit, the church in honor of St. Cassian, which has been stripped bare,[2] with houses, vineyards, land and woods, fields, pastures, trees, both fruit and others of different kinds, and water, with everything that generally and as a whole belongs to the place and to the church. As you define the boundaries, it appears to be located next to the above mentioned mountain called Amiato, so they begin from the ford, and at the foot [of the mountain] run along the bank, that is, from the village of Piano, up to St. Mary called Cotalia, and come up to the rock Cupula, and thence extend to the torrent Borsalino, thence to Ministrone and descend to the Paglia river; and from another part of this [mountain] it [the boundary line] descends to the torrent called Siena, and via this stream it reaches the Paglia river. Likewise, we concede and confirm to you the wood called Senatule and the wood called Caiolo-pelli located there, with everything belonging to them and with their rights of adjacency. By our apostolic authority we ought to confirm to you in the afore-mentioned monastery all of these things as a unit.[3]

Influenced by your prayers, therefore, we are granting your

requests for the love of Omnipotent God, out of fear of St. Peter, and for the redemption of our soul, in order that through your holy prayers we may merit grace and compassion. Indeed, we have acceded to your petitions so that from this first year of the indiction [4] forever after by your own ability and right you may defend and appropriate to your own uses the said places and church with all that belongs to them, which your monastery and your holy congregation is permitted to possess without any annual [payment].

Enjoining under the pain of apostolic censure by calling upon the divine judgment as a witness and upon the prohibition of anathema that no king, margrave, count, viscount, bailiff, nor any great or small person shall dare to disturb you or your successors or to engage in any sort of controversy, but that you and your successors shall be permitted to hold these possessions securely and quietly and to possess them forever.

If, however, anyone, contrary to this privilege of our piety, shall attempt to do aught against you and your successors and the fear of God—unbelievable as it seems—and shall not observe all details as set forth above, let him know that he has been excommunicated by our authority and that of St. Peter Apostle, that he is separated from all Christian society and is bound by the chain of anathema until he shall reach the point of correction; moreover, he shall make composition by payment of 300 pounds of unalloyed gold,[5] half to the papal treasury and half to the above-mentioned monastery.

If, however, any shall be an observer and guardian [of this], let him merit attaining the grace of benediction from our most compassionate Lord God.

Written by the hand of John, secretary of the Holy Roman Church. In the month of November, in the above written year of the indiction, the first.

✠ FAREWELL. Sylvester, Gerbert, Roman bishop

JL 3925. Kehr, *Italia pontificia*, III, 239, No. 6, and p. 237. This is translated from Bubnov, I, 336-37. The text of this privilege is corrupt, although the copy indicates no gaps.

1. Montamiato, or San Salvatore in Montamiato, diocese of Chiusi, commune of province of Siena, reputedly founded in 747 by the Lombard King Ratchis, but no authentic documents are known before 770. The monastery was situated at an altitude of 2,700 feet on this mountain, which rises isolated between the valleys of the Ombrone and the Paglia rivers. *Enciclopedia italiana*, I, 12f.; II,

964f.

2. *Ininter* in text, but I suggest *inanitum* [stripped bare] because the abbey's property had suffered depredations at the hands of Count Hildebrand. Ewald, "Zur Diplomatik Silvesters II," NA, IX (1884), 343.

3. *In integrum.* Even though the property might be widely scattered it was considered a unit for certain purposes such as taxation.

4. September 1, 1002-August 31, 1003.

5. This is an enormous fine, but apparently characteristic of documents influenced by Italian law. Ewald, "Zur Diplomatik Silvesters II," NA, IX (1884), 344.

260. ROME. December, 1002

Sylvester II to Odo, bishop of Gerona, confirming the possessions of the bishopric of Gerona

SYLVESTER, BISHOP, SERVANT OF THE SERVANTS OF GOD, [sends greetings] to [you] beloved son Odo,[1] bishop of the holy church of Gerona, and to your successors forever.

A desire which, etc.[2] And, therefore, because you have asked us that by the protection of apostolic authority we should strengthen the aforesaid bishopric of the church of Santa Maria of Gerona and should confirm that all property belonging to it ought to continue by unceasing right undisturbed as such, to wit, as much as it appears to have within the walls of the city of Gerona or in its county, together with the church of St. Felix Martyr[3] and St. Narcissus which is near the gate of the city of Gerona with all of their appurtenances, and the church of Santa Maria, that popular speech calls Labisbal,[4] (the bishop's), together with its alod and the fiscal[5] land that they call Fontanetus and Fonte Edeta, and Apiliares, and Ventinco, and the wall and little wall of Palatiolo, and the spring itself; all of these with their tithes and first-fruits and offerings, and the obligations due the fisc, and that alodial land that they call the Walls[6] of Rufinus with its boundaries and bordering lands, and all the parish churches and dependencies that are in the county of Gerona, with the tithes, first-fruits, and offerings of the faithful, and the alodial land that belongs or appears to belong to these churches, and one third of the money coined[7] in the city of Gerona, together with the tax paid by the Jews,[8] and one third of the customs of the markets[9] of the aforesaid city and of its county, and a third part of the pasturage[10] of the said county; and in the county of Besalú[11] the alod called Báscara and the alod of Crispiano with their boundaries and borders; and the cell of St. Lawrence that is above the fortified village of Bobeta, just as Fredolo holds it through royal documents; and the church of St. Martin, in the place called Calidas with everything it appears to have; and all the parish churches, and their dependencies in the county of Besalú that belong or ought to belong to the aforesaid see, with tithes, first-fruits, offerings and alods belonging to these churches, with one third of the customs, and their market and their pasturage tolls; and in the city of Ampurias,[12] as much as the said see possesses with the taxes from the port;[13] and in the aforesaid county of Ampurias the alod called Uliano with boundaries and adjacent land and with the obligations due the fisc, and the churches built there with tithes and first-fruits and offerings belonging to these churches; and the church of St. John in Bederga with tithes, first-fruits and offerings, and the alods belonging to these churches; and in the county of Pedralbes,[14] the church of St. Mary with tithes, first-fruits, offerings, and its alods; and all the parish churches with their dependencies in the said county of Pedralbes with their tithes, first-fruits, offerings and alods; and one third of the tolls from the market, and one-third of the pasturage; and by this page of our privilege we confirm that it exist without any [imposition of] servitude by any person or dominion [over it]. Therefore, having been influenced by your prayers we, enjoining through the authority of this privilege of ours, decree that all places, etc., thus so that no judge, no margrave, etc. Whoever, indeed, [shall be] a preserver, etc.[15]

Written by the hand of Peter, notary and secretary of the Holy Roman Church in the month of December, in the first year of the indiction.[16]

FAREWELL.

JL 3926. This is translated from Olleris, pp. 169-70. The original privilege apparently existed in Gerona until the War of the Spanish Succession, disappearing between 1688 and 1711. Ewald, "Zur Diplomatik Silvesters II," NA, IX (1884), 334, n.2; H. Bresslau, "Papyrus und Pergament in der päpstlichen Kanzlei," MIOG, IX (1888), 3, n.3.

In 977 Bishop Miró Bonfill (Letter 33) had placed the church of Gerona under the papacy's protection, agreeing to a yearly payment of 2 *solidi* as evidence of this relationship. Marca, *Marca hispanica*, p. 912.

1. Bishop of Gerona, 995-1010. Florez, *España sagrada*, XLIII, 144-69; Villa-

nueva, XIII, 81-89. He may have attended the Roman synod held by Sylvester II, December 3, 1002. Olleris, p. 264.

2. *Liber diurnus* (ed. Sickel), 101.

3. Although originally a monastery, whose abbot at this time was Bishop Arnulf of Vich, this church became a collegiate church that was important for centuries and noted for its liturgical and legal manuscripts. Florez, *España sagrada*, XLV, 255ff., 259ff.;*Enciclopedia universal ilustrada*, VIII, 666.

4. The vernacular form here indicates that the detailed portion of this privilege was drawn up in Spain.

5. Emperor Charles the Bald had granted legal sovereignty over the Spanish March to Count Wifred I the Old, confirming to him all the property the latter held privately, which thus became the crown or fiscal land of the counts, as well as all the land not held by anyone, which was, of course, the uncultivated land, the *terras heremas*. Balari, *Orígenes históricos*, pp. 337ff.

6. Roman ruins (walls) built originally by a Rufinus. Probably the alod was given to the See in 968 by Bishop Miró Bonfill (Letter 33). Marca, *Marca hispanica*, p. 889, Appendix cvi.

7. This right, allowing the See of Gerona a profitable seigniorage of 33⅓ per cent, had been granted to Gerona in 934 by Count Suniefred (Sunyer), father of Count Borrell II, and was a right maintained during the whole period of the Catalonian counts. Marca, *Marca hispanica*, pp. 846-47, no. lxxi; Rovira III, 53f., 280-82, 331, 339-40. Cf. R. S. Lopez, "An Aristocracy of Money in the Early Middle Ages," *Speculum*, XXVIII (1953), 16-17.

8. At this time in Catalonia a special tax on Jews seems to have been peculiar to Gerona, although in Barcelona they were subject to some disabilities. Rovira III, 276, 323; IV, 251f.

9. The bishopric assumed the office of tax collector of the market imposts in city and county wherever goods and produce were sold or transported, and it was granted the right of keeping one third of the total collections in payment for its efforts. Balari, *Orígenes históricos*, p. 650; Rovira III, 50, IV, 272-73, 282.

10. In addition to local pasturage this included the impost of *peatge* or *raficas* on transient animals, especially migratory flocks of sheep, so important in medieval Spain. Thus, in Gerona, the count owned the uncultivated lands, *terras heremas* (n. 5 above), and farmed out this impost to the bishopric of Gerona for which it received one third of the total. The count's right to a pasturage impost was in contrast to the community right in both pastures and woods existing in many places. Rovira IV, 277f.; C. Parain in *Cambridge Economic History*, I, 122f., 135; R. Smith in *Cambridge Economic History*, I, 357ff.

11. The most important of the four counties forming the diocese of Gerona (the others being Roussillon, Gerona, and Ampurias). It included land from the upper valley of the Fluvian river to the lower Ter. Kehr, "Papsturkunden in Spanien," ABG, n. f. XVIII (1926), 146; Rovira IV, 385, map.

12. A small Catalan county northeast of Gerona, extending to the Mediterranean. Originally it consisted of Ampurias and Rosselló or Roussillon, but the two parts were inherited separately in 991 by Hugh and by Guislabert, sons of Count Gausfred. Rovira III, 274, 561-62.

13. Port dues and anchorage. Rovira, III, 51.

14. *Enciclopedia universal ilustrada*, XLII, 1248, does not list a county of Pedralbes. However, the close association of Pedralbes here with Besalú and Ampurias suggests that the northern half of the county of Ampurias at this time was called the county of Pedralbes (Perelada) with its center in the town of Pedralbes (Perelada). Map in Rovira, IV, 385.

15. See Letter 240, n. 1.

16. September 1, 1002-August 31, 1003.

261. ROME. December, 1002
   *Sylvester II to Odo, abbot of Sant Cugat del Vallés, confirming
   possessions of the monastery*

SYLVESTER, BISHOP, SERVANT OF THE SERVANTS OF GOD, to Odo,[1] beloved son, religious and venerable abbot of the monastery of Sant
Cugat Martyr,[2] founded in the county of Barcelona in the place
called Octaviano, both for your sake and that of your successor
abbots in the same venerable monastery in perpetuity.

Because whatever is known to belong among reasonable desires
ought to be granted, the authority of our apostolate ought not to be
denied toward strengthening the devotion of the faithful. Therefore,
your excellent and praiseworthy grace has asked us that by apostolic
authority through this privilege we grant and confirm to you and
your successor abbots forever the abovenamed monastery with everything adjacent and pertaining thereto with its boundaries and
adjacencies.

And therefore, favoring your pious desires, we by apostolic authority decree that this aforesaid monastery of Sant Cugat Martyr with
all of its possessions henceforth and forever shall be subject to the
jurisdiction of no one except you and your successors. For we
confirm to you and your successors the aforesaid monastery with its
boundaries and adjacencies, and with everything enumerated below,
to wit:

The alod on which the monastery is situated;[3] on the east it ends
at the boundary or below the boundary of Cerdaniola, on the south,
indeed, it faces the mountain ridge called Querol or Montagut[4] and
the alod of the monastery of St. Peter of the Maidens[5] and the
boundaries of Aqualonga, on the west it likewise faces the boundaries
or below the boundaries of Aqualonga and of the fortified village
of Llobregat, on the west-northwest it faces the boundaries and below
of Ter and Llobregat. And in the village called Milás the cell of St.
Felix with its boundaries and adjacencies, and the alod of Bodigari
that belonged to Antonio, son of Ildemar,[6] which you yourself gave
to the said monastery through a charter of gift. And in another place
within the district of the fortified village of Aramprunyá[7] the church
of St. Mary and St. Peter with its pool called Castell de Fels[8] with
its boundaries and adjacencies; and the alod of Gaiano or Sales;[9] and

the alod that extends from Montepetroso to the sea and to the river Llobregat, with its boundaries and adjacencies. And within the district of the Castle of Cervelló the cell of the Holy Cross and St. Sylvester with its boundaries and adjacencies [10] together with other alods that are within the districts named above. And within the boundaries of the Castle of Subirats the cell of St. Mary and St. John that they call Monistrol [11] with its boundaries and adjacencies, and the alod called Espiells [12] with its boundaries and adjacencies. And the fortified village of Masquefa with boundaries and adjacencies, together with the church of St. Peter founded there, with tithes, first-fruits, and offerings of the faithful; and the alod called Castelet within the boundaries of the said fortified village of Masquefa, and of Piera and Pierola with its boundaries and adjacencies, and the cell of St. Mary together with its springs situated within the limits of Piera and Pierola and of Claramunt with its boundaries and adjacencies.[13]

And within the district of the castle of Olerdola [14] at the towers called Becias the alod that belonged to Bonfill and to Prouizio; [15] and the alod of Avinyó that belonged to Maior; [16] and the alod in Magrinyá [17] that belonged to Petrario and to Teudisclo the judge or to Baio, and the alod called the Vila de Lops that belonged to Judge Teudisclo,[18] with its boundaries and adjacencies, and the alod that belonged to the [Arch] deacon Seniofred.

And within the district of the Castle Santo Stefano the cell of St. Stephen with its boundaries and adjacencies, and the cell of St. Oliva [19] with its boundaries and adjacencies in length from the Villa-domenio to the sea, together with its ponds, and in width from the Guardia de Banyeres [20] to the Villa Domabuis [Tornabuis?].

And within the districts of the Castle Fonterubio, Montagut, Piniana and Querols the alod there that Ansulf [21] gave. And within the district of Castle Lavid the alod there that Azius and his wife Druda gave. And on Monte Olorda and within its boundaries the tower with the alod there that [Ennego] Bonfill gave. And in Duo-decimo or in Mizano, and within the wall of the city of Barcelona, the houses with their yards and gardens and kitchen gardens [?] and as much land in the territory of the said city as the aforesaid monastery appears to possess; and the alod of Toldell with its boundaries and adjacencies, and the church[es] of St. Lawrence and St. Stephen that are built on the mountain called St. Lawrence, with everything they appear to own, and the cell of St. Felix in Valrano [22] with its boundaries and adjacencies, and as much as this home of monks owns within the districts of Tarrasa and of Castellare and in Arraone and in Barberano and in Palou Avuzide [23] and with its boundaries, and in Cananilias and in the village Mogoda and within its boundaries and in the Palou Saldani and within its boundaries, and in Calidas [Calders, Caldario?] and within its boundaries, and in the Palou de Aries and within its boundaries and in Upper and Lower Lisano, and in the parish of Parets [24] and within its boundaries; and in Molliedo and within its boundaries and in Gallechs and within its boundaries, and the alod of Plegamanus with boundaries and adjacencies just as Bonfill [25] made donation there; and the alod of Rexach with its boundaries and adjacencies just as Count Borrell [II] made donation there; [26] and the alod that the said monastery has in Badalone [27] and within its boundaries; and in Palumbare and within its borders; and in Horta and its boundaries; and near Ripoll; and in Palou and in its boundaries, and in Valldario [28] and within its boundaries; and in the village Granollers [29] and within its boundaries; and in Laurona and within its borders; and in Upper and Lower Corró and within their boundaries; and in Mesarata and within its boundaries; and in Canoves and Samalus [30] and within their boundaries; and the cell[s] of St. Genese, St. Martin and St. Felix which are at the top [?] [31] with their boundaries and adjacencies; and the village called Rifa with its boundaries and adjacencies; and the village of Vitaminea called Palou with its boundaries and adjacencies, and with the churches of St. Stephen and St. Mary built there, with the tithes and first-fruits, and offerings belonging to the churches; and the hamlet called Teudbert with its boundaries and adjacencies; and the cell of St. Genese and St. Eulalia called Monastirols or Tapiolas with its boundaries and adjacencies, and in Vallgorguina with its boundaries and adjacencies, and the valley of Ildefredi with its boundaries and adjacencies.

And in the county of Manresa the fortified village of Cleriana with the church of St. Mary [32] there with its boundaries and adjacencies and with its tithes and first-fruits, and the cell of St. Mary near Aqualada with its boundaries and adjacencies, and the cell of St. Felix near the fortified village of Oddeno.

And in the county of Vich all of the alods that the aforesaid monastery seems to have there with their boundaries and adjacencies. And in the county of Gerona, the alod in Esterria that belonged to Abbot Landrico.[33] As much of the tithes, first-fruits, and offerings of the already mentioned churches to the said monastery and the places and alods with all their borders, limits, and adjacencies, and their appurtenances, [just] as this monastery possesses within these counties enumerated above, and with God's aid [will acquire] after the present time, which is the first year of the indiction.

We confirm through the notification by this privilege that you and your successors, with the fear of God, are to hold, control, and manage forever the villages, alods, tithes, first-fruits and churches with all of their appurtenances that the monastery has long possessed, as is read above. In such a way that no king ever, nor any bishop nor any man belonging to any order or ministry shall dare to take upon themselves in a troublesome way the causes of this same monastery, nor assume legal jurisdiction over any of their men for any cause; and all of these things shall persist thus forever as we have commanded: enjoining by apostolic censure under the witness of divine judgment and the prohibition by anathema that none of our successor pontiffs shall presume ever to exhibit any forceful invasion of the property of this monastery.

After the death of the abbot, indeed, no one may establish an abbot there except one whom the agreement and common wish of the brothers of this congregation shall have elected according to the Lord and the Rule of St. Benedict, if a worthy person shall be found there, and no one shall attempt to receive a reward or gift for his consecration. If the bishop of the diocese to which this place belongs is unwilling obligingly to ordain him, he may, through our authority, be ordained freely by our Roman Mother Church or by whatever bishop may come.

If anyone, by wicked boldness however—though God forbid—shall presume to transgress these things that have been established for the honoring of our Lord Jesus Christ for the durability of the aforementioned monastery, let him know that he has been bound by the chain of anathema and with the devil and all the wicked he is doomed to the punishment of everlasting fire. But he who out of pious respect

shall be truly a guardian and observer [of this privileges of ours]
shall merit attaining from our most merciful Lord God for ever and
ever every sort of benediction, grace, the absolution of all his sins,
and the blessedness of the heavenly life with the saints and the elect.

Written by the hand of Peter, notary and secretary of the Holy
Roman Church, in the month of December in the first year of the
aforementioned indiction.

℞ FAREWELL. Sylvester, Gerbert, Roman bishop [34]

I HAVE SIGNED

[BULLA] [35]

JL 3927. This is translated from F. Fita, "Patrología: Bulas inéditas de Silvestre
II," BAH, XXXVIII (1901), 477-84. The papyrus original of this privilege,
consisting of the lower part and a few shreds of the upper part, exists in the
Archivo de la Corona de Aragon in Barcelona. A portion of it is shown on the
plate facing p. 364, and it is reproduced as Plate IX in Kehr, "Ältesten Papsturkunden Spaniens," ABB, 1926, No. 2, with a transcription on p. 54.

1. Abbot of Sant Cugat, December, 985-September 1, 1010. He was also bishop
of Gerona. See Letter 260, n. 1.

2. San Cucufate in Castilian, a *municipio* in the province of Barcelona, the
partido judicial of Tarrasa. *Enciclopedia universal ilustrada*, LIII, 1443-46.

3. The documents of Sant Cugat were destroyed by Saracen al-Manṣūr and
his troops in July, 985. In February-March, 986, the new Abbot Odo traveled
to northern France and secured from King Lothair a diploma confirming the
property of Sant Cugat. Marca, *Marca hispanica*, col. 937; L. Halphen and F. Lot,
Recueil des actes de Lothaire et de Louis V (Paris, 1908), No. li. (Halphen and
Lot incorrectly date the diploma 984[?].) Although nearly identical to Sylvester
II's privilege, occasionally it contains additional information, such as the fact
that Count Sunyer (father of Count Borrell II) had granted this alod to Sant
Cugat and had defined its boundaries.

4. In the one-time vicarage of Villafranca del Panadés. Rovira, III, 327;
Enciclopedia universal ilustrada, LXVIII, 1359.

5. San Pedro de las Puellas, nunnery located within the present limits of the
city of Barcelona, built in 945 at the instance of Count Sunyer of Barcelona.
Enciclopedia universal ilustrada, VII, 731.

6. On August 25, 992, an Ato (Antonio?) son of the defunct Eldemar
(Ildemar?) sold land, etc., to Abbot Odo, in the district of Cerdianola at Budigas
(*Bodigari?*) and at Terrs (Terrarios). Màs, IV, Nos. CLXXVI, CCXXXIX,
CCXLVII.

7. Erapriniano, or Eramprunyá, called also Rosanes and Rodanes. This had
been given by Count Borrell II before 986. Màs, IV, No. CCCLXVIII.

8. Màs, IV, No. XCV, a.975; No. CXXI, a. 980, that mentions five churches
at Castle Fels—St. Mary Monastery, St. Michael, St. Peter, St. John, and St. Mary;
and No. CLXI, April 8, 986.

9. Also in the district of the castle of Aramprunyá, acquired in 954 by
exchange of land with Count Borrell II. Màs, IV, Nos. MCCCXXXVII and
CCCLXXXXIII.

10. Màs, IV, Nos. I, XXIII, XLIV, LIX-LXI, all of which refer to land in
Cervelló that belonged to Sant Cugat. In 993 Count Borrell II left half of his

alods and houses here with the churches, tithes, and first-fruits to Sant Cugat. Marca, *Marca hispanica,* col. 946, No. CXLI. Holy Cross, a small nunnery, belonged to Sant Cugat as early as the year 915. Some distance from it was the church of St. Sylvester. Màs, IV, No. IX.

11. Monistrol de Noya in the county of Barcelona belonged to Sant Cugat by the year 992. Màs, IV, Nos. CCXLI, CCXLII.

12. The *espiells* (Castilian, *spicellos*) were observation places built near the sea or the frontier. Such places were sometimes called *guardia, guardiola, miralles.* Their numerous locations on the map indicate the gradualness of the Christians' advance against the Saracens in the Iberian peninsula. Balari, *Orígines históricos,* p. 285; Rovira, III, 330.

13. All of the places named in this sentence were in the ancient vicarage of Villafranca del Panadés. *Enciclopedia universal ilustrada,* XIII, 629B.

14. The region of Olerdola (Olerdula), overlooking the plain of the Panadés, was of great strategic importance against the Saracens at the end of the tenth century and during the eleventh. M. Milá y Fontanals, "Apuntes históricos sobre Olerdula," *Memorias de la Academia de Buenas Letras* de Barcelona, II (1868), 516f.; Milá, "Olerdula: Appendice," MABL, III (1880), 589ff.

15. Màs VI, No. MCCXLIV, March 30, 998. Two separate pieces of land are intended, one owned by Ennego Bonfill and one owned by Prouizio. Ennego's land extended "from the summit of Granada to Subirats and to the towers belonging to Prouizio" so that the latter's alod appears to have been situated in Subirats.

16. In the suburbs of Barcelona, in Villafranca del Panadés. *Enciclopedia universal ilustrada,* LXVIII, 1359.

17. In the district of Olerdola. A Baio appears as executor of a Longovard's will, making Sant Cugat a beneficiary, and a Baio is referred to as defunct by 1013. Màs, IV, No. CCXLV, May 13, 992; No. CCLXXXVII; No. CCCLXXXII.

18. Màs, IV, No. CCXL, February 17, 992. The alod was bestowed upon both Sant Cugat and San Pedro de las Puellas (n. 5 above), and was near the walls of Barcelona, adjoining the district of the Castle of Olivella and extending through the mountainous region, now the *partido judicial,* of Villafranca del Panadés. *Enciclopedia universal ilustrada,* LXVIII, 1359.

19. In the *partido judicial* of Vendrell, diocese of Barcelona, containing the ruins of a castle of this period. *Enciclopedia universal ilustrada,* LIV, 161B.

20. Province of Tarragona, 6 kilometers from the present Vendrell. *Enciclopedia universal ilustrada* VII, 568B; Carreras, "Lo Montjuich de Barcelona," MABL, VIII (1903), 480, Appendix XVIII.

21. Màs IV, No. CCL, January 6, 993, given by the executors of the estate of Ansulf, who is here called a "vicar," i.e., the count's deputy. This was a fortified place called Cleriana, in the northern part of the province of Tarragona, in Villafranca del Panadés, on the left bank of the River Gayo. Sant Cugat had also received other gifts of land at Cleriana from Sendered. Màs, IV, No. CCX, April 7, 990.

22. A valley through which ran a public road. Màs, IV, No. CLXXXII, March 10, 988.

23. This is S. Stefano de Ripollet. Fita, "Patrología: Bulas inéditas de Silvestre II," BAH, XXXVIII (1901), 480, note.

24. Parets del Vallés. June 10, 993, Ermengard Bonadona and Na Ellregodo made a gift to Sant Cugat here, that was bounded by a road going to Gallechs (Gallegos) in Vallés. Màs, IV, No. CCLIII.

25. Màs, IV, No. CCVII, February 19, 990.

26. Màs, IV, No. CLXXXII, November 27, 983. More land in the district of

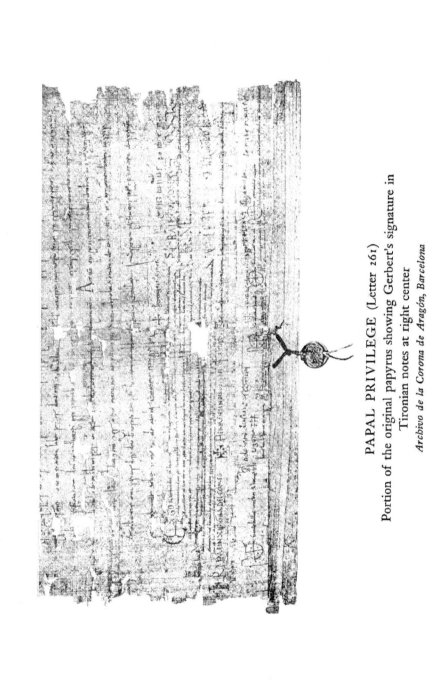

PAPAL PRIVILEGE (Letter 261)
Portion of the original papyrus showing Gerbert's signature in
Tironian notes at right center
Archivo de la Corona de Aragón, Barcelona

Rexach at Vall Major was given by Borrell II to Autemir who sold it to Sant Cugat, November 13, 998 for 12 *solidi*. Màs, IV, No. CCV.

27. *Betulone*, property, consisting of a tower, houses, land, trees, and vines, that had belonged to the Archdeacon Seniofred (Lobet, see Letter 32) and had been given to Sant Cugat by his executors. Màs, IV, No. CCLXXIII, August 2, 996.

28. Near Granollers and the River Vallés. Màs, IV, No. CCLXIII, a.995.

29. In the province and *partido judicial* of Barcelona, containing now 31 *municipios*. *Enciclopedia universal ilustrada* XXVI, 1091B-97B.

30. *Municipio* in Granollers. *Enciclopedia universal ilustrada*, XVI, 1091B.

31. *Ad ipsa cute*. This is mentioned in Lothair's diploma to Sant Cugat as the "churches of St. Genese and St. Martin and St. Felix that are at the falls[?] (*ad ipsum Fallium*)."

32. In 981, Sant Cugat owned an altar dedicated to St. Mary in Buco (Bruch?) in the county of Manresa. Màs, IV, No. CXXVI.

33. Abbot of Sant Cugat in 967, called also Teudericus. Villanueva, XIX, 31.

34. Signature in Tironian notes, reproduced facing p. 364 and by Kehr (see introductory note above). Noteworthy is the lack of the authentication by the librarian or other papal official, even though this is an original privilege.

35. The bulla (of lead), now reattached to this papyrus original, still exists in the Archivo de la Corona de Aragon. For another bulla, probably authentic, from one of Sylvester's documents see Letter 237, n. 8. H. Bresslau, "Papyrus und Pergament in der päpstlichen Kanzlei bis zur Mitte des 11. Jahrhunderts," MIOG, IX (1881), 1-2.

262. ROME. 999-1003

Sylvester II to Odilo, abbot of Cluny, and his monks, confirming the ecclesiastical grades properly bestowed by an ex-bishop, but quashing the others

SYLVESTER, BISHOP, SERVANT OF THE SERVANTS OF GOD, sends loving greetings and apostolic benediction to Odilo,[1] his son and illustrious abbot, and to the whole congregation entrusted to him.

At all times we entrust ourselves to your most holy prayers, and we sincerely entreat that you deem us worthy of them because, whithersoever we succeed, you by no means will fail to experience the benefits. Therefore, to those questions presented to Our Authority for discussion through your monk Gerbald, we are giving you an answer by the following decision in accordance with our apostolic authority and with the advice of our brother bishops.

For we know that that bishop was ordained in Catholic fashion and accepted the episcopal office in accordance with reason; but after he had been led by divine love to renounce secular honors and offices, he was not permitted to exercise the same functions which he had previously performed as a secular clergyman.[2]

Wherefore, because he did nothing rashly nor presumed anything against Catholic authority, but acted obediently and uprightly by the permission of his fellow bishops and of his abbot, and because good intentions are not contrary to God, it is our will and we so decide that whomever he advanced to any ecclesiastical grade and blessed, are blessed and are functioning in their grades in conformity with our permission and benediction. Those who haughtily and presumptuously refuse to continue in the same grade in which he ordained them, are suspended from the grade that they received after his resignation, but may freely enjoy the grade they previously had. Henceforth, the said bishop shall not presume to repeat his actions.

FAREWELL.

JL 3929. This letter is translated from Olleris, pp. 152-53.

Although this letter was written as the result of a synodal decision it still is not possible to date it more definitely since Sylvester II held a synod soon after his consecration, and thereafter at least twice yearly. Abbot Odilo was at Farfa in Italy, December, 999-January, 1000, or possibly a little earlier, suggesting the reforms for the abbey of Farfa.

1. He had succeeded Mayeul (Letter 76, n. 1) in 994, as abbot of Cluny. He died January 1, 1049. Jotsald *Vita Odilonis*, PL CXLII, 897-940; Manitius, II, 138-47.

2. The bishop in question had resigned to become a monk.

263. ROME. Middle of 1000-1003
Sylvester II to Archbishop Arnulf of Rheims, ordering him not to deny the Eucharist to any who die penitent and to continue burying the dead in the ancient cemetery of St. Remi

SYLVESTER, BISHOP, SERVANT OF THE SERVANTS OF GOD, sends greeting and apostolic benediction to Arnulf, archbishop of Rheims.

Recently it came to our notice that there is a disagreement among your citizens relative to a place of burial, since some desire to be buried in the city, some outside in the ancient cemetery of St. Rémy,[1] and that, therefore, those liking a burial place within the city are denying the Eucharist to dying persons who have requested burial in the aforesaid cemetery outside the city.

However, the canons assert that no one on the point of death ought to be denied the Eucharist, with the exception only of those who have been excommunicated and are unwilling to make satisfaction.

For to those of keen perception it seems evil and wicked when a person has irreligiously abandoned a brother on his deathbed by withdrawing from him whatever heals and revivifies.

By apostolic authority, therefore, we command that the dying be not prejudged, and that the Eucharist be denied to no one who, at the point of death, professes repentance. To all who so desire let it be granted that they be buried in the ancient cemetery of St. Rémy without opposition so that the living may possess the sure expectation of being buried and the dead may rest in peace in the spot they long for.

JL 3932. This is translated from P. Ewald, "Mitteilungen. IV. Drei unedirte päpstliche Schreiben," NA, VIII (1883), 364.

Since Sylvester II supposedly restored Arnulf to his archbishopric of Rheims only in December, 999, this letter must have been written later and sufficiently later to allow time for Arnulf to have returned to Rheims and to have functioned for a while as archbishop, and for the complaint against him to have been carried to Rome.

1. Lesne (III, 123-35) discusses cemeteries and burial rights in the tenth century but does not mention this argument at Rheims, nor either of these two cemeteries. The monastery of St. Rémy was outside the walls and two miles distant.

264. ROME. March, 1003

Sylvester II to Emma, countess of Poitou, confirming the possessions of the monastery of St. Peter of Bourgueil-en-Vallée, and exempting it from partial control by the bishop

SYLVESTER, BISHOP, SERVANT OF THE SERVANTS OF GOD, to Emma, countess of Poitou.[1]

You have poured into our ears the news that through a generous God and the encouragement and urging of the venerable Abbot Gauzbert [I] [2] you have built a monastery in the district of Angers in a place called Bourgueil [3] in honor of the Holy and Individual Trinity and of St. Peter, prince of the apostles, and that you have enriched it with lands and endowed it with wealth. And I discover that you have done this [i.e., informed us] in order that by [our] aid it may be made into a whole for the rectors of this place and be sustained by [our] support and flourish under our protection. For you know the words spoken to Peter: "You are Peter and upon this rock will I build my Church" [Mat. 16 : 18]. Thus, there is nothing more solid than something made firm upon the foundation of this rock. Because you have petitioned us to strengthen the above-mentioned monastery with all of its possessions by the authority of apostolic privilege, and since we have been influenced by your prayers we therefore freely grant our assent.

Therefore, conditioned upon the willingness of Rainaud, bishop of Angers, we decree that the bishop of no city shall presume to celebrate a council in this same monastery without the consent and wish of the abbot and monks of this place.

It is granted to the monks of this same place, indeed, to carry on the election of the abbot who is not to be an outsider but one of their own whose life and habits are according to God. After his election they shall present him to the duke of Aquitaine [William V] and his sons who shall bestow the gift on him without any contra-diction or opposition.

If, however, any abbot, filled with cupidity and aided by secular power, shall wish to enter this abbey by force and shall dare to contravene the above decree, let him fall into the dread judgment of God, and let him and all consenting to, or associating with, his desire know that they have been excommunicated by myself and by the power of my successors, whoever they may be, flourishing in this sacred seat till the end of time and having the power of binding and loosing. Thus, the sacrament of Christianity and of baptism will avail them nothing for the salvation of their souls, but with Judas the traitor, Nero the impious, and Julian the Apostate let them take possession of the infernal regions, and after the Great Judgment Day let them continue in hell permanently without end as associates of the devil and his angels, unless they shall have repented and shall have come for correction.

If, however, the county of Angers or even the whole province shall by any chance be put under a sentence of excommunication, to this monastery shall be reserved the permission of carrying on the ministry of the divine office. The churches of this monastery, wherever situated shall be exempt from obligation to any bishop, archdeacon, or any other person, excepting only payments for holding [?] synods and for entertaining ecclesiastics, each of which is called in common speech, respectively *circada* and *parata*.[4]

By apostolic authority we decree that all of the property, movable and immovable, indeed, that you or any good men have bestowed or will have bestowed shall be owned by the monks of this place forever. We shall enumerate them with appropriate description: The manors of Bourgueil with the church of St. Germain [5] with all the revenues [6] belonging to the manors and to the church. The church of Chouzé-sur-Loire [7] with its port and whatever belongs to it. In the district of Tours three *quartas* [8] of the benefice of the knight Corbon; likewise four *quartas* of the manor of Souliac which belonged to the same knight. Also, a half of a manor of Cassanias with half of the church of St. Mary and all the revenues belonging to the same half. Also, the half of St. Hilary with half of the manor of Vosalio and all their revenues. Also, certain purchases, namely, the village of Cré [?] [9] with the things that belong to it. Also the church of St. Denis [10] in the manor Golnaica and whatever belongs to the church and to the altar. Also villages with the following names: Booras [Bourras?], Canatias, Loliacum, and whatever belongs to them. The church in honor of St. Hilary with the manor of Fusciaco and those things that belong to it. Also, the church in honor of St. Mary in Beaumont [11] with its tithes and revenues, also vineyards, fields, houses, wherever they border upon the circuit of the castle of Fontenay, property in the neighborhood of the monastery of St. Peter of Bourgueil that you have given or will give in the future. Let the monks of this same place hold and possess them without disturbance.

Likewise, the church in honor of St. Stephen [12] with the village called Lotias. Also, the whole village of Cassanus, also the church of St. Christopher [13] with the whole village and the fair with full justice [14] and the customs dues entirely free from the power of any person. Also the village called ad Broolium [Breuil?] a Befredi. And the church of Oziacho [Ozillac?] with the whole village. Also these villages: Podium caninum, Valregia, Lemovicmaria [Limoges?], Podium Lotardi, Diddone, Vineda, the manor of Ledramnus and the alod near the above named village of Cassanus. The church in honor of St. Martin with the whole village named de Villaris [Villiers or Villers?]. Also the two villages of Drogiaco and Turtim. Also four *quartas* in the village of Odrunaco in the district of Alniasi. Two churches, one in honor of St. Peter, the other of St. Nazaire [15] located at Ingolmas on the seashore. Also the prebend of St. Martin, the gift of the abbot, and whatever those who serve within receive. Also, the prebend of the village of St. Martin of Candes [16] with the churches, homes, and fields belonging to it. Also a third part of Longueville on the Seine river.

We who are adorned with divine inspiration confirm by this privilege of apostolic authority all of the above-written things—churches, manors, payment of tenths, villages, male and female farmers, cultivated and uncultivated lands—and altogether everything that you and other good men have given or will give in the future to the said monastery of St. Peter, as enumerated in charters, so that the monks living there shall hold and possess them forever for their food and stipends so that no powerful person shall presume to remove any of it from the control or possession of the aforesaid monastery, or to impose injurious customs [17] on either their land or their possessions but rather they shall be allowed in quiet possession to exert themselves according to the way of life prescribed by the Rule.

Whoever, on any occasion, shall attempt to break the prescription of this decree will incur the supreme punishment of everlasting damnation and the headlong descent of excommunication pronounced by the Immeasurable Divinity, [together] with all transgressors of the holy law, unless he shall have made amends by compensation. Whoever, indeed, out of pious consideration shall be a guardian and observer of this privilege of ours, shall merit the grace of benediction by the compassionate Lord, and the achievement of becoming a partaker of the life eternal.

Written by the hand of Peter, notary and secretary of the Holy Roman Church, in the month of March in the first year of the indiction.

✠ FAREWELL. Sylvester, who is also Pope Gerbert.[18]

JL 3940. This is translated from Bubnov, I, 323-35.

1. Emma, the sister of Count Eudes I of Chartres and Blois, was the widow of Duke William IV (*Fièrebrace*) of Acquitaine. Lot, *Hugues Capet*, pp. 174, n. 3; 180, n. 2; 182, n. 3.

2. Or Joubert, a relative of Countess Emma. Lot, *Hugues Capet*, p. 423. Probably Abbot Gauzbert accompanied Emma to Rome since he secured from Sylvester II a privilege for St. Julien of Tours (JL 3935, text now lost). See Appendix C, No. 57.

3. Lot, *Hugues Capet*, pp. 423-26, prints the original grant of Count Eudes (drawn up February 12, 996 at the siege of Langeais), approving Emma's foundation of a monastery on the property-complex of Bourgueil (now dept. Indre-et-Loire, arrondissement Chinon) that had been given her as a dowry by their father Thibaud.

4. The obligation to furnish hospitality to a bishop or other ecclesiastical official on his round of visits to his diocese.

5. On the left bank of the Vienne river, southeast of Candes.

6. *Utilitatibus* (nom. sing. *utilitas*).

7. Dept. Indre-et-Loire, arrondissement Chinon, canton Bourgueil, between Bourgueil and Candes.

8. A land measure used especially in Poitou and the region around Tours. DuCange, V, 545-46.

9. *Croolio*. Either Cré, dept. Maine-et-Loire, canton Chateauneuf-sur-Sarthe; or Cré-sur-Loir, dept. Sarthe, arrondissement and canton of Flèche.

10. Perhaps St.-Denis-Hors, dept. Indre-et-Loire, arrondissement Tours, a suburb of Amboise, on the left bank of the Loire.

11. Probably Beaumont, dept. Indre-et-Loire, south of Bourgueil, between the Loire and Vienne rivers.

12. Perhaps St.-Etienne-de-Chigny, dept. Indre-et-Loire, arrondissement and canton Tours.

13. St.-Christophe, dept. Indre-et-Loire, arrondissement Tours, canton Neuvy-le-Roi.

14. Frequently fairs were held on a day preceding and on a day succeeding a particular saint's day, which itself might be celebrated with a market. The right of "full justice" resulted in the income which accrued from the judging of all disputes and crimes occurring during the fair. Newman, *Domaine royale*, p. 33, n. 1.

15. Dept. Loire-Inférieure, at the mouth of the Loire.

16. Dept. Indre-et-Loire, arrondissement and canton Chinon, at the confluence of the Loire and the Vienne rivers. St. Martin died at Candes.

17. Payments or claims not already in existence at the time of this privilege. Cf. the later *malos usos* in Catalonia. Smith in *Cambridge Economic History*, I, 349.

18. The signature is unlike Sylvester II's other signatures, but this is the last one known, and he may have changed it a little. In the Cartulary of St. Peter of Bourgueil following the signature was a notation of the copyist: "Let our successors know that this document was written on papyrus." Bubnov, I, 325.

APPENDICES

APPENDIX A

FAMILY ORIGIN OF THE EMPRESS THEOPHANU

According to the document recording the marriage gift of Otto II to his bride Theophanu (variously spelled Thephanou, Thephania, Theophano, Theophanu), dated April 14, 972, she was the niece of John I Tzmisces, an Armenian noble related to Emperor Nicephorus II Phocas, who raised himself to be co-emperor of Byzantium with Basil II and Constantine VIII (Letter 119). This document (DO II 21), is reproduced in colored facsimile by Schlumberger.[1] Had Theophanu been the daughter of a Byzantine emperor such a relationship would certainly have been mentioned in as official a document as this concerning the wedding gift, especially since this diploma was based on the one used earlier for the Empress Adelaide in which Adelaide is called "the daughter of King Rudolf of divine memory."[2] Thietmar (ii.ix) states that Emperor John Tzmisces sent as Otto's bride "not the desired maiden, but his [Tzmisces'] niece, called Theophanu." Otto I had been negotiating since 967[3] with the Byzantine emperors, first Nicephorus Phocas, then John Tzmisces, for a Greek princess to be Otto II's bride.

---

[1] *L'Epopée byzantine*, I (Paris, 1896), between pp. 202-3.
[2] Schramm, "Kaiser, Basileus und Papst," *Historische Zeitschrift*, CXXIX (1924), 435.
[3] *Continuatio Reginonis*, a.967, MGSS VI, 620.

Germanic custom prescribed that the first daughter be named for the paternal grandmother, and the second for the maternal grandmother. Otto II and Theophanu named their eldest daughter Adelaide for Empress Adelaide. Their second daugther, born in the summer of 978, they named Sophie. Therefore, Theophanu's mother apparently was Sophie who was the sister of John Tzmisces and a niece of Nicephorus Phocas.

Because Liutprand of Cremona, who in 968 headed a second embassy to Nicephorus Phocas to secure a Greek wife for Otto II, writes of his speech to Nicephorus, "My lord [Otto I] sent me to you so that you will declare to me with an oath whether you are willing to bestow in marriage upon his son, my lord, august Emperor Otto, a daughter of Emperor Romanus and Empress Theophanu,"[4] many modern historians designate Theophanu as the sister of Anna (b. 963) who married Vladimir of Kievan Russia in 989. Until recently however, no one was ever able to find in the sources even an allusion to any other daughter of Romanus II than Anna.

Then, Vasiliev[5] discovered in the account of the Russian Princess Olga's reception at the Byzantine court on September 9, 957, described in Emperor Constantine VII *De ceremoniis aulae byzantinae* (Ceremonial book), a reference to the Emperors Constantine VII and Romanus II and *their* (italics Vasiliev's) children. Romanus II's successors to the throne were his two sons, Basil II and Constantine VIII, who were born in 957/58 and 960 or 961 respectively. Therefore, Romanus II's oldest child must have been a girl, and since the child sat during the ceremony, Vasiliev concludes that she was at least seven years old in 957. Hence, she was born in 950 or earlier and was at least five years older than Otto II who was born in 955. Consequently, Vasiliev maintains the view, with more justification than in the case of other historians, that Otto II's wife Theophanu was the daughter of Romanus II.

Actually, this reference in the *Ceremonial Book* to Romanus's child older than Basil II serves to strengthen confidence in Liutprand's reference to a daugther of Romanus as the bride desired for Otto II. Surely, Otto I was not asking for Romanus's daughter Anna, who

---

[4] *Relatio de legatione constantinopolitana,* PL CXXXVI, 913.
[5] "Hugh Capet," *Dumbarton Oaks Papers,* VI (1951), 244f.

was only four years old when the first German embassy arrived in Constantinople in 967, but for a girl of marriageable, or near-marriageable age. Otto I hoped she would bring to his son control over Byzantine territories in Italy, just as Adelaide had brought to him control over much of the Italian peninsula. Nicephorus Phocas hoped to use his stepdaughter as a reward to the Ottos for abandoning pretensions to Byzantine territories in Italy. In 969 during the impasse resulting from these conflicting desires Nicephorus was murdered.

The new emperor, John Tzmisces, planned to marry Romanus's widow Theophanu, but the Patriarch Polyeuctus prevented this, and so, instead, Tzmisces married Romanus's sister Theodora, thus becoming uncle-in-law of Romanus's children. Otto I sent another embassy to congratulate John and to press the suit for a Greek bride for Otto II. John complied by sending his niece Theophanu, who was not the girl Liutprand had tried to secure for Otto II, i.e., Theophanu was not the daughter of Romanus II. What happened to this daugther? I suggest that she died between 968, the time of Liutprand's embassy, and the end of 971, the time of Otto I's next embassy under Archbishop Gero of Cologne.

Otto III also sought a Greek wife, and in January, 1002, his betrothed, the Princess Zoë, arrived in Italy for their marriage. She was the daughter of Constantine VIII so that if Otto III's mother Theophanu, had been Constantine VIII's sister, Otto III would have been marrying his first cousin. This would have been uncanonical according to both eastern and western church laws. Neither Gregory V nor Gerbert, both so vigorously opposed to the marriage of Robert II of France to his more distant cousin Bertha, would have sanctioned such a marriage. So, for this additional reason, it appears that Theophanu was not Romanus II's daugther, nor was she closely related to his family (the Macedonian House).[6]

---

[6] One of Romanus II's sisters was named Theophanu, but she was not the "daughter of Romanus and Theophanu" mentioned by Liutprand, nor the "niece of John Tzmisces" mentioned by Thietmar and the marriage gift document of Otto II. She was John's sister-in-law by his second marriage to Theodora. M. Uhlirz ("Studien über Theophano," DA, VI (1943), 442ff.) seeks to prove that Otto II's wife, Theophanu, was the granddaughter of Romanus I Lecapenus and thus a cousin of Romanus II. This is contrary to both Liutprand and Thietmar, and would have resulted in an uncanonical marriage for Otto III, since in this case Zoë would be his second cousin.

APPENDIX B

THE STRONGHOLD OF LAON ACCORDING
TO RICHER

Richer, in several instances, emphasizes the difficulty of capturing Laon because of its situation:

II.ix. [In the year 938, Louis IV] collected troops, equipped an army and, reaching Laon, where Heribert had recently constructed a citadel still held by a garrison of his men, the king besieged it. After disposing archers round about, the king attempted to capture it by missiles. In the melee, there were injuries to both sides since the garrison in the citadel likewise employed arrows and other missiles. Unsuccessful in terminating the siege through soldiers, the idea of using a machine occurred to him.

II.x. CONSTRUCTION OF THE WAR MACHINE. From very strong pieces of wood that were joined together he ordered a machine constructed like a rectangular house of the height of a man, having a capacity of twelve men. Its sides were made of wood of great strength, and its roof consisted of bundles of strong sticks woven together. Inside he had attached four wheels by which the machine could be propelled up to the citadel by those who were hiding inside. However, the roof was not flat but sloped from the top to right and left so that it might easily shed falling arrows. After it was completed it was filled with young soldiers who propelled it on its wheels right up to the citadel.

From their elevated position on the cliff the enemy attempted to destroy it, but they were repulsed with great injury by the archers stationed on every side. As soon as the machine was rolled up to the citadel, part of the wall was sapped and demolished. The enemy, frightened at the possibility that a crowd of armed combatants might enter through this breach, laid down their arms and implored the king's clemency. The king forbade any further combat, seized the garrison which was almost intact, except for those wounded in the melee, and substituted his own followers for defending the city.

ii.xxiii-xxiv. [In the year 940, Hugh the Great and Heribert of Vermandois besieged it during the absence of King Louis IV, believing that it was protected by only a small garrison.] However, they were unequal to the defenders who controlled the top of the hill, and were compelled to withdraw several times. They persisted, hoping to capture the city before the arrival of the king. [However, upon the arrival of the king they abandoned the siege.]

[In 948 Louis IV again found it necessary to recapture Laon.] it.lxxxiv. [After capturing the castle of Montaigu near Laon,] the king installed a garrison there and led his army to Laon. He prepared for the siege by utilizing strategic positions, and he attacked the forces on all sides. Frequently the attack was from the distance [i.e., with missiles], and nine times it was close at hand, but the king was not successful in any attack at that time. The winter season threatened and in that space of time a war machine could not be fabricated, without which the height of such a lofty hill could not be captured. Thus, by the king's order the army returned home, to reassemble after the winter. He himself retired without escort to Rheims. [Latouche (Richer, I, p. 271, n. 3) states that Richer invented this siege. Since Richer (ii.x) embroidered Flodoard's account of the war machine by actually describing it, possibly he may have described the machine mentioned in Letter 134 (n. 3), and have assigned it to the earlier siege.]

[In 946, three kings, Otto I, Conrad of Burgundy, and Louis IV, together had planned to capture Laon.] ii.liv. When in front of them they perceived the height of the hill and explored the situation of the city on all sides, they realized that it would be folly for them to fight there so they withdrew from this city and approached Rheims.

[According to ii.lxxxviii-xci, the city was finally captured only by a ruse devised by Richer's own father, but even then it was impossible to capture the tower. This was captured later by Hugh the Great (ii.xcvii) and turned over to Louis IV.]

APPENDIX C

SYLVESTER II'S PRIVILEGES, DECREES, LETTERS, AND ACTS WHOSE TEXTS ARE NOT EXTANT

1. April 9-15, 999? To the nunnery of the Holy Savior and St. Vitus of Elten. From: W. Erben, "Excurse zu den Diplomen Otto III," MIOG, XIII (1892), 572-74.
2. April 15, 999. Petitions Emperor Otto III in behalf of Bishop Teuzo of Reggio nell'Emilia. From: DO III 317.
3. End of April, 999? Summons Bishop Peter of Asti to a synod in Rome. From: Letter 248 (JL 3911).
4. May, 999. Presides over a synod at Rome, decreeing a sentence of penance against Margrave Arduin of Ivrea; and the summoning of Archbishop Giselhar of Magdeburg to Rome to answer the charge of holding two bishoprics. From: MG *Constitutiones* I, p. 53, No. 25; and Thietmar iv.xxviii.
5. May, 999. Summons Archbishop Giselhar of Magdeburg to Rome in accordance with the synodal decree. From: *Chronica episcoporum Merseburgensium*, MGSS X, 170.
6. May 7, 999. Petitions Otto III in behalf of Bishop Leo of Vercelli. From: DO III 324.
7. July 9, 999. At Benevento. Consecrates Heribert archbishop of Cologne, and bestows the pallium upon him. From: Lantbert *Vita Heriberti*, MGSS, 743-44.
8. August 14-15, 999. With Otto III presides over a council of the Romans? *Vita Burchardi episcopi*, MGSS IV, 833.
9. September 20-21, 999. Between Rome and Farfa. Confers with Otto III and his magnates on affairs of state. From: DO III 331.
10. September 22, 999. Farfa. With Otto III hears the complaints of Abbot Hugh of Farfa and orders Hugh to take his case to Rome for adjudication. From: DO III 339.

11. October 23, 999. Petitions Otto III to bestow an estate upon Siggo, Otto's chaplain. From: DO III 334; Brackmann, I, 142, No. *9.

12. October 23, 999? To King Olaf I Tryggvessön of Norway, commanding him to cease using runic letters. From: Johannes Georg Eccard (Eckhardt) *De origine Germanorum eorumque vetustissimus coloniis, migrationibus ac rebus gestis libri duo*, ed. C. L. Scheidius (Göttingen, 1750), p. 192.

13. November 3, 999? To Petroald, abbot of Bobbio, confirming the privileges granted by previous popes, exempting Bobbio from episcopal control, retaining it under papal protection, and (perhaps) confirming possessions. From: Cipolla, *Codice diplomatico di Bobbio*, III, 367, No. cccxi; Kehr, *Italia pontificia*, VI, Pt. 2, p. 252, No. *21, and p. 247.

14. November 3, 999. Petitions Otto III to confirm to Abbot Petroald the possessions of the monastery of St. Columban of Bobbio. From: DO III 335; Kehr, *Italia pontificia*, VI, Pt. 2, p. 252, No. *20.

15. Beginning of November, 999? Summons Bishop Peter of Asti to appear before a synod in Rome in December, 999. From: Letter 248 (JL 3911).

16. December 1?, 999. Creates Gaudentius (Radim) archbishop of St. Adalbert. From: DO III 339; Thietmar iv.xxviii.

17. December 2, 999. Consents to the judgment in a court, awarding the cell of Santa Maria in Minione to Abbot Hugh of Farfa, and agrees to order Peter, a papal secretary, to draw up a memorandum brief embodying the court's decision. From: DO III 339; Kehr, *Italia pontificia*, II, p. 62, No. *14*.

18. December, 999-January, 1000. Confirms the constitution for the monastery of Santa Maria di Farfa, prepared by Abbot Hugh. From: *Relatio constitutionis Domni Hugonis abbatis*, ed. Ugo Balzani, in *Fonti per la storia d'Italia*, Vol. XXXIII, Pt. 1 (Rome, 1903), pp. 55-58; Kehr, *Italia pontificia*, II, p. 62, No. *15*.

19. December, 999? To Bishop Ascelin of Laon, urging him to desist from treacherous actions against King Robert II, and Archbishop Arnulf of Rheims. From: Letter 253 (JL 3914).

20. December, 999. To Archbishop Giselhar of Magdeburg, commanding him to submit to examination by his suffragan bishops in a synod in the presence of the papal legate (Robert?). From: Thietmar iv.xxviii; and *Chronica episcoporum Merseburgensium*, MGSS X, 170.

21. December, 999. Accredits the Archdeacon and Papal Oblationary Robert as papal legate to Germany to investigate the case of Archbishop Giselhar. From: Same as in No. 20.

22. December, 999-March, 1000. To Vladimir, prince of Kiev. From: *Polnoe sobranie russkikh lietopisei, izdannoe po Vysochaishemu Povelieniiu Arkheograficheskoiu Kommissieiu. IX. Lietopisnyi sbornik, imenuemyi Patriarsheiu ili Nikonovskoiu lietopis'iu* (St. Petersburg, 1862), p. 68.

23. January-February, 1000? To an unknown (French cleric?) suggesting a Toledo Council as a precedent for celebrating the Feast of the Annunciation of the Virgin Mary on December 18th. From: Letter of Abbot Heriger of Lobbes, PL CXXXIX, 1134A.

24. March, 1000. To Leotheric, acknowledging him as the legally elected archbishop of Sens and conferring upon him the primacy of France and the pallium. From: *Chronicon S. Petri Vivi Senonensis auctore Clario monacho,*

in d'Achery, *Spicilegium* (1723), II, 473; and *Odoranni monachi S. Petri Vivi Senonensis Chronicon*, in A. DuChesne, *Historiae Francorum Scriptores*, II (1636), 641.

25. June? 1000? To Boleslaw I Chrobry, duke of Poland, confirming the ecclesiastical arrangements for Poland made in conjunction with Emperor Otto III. From: Anonymous (Martinus) Gallus, *Chronica Polonorum* i.vi, MGSS IX, 429.

26. October-November, 1000. To the suffragan bishops of Sens, commanding them to consecrate Leotheric as archbishop. From: *Chronicon S. Petri Vivi Senonensis* in d'Achery, *Spicilegium* II, 473.

27. January 1, 1001. To Bishop Rethar of Paderborn, confirming previous possessions and granting further privileges. From: *Vita Meinwercki Episcopi Patherbrunensis*, MGSS XI, 109-110; JL 3915.

28. January 13, 1001. Presides over synod which declares Archbishop Willigis's synod at Gandersheim schismatic, reaffirms Bishop Bernward's legal control over Gandersheim, requests that Willigis be reprimanded, and that German bishops be commanded to hold a synod at Pöhlde on June 21st. From: Thangmar *Vita Bernwardi*, MGSS IV, 768f.

29. January 13, 1001. Confirms to Bishop Bernward of Hildesheim the control over the nunnery of Gandersheim (by a written document?). From: Thangmar *Vita Bernwardi*, MGSS IV, 769.

30. January 13, 1001, or soon thereafter. To the bishops and princes of Germany recommending the papal legate, the Cardinal Priest Frederick, and calling for a synod at Pöhlde. From: Thangmar *Vita Bernwardi*, MGSS IV, 771.

31. January 13, 1001, or soon thereafter. To Archbishop Willigis of Mainz, upbraiding him for infringing the rights of others and requesting fraternal concord and obedience. From: Thangmar *Vita Bernwardi*, MGSS IV, 771f.

32. January 13, 1001. To Bishop Bernward of Hildesheim, confirming previous immunities. From: Hermann Lüntzel, *Die ältere Diöcese Hildesheim* (Hildesheim, 1837), pp. 151-54; JL 3921.

33. January 23?, 1001. To Bishop Bernward of Hildesheim, granting him ecclesiastical rights in the castle of Dahlum. From: Hermann Lüntzel, *Die ältere Diöcese Hildesheim* (Hildesheim, 1837), pp. 347-49.

34. January 23, 1001? To Stephen, king of Hungary, granting him the right of being crowned king, and of establishing episcopal sees in Hungary; sends him a crown. Also creates Gran an archiepiscopal see. From: *Passio s. Adalperti martyris*, MGSS XV, Pt. 2, p. 706; *Thietmar* iv.xxviii; *Stephani Regis Ungariae Vita minor*, MGSS XI, 228; *Stephani Regis Ungariae Vita maior*, MGSS XI, 232-34; JL 3909.

35. March 1-3, 1001. To Geribert, viscount of Barcelona, citing him to appear in Rome at Christmas. From: Letter 255.

36. March 7, 1001. Perugia. To Abbot Peter of San Lorenzo in Campo of Perugia. From: Kehr, "Papsturkunden in Rome," NAG, 1901, p. 251; Kehr, *Italia pontificia*, IV, 190, No. *3.

37. March 7, 1001. Perugia. Intercedes with Otto III on behalf of Abbot Peter of San Lorenzo in Campo, for confirmation of property and quashing emphyteutic leases. From: DO III 392; Kehr, *Italia pontificia*, IV, 190, No. *1.

38. April 4, 1001. Ravenna. Signs a decision of the imperial court, adjudging

Santa Maria in Pomposa and San Vitale to the church of Ravenna. From: DO III 396.

39. May 1, 1001. To Count Armengol I of Urgel, granting him permission to compel the monks of Sant Climent of Codinet to live a religious community life according to the Rule of St. Benedict, after being joined to Sant Andreu of Sintilias. From: Villanueva, XII, 214ff.

40. May, 1001? To Patriarch John of Aquileia, citing him to appear in Rome relative to his dispute with Bishop Andrew of Parenzo over the parish of Ruvigno (Rovigno). From: Privilege of Pope Sergius IV, a.1010 (JL 3966), in PL CXXXIX, 1499D-1501A; Kehr, *Italia pontificia*, VII, Pt. 1, No. *102, p. 28, No. *46; VII, Pt. 2, No. *113, p. 232, No. *3.

41. August-September, 1001. Paterno? or Rome? To all the German bishops, citing them to attend a synod in Italy (Rome?) at Christmas, 1001. From: Thangmar *Vita Bernwardi*, MGSS IV, 772.

42. September, 1001? To Patriarch John of Aquileia, citing him a second time to appear in Rome about Ruvigno. From: Same as No. 40 above.

43. December 27, 1001. Todi. Presides over a synod which hears the complaint of Bishop Bernward of Hildesheim, through Thangmar, and the report of the papal legate, Frederick. From: Thangmar *Vita Bernwardi*, MGSS IV, 773, 774.

44. 1001. Receives ambassadors from Prince Vladimir of Kiev. From: *Polnoe sobranie russkikh lietopisei, izdannoe po Vysochaishemu Povelieniiu Arkheograficheskoiu Kommissieiu. IX. Lietopisnyi sbornik, imenuemyi Patriarsheiu ili Nikonovskoiu lietopis'iu* (St. Petersburg, 1862), p. 68.

45. December 27, 1001-January 13, 1002? Todi. Petitions Otto III to bestow Herewarden upon Bishop Notker of Liége for St. John of Liége. From: DO III 240; H. Bloch, "Das Diplom Otto's III für das Johanneskloster bei Lüttich (DO III 240) und die Gründung des Adalbertstiftes zu Aachen," NA, XXIII (1898), 151-58.

46. Beginning of 1002? or April 5, 1002? To Count Ramon Borrell III of Barcelona, advising that he allow the monks of St. Benedict of Bages to choose their own abbot, and granting permission for them to do so. From: Villanueva VII, 281-83, 284-86.

47. January, 1002? To Patriarch John of Aquileia, reprimanding him for not appearing in Rome, and for the third time citing him to appear before Sylvester II. From: Same as No. 40 above.

48. March 8, 1002. Presides over a court which accepts a copy of the gift of his property by Eufemiano, father of St. Alexius, to the church of St. Boniface on the Aventine as having the validity of the partially destroyed original [forgery?]. From: A Monaci, "Regesto dell'abbazia di Sant'Alessio all'Aventino," ASSP, XXVII (Rome, 1904), 363-65; Kehr, *Italia pontificia*, I, 116, No. 3.

49. April 5, 1002. Presides over a general synod. From: Letters 255, 256, 257; Schramm, *Kaiser, Rom und Renovatio*, I, 182, n. 1.

50. April 5, 1002? To Patriarch Vitale IV Candiano of Grado, confirming patriarchal rights to him and metropolitan jurisdiction over the bishoprics of Venice and Istria. From: Privilege of Pope John XIX to Urso, patriarch of Grado, a.1029, PL CXLII, 1140A-1142A; Dandolo *Chronica*, in Muratori,

Rerum italicarum Scriptores, new ed., XII (Bologna, 1931), 201; Kehr, *Italia pontificia*, VII, Pt. 2, p. 50, No. *66.

51. Soon after April 5, 1002? To Duke Henry of Bavaria, requesting him to warn John, patriarch of Aquileia, to cease disturbing the church of Parenzo. From: Same as No. 40 above; Kehr, *Italia pontificia*, VII, Pt. 2, p. 232, No. *4; Brackmann, I, App. I, No. *27.

52. July-August, 1002? To Bishop Andrew of Parenzo, describing Sylvester II's efforts to secure the presence of Patriarch John of Aquileia in Rome and confirming the parish of Ruvigno, two castles, and a valley to Andrew. From: Same as No. 40 above; Kehr, *Italia pontificia*, VII, Pt. 2, p. 232, No. *5.

53. Probably September, 1002. To Bruno of Querfurt, granting him permission to evangelize pagans, creating him archbishop of the pagans ("peoples"), and bestowing the pallium upon him. From: *Bruno Vita quinque fratrum*, MGSS XV, Pt. 2, pp. 725, 726; *Gesta episcoporum Halberstadensium*, MGSS XXIII, 89; *Gesta episcoporum Magdeburgensium*, MGSS XIV, 388; Peter Damian *Vita Romualdi*, MGSS IV, 850.

54. December 3, 1002. Presides over a synod which adjudges the monastery of St. Peter of Perugia to be directly under the jurisdiction of the Holy See, not under that of the bishop of Perugia. From: Olleris, pp. 264-65; Kehr, *Italia pontificia*, IV, p. 67, No. 4.

55. December 3-4, 1002. To the abbot of St. Peter of Perugia, confirming its exemption from the control of the bishop of Perugia and its protection by the Holy See, in accordance with the decision of the Lateran synod of December 3d. From: No. 54 above; Ewald, "Zur Diplomatik Silvesters II." NA, IX, (1884), 345-46.

56. 1002-1003? To the abbot of St. Mary of Vangadizza, confirming its possessions and taking it under the protection of the Holy See(?). From: Privilege of Innocent II, April 9, 1139, PL CLXXIX, 419D-420A; Kehr, *Italia pontificia*, V, p. 193.

57. 999-1003 (possibly March, 1003). To Abbot Gauzbert I of St. Julien of Tours, confirming the possessions of the abbey. From: A. Salmon, *Recueil de chroniques de Touraine* (Société archéologique de Touraine, Collection de documents sur l'histoire de Touraine; Tours, 1854), pp. 228-29; JL 3935.

58. 999-January 23, 1002. With Otto III approves the substitution of canons for monks in the church of St. Paul in Rome. From: Raoul Glaber *Historiarum Libri quinque*, PL CXLII, 622ff.

59. 999-1003. To the abbot of St. Paul in Rome, confirming its possessions. From: Privilege of Anti-Pope Anacletus II, PL CLXXIX, 692-694D; Kehr, *Italia pontificia*, I, No. *11.

60. 999-1003. To the abbot of St. Mary of Arles. From: Edmond Martène and Ursin Durand, *Voyage littéraire de deux bénédictins de la congregation de Saint-Maur* (Paris, 1724), p. 61.

61. 999-1003. To the church of Rosellae, adjudging to it, as the result of a synodal decision, estates disputed by the church of Populonia. From: Bubnov I, 338; Kehr, *Italia pontificia*, III, p. 259, No. *2, and p. 269, No. *2.

62. End of 999-end of 1001. To Hugh Dissutus (Scucitus), or of Montboissier, or of Auvergne, granting him permission to establish the monastery of St. Michael of Chiusa. From: William *Historia Clusiensis monasterii*, PL CL,

1452A; Kehr, *Italia pontificia*, VI, Pt. 2, p. 122, No. *1, and p. 125, No. *14*.

63. 999-1003. To Viscount Gui of Limoges, summoning him to Rome. From: Ademar of Chabannes *Historiarum Libri*, MGSS IV, 132-33.

64. Easter, 1002 or 1003. Presides over a synod which adjudicates the dispute between Bishop Grimoard of Limoges and Viscount Gui of Limoges. From: Same as No. 63.

65. 999-1003. Takes the castle of Lescure under the protection of the Holy See. From: Privilege of Pope Sergius IV, March 30, 1010, PL CXXXIX, 1501C-1502A.

66. 999-1003. To the monastery of the Holy Cross of Fonte Avellana. From: Kehr, *Italia pontificia*, IV, 94, No. *1.

67. 999-1003. To the collegiate church of St. Mary of Cori. From: Kehr, *Italia pontificia*, II, 107.

68. 999-1003. To King Robert II of France. From: Masson, *Epistolae Gerberti*, p. 79.

69. 999-1003. To the monastery of St. Michael of Hildesheim. From: JL 4036, issued by Benedict VIII. The printed text is from a spurious document. See No. 7 of my list of Sylvester's spurious privileges.

70. 999-January, 1002. Petitions Otto III in behalf of the church of Aachen. From: DO III 240.

71. 999-January, 1002. To Emperor Otto III. From: Masson, *Epistolae Gerberti*, p. 79.

APPENDIX D

SPURIOUS PRIVILEGES ASCRIBED TO SYLVESTER II

1. May, 999. To Mazzeus de Mergantibus, a noble of Umbria, From: Kehr, *Italia pontificia*, IV, p. 50, No. †4.

2. December 1?, 999. Canonization of Adalbert of Prague, martyred by the Prussians. From: A. F. Czajkowski, "The Congress of Gniezno in the year 1000," *Speculum*, XXIV (1949), 346.

3. April 28, 1000. To the canons of the church of Santa Maria in Pisa. From: Kehr, *Italia pontificia*, III, p. 333, No. †11. Kehr (VI, 217) dates this "1001."

4. April 28, 1000. To the citizens of Pisa. From: Kehr, *Italia pontificia*, III, p. 357, No. †14.

5. 1001-1003. To Otto III, requesting him to confirm a document to Wido, bishop of Pavia. From: JL †3939, in PL CXXXIX, 285, and Olleris, p. 167. Kehr, *Italia pontificia*, VI, 217, dates this "1001."

6. 999-1003. To the monastery of San Zaccaria and San Pancratio of Venice. From: Kehr, *Italia pontificia*, Pt. 2, p. 177, No. † *12.

7. 999-1003. To St. Michael of Hildesheim. From: A. Brackmann, "Papsturkunden des nordens, nord- und mittel Deutschlands," NAG, 1904, p. 108.

8. 999-1003. Establishment of the observance of All Souls Day on November second as a Catholic festival. From: Ciaconi, *Vitae et res gestae pontificum romanorum et S. R. E. cardinalium... ad Clementem IX* (ed. Oldoin), p. 757, note by Oldoin. (Sylvester II may have formally accepted this observance which was actually started by Odilo of Cluny in 998.)

9. To Liutbert, bishop of Mainz. From: Bubnov I, 285; MS Leningrad O v. Otd. I No. 9, s. XII, fol. 18r. This is really JL 3443, a.887 or 888, issued by Pope Stephen V to Liutbert of Mainz.

10. To Odilo of Cluny, confirming Peterlingen to Cluny. From: Sackur, *Die Cluniacenser* (Halle, 1892), I, 218, n. 2. No such privilege is known to have been issued by Sylvester II. Actually, Pope Gregory V issued the privileges for Peterlingen (JL 3895 and 3896). See Brackmann, II, Pt. 2, pp. 186-88; NAG, 1904, pp. 438-40.

COMPARATIVE LIST OF LETTER
NUMBERS

Havet	Lattin		Havet	Lattin		Havet	Lattin		Havet	Lattin
1	8		30	38		59	67		88	94
2	9		31	39		60	66		89	103
3	10		32	40		61	68		90	104
4	11		33	41		62	69		91	102
5	12		34	42		63	70		92	105
6	13		35	43		64	71		93	95
7	14		36	44		65	73		94	96
8	15		37	45		66	72		95	97
9	16		38	46		67	74		96	98
10	17		39	24		68	75		97	100
11	18		40	47		69	76		98	101
12	19		41	53		70	77		99	106
13	20		42	48		71	78		100	112
14	21		43	49		72	79		101	107
15	22		44	50		73	80		102	108
16	23		45	51		74	81		103	109
17	25		46	52		75	82		104	110
18	26		47	54		76	83		105	111
19	27		48	55		77	84		106	113
20	28		49	56		78	85		107	114
21	29		50	57		79	86		108	118
22	30		51	58		80	87		109	115
23	31		52	59		81	88		110	116
24	32		53	63		82	89		111	119
25	33		54	60		83	90		112	120
26	34		55	61		84	91		113	121
27	35		56	62		85	99		114	122
28	36		57	64		86	92		115	123
29	37		58	65		87	93		116	124

Havet	Lattin	Havet	Lattin	Havet	Lattin	Havet	Lattin
117	125	143	148	169	178	195	197
118	126	144	152	170	179	196	198
119	128	145	153	171	180	197	199
120	129	146	154	172	181	198	200
121	130	147	155	173	182	199	195
122	131	148	156	174	183	200	203
123	132	149	157	175	184	201	205
124	134	150	158	176	186	202	206
125	135	151	159	177	189	203	216
126	127	152	150	178	190	204	217
127	136	153	161	179	191	205	218
128	137	154	162	180	192	206	207
129	133	155	163	181	221	207	213
130	138	156	164	182	224	208	212
131	139	157	165	183	227	209	215
132	140	158	166	184	228	210	219
133	141	159	167	185	229	211	220
134	142	160	168	186	230	212	223
135	143	161	169	187	231	213	208
136	144	162	170	188	193	214	209
137	145	163	171	189	117	215	210
138	146	164	172	190	194	216	211
139	147	165	174	191	204	217	201
140	149	166	176	192	214	218	226
141	150	167	175	193	202	219	222
142	151	168	177	194	196	220	225

ABBREVIATIONS

USED IN THE NOTES AND IN THE BIBLIOGRAPHY

ABB   Abhandlungen der Preussischen Akademie der Wissenschaften zu Berlin, Philosophisch-historische Klasse.

ABG   Abhandlungen der Gesellschaft der Wissenschaften zu Göttingen, Philologisch-historische Klasse.

ALMA   Archivum latinitatis medii aevi (Bulletin DuCange).

AMNG   Abhandlungen zur mittleren und neueren Geschichte.

ASR   Archivio della Reale Società romana di storia romana.

ASSP   Archivio della R. Società di storia patria.

BABL   Boletin de la Academia de Buenas Letras de Barcelona.

BAH   Boletin de la Real Academia de la Historia.

BEC   Bibliothèque de l'Ecole des Chartes.

BISI   Bullettino dell'Istituto storico italiano per il medio evo e Archivio muratoriano.

CG   Catalogue générale des manuscrits des bibliothèques publiques de France. Departements.

DA   Deutsches Archiv für Geschichte des Mittelalters, Weimar (continuation of Neues Archiv [NA]).

DACL   Dictionnaire d'Archéologie chrétienne et de liturgie, ed. by F. Cabrol and H. Leclercq.

DHGE   Dictionnaire d'Histoire et de Géographie ecclésiastiques, ed. by A. Baudrillart and others.

DO I, II, III Diplomata of Otto I, II, III, in MG Diplomata.

JE   Jaffé-Ewald, referring to Ewald's editing and numbering of papal documents in 2d ed. of Jaffé, Nos. 1066-3386.

JK   Jaffé-Kaltenbrunner, referring to Kaltenbrunner's editing and numbering of papal documents in 2d ed. of Jaffé, Nos. 1-1065.

JL   Jaffé-Loewenfeld, referring to Loewenfeld's editing and numbering of papal documents in 2d ed. of Jaffé, Nos. 3387-8432.

MABL   Memorias de la Academia de buenas letras de Barcelona.
MG   Monumenta Germaniae Historica.
MGAA   Monumenta Germaniae Historica. Auctores antiquissimi.
MG Dipl.   Monumenta Germaniae Historica. Diplomata regum et imperatorum Germaniae, I-III, 1879-1903.
MG Epp.   Monumenta Germaniae Historica. Epistolae.
MGSS   Monumenta Germaniae Historica. Scriptores.
MIOG   Mitteilungen des Instituts für oesterreichische Geschichtsforschung, 1880-1922; Mitteilungen des oesterreichischen Instituts für Geschichtsforschung, 1923ff.
MS L   MS Leyden Vossius quarto latin 54, s. XIin.
MS P   MS Papire Masson (lost).
MS V   MS Vallicelliana, Rome, G. 94, s. XVIIin.
NA   Neues Archiv der Gesellschaft für ältere deutsche Geschichtskunde, I-L, 1876-1936 (continued by Deutsches Archiv [DA]).
NAG   Nachrichten der Gesellschaft der Wissenschaften zu Göttingen, Philologisch-historische Klasse.
PL   Patrologia latina. See entry under Migne in Bibliography.
SBB   Sitzungsberichte der Preussischen Akademie der Wissenschaften zu Berlin, Philosophisch-historische Klasse.
SBM   Situngsberichte der Akademie der Wissenschaften zu München, Philosophisch-historische Klasse.
SBW   Sitzungsberichte der Wiener Akademie der Wissenschaften, Philosophisch-historische Klasse.

BIBLIOGRAPHY

Only the most frequently cited works, and those most significant for understanding the background and allusions of Gerbert's Letters are included here. Editions of classical authors cited in the notes are omitted. The Biblical references are to the Douay-Confraternity Version of the Bible (1953). Indentifications of the abbreviations will be found in a separate list on pp. 391-92.

Acta concilii sancti Basoli. Ed. by Gerbert. In MGSS III, 658ff. and A. Olleris, Oeuvres de Gerbert. Clermont-Ferrand and Paris, 1867, pp. 173-236.

Annales Hildesheimenses. In MGSS III.

Annales Quedlinburgenses. In MGSS III.

Annales Weissemburgenses. In MGSS III.

Balari y Jovany, José. Orígenes históricos de Cataluna. Barcelona, 1899.

Barse, Louis. Lettres et discours de Gerbert, traduit pour la première fois, classés dans sa biographie, expliqués par l'histoire du Xe siècle. 2 vols. Riom, 1847.

Barthélemy, Edouard de. Gerbert: Etude sur sa vie et ses ouvrages, suivie de la traduction de ses lettres. Paris, 1868.

Becker, Gustav. Catalogi bibliothecarum antiqui. Bonn, 1885.

Bloch, Hermann. "Beiträge zur Geschichte des Bischofs Leo von Vercelli und seiner Zeit," NA, XXII (1897), 13-136.

Böhmer, Heinrich. "Willigis von Mainz: Ein Beitrag zur Geschichte des deutschen Reichs und der deutschen Kirche in der sächsischen Kaiserzeit," Leipzig, 1895. Leipziger Studien aus dem Gebiet der Geschichte, Vol. I, No. 3.

Böhmer, Johann. Regesta imperii. II. Sächsisches Haus: 919-1024. Part III: Die Regesten des Kaiserreiches unter Otto III. 980(983)-1002. New ed. by Mathilde Uhlirz. Graz, 1956-57.

Boethius. De arithmetica. In PL LXIII, 1079-1168; also ed. by G. Friedlein. Leipzig, 1st ed., 1867; 2d ed., 1894.

Boethius. De musica. In PL LXIII, 1167-1300.

Bouange, Guillaume. Saint-Géraud et son illustre abbaye. 2d ed. 2 vols. Aurillac, 1870.

Boyd, Catherine E. Tithes and Parishes in Medieval Italy. Ithaca, N.Y., 1952.

Brackmann, Albert. Germania pontificia. Vols. I, II. Berlin, 1911. Regesta pontificum Romanorum.

Brutails, Auguste. "Bulle Originale de Silvestre II pour la Seo de Urgel (Mai 1001)," BEC, XLVIII (1887), 521-26.

Bubnov, Nikolai Mikhailovich. Gerberti opera mathematica 972-1003. Berlin, 1899.

———. Sbornik pisem Gerberta kak istoricheskii istochnik (983-997): Kriticheskaia monografiia po rukopisiam. 2 vols. St. Petersburg, 1888-90.

Bzovius, Abraham. Silvester II Caesius Aquitanus pontifex maximus. Rome, 1628.

Cambridge Economic History of Europe, from the Decline of the Roman Empire. Vol. I. The Agrarian Life of the Middle Ages. Cambridge, England, 1944.

Carey, Frederick M. "The Scriptorium of Reims during the Archbishopric of Hincmar (845-882 A.D.)," in Classical and Mediaeval Studies in Honor of Edward Kennard Rand. New York, 1938. Pp. 57-60.

Carreras y Candi, Francisco. "Lo Montjuich de Barcelona," MABL, VIII (1903), 195-450.

Chevalier, Ulysse. Repertoire des Sources historiques du moyen âge. Topo-bibliographie: 2 vols., Paris, 1894-1903; Bio-bibliographie: 2 vols., Paris, 1905-7.

Ciaconi [Chacon], Alphonse. Vitae et res gestae pontificum Romanorum et S.R.E. cardinalium ab initio nascentis ecclesiae usque ad Clementem IX. P.O.M. 2d ed. by Augustin Oldoin. Vol. I. Rome, 1677.

Cipolla, Carlo. Codice diplomatico del monastero di S. Colombano di Bobbio fino all'anno MCCVIII. 3 vols. Vol. I, ed. by C. Cipolla; Vol. II, ed. by C. Cipolla and G. Buzzi; Vol. III, ed. by G. Buzzi. Rome, 1918. Fonti per la storia d'Italia, Vols. 52-54.

Colombier, H. "Regestum de Gerbert," *Etudes Religieuses, historiques et littéraires par des Pères de la Compagnie de Jesus.* 4th ser., IV (1869), 299-316, 445-58.

Darlington, Oscar G. "Gerbert, 'obscuro loco natus,'" *Speculum,* XI (1936), 509-20.

———. "Gerbert, the Teacher," *The American Historical Review* LII (1947), 456-76.

Daux, Camille. "La Protection apostolique au moyen-âge," *Revue des questions historiques,* LXXII (n. s. XXXVIII) (1902), 17ff.

Delisle, Léopold. "Bull de Silvestre II pour Théotard, évêque du Puy, datée du 23 novembre 999," BEC, XXXVII (1876), 79, 108-11.

De Vic, Claude, and Vaissete, J. Histoire générale de Languedoc. 2d ed. Toulouse, 1872. Vol. IV.

Dionysius Exiguus. Collectio canonum ecclesiasticorum. In PL LXVII.

Dollinger, Philippe. L'Evolution des classes rurales en Bavière depuis la fin de l'époque carolingienne jusqu'au milieu du XIIIe siècle. Paris, 1949. Publications de la Faculté des lettres de l'université de Strasbourg, Fasc. 12.

D'Ooge, M. L., trans. Nicomachus of Gerasa: Introduction to Arithmetic. *See* Nicomachus.

Dopsch, Alfons. The Economic and Social Foundations of European Civilization. New York, 1937.

DuCange, Charles. Glossarium mediae et infimae latinitatis. 7 vols. Paris, 1840-50.

Duchesne, André. Historiae Francorum scriptores. Vol. II. Paris, 1636, pp. 789-844.

Duckett, Eleanor S. Alcuin, Friend of Charlemagne. New York, 1951.

Ewald, Paul. "Zur Diplomatik Silvesters II," NA, IX (1884), 323ff.

Fita, Fidel. "Bula inédita de Silvestre II," BAH, XVIII (1891), 247-49.

———. "Patrología: Bulas inéditas de Silvestre II y Juan XVIII," BAH, XXXVIII (1901), 477-84.

Florez, Enrique, and others. España sagrada. Teatro geographico-historico de la iglesia de Espana. 51 vols. Madrid, 1747-1879.

Gams, Pius Boniface. Series episcoporum ecclesiae catholicae. Regensburg, 1873-1886; 2d ed. 1931.

Giry, Alexandre. Manuel de diplomatique. Paris, 1894.

Goerz, Adam. Mittelrheinische Regesten; oder Chronologische Zusammenstellung des Quellen-materials für die Geschichte der territorien der beiden Regierungs-bezirke Coblenz und Trier in kurzen Auszügen. Vol. I. Coblenz, 1876.

Gregory I, Pope. Registrum epistolarum. In MG Epp. Vols. I-II. Ed. by P. Ewald and L. Hartmann. Berlin, 1899. Also in PL LXXVII, 477ff.

Gregorovius, Ferdinand. History of Rome. 2d ed. rev. Vol. III. London, 1903.

Havet, Julien. Lettres de Gerbert (983-987), publiées avec une introduction et des notes. Paris, 1889. Collection de Textes pour servir a l'étude et a l'enseigne-ment de l'histoire.

Hincmar, Archbishop. Opusculum adversus Hincmarum Laudunensem. In PL CXXVI, 307ff.

Hirsch, Hans. "Untersuchungen zur Geschichte des päpstlichen Schutzes," MIOG, LIV (1942), 364-433.

Holland, Leicester B. Traffic Ways about France in the Dark Ages (500-1150). Allentown, Pa., 1919. Ph.D. Dissertation, University of Pennsylvania.

Holtzman, Robert. Geschichte der Sächsischen Kaiserzeit (900-1024). 3d ed. Munich, 1955.

Hyginus, Caius Julius. Hygini astronomica. Ed. by B. Bunte, Leipzig, 1875.

Jaffé, Philipp. Regesta pontificum Romanorum ab condita Ecclesia ad annum post Christum natum MCXCVIII. 2d ed. by F. Kaltenbrunner, P. Ewald, and S. Loewenfeld. Vol. I. Leipzig, 1885-88.

Johnson, Edgar N. The Secular Activities of the German Episcopate 919-1024. Lincoln, Neb., 1932. University of Nebraska Studies, Vols. XXX-XXXI.

Jordan, Karl. "Das Eindringen des Lehnswesen in das Rechtsleben der römischen Kurie," *Archiv für Urkundenforschung*, XII (1932), 15-110.

Kehr, Paul. "Die ältesten Papsturkunden Spaniens," ABB, Jahrgang 1926, No. 2.

———. Italia pontificia. 7 vols. Berlin, 1906-25. Regesta pontificum Romanorum.

———. "Das Papsttum und der katalanische Prinzipat," ABB, Jahrgang 1926, No. 1. Trans. into Catalan by R. d'Abadal i Vinyals in *Estudis universitaris catalans*, XII (1927), 321-47; XIII (1928), 1-12.

———. "Papsturkunden in Spanien. I. Papsturkunden in Katalanien. II. Urkunden und Regesten," ABG, n.f. XVIII (1926).

———. "Rom und Venedig bis ins XII. Jahrhundert," *Quellen und Forschungen aus italischen Archiven und Bibliotheken*, XIX (1927), 80ff.

Kölmel, Willi. "Rom und der Kirchenstaat im 10. und 11. Jahrhundert," AMNG, LXXVIII (1935).

Kurth, Godefroid. Notker de Liège et la civilisation au Xᵉ siècle. Paris, 1905.

Lair, Jules. Etudes critiques sur divers textes des Xᵉ et XIᵉ siècles. Vol. I. Paris, 1899.

La Salle de Rochemaure, Duc de. Gerbert Silvestre II: Le Savant, le "faiseur de rois," le pontife. Paris, 1914.

Latouche, R., ed. *See* Richer.

Lattin, Harriet. "The Eleventh Century MS Munich 14436: Its Contribution to the History of Coördinates, of Logic, of German Studies in France," *Isis*, XXXVIII (1948), 205-25.

——. "Lupitus Barchinonensis," *Speculum*, VII (1932), 58-64.

——. "The Origin of our Present System of Notation According to the Theories of Nicholas Bubnov," *Isis*, XIX (1933), 181-94.

——. The Peasant Boy Who Became Pope: Story of Gerbert. New York, 1951. German trans. by Wolf-Rüdiger Stechele with title Vom Hirtenjungen zum Papst. Aschaffenburg, 1959.

——. "Symposium on the Tenth Century. Astronomy: Our Views and Theirs," *Medievalia et Humanistica*, VIII (1955), 13-17.

Lausser, P. F. Gerbert: Etude historique sur le Xᵉ siècle. Aurillac, 1866.

Leflon, Jean. Gerbert: Humanisme et chrétienté au Xᵉ siècle. Abbaye S. Wandrille, 1946. Figures monastiques.

Lerche, Otto. "Die Privilegierung der deutschen Kirche durch Papsturkunden bis auf Gregor VII: Ein Beitrag zur Geschichte des päpstlichen Formelwesens," *Archiv für Urkundenforschung*, III (1911), 125-232.

Lesne, Emile. Histoire de la propriété ecclésiastique en France. Vols. III-V. Lille, 1936-40.

Le *Liber censuum* de l'Eglise romaine. Ed. by P. Fabre and L. Duchesne. 2 vols. in 1. Paris, 1905-10. Bibliothèque des Ecoles françaises d'Athènes et de Rome, 2d Ser., Vol. VI.

Liber diurnus Romanorum pontificum. Ed. by E. Rozière. Paris, 1869; ed. by T. v. Sickel. Vienna, 1889.

Lot, Ferdinand. Les Derniers Carolingiens: Lothaire, Louis V, Charles de Lorraine (954-991). Paris, 1891. Bibliothèque de l'Ecole des Hautes Etudes, Fasc. 87.

——. Etudes sur le règne de Hugues Capet et la fin du Xᵉ siècle. Paris, 1903. Bibliothèque de l'Ecole des Hautes Etudes, Fasc. 147.

——. "Etude sur le recueil des lettres de Gerbert," BEC, C (1939), 8-62.

Lowis, D. W. The History of the Church in France, A.D. 950-1000; Being a Study in Mediaeval Christianity. London, 1926.

Lunt, William. Papal Revenues. 2 vols. New York, 1934. Records of Civilization, XIX.

MacKinney, Loren. Early Medieval Medicine with Special Reference to France and Chartres. Baltimore, 1937. Publications of the Institute of the History of Medicine, The Johns Hopkins University, 3d series, Vol. III.

——. "Tenth Century Medicine as Seen in the *Historia* of Richer of Rheims," *Bulletin of the Institute of the History of Medicine*, II (1934), 347-75.

Macrobius, Ambrosius Aurelius Theodosius. Opera. Vol. I. Commentarii in Ciceronis Somnium Scipionis. Ed. by L. v. Jan. Quedlinburg, 1848. English trans. by W. H. Stahl. New York, 1952. Records of Civilization, XLVIII.

Manitius, Max. Geschichte der lateinischen Literatur des Mittelalters. Vol. II. Munich, 1923.

Marca, Pierre de. Marca hispanica sive limes hispanicus hoc est geographica et historica descriptio Cataloniae, Ruscionis et circumjacentium populorum. Paris, 1688.

Martianus Capella. Martianus Capella de nuptiis Philologiae et Mercurii. Ed. by A. Dick. Leipzig, 1925.

Màs y Domènech, Joseph. Notes històriques del bisbat de Barcelona. Vols. IV and VI: Taula del Cartulari de Sant Cugat del Vallés. Vol. IX: Rúbrica dels Libri antiquitatum de la Sèu de Barcelona. Barcelona, 1909-14.

Masson, Jean. Epistolae Gerberti primo Remorum, dein Ravennatum archiepiscopi, postea Romani pontificis Silvestri secundi. Paris, 1611.

Migne, Jacques Paul, ed. Patrologiae cursus completus; series latina. 221 vols. Paris, 1844-64.

Millàs Vallicrosa, Josep. Assaig d'història de les idees físiques i matemàtiques a la Catalunya medieval. Barcelona, 1931. Estudis universitaris catalans. Sèrie monografica, No. I.

Monumenta Germaniae historica. Hanover and Berlin, 1826-.

Newman, William M. Le Domaine royal sous les premiers Capétiens (987-1180). Paris, 1937. Dissertation, University of Strasbourg.

Nicolau y d'Olwer, Lluis, "Gerbert (Silvestre II) y la cultura catalana del sigle X," *Estudis Universitaris Catalans*, IV (1910), 337-58.

Nicomachus of Gerasa. Introduction to Arithmetic. Trans. into English by M. L. D'Ooge; with studies in Greek arithmetic by F. E. Robbins and L. C. Karpinski. New York, 1926. University of Michigan Studies, Humanistic Series, No. XVI.

Odegaard, Charles E. "Carolingian Oaths of Fidelity," *Speculum*, XVI (1941), 284-96.

Odilo. S.Adalheidae imperatricis epitaphium. In MGSS IV, 636-49; PL CXLII, 967-82.

Olleris, Alexandre. Oeuvres de Gerbert, pape sous le nom de Sylvestre II, collationnées sur les manuscrits, précédées de sa biographie, suivies de notes critiques et historiques. Clermont-Ferrand and Paris, 1867.

Omont, Henri. "Bulles pontificales sur papyrus (IXe-XIe siècle)," BEC, LXV (1904), 575-82.

Parisot, Robert. Histoire de Lorraine. Vol. I: Des Origines à 1552. Paris, 1919.

———. Les Origines de la Haute-Lorraine et sa première maison ducale (959-1033). Paris, 1909.

Picavet, François. Gerbert, un Pape philosophe. Paris, 1897. Bibliothèque de l'Ecole des Hautes-Etudes. Sciences religieuses, Vol. IX.

Pivec, Karl. "Die Briefsammlung Gerberts von Aurillac," MIOG, XLIX (1935), 15-74.

———. "Stil- und Sprachentwicklung in mittellateinischen Briefen vom 8.-12. Jh.," MIOG, Erganzungsband XIV (1939), 33-51.

Richer. Histoire de France (888-995). Ed. and trans. by R. Latouche. Vols. I, II. Paris, 1930, 1937. Les Classiques de l'histoire de France au moyen âge. An earlier ed. with title Historiarium libri IV, in MGSS III, 561-659. New ed. in MG in usum scholarum ex Monumentis Germaniae historicis recusi, VI (Hanover, 1877). Also in PL CXXXVIII, 9-170. Text and French translation by J. Guadet. 2 vols. Paris, 1845. Société de l'Histoire de France. Translation into German by K. v. Osten-Sacken. Berlin, 1854.

Rovira i Virgili, Antoni. Història nacional de Catalunya. Vols. III, IV. Barcelona, 1924, 1926.

Santifaller, Leo. "Saggio di un elencho dei funzionarii, impiegati e scrittori della Cancellaria Pontificia dall'inizio all'anno 1099," BISI, LVI (1940).

——. "Die Verwendung des *Liber diurnus* in den Privilegien der Päpste von den Anfangen bis zum Ende des 11. Jahrhunderts," MIOG, XLIX (1935), 225-366.

Sarton, George. Introduction to the History of Science. Vol. I. Baltimore, 1927. Carnegie Institution of Washington Publication, No. 376.

Schanz, Martin. Geschichte der römischen Litteratur. 2 vols. Munich, 1914-20.

Schlockwerder, Theodor. Untersuchungen zur Chronologie der Briefe Gerberts v. Aurillac. Halle, 1893. Dissertation, University of Halle.

Schlumberger, Gustav. L'Epopée byzantine à la fin du dixième siècle. 2 vols. Paris, 1896-1900; 2d ed., 1925.

Schramm, Percy. "Die Briefe Kaiser Ottos III. und Gerberts von Reims aus dem Jahre 997," *Archiv für Urkundenforschung*, IX (1926) 87-122.

——. "Kaiser, Basileus und Papst in der Zeit der Ottonen," *Historische Zeitschrift*, CXXIX (1924), 424-75.

——. Kaiser, Rom und Renovatio. 2 vols. Leipzig, 1929.

——. "Neun Briefe des byzantinischen Gesandten Leo von seiner Reise zu Otto III. aus den Jahren 997-998," *Byzantinische Zeitschrift*, XXV (1925), 89-105.

Schwartz, Gerhard. Die Besetzung der Bistümer Reichsitaliens unter den Sächsischen und Salischen Kaisern mit den Listen der Bischöfe, 951-1122. Leipzig, 1913.

Studtmann, Joachim. "Die Pönformel der mittelalterlichen Urkunden," *Archiv für Urkundenforschung*, XII (1932), 251-374.

Ter Braak, Menno. Kaiser Otto III. Ideal und Praxis im fruehen Mittelalter. Amsterdam, 1928. Dissertation University of Amsterdam.

Thangmar. Vita Bernwardi. In MGSS IV, 757-82.

Thietmar of Merserburg. Chronicon. In MGSS III, 723-87. 2d ed. by F. Kurze.

Tschan, Francis J. Saint Bernward of Hildesheim: His Life and Times. 2 vols. Notre Dame, Ind., 1942-51. The University of Notre Dame: Publications in Medieval Studies, Nos. VI, XII.

Uhlirz, Karl. Jahrbücher des deutschen Reiches unter Otto II. und Otto III. Vol. I. Otto II. 973-983. Leipzig, 1902.

Uhlirz, Mathilde. "Die italienische Kirchenpolitik der Ottonen," MIOG, XLVIII (1934), 201-321.

——. Jahrbücher des deutschen Reiches unter Otto II. und Otto III. Vol. II. Otto III. 983-1002. Berlin, 1954.

——. "Das Kloster Bobbio im Zeitalter der Ottonen," in *Luschin-Festschrift*, *Zeitschrift des historischen Vereins für Steiermark*, XXVI (1931), 21-35.

——. Regesta imperii. *See* Böhmer.

——. "Studien zu Gerbert von Aurillac," *Archiv für Urkundenforschung*, XI (1930), 391-422; XIII (1935), 437-74.

——. Untersuchungen über Inhalt und Datierung der Briefe Gerberts von Aurillac, Papst Sylvesters II. Göttingen, 1957. Schriftenreihe der Historischen Kommission bei der Bayerischen Akademie der Wissenschaften. No. 2.

Vasiliev, Alexander. "Hugh Capet of France and Byzantium," *Dumbarton Oaks Papers*, VI (1951), 227-51.

——. "Mediaeval Ideas of the End of the World: West and East," *Byzantion*,

XVI (1944), 462-502.

Vic. *See* De Vic.

Vignier, Nicolas. La Bibliothèque historiale. Vol. II. Paris, 1587.

Villanueva, Jaime. Viage literario à las iglesias de España. 22 vols. Madrid and Valencia, 1803-52.

Warren, Frederick M. "Constantine of Fleury, 985-1014," *Transactions of the Connecticut Academy, Arts and Sciences*, XV (1909), 285-92.

Werner, Karl. Gerbert von Aurillac, die Kirche und Wissenschaft seiner Zeit. Vienna, 1878; 2d ed., 1881.

Wiederhold, Wilhelm. "Papsturkunden in Frankreich," NAG, Jahrgang 1910, 1913.

Weigle, Fritz. "Studien zur Überlieferung der Briefsammlung Gerberts von Reims," DA, X (1953), 19-70; XI (1954/55), 393-421; XIV (1958), 149-220.

Wilmans, Roger. Jahrbücher des deutschen Reichs unter der Herrschaft König und Kaiser Ottos III (983-1002). Berlin, 1840.

INDEX

Date Due

Printed in the USA
CPSIA information can be obtained
at www.ICGtesting.com
LVHW061019130823
755052LV00025B/1180